ETHNOMETHODOLOGY AT PLAY

Directions in Ethnomethodology and Conversation Analysis

Series Editors:
Stephen Hester, Honorary Senior Research Fellow, Bangor University, UK
Dave Francis, Department of Sociology, Manchester Metropolitan University, UK

Ethnomethodology and Conversation Analysis are cognate approaches to the study of social action that together comprise a major perspective within the contemporary human sciences. Ethnomethodology focuses upon the production of situated and ordered social action of all kinds, whilst Conversation Analysis has a more specific focus on the production and organisation of talk-in-interaction. Of course, given that so much social action is conducted in and through talk, there are substantive as well theoretical continuities between the two approaches. Focusing on social activities as situated human productions, these approaches seek to analyse the intelligibility and accountability of social activities 'from within' those activities themselves, using methods that can be analysed and described. Such methods amount to aptitudes, skills, knowledge and competencies that members of society use, rely upon and take for granted in conducting their affairs across the whole range of social life.

As a result of the methodological rewards consequent upon their unique analytic approach and attention to the detailed orderliness of social life, Ethnomethodology and Conversation Analysis have ramified across a wide range of human science disciplines throughout the world, including anthropology, social psychology, linguistics, communication studies and social studies of science and technology.

This series is dedicated to publishing the latest work in these two fields, including research monographs, edited collections and theoretical treatises. As such, its volumes are essential reading for those concerned with the study of human conduct and aptitudes, the (re)production of social orderliness and the methods and aspirations of the social sciences.

Other titles in this series

Adjudication in Action
An Ethnomethodology of Law, Morality and Justice
Baudouin Dupret
ISBN 978-1-4094-3150-3

Ethnomethodology at Work
Edited by Mark Rouncefield and Peter Tolmie
ISBN 978-0-7546-4771-3

Ethnomethodology at Play

Edited by

PETER TOLMIE
University of Nottingham, UK

MARK ROUNCEFIELD
Lancaster University, UK

ASHGATE

Published by
Ashgate Publishing Limited
Wey Court East
Union Road
Farnham
Surrey, GU9 7PT
England

Ashgate Publishing Company
110 Cherry Street
Suite 3-1
Burlington, VT 05401-3818
USA

www.ashgate.com

British Library Cataloguing in Publication Data
Ethnomethodology at play. -- (Directions in
  ethnomethodology and conversation analysis)
  1. Ethnomethodology. 2. Recreation.
  I. Series II. Rouncefield, Mark. III. Tolmie, Peter.
  306.4'8'01-dc23

The Library of Congress has cataloged the printed edition as follows:
Tolmie, Peter.
  Ethnomethodology at play / by Peter Tolmie and Mark Rouncefield.
      pages cm. -- (Directions in ethnomethodology and conversation analysis)
  Includes bibliographical references and index.
  ISBN 978-1-4094-3755-0 (hbk.) -- ISBN 978-1-4094-3756-7 (ebk.) -- ISBN 978-1-4094-
7385-5 (epub) 1. Ethnomethodology. I. Rouncefield, Mark. II. Title.
  HM481.T65 2013
  306.01--dc23

2012038850

ISBN 9781409437550 (hbk)
ISBN 9781409437567 (ebk – PDF)
ISBN 9781409473855 (ebk – ePUB)

Printed and bound in Great Britain
by MPG PRINTGROUP

*This book is dedicated to
John Hughes, our friend and mentor*

Contents

PART III: 'GETTING OUT OF THE HOUSE'

PART IV: DOING STUFF TOGETHER

List of Figures and Examples

Figures

Examples

Notes on Contributors

Jacquelyn Allen-Collinson is a sociologist based in the School of Sport & Exercise Science at the University of Lincoln, UK. Her current research and supervisory interests cohere around sociological and phenomenological analyses of the lived sporting body and sporting activity, particularly distance running; the impact of serious injury and chronic illness on self and sporting identity; 'identity work' and the management of disrupted identity. She is also interested in autoethnographic and autophenomenographic approaches to the sociological analysis of sporting experiences.

Steve Benford is Professor of Collaborative Computing in the Mixed Reality Laboratory at Nottingham, and is an EPSRC Dream Fellow. He won the 2003 Prix Ars Elctronica for Interactive Art, the 2007 Nokia Mindtrek award for innovative applications of ubiquitous computing, and has received four BAFTA nominations. He was elected to the CHI Academy in 2012. His book *Performing Mixed Reality* was published by MIT Press in 2011. In his spare time, he plays guitar and tenor banjo with The Phil Langran Band, and with Alamootie and the Big Jig Ceilidh Band and electric guitar with Goose McCoy.

Phillip Brooker (Brunel University) is a research assistant with MATCH (Multidisciplinary Assessment of Technology Centre of Healthcare), working in the field of user-requirements for healthcare devices. He has recently completed a Ph.D. in sociology (entitled Computerised Research Technologies in Practical Research Settings), which is a video-aided ethnomethodological account of the work of two postgraduate scientific research projects in the fields of astrophysics and electrical engineering. He spends most of his spare time collaborating with friends on various musical projects linked to the usage of virtual music studio software.

Graham Button is former Pro-Vice Chancellor for Arts, Computing, Engineering and Sciences at Sheffield Hallam University. Prior to that he was the Laboratory Director for Xerox's Grenoble and Cambridge Research Centres. He has pursued ethnomethodological and conversation analytic research since 1973, gaining his Ph.D. at the University of Manchester in 1975. He holds a Royal Yachting Association and the Maritime Coastguard Agency Yachtmaster Ocean Certificate which means that he 'is experienced and competent to skipper a yacht on passages of any length in all parts of the world'.

Andy Crabtree is a Principal Research Fellow in the School of Computer Science and IT at Nottingham University. His work focuses on the relationship between computing systems and social interaction. It exploits 'ethnography' – i.e., empirical studies of human action in context – to uncover the interactional work that animates everyday activities in the home, at work, and in play. This kind of research is used to ground systems development in the naturally occurring and naturally accountable organization of human conduct.

Paul ten Have is a retired Associate Professor in the Department of Sociology and Anthropology at the University of Amsterdam. After his retirement, he took up voluntary activities in the natural environments of sea dunes, a country estate, and polder land, including acting as a nature guide. He is the author of *Doing Conversation Analysis: A Practical Guide* (2nd ed. Sage, 2007). His current research interests concern ethnomethodology, conversation analysis, medical interaction, and research practices. He initiated and maintains an informative website on ethnomethodology and conversation analysis: *Ethno/CA News* at http://www.paultenhave.nl/EMCA.htm

John Hockey was a mature student at Lancaster where he encountered John Hughes who threw at him Mead, Goffman, Schutz and Garfinkel – a teaching for which he is forever grateful. At present he is Research Fellow at the University of Gloucestershire and has published extensively across the sociologies of education, work and sport. His current research is in the application of phenomenology to sport. To his bemusement an article of his on the sociology of the senses was awarded a Sage prize for sociological innovation at the 2010 British Sociological Association Conference. He is still putting on over-priced running shoes daily and he is listening to Bill Evans lots.

K. Neil Jenkings is a researcher in the School of Geography, Politics and Sociology at Newcastle University. His current research concerns 'The social production of the contemporary British military memoir'.

Russell Kelly teaches occasionally at the University of Trier (Germany). Previously he was Senior Lecturer at the University of Central Lancashire. He was initiated into the ways of the Ethnomethodologist in the late 1970s by John A. Hughes. A year with Wes Sharrock and Rod Watson in Manchester in the 1990s polished the gloss, completed by Wes with the epithet, 'philosopher' (probably his proudest moment). Studies of nurse-patient interaction were presented in lectures to successive generations of nurse students, with occasional forays into sociological theory and methods. Emerging out of 'early retirement', he returned to the classroom to spread the word but Line Dancing succumbed to stiffening joints. He still has a Cowboy Hat.

Eric Laurier is a Senior Lecturer in the School of Geosciences, at the University of Edinburgh. Currently he is principal investigator on 'Assembling the Line: Amateur & Professional Work, Skills and Practice in Digital Video Editing', and 'The Cappuccino Community: Cafes and Civic Life in the Contemporary City' both funded by the ESRC. He also organizes the Scottish Ethnomethodology, Discourse, Interaction & Technology (SEDIT) Group at the University of Edinburgh. Over a number of research studies he has drawn upon video as a form of data for providing access to the details of visual interaction in public space, mobile settings and workplaces.

Michael Lynch is Professor in the Department of Science & Technology Studies at Cornell University. During the 1970s, he began to study ethnomethodology under Harold Garfinkel's supervision. Coincidentally, at that time he also took up fly-fishing in the mountains near Los Angeles. Since then, he has lived, worked, and fly-fished in Canada and the UK, and on the west and east coasts of the US. After returning to upstate New York in 1999, he has lived in Ithaca, noted for its waterfalls, deep gorges and isolation from urban civilization. His academic work includes studies of laboratory practices, courtroom tribunals, and the intersection between the two (court cases in which scientific evidence is featured). He has also written on other subjects, including birdwatching (also a casual recreational interest of his), but until now he has protected his interest in fly-fishing from the contaminating influence of academic analysis.

Mark Rouncefield is Senior Research Fellow in the School of Computing and Communications, Lancaster University and a recent holder of a Microsoft European Research Fellowship studying social interaction and mundane technologies. His research interests are in Computer Supported Cooperative Work and involve the empirical study of various aspects of work, organization, human factors and interactive computer systems design. He has a UKA Bronze (highly commended) and Silver medal in salsa dancing and, despite years of practice, is a truly dreadful blues guitarist.

Wes Sharrock has been at the University of Manchester since 1965. He has been Assistant Lecturer, Lecturer, Senior Lecturer, Reader and Professor in Sociology there. His main interests are in the philosophy of social science, philosophy of mind, sociological theory, and ethnomethodology. He is currently researching the construction of online ontologies in bioinformatics. Wes' leisure pursuits are sedentary, and include reading novels and listening to music.

Peter Tolmie is a Senior Research Fellow in the School of Computer Science and IT at the University of Nottingham. He was previously an Area Manager for the Work Practice Technology group at Xerox Research Centre Europe and began his career in research as an ethnomethodologist at Lancaster University, studying a range of topics relating to Computer Supported Cooperative Work.

He has published widely in the areas of Human-Computer Interaction and CSCW and has conducted studies of a highly diverse set of domains including retail finance, domestic settings, call centres, teleworking, bid management, game-playing, film and television production, and musical performance. He trained as a classical musician but spent the late 1970s and early 1980s playing in New Wave bands, much to the dismay of his erstwhile teachers. Nowadays he trains his children to punish the world instead.

Acknowledgements

We would like to thank all our authors for all their hard work, and for their tolerance of a couple of complacent yet fretful editors. We would also like to thank our editor at Ashgate, Neil Jordan, firstly, for going along with and encouraging the initial idea of this book, but mainly, we must admit, for persevering with us for so long in the face of all the outrageous and obvious half-truths we offered to secure deadline extensions. Well, we got there in the end.

Peter would like to thank his patient and forgiving friends and colleagues at the University of Nottingham, most notably Andy Crabtree, Tom Rodden, and Steve Benford, all of whom manage somehow to keep him in business despite him living in another country and mostly only being visible to them as a ghostly blur on Skype calls. He also owes a huge debt to Claire, Tris, Ellie, Lew, and Sanna, who have all been press-ganged into providing data for more than one of the chapters in this book (and who are still wondering when the bills will get paid). Mark has once again been a stalwart companion in this venture, not least because he knows how to prevaricate in ways that only public school boys ever master. He also really must say thank you to the people who are contemplating reading this book, just for thinking about it, and who will now hopefully not put it back on the shelf …

Mark would like to acknowledge the financial support of a Microsoft European Research Fellowship and a Xerox University Affairs project. As always Mark would like to thank his patient co-editor, Peter Tolmie, for his continued acceptance and tolerance of the theft of his original ideas and his kind, and largely wasted, attempts to keep him on the ethnomethodological straight and narrow. He would like to thank his friends and fellow researchers in Lancaster, Nottingham, Manchester and Cambridge (and Liverpool and Singapore) who, apart from the constant, stinging, personal and professional criticism, are all better friends than he probably deserves. Finally, as always, he thanks Caroline, for everything else and everything more.

Introduction
Overview: Garfinkel's Bastards at Play

Mark Rouncefield and Peter Tolmie

As we originally noted in *Ethnomethodology at Work* (Rouncefield and Tolmie 2011), ethnomethodologists seem to spend a lot of their time apologizing. This may just seem like paranoia (and it may indeed be paranoia) but the fashion has developed whereby we are required to offer some kind of apology for our research, for our methods, our findings, for ourselves and for being not quite what people want, or expect, or value. We have endured this with relatively good humour for some time but some kind of innate grumpiness (there were after all good reasons why Garfinkel referred to us as 'bastards') means that we are now growing rather tired of it and, consequently, we are perhaps rather less inclined to offer apologies for this work.

But we should probably, grudgingly, apologize for our title – *Ethnomethodology at Play* – and we offer our apologies both before you begin to read this book and when you have finished. We apologize initially for the use of the word 'play' – though we can think of none better – which is intended to offer a simple 'playful', ironic, contrast with *Ethnomethodology at Work*. Play is a commonplace word that many people might use in a variety of (slightly different) ways when commenting on or describing their leisure or sporting activities – and here we use 'play' as a simple ordering device for speaking of the various sporting, leisure and cultural activities that are described and analysed in this book. For sociologists in general we use our title, *Ethnomethodology at Play* to draw attention to, and to contrast it with, conventional sociological studies in the 'sociology of work and leisure' and the 'sociology of sport'. The empirical studies and analysis offered in *Ethnomethodology at Play* are also intended to demonstrate the breadth of ethnomethodological analysis – showing how no topic is beyond ethnomethodology's fundamental respecification. So the title and the book as a whole are offered as a corrective of sorts to the significant number of sociologists and researchers who know something about ethnomethodology but seem to think it is all about, or is just about, or can only be about, workplace studies. Although one of our reviewers suggests that this is '*akin to the claim that the moon is made of green cheese, i.e. so daft as to be unworthy of serious attention*' we know our audience and 'daft' doesn't even begin to describe the depths of misunderstanding and stupidity that we sometimes encounter. Finally, for those who actually read the book we also apologize, for what you might well come to see as the lies, prevarications or, more kindly, 'economies of the truth' presented in the preceding sentences. Those of you who make the effort and take the time to struggle with and through the book will quickly realize that far from offering a contrast with *Ethnomethodology at Work*, the 'message' and the approach in *Ethnomethodology at Play* is essentially similar (and this may well be what makes it an 'ironic' contrast). As we went to some trouble to argue in *Ethnomethodology at Work* all activities, even 'play', involve 'work' – they are all effortful accomplishments: '*For the ethnomethodologist there is no domain of human practice that is exempt from this. Human action and interaction does not just tumble from the sky ready formed. Instead, even the most mundane of actions have to be produced somehow, somewhere, somewhen. This is a job of work*'. So don't say we didn't warn you.

Now we'd like to present some comments on the origin and motivation for this particular book and those for whom the book is intended. This book had its initial origins in a piece of extraordinary and fortunate cheek, when the current editors, whilst struggling to finish off *Ethnomethodology at Work* suggested *Ethnomethodology at Play* as a companion volume and, much to their surprise, their publisher agreed. Regardless of this particular piece of good fortune the interest in sport, leisure and 'play' more generally also coincided with some changes in the editors' own research interests and research direction, and, in turn, some very important developments in the nature of computing. Put simply, we witnessed a change in the focus of computing development and research, away from the large machines and the desktops in offices and factories, towards the ways in which computing power is increasingly ubiquitous, embedded in everyday devices, like phones, televisions, washing machines, running shoes and so on. Similarly few people could have failed to notice the growth in the use of computer games of various kinds, the widespread use of social networking and the massive rise of 'apps' for just about every activity. In the new world of domestic and ubiquitous computing, understanding users and use became equally, or perhaps even more important for as Casey (1998) argues: '*New Technologies will succeed or fail based on our ability to minimize the incompatibilities between the characteristics of people and the characteristics of the things we create and use*'. As computing shifted out of commerce and industry, with their relatively simple demands of profit and efficiency, so it increasingly moved into the home and other areas, with a range of far more complex demands – such as fun, and joy and intimacy and obligation and community etc. – and, of course, 'play' – all of which pose far more difficult problems for both research and design. So this book is intended largely for all those students struggling to make sense of any particular 'play' (or leisure or sporting or hobby) setting as a precursor to some design effort and who have turned to established social science accounts and found them wanting. Similarly students of the 'Sociology of Sport' or the 'Sociology of Leisure' or 'Cultural Studies' may find the very different, incommensurable, presentation of their subjects intriguing and worthwhile. You are our imagined readers. Once more we asked, begged and blackmailed our friends to write for you, to document some of their research, to provide some instances of their less well known, more personal, 'this and that'.

For us, Sociology, as Livingston suggests, is '*the attempt to discover what is social about the social world*'. But the ways in which sociologists have attempted to bring serious attention to aspects of leisure, sport and 'play' more generally have tended to be rather predictable in that they have used these topics for further examination and rehearsal of explanatory themes and theories that they have found to be interesting and relevant elsewhere in Sociology. Until comparatively recently, few 'mainstream' sociologists have undertaken systematic analyses of sport, leisure and other cultural pursuits. Seater and Jacobson's (1976) survey of the 'intradiscipline status hierarchy' of sociological specialisms in the United States revealed that 'leisure, sport and recreation', ranked 35th out of the 36 specialisms. Whilst the 'Sociology of Work and Leisure' often features as an identifiable aspect of Sociology, 'leisure' often seems an empirically and theoretically impoverished residual category. One of the key reasons for this has been the perpetuation of a conception of sport and leisure as somehow being separate from the rest of 'real' life. The sociology of leisure only emerged as a sub-discipline in the 1960s, and has always encountered difficulties in defining its focus and boundaries. Initially the focus was on 'work and leisure' where leisure was treated as being influenced by industrial and societal changes such as the modernization of work, the reduction of work time and the 'long arm of the job' and where the relationship could be characterized as extension, neutrality or opposition (Parker 1971). So, attention was paid to how particular occupations produced particular uses of leisure, for example in the justifiably famous accounts of deep-sea fishermen (Tunstall 1962), and coalminers (Dennis et al. 1956). Since then sociologists have proposed other interesting classifications of leisure, for example according to whether leisure is spent as a consumer, as a citizen, as a member, or privately. Others, notably Stebbins (1992, 1997) distinguished 'serious' from 'casual' leisure. For Stebbins casual leisure is: 'defined as immediately, intrinsically rewarding, relatively short-lived pleasurable activity requiring little or no special training to enjoy it. In broad, colloquial terms, it could serve as the scientific term for the practice of doing what comes "naturally", and apparently, "… comes in at least six types, … play, relaxation, passive entertainment, active entertainment, sociable conversation, and sensory stimulation'. More recently, and reflecting trends in Sociology more generally, feminist sociologists (Deem 1986; Green et al. 1990) argued that Sociology neglected gender issues in leisure and even more recently, the sociological focus on sexualities, that produced, for example 'queer theory' has emphasized the hetero-normativity of sports and leisure activities (Cauldwell 2006; Skeggs 1999; Wellard 2002). But, and many of you readers are likely to have anticipated this comment, few of these accounts have told us very much about, documented or analysed, the leisure activities themselves. Instead the leisure pursuits were marginalized (at best) or sacrificed in pursuit of other disciplinary, political and theoretical goals. So, if we examine one particular example, Anderson and Taylor's *Standing Out while*

Fitting In: Serious Leisure Identities and Aligning Actions among Skydivers and Gun Collectors (2010) we find the following:

> One of the most enduring expressions within the skydiving argot is the maxim, 'Eat, Fuck, Skydive!' By designating skydiving as belonging to the same basic category as eating and intercourse, the expression underscores the sensual, hedonistic character of the experience and implies that people skydive for the same reasons that they engage in the other two activities … Intertwined with the foregoing themes in skydiving subculture is … an ethos of 'hyperheterosexuality' and male dominance. While skydiving culture has been changing in recent years in ways that may be reducing this patriarchal hegemony, the change is variable across the skydiving community, where hyperheterosexuality and male dominance continue to be strong, if not as hegemonic, as in the past.

We hasten to add that we have no doubt that this is 'good work' and is, indeed, quite fascinating (that's why we chose it), but it tells us very little about the actual activity of skydiving. In common ethnomethodological parlance, the activity of skydiving and all that is involved in doing it is simply used as a *resource* for the examination of other topics, in this case 'hyperheterosexuality', assuming that 'everyone knows' what skydiving involves.

We must stress here that there are any number of obviously good sociological studies that proceed in this fashion: attempting to provide explanations of sport and leisure by reference to particular 'known' and/or theoretical glosses of presumed aspects of society. Giddens (2006), for example, regards sport as a form of catharsis in the context of the uncertainty fostered by rapid social change. In a similar vein Elias, who suggests that (1986: 26) '*studies of sport which are not studies of society are studies out of context*', claims that excitement, reputedly the core emotion of civilization, is both provided for and controlled through organized sports. More recently Stranger's (1999) study of surfing argues that, '*the surfing aesthetic involves a postmodern incarnation of the sublime that distorts rational risk assessment*'. Of course we can understand and appreciate this kind of analysis but need to make two points that are perhaps otherwise neglected. Firstly, in most of these analyses the analysis of society generally precedes the analysis of sport that is often used merely to confirm details of the societal analysis – it effectively becomes the docile matrix for the exercise of a theoretical will. Secondly, whilst we can appreciate arguments that suggest that sport or leisure is more than a mere pastime but instead a setting for the interplay of individual and societal notions, we need to point out that before sport can become the 'postmodern incarnation of the sublime' or 'the interplay of material and embodied capital' it firstly has to be understood as a sport rather than as an unexplicated resource for apparently 'more important' sociological arguments about the character of modern society – and this is what many of these studies –'good work' though they are – patently fail to accomplish. If we take one final example to illustrate this point, Dant and

Wheaton's (2007) study of windsurfing, that begins with this trenchant and readily understandable description of learning to windsurf:

> Watching novices trying to sail a windsurfer can be funny. It looks as if it is impossible – just when they think they've got it, there's a loud splash and a muffled curse or two as the sailor falls into the water, closely followed by the mast and sail. After remounting the board, the sailor stands hesitantly, laboriously dragging the sail into an upright position before again trying to make progress forwards. They often topple over several times before anything like 'sailing' happens.

In the course of the article this is then analysed – or re-described – as '*a complex "material interaction" between the material capital that is in the objects of the kit and the embodied capital that is in the body of the sailor.*'

And so our comment here is essentially similar to one we raised in *Ethnomethodology at Work*; that sociological accounts of 'play' (leisure, sport etc.) as socially produced, shaped and constructed in various ways risks '*hiding the phenomena*' behind an analysis of the forces that supposedly shape the form, structure and experience of play. And each and every setting becomes just one more arena in which to observe societal forces and processes (of whatever kind) at work, trotting out once again the same old range of worn out explanatory theories and interests. These studies have 'lost their phenomena' – the real world, real life experiences of people as they go about their everyday activities. In these sociological accounts of sport and leisure, instead of examining the activities and interactions that make these activities the recognizably distinct phenomena they are understood to be – i.e. rugby, cricket, gardening, stamp-collecting whatever – by those who partake in them, a theoretical analysis of the forces which allegedly shape that work takes precedence, or rather, is offered instead, and the setting becomes just another incidental area in which to observe such forces and processes at work. Sociology appears less interested in the phenomena itself than with internal, sociological, theoretical, debate. In an unfortunate likeness to playground disputes this often amounts to little more than who has the best theory, the deficiencies of other theories, what other theoreticians should do etc. Sociology seems to presume that its problems are *theoretical* in the sense that getting a fit between theory and 'the world' lies in the sophistication (or lack of it) of their theories. As Watson (1994) comments it is as if; '*persons live out the lives they do, have the children they do, feel the feelings, think the thoughts, enter the relationships they do, all in order to permit the sociologist to solve his theoretical problems.*' But really their problems lie in the fact that they have made the phenomenon *disappear*, what Garfinkel (2002) calls the 'haecceities', the 'things', the doings, the 'thisness and that's' that characterize ordinary activities go absent. And such accounts are usually utterly impoverished, discussing things in ways that ordinary people find hard to recognize, causing people to reflect (to steal that well-known phrase from Star Trek) 'Its life Jim, but not as we know it'. Consequently, it is no surprise that, as Atkinson commented some time ago: '*... sociologists still have a great deal of trouble in convincing a more general public that their "expert" claims about how the social world works should be taken any more seriously than those of anyone else*' (Atkinson 1978: 168). These difficulties will remain for so long as we search for *explanations* of *the* realities underlying commonsensically available appearances of social order in preference to an examination of how such appearances are interactionally produced, managed, recognized and used, as Crabtree et al. (1999) make plain:

> Ethnomethodology is not in the business of explanation as that notion is understood in the social sciences. The business of explanation – of abstracting from witnessed appearances and constructing master narratives or models according to the rules and procedures governing the production of factual knowledge of a calculable status – trades on, offers accounts of and about, rather than makes visible, the social practices in and through which members produce and manage the daily affairs of a setting. Thus ethnomethodology eschews explanation and urges the researcher to treat practice as a topic of inquiry through and through rather than a resource for building explanatory constructs. (Crabtree et al. 1999: 670)

This book offers a specifically ethnomethodological understanding of 'play'. Whilst we believe that this book is the first *collection* of ethnomethodological studies of various forms of 'play' it is obviously not the first time that ethnomethodologists have considered this particular range of topics, and nobody needs to look very far to find good examples. So, for instance, Garfinkel in 'Instructions and instructed actions' in *Ethnomethodology's Program: Working Out Durkheim's Aphorism* (Garfinkel 2002) presents us with this account of assembling a chair, including the loud comment, 'Do I have all the parts?'. Even for those not accustomed to recognizing birds by their song this is obviously the instantly recognizable and heartfelt cry of the occasional DIY enthusiast and probably everyone who has ever attempted to assemble any Swedish 'flat-pack' furniture.

> … The text has a readable beginning; an in-course serial arrangement of steps; an aimed for terminal step. And so on.

> That's a docile text.

> Now the rest of the parts fall out, and my wife warns me: Please finish that thing before this evening; we're having company. Now I understand that the sheet of stuff is itself a detail of the work I take up in which I'm picking over the parts and beginning on the thing to find, with these instructions, not only what 'first' looks like but what the first that is going to look like the thing that I'm making it happen that it looks like.

Thus I'm looking for this connecting piece in frame one. As soon as I see frame one I have the problem of *getting on the page* at frame one. Getting on the page? At frame one? DO I HAVE ALL THE PARTS? Nowhere on this sheet does it say: Before you begin count the parts.

Other 'classic' examples of ethnomethodological treatments of sport and leisure and 'hobby' activities include Girton's (1986) study of 'Kung Fu: Toward a Paradoxical Hermeneutic of The Martial Arts', in Garfinkel's (ed.) *Ethnomethodological Studies of Work*; Sudnow's examination of the learning of jazz piano in *Ways of the Hand* (1978), Law and Lynch's exploration of certain facets of birdwatching; *Lists, Field Guides, and the Descriptive Organization of Seeing: Birdwatching as an Exemplary Observational Activity* (1988) and finally Livingston's (2008) various analyses of playing checkers, making origami models and assembling jigsaws as instances of skill and reasoning: *'Our interests in skill and reasoning lie as much in activities such as dancing the tango, performing close-up magic, and playing soccer as they do in arguing legal cases and deducing theorems of formal logic.'* But there is also a host of other, perhaps less well known, studies of leisure and sport that draw on ethnomethodology such as Kew's (1986) work on rugby and its examination of 'rules' in sport; Laurier's study of Houdini's magic tricks (2004); Burke et al.'s (2008) analysis of high-altitude climbers; Macbeth's (2012) research on basketball; or Fele's (2008) analysis of 'teamwork' in playing football, of how a team is a team, specifically the activity of lining up for kick-off: *'A team is a grouping of persons who display "being a team," its typical conformation, to themselves and to others. It is an evident, obvious phenomenon which consists in the embodied and visible nature of these scenic characteristics, and which, precisely because of its obviousness and its self-explanatory nature, is a phenomenon taken for granted'*. Lastly there is a whole series of ethnomethodological studies of 'playing' with pets (or companion animals) including cats, dogs and horses, but the most notable of these is probably Goode's brilliant *Playing with My Dog Katie: An Ethnomethodological Study of Dog-Human Interaction* (Goode 2007). Goode concludes his study by writing:

This book is an attempt to display in detail a guardian playing with his dog, an instance of *just that*. That people play with dogs is in itself, in its own right, a 'miracle of everyday society'. I am not saying that play between companion dogs and their guardians is (or is not) socially or politically important or consequential. It is more like when Sacks watched and analysed a videotape of a couple greeting each other at the door. He was not doing so to advance a political agenda- to change how people greet each other at doors, for example. He did it to discover and appreciate the incredible details in and of the simplest things we do, and that is what this book is about.

And that – 'the incredible details in and of the simplest things we do' – is what this book is about too.

What might surprise some readers at this point is the apparent omission of any mention of a seemingly tightly allied body of literature growing out of conversation analysis (CA) and membership categorization analysis (MCA) as first initiated by the works of Harvey Sacks (1992). Our reasons for not giving equal emphasis to CA is that CA, ultimately, does what it says on the tin: it analyses conversation. Inspection of the chapters presented in this volume will make it clear to the reader that, whilst a number of them make use of various instances of naturally occurring talk and some also do draw upon particular concepts that were first articulated in CA such as adjacency pairs and membership categorization devices, none of them make conversation their primary topic. Instead the authors draw upon their own expertise in the domains they are discussing to draw upon a whole constellation of activities including talk in order to explicate the orderly production of certain phenomena such as line dancing, running, cooking, fishing, sailing, and so on. As we shall be discussing further below this way of proceeding constitutes a well-established approach to ethnomethodological work that Garfinkel termed 'hybrid' studies (Garfinkel 1996). Ethnomethodology puts a strong emphasis upon the acquisition of competent membership in a setting in order to be able to adequately articulate the work and reasoning within the setting. There is no-one better placed for this than the existing practitioner and the hybrid status of the practitioner-ethnomethodologist is recognized in the term 'hybrid' studies. There are, of course, other ways in which ethnomethodologists go about acquiring adequate membership apart from being existing practitioners but what tends to get brought to the fore by 'hybrid' studies is a fundamental distinction that has grown between CA and ethnomethodology. Whilst CA goes about trying to unravel the orderly character of unfolding conversation ethnomethodology takes as its topic the accomplishment of human action which rarely turns upon conversation alone. Thus, for many ethnomethodologists there is a suspicion that CA tends to lose a good measure of the phenomena through an undue focus upon just one part. We do not want to rehearse and further fuel that debate here as this book is not (surprisingly for ethnomethodologists some might say) primarily interested in polemics and critiques. It is about studies of human accomplishment of certain kinds of recognizable sport and leisure activities. Those who wish to understand the debate we have alluded to here would be well-advised to look at Lynch's (1993) volume entitled *Scientific Practice and Ordinary Action*. However, it should be recognized that there are some well-founded studies of play in CA that the interested reader could explore in further detail should the approach be something they wish to examine more closely. First and foremost amongst these is the work of Harvey Sacks (1992) who looked in detail at some of the organizational features of children's play (cf. for example *On Some Formal Properties of Children's Games* and *Button Button Who's Got the Button*). A significant corpus of the somewhat later CA material regarding this topic is the work of Marjorie Goodwin. She takes as her mission showing how talk (and other activities) in play represent resources through which children display interactional competence and make sense of one another's actions: 'how competent members use talk socially to act out the ordinary scenes of their everyday life' (Goodwin 1990). She assembled an impressive body of CA work on girls games like hopscotch, and jumping games etc. (1990, 1998, 2002), to detail how a range of social activities including directives, dispute, gossip, etc. were organized as part of the ongoing flow of talk and interaction. Goodwin's analysis then broadens (somewhat problematically for ethnomethodologists) to embrace other, particular, aspects of games such as the emergence and enforcement of rules as part of a larger sociological argument about gender differences in 'play': whether in play girls are 'naturally 'cooperative' whilst boys are naturally 'aggressive' (they aren't). For more recent CA treatments of the topic the reader might look to the work of Carly Butler (2008) which focuses upon playground interactions, building upon the vein of work established by Goodwin.

So, as can be gathered from the above, all of the chapters in this book are primarily concerned with taking an *ethnomethodological* stance as a starting point for their analyses. But, as with *Ethnomethodology at Work*, we don't propose to give you anything more than a basic grounding in what ethnomethodology 'is' – and suggest, once again, that you do some work, and some reading, of your own. Any, ethnomethodological analysis proceeds through the faithful description of the social practices through which the witnessed activity was observably produced and achieved. As Benson and Hughes (1991) write: '… *the analytic task is … to explicate and describe the members' methods that could have been used to produce "what happened in the way that it did"…*' (Benson and Hughes 1991: 132). Ethnomethodology involves a fundamental revision of sociology's traditional views on social order, of the sorts of questions to be asked about it, and of the kind of empirical research to be done. We believe that such an approach, as Armour (1997) suggests: '… *takes seriously the great questions of sociology: How do actions recur and reproduce themselves? How is it that interaction displays properties of patterning, stability, orderliness? How does social life get organized?*' For ethnomethodology this orderliness is worked at and developed from within the activities, treating social facts as interactional accomplishments and social order as a local production. The focus is on the 'local production of social order' – how participants within the settings locally produce or accomplish the production and recognition of social action:

> We are concerned with how society gets put together; how it is getting done; how to do it; the social structures of everyday activities. I would say that we are doing studies of how persons, as parties to ordinary arrangements, use the features of the arrangement to make for members the visible organized activities that happen. (Garfinkel 1967)

Accordingly ethnomethodological studies do not lead to the disappearance of the phenomenon because they explicate the methods members themselves use as they routinely and in taken for granted ways display their knowledge of and understanding of the facticity of the social world as organized and ordered.

The orderliness of social life is the achievement of ordinary social actors, the outcome of what they do, and their commonsense knowledge of social structures. Recognizable features of an activity or setting and their display are then 'locally' produced and produced in the ways the activity is being done by those engaged in it. That something is recognizable as 'this' activity or setting – that it is regarded as birdwatching, flyfishing, trainspotting or salsa dancing for example – in the first place is a local production:

> … activities whereby members produce and manage settings of organised everyday affairs are identical with members' procedures for making those settings 'account-able'. When I speak of accountable, my interests are directed to such matters as the following. I mean observable-and-reportable, i.e. available to members as situated practices of looking-and-telling. I mean, too, that such practices consist of an endless, ongoing, contingent accomplishment: that they are carried on under the auspices of, and are made to happen as events in, the same ordinary affairs that in organising they describe; that the practices are done by parties to those settings whose skill with, knowledge of, and entitlement to the detailed work of that accomplishment – whose competence – they obstinately depend upon, recognise, use and take for granted: and *that* they take their competence for granted furnishes parties with a setting's distinguishing and particular features, and of course it furnishes them as well as resources, troubles, projects and the rest. (Garfinkel 1967: 1–2)

For ethnomethodology, members use their commonsense cultural knowledge in simultaneously producing and recognizing settings and courses of activities. That is, in the course of producing 'orderly phenomena' members exhibit and put to practical use their commonsense knowledge of social structures. In studying members' methods – the 'machinery' that constitutes members' cultural competence – ethnomethodology displays an indifference to mainstream sociology's fundamental concern to explain *why* it is that things happen as they do. Instead it replaces it with an emphasis on the description of *how* people accomplish activities: '*Ethnomethodology does not take as its puzzle the fact that people act in stable, regular ways (such that we have the problem of what keeps them behaving like that) but the quite different one of how it is that the stability and regularity of conduct is recognizable and discoverable, and recognizable and discoverable from within its own midst*' (Sharrock and Watson 1988: 62). Rather than producing sociological theories, ethnomethodology attempts: '*… to describe the operational theories, or theories-in-use, that members deploy in attending to the appearances of their surroundings, in constructing their situated courses of action*' (Sharrock and Watson 1988: 127). That's all you're going to get. If you want more we suggest you go and read *The Ethnomethodologists* (Sharrock and Anderson 1986) or *The Perspective of Ethnomethodology* (Benson and Hughes 1983). If you are in a hurry, read Chapter 1 of Lynch's *Scientific Practice and*

Ordinary Action (Lynch 1993) or the Introduction to Button's *Ethnomethodology and the Human Sciences* (Button 1991).

We also will not offer much of an account of the methodological approaches or data collection choices of our authors. We still refuse to fetishize data collection techniques, though some of our authors offer their own accounts or pointers as to their chosen approach. Most involve some form of 'ethnomethodologically-informed ethnography', usually carried out as a form of 'auto-ethnography' and involving a range of collection techniques such as audio and video recording, photographs and logs or journals. If you feel you want to know more we recommend Randall et al.'s (2007) *Fieldwork for Design* and Crabtree et al.'s (2012) *Doing Design Ethnography* – and apologize for plugging our own books. What is more interesting about this collection of studies, as we pointed out above, is that each is an example of a 'hybrid' ethnography. This claim relates to the fact that Garfinkel (1996) once had the notion of ethnomethodology as a 'hybrid' discipline, whereby ethnomethodologists would develop the skills to become practitioners within the setting. With a very few exceptions, such as Sudnow and Livingston, when looking at ethnomethodological studies of the world of work, this has been rare. But each study here is a hybrid study, a study of aspects fly-fishing, or bird-watching, or rock climbing, or distance running or whatever by enthusiasts who, as it turns out, just happen to be ethnomethodologists. How useful or successful this is remains open to debate. As Goode writes of his own research and analysis of playing with his dog Katie, guidelines for research practice:

> ... are ideals that researchers attempt to observe to the greatest degree possible. They are practical guidelines. Thus, in line with the policy of ethnomethodological indifference, I tried to display and analyze play in terms intrinsic to actual instances of it and not to import theory into my analysis. Of course I have failed in this because such a thing is not possible. Particularly for an ethnomethodologist with a Ph.D. What is gained is in the attempt.

Looking to how the book is organized the reader will see that the chapters are loosely grouped together into four different sections: domestic pleasures; having a hobby; getting out of the house; and doing stuff together. This particular group of headings came out of a long discussion between the editors early on in the conceptualization of this book. We had, originally, hoped to organize the book along similar lines to those we had adopted in *Ethnomethodology at Work* (Rouncefield and Tolmie 2011), that is to say, along the lines of 'epistopics'. Here is how we described the matter then:

> There are certain recognizable features of work and the workplace that just anyone knows. These are things like: there's usually some kind of a division of labour; people calculate and/or measure things; people make plans; they schedule things; they have meetings; they talk to customers; they use documents and tools and technology; they read things; and so on. These are the mundane social 'facts'

people orient to. Their facticity is as much taken for granted by the sociologists
who would talk of work, as it is by the practitioners themselves. What we have
sought to do here, in the usual perverse way of ethnomethodologists, is to
respecify these seemingly mundane facts as topics for investigation in their own
right. (Rouncefield and Tolmie 2011: xxii)

Now, whilst the notion of epistopics as an organizational tool for materials relating
to the study of work is reasonably useful, in this volume we had set ourselves
the task of bringing together a selection of enormously diverse chapters treating
of, if you like, everything that people would set aside as standing in contrast
to the workplace. As we have already mentioned we pursued this course quite
deliberately, not only to make a distinctive volume from the previous collection
of papers we had published, but also to put to bed once and for all the confusion
about what ethnomethodologists mean when they talk about 'work' by presenting
a volume of papers treating topics clearly beyond the workplace yet just as
replete with 'work' by members as anything you could find in workplace settings.
However, the problem with bringing together such a diverse set of materials is
that it is very hard to uncover a set of obvious, taken-for-granted 'facts' about
such activities that might relate to all of them equally. Additionally, the related
disciplines being drawn upon here span a wide range of different interests, each
with their own favourite themes and concepts. Some crude tropes can be seen to
cover a large swathe of our materials such as 'gender' and 'class'; some cover a
smaller sub-set of the chapters, such as 'nature versus culture' in anthropology, or
'theory-laden perception' in studies of science and technology, or 'gaze' in studies
of tourism and leisure; and some others are hugely specific to their own domain
such as 'sighting' in yachting, 'sampling' in remixing, and 'busking' in music.

Confronted with this rather bewildering array of potentially addressable
concepts, and the fact that asking our authors to address them would be hugely
constricting and would potentially result in us finding no willing contributors at
all, we decided instead to locate authors we knew had already made forays into
ethnomethodological writing about non-workplace topics and to invite them to
write about the things they *did* feel particularly able to address. This was further
shaped by us approaching authors we already knew would provide us with a
diverse body of materials rather than just ten chapters about differing aspects of
line-dancing or kung-fu. The one additional organizational element we brought to
bear was to try and get some balance of contributions across four different 'folk
locutions' about non-workplace activities that we felt might be useful. What these
folk locutions amount to is nothing more than what anyone might say about the
kinds of things people get up to when they are not out and engaged in their paid
occupations. There are of course, many of these, but we felt that 'messing around
in the house' (which we rephrased as 'domestic pleasures'), 'having a hobby',
'getting out of the house' (which we felt carried slightly more active connotations),
and 'doing stuff together' with other people you know or with whom you share
some interest, covered a good spread of the things we were after. We claim no

particular analytic purchase for these categories at all and make no particular use of them in that way here. They were principally adopted as a means for finding an effective variety of contributions. We have retained them in our presentation of the volume because we feel they provide a strongly recognizable set of groupings at a vulgar, commonsense, everyday kind of level, hence the coinage of the term 'folk' locutions. Additionally, for a book with some pedagogic aspirations, we felt this commonsense recognizability of arrangement to be a virtue. Do not therefore expect there to be a strongly distinctive analytic focus within each of the different sections in this book. Do not, in addition, imagine we feel the placement of each chapter within one section or another to be some absolute form of classification. Clearly, depending upon the language game, virtually any of the chapters could be reconceived as belonging in any of the sections. If you are in the business of listening to birds it is pretty hard to do that effectively without getting out of the house; music-making is, for many, something they might call their 'hobby' and, as a means of diversion, might also count as a domestic pleasure; reading is something you might do anywhere, including out in the countryside or sat at a café. Here are our own rather idiosyncratic reasons for adopting the placements we have used here.

Chapters 1 and 2, about cooking and reading respectively, are distinctive for their massively recurrent visibility, day in and day out, in people's homes. All of the other matters discussed in the book are, however frequent, not so utterly embedded in people's everyday routines as these. Yet, at the same time, they can and do regularly get oriented to as aspects of life delivering scope for relaxation and pleasure. The heading 'domestic pleasures' attempts to recognize the utter mundaneity and routine character of such things. Part II of the book contains four chapters altogether, covering the identification of birds by their songs, fly-fishing, yachting, and remixing music, Most of these take place out of doors, though remixing music does not. What is distinctive here is the highly specific character of the pursuits and their capacity for generating notable passions about them amongst their protagonists such that they might ordinarily be described as hobbies rather than just pastimes. In particular, each of these chapters brings into view the exercise of particular bodies of expertise that are often acquired over quite considerable lengths of time. Part III takes as its theme activities that are used to quite specifically get out of the house and into the open environment. The chapters here are quite diverse, covering family days out on the one hand, and the sporting activities of running and rock-climbing on the other. What brings these chapters together is a set of conventional tropes regarding the pursuit of activities out of doors, such as engagements with the natural world and associated notions of escaping the confining character of life in modern societies. As might be expected from an ethnomethodological text such grand narratives are firmly set aside in favour of understanding these activities as actual situated accomplishments. The final part of the book groups together chapters covering activities that are normally undertaken in the company of people with whom one may only have a passing relationship, the relevance of being together arising from the pursuit of the activity itself. This is not to preclude the possibility of these being things that one might do with family and friends, but rather to acknowledge the potential scope of interactions that could pertain. Irish Music Sessions, Line Dancing classes and café visits all include within them the regular likelihood of encountering and having to interact with people you have never encountered before but with whom some kind of mutual collaboration may arise.

If you don't like these allocations or don't agree with them, that's okay, because they are doing no especially important work in any case. What you do get out of us having done this is a good spread of chapters. Read them in whatever order works best for you. Here, in summary, is what each chapter sets out to address:

The first chapter takes as its theme the hugely omnipresent matter of cooking food. In this particular case it is about cooking for pleasure and the specific data drawn upon relates to cooking a meal for friends. However, in the process of detailing the range of mundane work involved in preparing food it reveals the depth to which cooking is intertwined with numerous other elements of the ordinary everyday social organization of the home and the relationships within it. Thus the chapter speaks of aesthetics and pleasure but at the same time speaks also about what is clearly one of the cornerstones upon which everyday life is constructed.

Chapter 2 tackles another massively visible phenomenon: reading. Once again, as is always the case with ethnomethodological studies, it has at its core observations of actual lived human practice, in this case primarily the reading of a bedtime story. Here, too, the business of reading is found to be completely bound up with the broader social organization of the home within which it happens. By focusing upon the mundane practices and pleasures involved in 'reading to' and 'being read to' it sets aside all of the political and technological debates that current rage around the topic of reading and the changes taking place in the constitution of the medium and instead reveals the artfulness of reading as an embodied course of action that makes manifest a range of assumptions people make about how their home is organized and what the rights and responsibilities of those within it might amount to. It also brings into view how familial relationships are actually articulated through matters such as these and what gross tropes such as 'intimacy', 'pedagogy' and 'recollection' might look like as features of actual human practice.

In Chapter 3 the principal topic is birdsongs and the practices used by people in order to identify birdsongs as and when they are encountered. The materials within the chapter are used not only to explicate the range of ethno-methods involved in being able to recognize birdsongs but also to explicate the distinct competences involved in being an 'expert' or a 'novice' and the work involved in acquiring both 'expertise' and 'membership': in this case membership of the 'birder' community. Along the way the chapter also explores how birders make use of expectations and 'candidate identifications' in order to produce accountably adequate propositions regarding just what it is they might be hearing.

Chapter 4 examines the practices associated with fly-fishing to explicate matters of visual perception. The matter of visual perception is again taken not as a question of general interest, but rather as something where 'seeing' is organized around specific practices relevant to the specific job of fly-fishing in specific situations. The arguments put forward within the chapter are deliberately juxtaposed with those put forward in an earlier ethnomethodological piece regarding 'cultures of seeing' in order to elaborate aspects of seeing as a 'novice' and seeing as an 'expert'. The chapter works through a real-world examples in order to talk about just what practices and knowledge might be involved in actually 'seeing fish' as a fly-fisherman in situ in order to elaborate something that *is* of broader interest as well: how professional or developed sensibilities are 'cultivated' through the regular pursuit of specific bodies of organized practice. It ultimately presents 'seeing', for the expert, as something that is embedded in competences that stand wholly apart from what might ordinarily be though about as visual perception at all.

In Chapter 5 we move on to the cultivated and organized practices associated with the work of yachting. As the authors point out yachting is notable in particular for the extent to which the associated practices, methods and tools are rationalized and subjected to technical and mathematical calculation just in order to keep oneself safe and afloat. The chapter examines the inter-related skills of navigation and sailing in order to explore how these skills draw upon the successful *in situ* and *practical* application of formalisms acquired as part of the business of learning how to sail – making a robust distinction between formalisms as articulated in instructional handbooks and the work of actually rendering them meaningful and useful in the specific situations of their use. The chapter makes its argument by first of all presenting the formalisms of navigation as they might encountered in written texts and courses. It then presents both the formalisms and actual work involved in sailing a boat in order to demonstrate how mastery and application of the formalisms resides not so much in literal and unreflective application as in knowing application that elaborates beyond the formalisms themselves according to circumstance in order to make them fit to purpose for the occasions of their use.

Chapter 6 explores certain aspects of remixing music as a hobby that is collaboratively accomplished using digital technology in the hobbyists' homes. Remixing as a hobby draws upon a potentially limitless body of activities and possibilities but somehow, nonetheless, still results in the end in some specific, concrete, completed remix. The chapter takes the practices involved in arriving at this state of apparent completion as its principal topic and works through specific materials in order to reveal the nature of the collaborative work and associated bodies of reasoning in play here. It does this by means of exploring some distinct yet relevant features that provide for the character of the work, such as being able to simultaneously display creativity whilst somehow rendering the original source 'identifiable', the honing down of possibilities and shaping of materials into something that begins to take recognizable shape as something in particular in ways akin to what Garfinkel, Lynch and Livingston (1981) termed a 'potter's object', and the work towards completion articulated through collaborators' interaction and talk.

Moving back outdoors again, Chapter 7 presents an investigation into something experienced by most of us at some point in our lives: family days out. The chapter makes use of a specific example where a family plan for and then actually undertake a day out at a nature reserve in France. The principal objectives of the chapter revolve around: a) demonstrating the distinctiveness between the actual mundane work involved in going about such undertakings and the heavily theorized workings up of such activities in other kinds of social scientific literature; b) presenting in detail how the accomplishment is animated quite specifically as a *sequential* accomplishment where the ordering of the sequence is central to how it is brought about; and c) revealing how such endeavours do not stand apart from but rather work as another canvas upon which ordinary, everyday familial relationships, rights and responsibilities are made visible. Thus, as well as being about the specific practices involved in getting out of the house together as a family, it is about the practical realization of the *moral order* of the home, something that features strongly in a number of the chapters in this book.

In Chapter 8 we examine the doings of a very different kind of cohort: rock climbers. Here the author uses specific materials drawn from the practical accomplishment of two different kinds of climbing games to examine the praxiological haecceities of what is involved. In particular the chapter seeks to explicate just how climbing works as an embodied, *interactional* phenomenon. Specific matters of attention here are: how rock climbers conceive of, deal with, and anticipate 'problems'; the importance of the tactile aspects of rock-climbing to its effective accomplishment, including the tactile properties of a climber's gear; the work involved in 'seeing' a route or features of a rockface (which brings into view again the topic of developed competence discussed in chapters three and four); and, of course, the actual work of climbing itself.

Chapter 9 looks at how distance running is trained for as a joint accomplishment. It draws upon the running biographies of two running partners who have been running together for many years, presenting numerous anecdotes and vignettes in order to illustrate what running together looks like as a body of lived work in the landscape. Features of particular moment within this accomplishment prove to be things like listening for one another and one another's footfalls in order to manage pace, the situated 'seeing' of one another's condition in order once again to manage matters such as pace, the work of route selection and leadership, and the management of running together as an activity that necessarily has to unfold in public spaces where all manner of different contingencies might arise. The chapter also points out the levels of complexity involved in running together as collaborative work when compared to other cognate activities such as running alone. Once again we see here how something construed of routinely as a leisure pursuit, about 'play' if you like, is nonetheless something premised upon significant bodies of interactional work.

Chapter 10 returns to the topic of music-making, but this time outside of the home and 'down the pub'. Here the interest is centred upon the working practices adopted by those who play instruments in Irish music sessions. The chapter works through some of the broader organizational features manifest in sessions before exploring in detail the specific ways in which musicians make use of a highly developed turn-taking system in order to manage the production of tunes and sets of tunes with one another. Central to the chapter's argument is the way in which the turn-taking system solves the specific organizational problem of producing music in a pub setting, with a cohort of players that is continually in flux. In this respect the practices that have evolved are compared to the turn-taking system that has evolved as a means of producing coherent and ongoing conversation where certain similar problems confront both would-be speakers and would-be players of musical instruments. Ultimately it returns us to a core concern in Sacks et al.'s original *A Simplest Systematics for the Organization of Turn-taking in Conversation* (1974): the use of turn-making to manage the *sequencing* of ordinary situated human action.

In Chapter 11 more working together with others of varying degrees of acquaintance is explored in the context of a line dancing class. The author uses the unfolding organization of a class into different sessions in order to explicate a number of the workaday aspects of how line dancing is accomplished as an *in situ* activity in and through the specific practices of the dancers involved. The chapter explores along the way both the constitution of the venue as an environment within which line dancing may unfold and the specific ways in which different dancers make manifest their competence and membership. It also looks at the work associated with preparing for a line dancing class and some of the ways in which instruction is brought about, both as a body of formalisms and a body of *in situ* practices that render those formalisms meaningful.

The final chapter, Chapter 12, explores the interactions between regulars and staff at cafes. As a category the 'regular' is under-explored in the literature and the chapter uses a range of materials to explore how being a regular is something that is made visible within the relationships between people, the kinds of orientations that pertain towards regulars and between regulars and other people, and how 'being a regular' is maintained through the ongoing interactions between regulars, staff, and other regulars. In particular the chapter emphasizes the ways in which relationships, including those proposed by the notion of a regular, are not simply established once and for all but are rather ongoing accomplishments within each new set of interactions that arise. These reflections are further elaborated through consideration of such matters as how being a regular relates to the order of service, the kinds of interactions that unfold when regulars arrive at a café or depart, notions of intimacy that arise within the relationship associated with being a regular and the kinds of rights and responsibilities that go along with that, and how matters of absence come to be accounted for when the absent party is understood to be a regular rather than just another customer.

Finally, having originally eschewed the possibility of making epistopic treatments work for the structuring of this volume, we should point out that, having now collected all of these chapters together for you, you are going to find that there are, indeed, arising epistopics that *do* seem to cut across a broad selection of the chapters here and that might be worthy of further reflection. These epistopics include matters such as 'planning', 'calculation and measurement', 'record-keeping', 'timing', 'space and place', 'expertise', 'seeing', and so on. What is interesting about all of these is that they are, in fact, the same kinds of epistopics we presented in *Ethnomethodology at Work*. What better way could there be of underscoring the false distinction people make about 'work' and 'not-work' than the fact that, for ordinary people organizing ordinary everyday pursuits in the workplace, at home, or wherever, the business of actually accomplishing them is subject to reasoning in remarkably similar terms.

PART I
Domestic Pleasures

Chapter 1
Cooking for Pleasure

Andy Crabtree, Peter Tolmie and Mark Rouncefield

Introduction: Garfinkel's Bastards Eat Tarte Tatin

Cooking is a mundane feature of everyday life, done by people around the world as a matter of necessity and, for some at least, as the business of pleasure. It seems surprising therefore that food, eating and cooking has, at least until relatively recently (the 1980s), been largely neglected by Sociology (Beardsworth 1997; Murcott 1983). In anthropological analyses food has long featured in ritual and supernatural features of consumption ((Crowley 1980 (1921); Richards 1932) as well as in Levi-Strauss' famous culinary triangle – the raw, the cooked and the rotten. For Levi-Strauss (1970) food practices in general, including cooking, represent a primary binary opposition in society between 'nature' and 'culture' and also contribute to other oppositions such as 'the raw and the cooked' such that cooking represents a cultural transformation of the 'raw' and, thereby, defines culture. Where cooking and eating has featured in sociological analysis it is often as an instantiation of some wider social process, such as the 'civilising process' (Elias 1969), or class and social structure (Goody 1982) or patriarchy and the subjection of women (Charles and Kerr 1988; Murcott 1983). As Charles and Kerr suggest; 'Food practices can be regarded as one of the ways in which important social relations and divisions are symbolized, reinforced and reproduced on a daily basis'. The 'turn to consumption' has, not surprisingly, surfaced some interest in food and more recently food (especially 'fast food') and eating has featured as part of an analysis of the 'McDonaldization of society' (Ritzer 2008) or as part of a discussion of societal obsessions with body shape (Coveney 2006; Short 2006).

This chapter, perhaps not surprisingly, approaches the topic differently, explicating the mundane work involved in making a meal and the enjoyment members who do cooking for pleasure find in the enterprise. It focuses specifically on the mundane competences involved in figuring out what to eat and the considerations that are brought to bear upon this most ordinary of daily concerns, including matters of domestic routine, lifestyle, diet, work-home-life balance, etc. We then examine the sourcing of food and the different orders of working knowledge implicated in finding foodstuffs and assembling ingredients. After this comes the core business of 'alchemy': the skilful use of heat, knives, pans, spices, herbs and seasoning; the subtle art of working with colour, texture, taste, smell and even sound, to transform base ingredients into edible delights. Finally we turn to the pleasure of eating and the values that members bring to the table and exercise in eating together in the course of ordinary everyday *degustation*.

The data used in this chapter relates to observations of a professional man in his early 40s, preparing a three-course meal for friends. The man in question is an enthusiastic amateur cook who cooks for pleasure for both his household and for guests on a regular basis. The example provides us with a selection of interesting vignettes, displaying manifest and taken for granted kitchen competence. In this case cooking was being undertaken for the sheer pleasure of it rather than as a necessary obligation, yet the example is replete with features that exhibit the ordinary organization of household activities and the relationships of the people who inhabit them, underscoring the ways in which these matters are not just embedded within ordinary everyday life but are rather yet another canvas upon which the working up of ordinary household considerations get played out.

The examples are organized around a regularly unfolding sequence that relates to (and encompasses) the actual work of cooking:

1. Cooking and eating as a part of the weekly routine. A great deal of what gets eaten, and how what is going to get eaten is arrived at, is bound up with ordinary weekly activities and considerations such as 'what shall we eat on Sunday?', 'what shall we eat the rest of the week?', 'who's going to be here when?', 'who routinely eats what?', 'what needs to be got out of the freezer?', and so on.

2. Deciding what to eat right now, where broader considerations get honed down to specific matters of 'what do people want to eat just now?', 'what's actually to hand?', or even things such as baking and making things for the sheer pleasure of it or just to pass the time and keep others in the house entertained.

3. Shopping to a purpose. This reflects the fact that, once decisions have been made about what to eat, somehow the decision has to be provisioned by physically bringing the things required together. Much of this inevitably implicates shopping and that itself often implicates the making of a list, though shopping can also be about a more general purpose provisioning for the week with just what to eat right now being framed by what was purchased in the weekly shop.

4. Preparing things for cooking. Once ingredients have been sourced in one way or another and brought to the kitchen they usually need preparing in various ways. The work here can also be about creating the right ambience for cooking to take place. Inevitably the work of preparation often turns out to be interleaved with the work of actually cooking a dish, but in most cases preparation of some kind is a necessary preliminary to the actual heating and assembling of food. Considerations that feature in cooking such as the look of things, their consistency, and their smell, can also play an important part here.

5. Cooking the things prepared. This refers to the actual working upon of prepared foodstuffs in the company of heat such that things are bound together or transformed in some fashion so that they are ready for the actual business of eating.
6. Serving the food. Once food has been cooked, and prior to eating, it needs to be physically moved from the places where it has been cooked and apportioned in various ways so that all the parties to the eating can actually go about the eating of it.
7. Eating the food. Once food is on plates and people are gathered around the table or wherever to eat it, the business of consuming it can occur.

The first three and the last three features of the above sequence have some interchangeability according to circumstance. Reasoning about what to eat and shopping, for instance, can happen at the same time. Preparation and consumption can be comingled with some kinds of dishes, such that all of the four latter components can be going on more or less simultaneously. What does break down separately is the presence of a decision-making process, with the associated work of provisioning those decisions, and the subsequent assembly and consumption of food that brings those decisions to fruition. The organization of the data here is purely bound up with recognizing the specific sequences that were observed on this particular occasion of production.

A) Deciding What to Eat

Discussions about what to eat generally take place within the context of the household routine, being shaped not only by what people fancy eating but also by what is currently available within the house. Here the decision is a more spontaneous affair (Example 1). Where options are relatively open, as they are in this case, negotiations between the parties have the character of 'specific vagueness' (Crabtree et al. 1997) about them, with an iterative process of narrowing down until some specific kind of choice is made. Here it moves from things not to even be considered (e.g. marrow), to matters such as meat/not-meat, Indian/Chinese/French, until specific dishes are arrived at, i.e. pumpkin soup, chicken curry and tarte tatin.

Example 1: Deciding what to eat
A: Any – any preferences yourself? Let's have some candidate dishes. Things we might cook.
P: Is there stuff you detest? So eliminate them completely from the picture.
M: Well I'm not too keen on marrow.
A: Well you're alright coz it's not marrow season.
M: I bloody hate marrow.
A: I don't mi- At this point in time anything's up for grabs. If you want Chinese we can do Chinese. If you want Indian we can do Indian.

M: I prefer Indian.

A: You prefer Indian?

M: How are you on Indians?

P: Oh I like Indian.

A: So errr: So hows about we do er- some curried pumpkin soup.

M: Yeah! Sounds good.

A: Which is a nice starter and goes well with a curry. … we could have chicken curry

…

…

A: What about pudding? (*heading back into living room*)

M: I don't really like puddings (*laughing*).

A: Ahh no. They're too sweet aren't they? They're vile actually

M: Don't you do /(   )

P: /I quite like-

M: Tarte tatin

A: I do. I can do tarte tatin. I do a fantastic tarte tatin if you want it. Tarte tatin and a curry?

M: Sounds alright to me.

P: Yeah.

B) Shopping to Purpose

The meal calls for things that have to be actively sourced from outside of the home. That means there will have to be a shopping expedition, involving some measure of forward planning, constituted around the work of assembling a shopping list. In Example 2 we see the ways in which this kind of work unfolds. One feature is about *projection*: knowing what the dish to be cooked will call for. This can involve consultation of recipes, but it can also be grounded in ordinary recollection of what it takes to make a dish. Another feature is *verification*: checking whether you have the required ingredients, in enough quantity, and whether they are 'good enough'. This can itself lead to another feature, the ongoing *revisability* of a proposed menu as its production is thought about in greater detail. Thus we see A move here from having apples in the tarte tatin to pears, and deciding to buy onions as this will be less unpleasant than digging onions in the rain. These elaborations also move into thinking about the surrounding work of preparation and other meal accompaniments, such that A is moved to not only consider whether beer is needed but to also then ensure it goes in the fridge. Indeed, assembly of the meal and its surrounding paraphernalia has already begun by this stage with the bringing in of the pumpkin from outside, and is further realized by A getting a tub of tag (curry base sauce) out of the freezer. Notice also how the work of preparing a list here is informed through and through by 'how we routinely do shopping lists around here'. So we see A tear a sheet off the pad on the notice board where some things needing purchasing have already been recorded. A then uses this as a place for adding things. All of this itself attests to another common part of the planning process: the active making of a record that can then provide a situational prompt beyond the confines of the home.

Example 2: Making a shopping list

A *getting tub of tag from the freezer and putting on side by cooker*: We'll want some chicken. I'll nip down to the butchers and see if he's open, and if he's not I'll nip up to the next village, and grab something

P: Okay

A: Er, we'll grab some chicken breasts and er I'll nip up to the allotment and grab a couple of things, some onions. What else do we need?

A: So we need some puff pastry, we need two apples, Pears! Pe- pear tarte tatin.

M: Pear tarte tatin?

P: Ooh yeah.

A: We can do that can't we?

…

A:. *Tearing sheet from pad on noticeboard and holding it up*: That's what I've already got on there this week.

Figure 1.1   Getting the shopping list

A *takes the list to a chopping board on side and rests on it with pen poised*: Er: right, I want some chicken breasts don't I? (*writes under previous items on list*) I want some er (*pen poised for a moment*) Some chicken breasts. Puff pastry (*writes underneath other items on list*) Erm.

A: How am I doing for sugar (*walks over towards shelves on other side of kitchen*) (*peers in jar and in packet*). Got some more there, great.

…

A *writes on list under prior items*

A: Yeah, so let me check that then, have we got everything we need?

…

A: I might actually buy some bloody onions to save me going and fucking about on a dirty horrible day and getting stuff from the allotment.
Adds onions to the list
A: (*Looking around kitchen*) Er, I think that's it isn't it?
A: (*Thinking through items out loud and holding out fingers as he does so*) Chicken. Er, so I've got the squash there.
…
A: (*Tapping pen on side as thinking*) Erm, alcohol. We've got some beers about if we're having a drink (*looks over to fridge*), or some wine. We might want to put some beers in the fridge.
A gets pack of beer from top of fridge and puts into fridge. A goes back to side and picks up list and looks at it.
A: I think that's it

Production of a shopping list implicates the actual activity of shopping (not presented here). Many topics fall out of the work of shopping that move beyond just the sourcing of food, particularly the provided-for legibility of shopping environments (expectable and accountably appropriate places for the placement of baskets, vegetables, chilled cabinets, checkouts, and so on). This includes the ways in which shoppers come to know their local shops and appropriate trajectories through them, the practiced competence of selection and the relationship between that and a projected recipe.

C) Preparing Things for Cooking

Creating the right kind of ambience   Something that particularly plays into the pleasure of cooking is the way in which those about to undertake cooking will devote attention to making the environment and its complements 'right' for the doing of that kind of work. A's cooking for friends displays a number of these kinds of considerations, including: putting drink into the fridge in anticipation of it being wanted once food preparation is under way; making sure his friends have drinks whilst he is preparing the food; and setting some music going.

Example 3: Serving drinks and setting the music going
A: (*Going into kitchen and moving things around on side*) Right. Right right right. Soup! Drink even.
Turns round and walks over towards fridge.
A: Tea or beer or (*shrugging shoulders*).
M: Beer will do me.
A: Beer?
A goes to fridge and gets out bottle from top shelf and hands it to M.
…

Music starts playing. A pushes on left hand volume reduce button under iPod, clicking repeatedly until volume is fairly low but still audible.
A: Right, soup.

Assembly of what's needed   Once matters of ambience and its like have been dealt with cooking involves a significant amount of assembly. A range of things have to be brought together, both ingredients themselves and the apparatus for working upon them in order to transform them into a meal. In Example 4 we see how this business of assembly is an ongoing process that runs throughout the stages of initial preparation and of cooking. In this case everything is brought together in phases according to need: first of all for the preparation of the rice, then the chicken, the pepper, and the chillis. In each case there is a surrounding set of accoutrements and practices that are brought to bear, with the larger set of overall ingredients being assembled itself to one side of the chopping board. At the same time, because the rice is already under way as other things are being worked upon, there is a regular stepping out of these activities to monitor the progress of the rice.

Example 4: Getting the curry going
A goes to cupboard and gets out wide pan and puts it on the hob.
A: So we want one of them, and we want some rice don't we.
Goes to same cupboard and gets out a saucepan and puts that next to the other pan on the hob
Puts jar on chopping board, then turns round and walks over towards the shelves, gets knife out of block and then sharpener from rack and sharpens the knife.
Puts knife down next to chopping board and hangs sharpener back up on wall.
A: What am I going to do? Chicken.
Rinses chicken breasts under tap then brings them over to chopping board, lays them down, and turns them to and fro inspecting them. Uses knife to trim off fat from one breast. Puts fat over to left of board and starts to cut the breast into strips.

Figure 1.2   Cutting up the chicken

Lays strips of chicken side by side and cuts across them, making smaller pieces. Prepares other breast in a similar fashion. Goes to sink and washes his hands. Takes towel off back of chair and dries his hands.
Goes to drawer to right of cooker and gets out roll of plastic bags and tears one off. … Pulls mouth of bag open then puts in chicken breast remaining in sink. Washes his hands again and flips bag over a few times and ties it up. Comes over to the table.
A: Can I just get you to pop that in the freezer M? Top shelf?
M: Yeah.
A hands him bag of chicken. M takes to freezer and starts to open door then pauses.
M: In here?
A: Top. Top shelf.
M opens door wider.
A: That's it, yeah.
M puts chicken into freezer and closes door.
A: Cheers
A goes back to chopping board and continues to cut chicken into smaller pieces, mounding cut segments up at back of board. When A finishes cutting chicken he shifts it all into single mound in centre of board. Then goes and puts knife in sink. Puts trimmings into bin, rearranging binbag in bin as he does so. Then washes hands at sink. After this he rinses the knife, squirting some washing up liquid on it and rubbing it with sponge. Puts knife on draining board and continues to wash other items in sink … Goes and dries hands on towel on chair.

…

A: Right. What am I doing next? (*Takes sip of drink*) Get the rice on actually.
Opens up bottom of oven and gets out saucepan. Takes rice pan to tap and runs water into the pan
A brings back pan and puts it on hob.

Figure 1.3   Putting the pan on the hob

Shifts position of other pan and slides the rice pan to the back
Turns on heat under rice pan
Gets pinch of salt from tub on side and adds it to the rice
A: (*to M*) Sorry M. On the top bit, there's a block of creamed coconut in it.
M opens fridge gets out block of creamed coconut and passes it to A
A: Cheers M.
…
A: (*Pausing mid-stride across the kitchen and turning towards the fridge*) Ah! Chillis! (*points to fridge*).
A: (*Pointing to fridge still*) In there in the salad box there's some chillis.
M: (*Opening door to fridge and reaching down to bottom*) In the salad box in here?
A: Yeah.
M pulls open the salad box and rummages around, looking for the chillis. M finds them and hands A the pack of chillis
…
A goes to the cupboard under the chopping board and gets out a sieve. He puts the sieve down next to the chopping board
A: Preparation is everything, ain't it? Y'know. That's what we're about here. And anticipation as well, or y'know. The rice is cooking, I need to drain it in a bit, and- It's getting everything to hand isn't it? The order of things.

Observe in the above example how much of the work is about getting things to hand, before you even get into the actual business of cooking. Notice too how A makes free use of M's proximity to the fridge to draw upon his labour. Cooking, in one way or another, is often a collaborative enterprise. Another thing visible in the above data is that, as well as starting off with a logical arrangement of ingredients and artifacts when the cooking first begins, people work to maintain a coherent and orderly arrangement of things *throughout* the preparation and cooking process. The whole way through the cooking process A preserves a continual orderly arrangement of objects upon his chopping board. Notice too how the placement of things on the shelves, pans in the cupboards, knives in the chopping block, the bin by the door, and so on display the extent to which the crafting of an orderly arrangement of prerequisites for cooking is underpinned by a broader presumptive understanding that members have about the organization of their home and the ways in which that should routinely maintained. The preservation of this kind of order in homes is ultimately a *moral* order, with any kind of breach being subject to account.

Using recipes   The use of recipes is not an overt part of all cooking activities. However, here recipes *were* an integral part of how the cooking was accomplished. In Example 5 we see A using a recipe as an important part of ensuring precision and providing for ongoing verification as the cooking progresses. We see in the practiced use of the recipe book how it is positioned to enable the articulation of both measurement and verification through *episodic constellations of activity*.

During preparation A reads a coherent segment, such as that pertaining to the measurement of butter, then engages in the work of actually measuring those things, then uses the book as a point of reference to verify what he has done, and then he moves on. During cooking A used the book as a description of both how to enact the process and of what it was he might be looking for as the food underwent transformation. Notice also here how certain aspects of local reasoning can become critical to the way a recipe is worked, for instance the use a fan-assisted oven and its effects and cooking with a thick-bottomed pan.

Example 5: Referring to a recipe

A goes into living room. Goes to bookshelf and lifts down Rick Stein recipe book, carries it through to the kitchen and places it on the kitchen table, then leafs through trying to find the recipe. Finds it.

A: There we go.

Presses book down firmly at open pages and smoothes along the centre binding.

M: Ooh.

A: That look like what we're after? *Pushes book towards M who looks more closely at the photo page.*

M: It is.

A: So I'm going to need to do some weighing on this.

A goes to cupboard beneath chopping board and gets out scales, puts the scales onto the chopping board. A peers at recipe book.

A: So we want seventy-five grammes of (*heading back over to scales*) softened butter. *Moves butter onto chopping board and opens out wrapping. Gets knife from back of board and cuts off a portion of butter. Struggles to lift it off the paper.*

A: Erk, come here you beast.

Places knife underneath to prise it up. Lifts block up and places it on the scales.

A: What does it say about the temperature M?

M stands over recipe book and looks at the recipe.

M: Ermmm Preheat the oven to one hundred and ninety.

A: (*Still peeling a pear*) One ninety. So this fan oven (*pauses peeling and adjusts knob on oven*) you've got to knock twenty off of it. … *He turns the knob to position.* Coz they cook hotter.

Studies recipe for a while, drying hands.

Figure 1.4   Checking the recipe

A: (*Reading out*) Place the tarte tatin dish in the frying pan over a medium heat and cook for twenty to twenty-five minutes (*drops towel onto back of chair and heads to cooker*) shaking- twenty to twenty-five minutes, shaking it gently.
Goes to hob and turns on heat under frying pan.
A: So we'll give it a good whack of heat. Get the pan hot, coz it's a thick bottomed pan. It takes a bit of heat to get it going.

Measuring things out and reasoning about quantities   An important counterpart of the use of recipes, already visible in the above, is the measurement of ingredients. Indeed, cooking is replete with both tight and approximate judgments regarding the quantities of different things, and physical measurement is a part of this larger body of reasoning. Measurement provides a solution to the ongoing cook's problem of 'how much'.

In Example 6, A, in practiced fashion, demonstrates the ordinary work that goes on to makes scales usable for effective measurement. The problem one has when measuring loose ingredients is that the bowl or the scales pan has a weight of its own that has to be taken into account. What A demonstrates here is that for accomplished practitioners, this is a taken-for-granted aspect of making use of the scales. We can also see in example 6 the work of repair undertaken to make sure the quantities specified by a recipe are respected, using a spoon to return sugar to the bag. This shows the practical realization of the adaptability of recipes to need. Here we see something else as well: the re-articulation of certain instructions in locally meaningful ways, such that certain measurements can be deemed close enough.

Example 6: Measuring the sugar for a tarte tatin

A rinses sponge under tap and takes over to wipe scales. Puts sponge on draining board then gets towel from the chair and brings it over and dries the scales. Puts towel back on chair. Pauses for a moment then picks up small bowl from the draining board. Inverts it and peers into it.

A: That's dry.

Takes it over to the scales and puts it on them and resets the scales to read zero.

A: (*Walking over to look at recipe*) Sugar. One seventy-five of sugar.

...

A: (*Pouring more sugar into bowl*) One thirty-two (*carries on pouring*) One seventy-seven, one seventy-eight

Puts bag of sugar down on board. Goes to look at recipe.

A: One seventy-five, we'll take a bit out of there.

Lifts some sugar out of bowl with a teaspoon.

Figure 1.5   Measuring the sugar

Tips it back into the bag.

A: (*Looking at readout on scales*) That's it isn't it? Oh, that'll do.

Picks up bowl and shakes it, then tips it over the butter in the pan.

A: I think it was saying one seventy-three there wasn't it?

P: Yeah, one seventy-three.

A: So we're a touch under on butter and a touch under on sugar. That'll do (*puts bowl over to side*) It won't matter.

Shaping and cutting food to size   A great deal of the work being related here involves the 'working' of food in terms of making the food the right size or shape to solve considerations of texture and consistency, or other concerns bound up with how the food will behave and cook in the pot etc, or how it will feel in the mouth. All of these matters impact on work undertaken to shape and cut food in appropriate ways. For A there is a great deal of knife work involved in all of the dishes he prepares. Example 7 shows just how much knowing manipulation of both the knife and the food itself can be involved in the apparently simple matter of peeling and cutting some pears.

Example 7: Cutting up pears

A goes to table and takes two pears out of bowl.

A: (*Walking over to chopping board*) We'll try these for starters and see how many more we need ...

Cuts along the length of the pear, peeling off a strip of skin, working his way around the pear …

Figure 1.6   Peeling the pears

Finishes removing the skin from the first pear and puts it down behind the other pear at the back of the chopping board. Then he picks up the other pear and peels it in exactly the same way. Note how he holds the pear in his left hand, and uses that hand to twist it round each time one strip is finished, whilst holding the knife flat to the skin and drawing it along the pear just beneath the skin with his thumb pressed firmly against the end of the pear, drawing the knife closer and closer to his thumb each time until the skin falls…

Comes back to the chopping board and takes larger knife out of the knife block.

Positions a pear so that it is facing him with the stalk end to the rear and rests the knife along the length of it.

Figure 1.7　Cutting up the pears

Presses the knife lightly into the flesh of the pear, then, still holding the knife into the flesh with his right hand he taps firmly on the knife with his left hand and it falls in half. Pushes the two halves slightly to the right and gets the other pear and does the same. Puts the large knife to the rear of the chopping board and picks up the small knife he used previously to peel them.

Picks up one of the halves and puts it in his left hand and begins to cut out the core, using the small knife in his right hand. This involves drawing the knife down the length of the pear from the stalk end with the tip inserted into the flesh at an angle under the stalk, following the outline of the core around the bulb of the part with seeds. As he reaches the end he turns the pear round with his left hand and goes back towards the stalk along the other side of the core and stem.

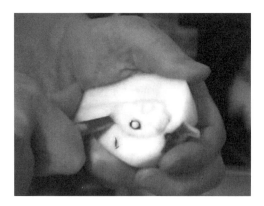

Figure 1.8　Cutting out the core

A: Get rid of that stringy bit that runs right up it.
Gets to the end then works his way back along the same side, pushing the knife in a little deeper.
A: It's not good eating.

Assembling a dish – the interleaving of preparation and cooking   The data shows that there is no neat process where all the food is first prepared and then all the food is cooked, but rather an interleaving of these two activities, with cooking starting after just some preparation has been undertaken and then preparation continuing whilst a first part of a dish is being cooked, preparation and cooking working side by side. In Example 8, we see that, whilst A is putatively engaged in a solo cooking endeavour, it is utterly unremarkable for him to call on others in the kitchen to assist him. M, who is sat beside the fridge, is co-opted to help and needs quite precise instruction as to where to place things or to find things because he has no local knowledge about the routine and ordinary ways in which A's household organize their fridge.

Example 8: Helping out with things from the fridge
A picks up block of pastry and looks at it. Squeezes it with his fingers, then gets a plate from the draining board. Takes both plate and block of pastry over to M.
A: Can you pop that into the fridge for a few minutes? It's just a bit (*tossing the pastry up and catching it and putting it on the plate*) soft.
M takes the plate from him and puts it in the fridge.
A: I think there's some cre- (*grabbing towel from back of chair*) some cream in there (*gesturing to fridge*), in the fridge M.
M: Okay ...
M: Ohhh. Cornish clotted cream?
A: That's the one.

Keeping things clean and tidy – preserving the moral order and facilitating re-use   Something that goes right to the heart of a whole swathe of ordinary assumptions people make about the organization of their households and appropriate ways of maintaining that organization, is the attention paid during cooking to matters of tidiness and cleanliness. Throughout the cooking process A engaged in cleaning tasks that were bound up with the ongoing facilitation of the cooking. Primarily this focused on thing like the cleaning of knives, which he did after use and in an appropriate lull in other activities, before returning the knives quite purposefully to the knife block which rendered them available for re-use. This makes evident sense when the cooking is still in progress as it avoids the need to suddenly uncover the need for a knife and having to clean it then and there and put everything else on hold. However, it also demonstrates a more fundamental assumption: that, even though they could be left unwashed, utensils are cleaned between the preparation of different things rather than having the residues of one thing mixed with another. This was visible in A's attentiveness to cleaning the chopping board as well. Notice also how the very constitution of kitchen spaces provides for these kinds of things, from relatively static arrangements such as the proximity of sinks and draining boards to areas where cooking takes place, to more household elective matters that are nonetheless remarkably static once the election has taken place, such as the positioning of rubbish bins, knife blocks, utensil pots and drawers, and even where towels get hung. What this demonstrates is the extent to which there is a *topological* organization to these matters.

D) Cooking the Things Prepared

Using the senses   At this point we move on to considering one of principal alchemies of cooking: the transformation of prepared ingredients into an actual dish to be eaten by means of applying heat. One of the most important parts of how cooking is managed as an activity by those who undertake it is through the application of various senses in a mundane fashion in order to inform various judgments about what should be done with the food, what stage of transformation food may have reached, what that might imply for what happens next, and whether food has reached the point where it is ready for consumption. Example 9 demonstrates how the various senses provide for the accountable characteristics of a tarte tatin and what would make it 'right' or otherwise.

> **Example 9: Discussing what makes a dish right**
> A: And the actual cooking of something, you're talking about colour, and taste, bite, smell, and all those things. Trying to nail those down.
> M: It applies to specific dishes. Tarte tatin has a specific – well it has taste and smell but there's also something to do with the bite. The crunch and the softness of the pear, but it's not so soft that it's disappeared. There's still a hardness there.
> A: It's a fruit ain't it?
> M: Yeah. The colour of the sauce and the taste of the sauce, but also the pastry. Different parts of the pastry tasting, crunching –
> A: Differently?
> M: What's the word for that? Not to do with taste but with like the feel of it in your mouth?
> P: What would make it wrong for a tarte tatin? What would offend you?
> A: Soggy fucking pastry.

Using the tongue – monitoring flavour   In Example 10 it is the tongue that is brought to bear. A is tasting the curry to assess the adequacy of its flavour. This is not about monitoring readiness, it is about making a judgement about a balance of tastes.

Example 10: Using the sense of taste

A turns heat down under pan and moves it over to right. Opens bag of coriander. Gets
out a pinch and throws it into pan ...
Stirs in the coriander, moving the pan back over the heat.
Grabs teaspoon from chopping board and dips it into the pan.
Lifts the teaspoon to his mouth and tastes.
Dips it in again and does the same.
Puts teaspoon down on chopping board and stirs the pan.
Picks spoon up again and dips it in as stirring and lifts it up to taste.

Figure 1.9   Tasting the curry

Stirs the pan some more.
Tastes it again.
Dips and tastes again.
Puts teaspoon back on chopping board and carries on stirring.
Grabs a pinch of salt from jar behind board and sprinkles it into the pan.
Stirs it again.
Reduces the heat a little and carries on stirring.
A: The best thing we can do with this is leave it.

Using the nose – monitoring progress and readiness   One of the prime arbiters
of cooking-in-action is the nose. Cooks use the nose in a variety of ways to make
all kinds of judgments. In Example 11 the nose is pressed into service as a basis
for monitoring what stage has been reached and monitoring whether the next stage
can be commenced. Here A uses his nose in order to assess what ingredients are
beginning to become pronounced, understanding that this carries implications
regarding how different ingredients are responding to heat and beginning to
mingle. He uses this also as a means of drawing M into such assessments (or
at least into affirming his own) and this in turn becomes the grounds of a fairly

extended piece of talk about smells and tastes and what they indicate about the things one is cooking.

Example 11: Sniffing the pears
A sniffs at pan on hob.
A: (*To P*) Get your nose in that.
P sniffs pan, then M has a sniff.
M: You can smell the sugar can't you.
A: And you're starting to smell the fruit.
A has another sniff.

Figure 1.10   Sniffing the pears

A: Can you smell the pear in there? Coming through now?
M comes over and has another sniff.
M: Yes. There's butter – The smell of butter is quite strong.
A: Yes.
M: But there's –
A: It's starting to come through. The sweetness is there and then the fruit is just percolating through in it. And that just becomes stronger and stronger as you go. So here's a thing, with S. Y'know, one of the first things she often says is – er when she comes in the door is. That smells good.
M: It smells nice, yeah. That's the first – well, before you even see anything you get the smell.
A: Yeah, yeah. And that frames things in a sense as well. It's not just 'that smells good' but 'that smells good, what we having?', y'know, 'is it ready?', y'know?

Using the eyes – monitoring progress and readiness   Of course judgments about progress and readiness do not turn solely upon the use of people's noses and tongues, vision plays an important part as well. In Example 12 we see A continually assessing the progress and ultimate readiness of the pears he is cooking in a caramel sauce on the basis of colour. He has an understanding of what colour he is looking for because he has an idea of just what shade of brown a caramel sauce should be. Indeed, in this case he is looking not for the ultimate shade of brown but the right in-between shade to allow for it to finish off as the tarte tatin is cooked in the oven. This is a subtle judgment that rides in good part on prior experience but it is the central focus of A's assessments of the food and its readiness.

Example 12: Watching the pears

A: (*gesturing to pan*) Now basically what you're doing there is to – because all together it gets cooked for about forty-five minutes – you're just making a caramel sauce. You're just doing fruit in a caramel sauce with a lump of pastry on top, soaking it all up, y'know? It ain't complicated.

Leans over pan and studies it.

Figure 1.11   Watching the pears

Leans further in and sniffs.

A: Once the fruit starts to go it smells divine.

Looks at recipe book

A: (*Reading out*) Forty-five minutes shaking gently now and then till butter and sugar have amalgamated with the apple juice to become a rich toffee sauce and the apples are just tender. Okay.

Turns back towards cooker.

A shifts the position of the pan on the hob again and shakes it a little.

Bends down and peers at it closely.

A shaking pan then turning heat down a little.

A: Let's turn the heat up again (…) to get a bit more (…) It's starting to need a little bit more colour.

Using the ears – monitoring progress and controlling through heat   In fact, the monitoring of the progress of cooking exercises all of the senses to varying degrees. Thus we also find that hearing can become a feature of certain judgments. In Example 13 A brings attention to a potential problem with how the dish is cooking, namely that it is 'going too fast', it is 'too busy'. This typically refers to the bubbling sounds that come from a pot, though for some dishes it could be judgments about sizzling, hissing, and so on.

Example 13: The sound of food

A stirring contents of saucepan with a wooden spoon.
A: Can you hear that? (.) it's going too fast.
Stirs contents of pan again.
A: Too busy.
Turns down heat under pan. Stirs contents of pan around again. Leaves wooden spoon in pan ...
Stirring pan with spoon.
A: That's a nicer sound now.

Using the ears and the eyes together – monitoring progress and controlling through heat   Of course, it is rarely just one sense in isolation that is brought to bear upon specific in-the-course-of-cooking reasoning. Example 14 demonstrates this point. Here A reasons about both the pace of bubbling and the turning of the sauce to a caramel colour to make judgments about heat.

Example 14: Working with the bubbling of food

A Shakes the pan to and fro slightly on the hob and changes the angle, twisting the handle to the right
Shakes it some more then moves the pears in the pan with his fingers.
A: The trick with this in a lot of respects is … It's not to be too gentle with it. Coz you see how it's going now (*pointing into pan with little finger*).

Figure 1.12   Pointing to the bubbling

A: You see all that bubbling, and you're thinking, like, When you first do it, and you think like.

M: It's going to burn.

A: Yeah. You think it's going too fast. So you turn it down. And when you've turned it down it never goes that rich caramel colour.

Using the hands – monitoring progress and readiness   So taste, smell, sight, and hearing can be implicated in various ways in the assessment of how food is cooking and what kinds of other actions might need to take place. However, it does not stop here: the sense of touch is also applied in numerous different and subtle fashions. Thus we see in Example 15 how A actually prods at the pears to see if they feel 'soft', judging where they have got to in the cooking process and whether the heat might need to be changed.

Example 15: Assessing consistency in cooking
A prods pears gently in the pan with his fingers.
A gets a knife from the draining board and brings it over to the cooker.
He wipes the blade between two fingers then prods one of the pears a few times with it.

Figure 1.13   Prodding for consistency

Then he prods another one. And then another.
A: I'm just seeing if they're softening a touch.
Works his way around the other pears in the pan, prodding them in the same way.
A: They are softening. I think they'll be nice in bit. (*Carries on prodding*) That'll do.

Example 16 is a more complex case, a combination of senses working together to make judgments about when rice might have finished cooking. This is about more than taste. It is primarily about a texture in the mouth, a softness to the bite that indicates it has finished cooking. The sensation of feelings 'in the mouth' of softness, hardness, graininess, smoothness, and so on, is a critical component of reasoning about the pleasures of food and appropriateness of cooking practices, with cooks being openly accountable for having got the consistency 'wrong'.

Example 16: Checking the rice
A comes over to hob, picks up spoon from edge of pan, and stirs the rice. Lifts some out of the water and inspects it. Picks a few grains up from the tip of the spoon and eats them.
Taps spoon on side of pan. Goes to put on edge of pan, then changes his mind and stirs it again and picks some up and tastes it again.

Figure 1.14   Checking the rice

Pauses a moment, then picks up a few more grains and tries those. Drops rest back in pan, taps spoon, and rests it down again.
A: Nearly ready that.

Using time as a feature of judgment   Timing proves to be especially critical in cooking, with cooks constantly concerned with, and monitoring, just how long different things have been cooking. In Example 17 A elaborates on some important aspects of this, that timings in cooking are a contingently used resource rather than something to be taken as an absolute. Times implicate points of assessment and reasoning at best, but the other arbiters are also brought to bear upon any decisions rather than 'it's had ten minutes, it must be done'.

Example 17: Thinking about time
M: Well cooking is about timing.
A: It is, isn't it?
M: A production line. That's what I do. I don't cook, I assemble things.
A: Well there is that about it.
P: There definitely is.
A: Assembly is a feature of working it isn't it? It's like 'are me onions soft enough now to do the next bit?' There's a set of skills you use and judgements to bring it to the appropriate – You couldn't use a clock to do it. You couldn't say after thirty seconds that – 'Y'know? There's a perception of the right time that trades on colour and all the rest of it.
A: (*Turning heat down under pan*) I think we might just crank it down a touch with that now.
A: It's getting happy and excited en't it?
M: Mmm. It's bubbling away.
A: (*Shaking pan*) What time did we put it on? About five minutes ago?
M: More seven minutes really.

A Shakes pan some more.
A: It ain't been on ten minutes has it?
M: No. Six and a half.
A: Right. Timing again. Well what – It doesn't matter if it's to the nth …
M: Yeah, one way is to do it by time, the other is to do it by colour.
A: I would always work off colour. I think time – Time can only be treated as a guide.

In Example 18 A uses the judgEment that the pears for the tarte tatin have been cooking for 'about ten minutes' as grounds for changing the heat under the pan, using the account that it is at about this point in time that it will otherwise start to 'blow itself over the edge of the pan'.

Example 18: Changing the heat
A Shaking and shifting position of pan on hob.
A: So that's about ten minutes that's had in't it? (*Goes to turn heat down*).
A: It's going to get too excited and start to blow itself over the edge of the pan in't it?

Filling in the pauses in-between   One of the aspects of cooking many dishes that cooks prove to make use of in a variety of ways is that dishes often do not require continual attention. Thus, it falls out that cooks will find themselves with idle time between moments of working with the food in some way. However, there are accountable matters to attend to here and this is one of the things that will keep a cook's eyes on the clock. One's principal responsibility when cooking is to maintain the due progress of the work in hand. Other activities therefore have to be easily accommodated within the spaces between or trouble may ensue since cooks are called to account for not paying proper attention and letting things burn or get ruined. In the course of our observations we saw A use a number of different things to fill in these spaces in cooking. On every occasion, his friends being present at the time, these were taken to be opportunities for interaction and most particularly for occasioned conversation. They also afforded him time to do washing-up and drying of items that might be needed subsequently. He also took these spaces as opportunities for drinking the wine he had poured himself at the start. Indeed, pouring of drinks to imbibe whilst cooking is, in part, an anticipation of exactly these kinds of opportunities coming along.

E) Serving the Food

The work of serving   Once the cooking is all done a cook's work is not yet finished. There is the small matter of getting the food out of pots and pans etc and to the table and under people's noses, ready to eat. This can involve varying degrees of ritual, but it is always a part of the work. In Example 19 we see A working on the serving of the tarte tatin. Notice here the added complication of having to invert the contents of the pan onto a plate prior to serving because the whole thing is effectively cooked 'upside down'. This involves further knife work, but also some dexterity with plates, their positioning, and the rapid inversion of the pan and plate to avoid spillage. This is made harder by the fact that the pan is only recently out of the oven so it requires handling with oven gloves. Hence A's comment: 'this is where it can all go wrong'. However, there's something else going on here as well. This is a dish being prepared for friends, and the recipients of the dish are accountable for how they respond to the food put in front of them. A plays to this point here by introducing an element of showmanship about it all. Notice how he first of all takes a peek once it's been turned over. And notice how he then holds it out for all to see with a flourish. And note, in turn, how once it comes to the table this prompts the implicated second part of all this work of presentation when M says 'It looks fantastic'.

Example 19: Working the serving of food
A holding top of pastry in pan in place and cutting around edges with knife.
A: You can feel a bit of resistance, like something's really caramelized quite nicely
M: Mmm.
A: Whether it has we're going to find out ...
A: Right, the next – oh shit, that's what I was going to do innit?
A grabs plate from drainer and puts it next to chopping board.
M: Weren't you going to turn it over?
A: Yes.
A grabs oven gloves from chair.
A: This is where it can all go wrong.
Picks pan up with oven gloves and holds plate against side of pan. Inverts plate on top of the pan. Holds the plate down with his left hand. Then he inverts whole lot and gives it a downward/upward shake.
A: And …
He holds the plate with pan resting upside down on top of it towards the table.
A: Is it all just going to drop off?
A puts the oven gloves down but picks them up again and grabs the handle, still holding the plate up with his left hand. He lifts the pan a bit and peers underneath.

Figure 1.15   Turning the tarte over

A: Do we have a tarte tatiin?
He lifts the pan right off and holds the tarte out towards M and P to show them it on the plate.

Figure 1.16   Success – the tarte tatin

...
M: It looks fantastic.

The shared work of serving   Serving food is a collaborative activity. There are numerous features of comportment and bodily orientation relating to the passing of plates and cutlery between people, and in Example 20 we see how this collaborative work can sometimes become more explicit with certain parties being called upon to directly assist with the serving. In this case A is unwilling to risk a balanced portion of tarte tatin, dripping sauce, being carried any distance across the table so he enlists the help of M, who is asked to hold plates in close position to the plate he is lifting portions from.

Example 20: Helping out with serving

A cuts a slice then goes to lift with the blade of the knife. It doesn't lift. He cuts the edges of the slice again. Then he goes to lift onto a plate
A: M, can you pick your plate up?
M holds the plate over the larger plate and A lifts the slice onto it.

Figure 1.17   Helping out with serving

After this he scrapes the bits left on the bottom of the plate up and with the knife and puts them on top of the slice.
A: We'll dish some of this caramel sauce out in a minute.
A cuts the tarte to make another third.
A: P? Oh M, can you do the honours again?
P passes M his plate and M holds it up as before.

Expressions of enthusiasm   As we noted above, the presentation of a dish usually implicates some kind of positive response from its recipients. This is especially the case with guests. Indeed, the kinds of responses expected and delivered mark out, in part, people as guests rather than inhabitants or family members etc. For a guest to take food without comment is potentially accountable as being 'rude'. What we see in Example 21 is the way in which guests demonstrate this understanding even in the absence of any overt presentation of the food. This example precedes A's inversion of the tarte but even now, and before A has done anything much other than get it out of the oven and put it on a trivet to cool, M still offers up the remark 'it looks great'.

Example 21: Responding to a well-turned-out dish

A: (*standing up from table*) And with that gentlemen (*wiping hands on towel*) that can come out (*grabs oven gloves from back of chair and pulls them on*). Bends down and opens lower oven door. Reaches into oven, turns handle of pan slightly with oven glove then grabs the handle and lifts it out.

Figure 1.18   Getting the tarte from the oven

Lifts it up towards top of oven.
M: Oooh!
P: Mmmmmm!
A: Now we're going to let it cool.
Places pan on top of hob. Studies it as he reaches down to shut the oven door.
A: You see tha – We could have given that a bit more welly, you know, when it were on here (*pointing to top of hob*) Turns oven off.
A: It's nice (*gesturing to tarte in pan*) It is nice and brown but it could have – we could have given it a bit more. And now –
M: It looks great.

F) Eating the Food

Expressions of enthusiasm – expressions of gratitude   We now move to the final part of the business: the eating. In Example 22 we see an extension of the points we have just been making regarding how guests understand part of the business of being a guest is to offer compliments regarding the food as it is being served. What happens now is a series of expressions of pleasure and gratitude during the actual course of eating the food. Again, this is routine practice for being a guest and a potentially exceptional practice for being an inhabitant. It is not that inhabitants do not use such expressions, but they are not something they are expected to do all of the time. Indeed, it would become odd in itself if a member of the household offered up expressions of delight at every morsel of food they were given (rather in the fashion of Garfinkel's infamous children as lodgers). Thus such expressions get used by inhabitants as a way of recognizing particular cases of merit and effort, such as special family meals.

Example 22: Eating
A: So you could – That caramel sauce, well that caramel recipe I've got here, you could make less of it – you make a third less of it and make a drier, tighter – tighter – so it'd cling more to your fruit if you know what I mean, it'd be more toffee if you will. But, it's so fucking good that why would you bother?
A: Right, go on P. Get eating.
A: Get some cream, P. Get some cream.
M: Yum, yum. Mm, pastry's nice.

At the same time, along with the kinds of comments one gets from guests, cooks are able to engage in various kinds of post-cooking assessments regarding what might or might not have worked with a meal. We saw A saying earlier about the tarte tatin 'It is nice and brown but it could have – we could have given it a bit more'. This is a potential criticism. Self-criticism like this is unproblematic. However, for a guest to make this kind of comment would be a very different matter, with very different consequences.

Conclusion: Cooking and Family Life

What our data suggest is the way in which the production of food is possessed of various accountable characteristics that form a part of how the constellation of relationships within a household get managed and maintained. What this discussion needs to be set against is just who might be able to actually call these different features to account and in what circumstances, regardless of whether they are connoisseurs of such desserts. What we have seen in the examples is that there is already a dividing line between guests and hosts on this score, not to mention between cooks and recipients. But it goes further than this. Different children (e.g. those known to be 'fussy' or not) have different rights of expression and calling to account with regard to their parents. Partners and spouses may have further rights, but even then rights of criticism vary. So what we have here is the eating of food being a vital domain for the constitution of household relations. Small wonder then that so much emphasis can come to be put upon certain family meals such as Sunday dinners.

In this conclusion we want to move on from the production (and obviously consumption) of pumpkin soup, chicken curry and tarte tatin to consider the interleaving of cooking and family life. A strong aspect of how cooking is a feature of the broader social organization of the home is the way in which provisioning for cooking informs the rest of the household routine, yet how, at the same time, this provisioning is informed by the ways in which the rest of the routine is accomplished. So, in Example 23 below, A and his guests are discussing the relationship of cooking to their family routines, including matters such as the occasioning of shopping, cleaning, tidying, and even the timing of other activities. The logic of provisioning is interleaved with the organization of other activities. Different kinds of cooking and eating patterns get constituted around other ways in which household life is organized throughout the week, such that Friday night could be 'pizza night', or Sunday lunch treated as something special.

Example 23: Reasoning about the cooking routine

A: ... The routine is being with your family. Occasionally extends to having guests and doing special events. Things like that, but that's all wrapped up again in part of daily life and relationships ...

A: Yeah, Sunday's for me are often, and particularly at this time of year, cooking days. And it's wonderful, like Sunday morning's she'll get a bit of a lie-in and I'll get up and start cooking stuff, make a few dishes. Sunday's also a special thing, not in a religious way, but it's like, we'll have a nice meal because I've got more time. So we always say: 'what are we having for Sunday tea?'.

Reasoning about cooking is informed through and through by the constitution of the different relationships between various members of the household. So it can fall down to having to manage a variety of different tastes and preferences with, significantly, those preferences having a right to be voiced and the person doing the cooking being held accountable to their recognition. In Examples 24 and 25 it can be seen that aspects of familial relationships can also be found at the dinner table with cooking and eating being just another opportunity for such considerations to get occasioned.

Example 24: Bringing family relations to the table

A: Yeah, It's recognizing that it's not just some technical skill being exercised on a bit of food or with some pans and stuff, it's really integral to

M: Family life, yeah ...

A: It's woven into a whole set of familial concerns.

P: And it's accountable to those concerns, not just to itself.

Example 25: Bringing the family together

A: It gears into a whole bunch of things that are really important, and if you didn't do it – If I didn't cook, and S didn't cook, I don't know what our lives would look like if you know what I mean. Things really turn upon it. This is our meal. We sit down, and we're doin' nowt in some respects, but we sit down to eat and we have a conversation. We're cooking – while we do it we're not just talking about it we're talking about us and our everyday lives, y'know. And it goes all the way through it. ... So for us dinner is – It's not just food, it's an opportunity to be together. Talk about the shit in our lives.

The good things in our lives. Project, plan, all the rest of it, y'know? Yeah. So it's a very, very precious thing.

In these final examples, we have arrived at the point of summing up the importance of what we have been saying. Here A discussed how significant the meals he has with his wife are in terms of the preservation of their relationship and the forum it provides for them to 'work' their relationship through a variety of interactions about what has been happening with their lives, what things they plan to do, and so on. This is the very stuff of family life that provides for its ongoing realization and, without it, it is just a bunch of people living together without commitment or responsibility, offering up politenesses about food because that is the limit of their ordinary rights.

Chapter 2

Reading for Pleasure: Bedtime Stories

Peter Tolmie and Mark Rouncefield

Introduction: … 'Once upon a time'…

Reading is a commonplace activity, visible across all walks of life and in virtually all human settings. The acquisition of the capacity to read is emphasized from an early age and having a literate population is a foundational concern for most modern nations. Early sociological interest in reading (Dulin 1974), in reading as a process and as an activity, outlined the various ways in which sociological issues, the 'usual suspects' of class and gender and social groupings, impacted on what, why, how and when people read – though there was little obvious interest in the activity of reading itself other than as yet another instantiation of other, wider, more important social processes at work. More recently the focus of research on reading has largely moved away from an interest in the actual activity of reading towards an interest in the form, the physical mechanisms, the technologies, by which reading is accomplished – that is, the shift from books to various forms of electronic devices such as the Kindle (Marr 2007; Thompson 2005) – often accompanied by scare stories telling us that such devices are 'making us stupid' (Carr 2008) or 'lazy' (Collins 2011). So a debate has begun to open up regarding the changing character of reading as more and more of people's reading apparently takes place through the mediation of various digital devices. Yet in all of these arguments reading is often taken to be of a piece whilst, in fact, people read for an enormous variety of different reasons in different contexts (see Rooksby 2011 for an analysis of reading in workplace settings). Reading *for pleasure* is something that in many ways is far more circumscribed. It can still be witnessed in many settings: in waiting rooms, on trains, in buses, on beaches, in worker's lounges, even at people's desks at lunchtime. However, it remains a predominantly domestic pastime.

Ethnomethodologists have long been interested in explicating ordinary reading practices and the various mundane competencies exhibited in and through them. Ethnomethodological approaches to reading, that examine reading as a practical social accomplishment, were perhaps first explored in McHoul (1978) *Ethnomethodology and Literature: Preliminaries to a Sociology of Reading –* '*a sociology of literature, or more precisely of reading, would take as its topic the methodical ways in which members go about making sense of the written traces of other men in society*'. McHoul documents members' procedures in performing reading work, examining how indexicality, reflexivity and the documentary method impact on reading as a social accomplishment. '*Once embarked upon reading, the reader encounters individual utterances which act as evidences of an underlying pattern of meaning ... (mutually informing) ... until the end of the work is reached and a final interpretation of 'what the whole work is about' is arrived at.*' Similarly, Livingston (1995) in *The Anthropology of Reading* illustrates how reading's 'work' is the continual "labor" of finding and sustaining a relationship between a text and its reading. The unremarkable character of reading's work lies in its accomplishment:

> When readers read they are actively engaged in an activity which might be said to consist of 'work'. They are doing things while reading, and what they are doing is 'work'. For the most part, this work is so familiar and ordinary that it does not cause readers to reflect on what they are doing.

In *Structuring Writing for Reading* Paul Ten Have (1999) presents an ethnomethodology of artful textual practices, textual devices – such as paragraphs or footnotes – that are used by writers to structure the activities of readers – that act as a resource to readers and influence how a text, a story, is read. As Ten Have suggests the accomplishment of reading involves rather more than simply being able to piece together and recognize words in a sentence: '*... reading involves "following" more complex forms of organization than "just" the ways in which words can be seen to form a sentence ... reading involves more than recognizing and understanding sentences; it requires complex structuring operations.*' Accordingly, he argues that writers need to provide a range of structuring devices to make things easier for the reader. But even studies of reading embracing approaches seemingly sympathetic to ethnomethodological concerns sometimes appear to have been hijacked in the interests of conventional sociological topics. So, for example, Anita Webb's (2007) *A Father, a Son and a Storybook* uses conversation and discourse analysis to document and analyse recorded conversations and interactions between a father and his four-year-old son during reading sessions. But the focus of interest is on the role gender, genre and adult/child power relationships play in reading.

Our focus here is on reading 'bedtime stories', with an emphasis on what Heap (ref) calls reading '*simpliciter*', the practices of mundane or lay reading, rather than reading '*cultura*', the cultivated practices of professional reading, the reading of literature critics. In this chapter we use data gathered in domestic environments that concentrates upon the actual situated practices of one aspect of reading for pleasure – reading stories to children at bedtime. Instead of engaging in the grand debates outlined above we adopt a position of ethnomethodological indifference and explore, instead, how reading is actually accomplished in these settings as a part of the daily fabric of life: how it fits within the domestic routine; who can do it where and when; how it is actually visibly done; how its visible character ramifies for others in the household; and, most importantly, how it is manifestly about leisure and pleasure rather than about remuneration and obligation to others.

In doing this we touch on some of the pleasures of *reading to* and *being read to* and articulate a range of considerations regarding how reading actually gets done that are of moment regardless of the political and technological agendas that many sociological accounts would wish to bring to bear.

In this chapter we consider some videotaped data about reading and the ways in which it constitutes socially organized phenomenon within the home. As with any body of practice, there are manifest, situated logics that attach to how people reason about their reading practices and these are accountable to the moment, to the social organization in play. The analytic focus is upon manifest, accountable reasoning and practice. The data displays the socially organized character of reading; how reading is not just a matter of consuming words off the page but rather and also about accomplishing a range of possible activities within the home environment such as: 'relaxing', 'killing time', 'informing', 'having a break', or, in this case, 'putting to bed'. We are therefore hinge our discussion of the data around our observations of bedtime reading because these most clearly demonstrate the placement of a particular household activity within a routine whilst at the same time bringing into view a wide variety of the organizational characteristics of reading from matters of embodiment to spatiotemporal placement, from affordances to visibility and coordination.

Book Reading as Embodied

Many aspects of reading as a social phenomenon can be seen to turn upon its physical embodied character. In the following observations the mother (M) is reading a bedtime story to her daughter Sarah (S):

> *M picking up the book to sit down as S reaches out to her*
> *M gets ready to open the book*
> *M flicks through the pages*
> *M opens the book*
> *M lifts out the bookmark*
> *M puts the bookmark on the arm of chair*
> *M sorts out the dust jacket*
> *M positioning the book to read*
> *M holding the book in place as asking S to recall the last part*

Figure 2.1   Positioning the book to read

M flicking back to the prior chapter.
M flicking back to the current chapter.
M: (*starting to read*) Chapter twelve. Cold air burned in Torak's throat as he tore through a willow thicket …
M: … If he tried to swim over he'd be seen and be speared like a pike. He had to get back to (*grabbing the edge of the page to turn it*)
… the cover of the (*turning the page*) …
M shifting to holding the book with just one hand
M: … The booming of the horns suddenly cut off. (*Shifting the book again*)
M: … Through the (*shifting her hold on the book to turn the page*)
M: … Big and dark (*opening at a new page [note it's visibly the last couple of pages of the chapter]*).
M flicking to and fro
S: More story.
M flicking forward page by page – note the finger still held in place at the beginning of the chapter

Figure 2.2   Flicking through the pages

M: It's a long one
S: (*As M flicks back*) You could stop in the middle of it.
M: I could read up to (*pointing out section marker on page*).
S: Up to (…) there.
M: Up to that one? (*pointing*).
S: Yes (…) There (*pointing*).
M flicking back to the chapter beginning – note how she held her thumb in place. Reading on …
M: … she still had her knife pointed straight at him (*M raises her hand*).
M: Right. That's where I'm stopping (*M reaches over and gets the bookmark from the arm of the chair*).

Figure 2.3   Stopping reading

The data clearly illustrates some ways in which reading is embodied such as the manner of sitting; of holding one's arms; of holding one's hands; the angle of the head; the direction of the gaze; the actual relation and orientation to the book being held; and how each of these proceeds dynamically in order to accomplish something that amounts to 'reading to your daughter' and 'being read to by your mother'.

To begin with the mother picks up the book and sits down. She sits in the angle between the arm of the chair and the back, with a cushion behind her, knees and legs somewhat raised, in such a way as to be able to easily accommodate her daughter resting against the arm that is nearer to her, enabling her daughter to sit 'with' her in such a way that they can share the book. For the Mother this ensures that both arms are free both for the manipulation of the book and (perhaps equally important) for cuddling her daughter. These things are artful competences that make up part of the reading of bedtime stories. The daughter quickly comes to echo the position of her mother, knees drawn up, slightly angled in the opposite direction, leaning against her mother in front of her left arm. Mother and daughter, with some slight shifting around, hold these positions throughout the course of the reading.

The mother positions her arms as she is reading to her daughter so as to support being able to hold one side of the open book with her right hand, the other with her left, whilst also encompassing her daughter with her left arm, holding the book open in such a way that both parties can see the open pages. This position is adopted the moment the mother sits down with the book, and is held throughout. The arm position supports being able to occasionally hold the book with one hand whilst she rests her hand on her daughter's head. This way of cuddling and reading is not a position that is negotiated by either party or in any way made notable or accountable. They both fall into it in the ordinary way of things. This then is a constituent feature of how many parents go about reading to their younger children and the pose is visibly appropriate at a glance as a way in which the relationships between different members of a family are made manifest.

The way in which reading is an embodied activity is also noticeable in how the mother picks the book so that it is already oriented for opening, already presented in the right way for reading. Her grip on the external edges of the cover facilitates opening; opening the book just wide enough facilitates running a thumb along the edges of the pages so that the placement of the bookmark can be got to and the thumb slipped in; then, as the thumb is slipped in between two pages the book can be opened right out at the correct place and held like that with one hand whilst the bookmark is lifted out. Then the book is opened out completely, each hand gripping the block of pages on its side of the book, with the book held just above the knees and angled so that the eyes can engage with it without having to unduly tilt the head. This just documents the work involved in having the book ready for reading. Once the reading is under way a whole new set of manipulations become necessary: sliding a finger of the right hand along the edge of the right hand page to separate it from the page below and lift it slightly as one sees that the bottom of the right hand page is approaching; sliding the finger completely beneath the page as you arrive at the bottom; flipping the page over as the last word is reached so that there is no pause between one word and the next across the page turn. Along the way there is some discussion about whether another chapter should be read and this too involves some work with the hands to augment the verbal negotiation: closing the book up to facilitate flicking of pages for looking ahead, whilst not so much that the pages themselves cannot be seen; actually flicking ahead whilst simultaneously keeping the thumb in between the two pages at the start of the chapter she has just reached; opening the book out to display a section marker; pointing at section markers on the page (whilst still retaining the grip on the book and the place with the thumb); repeating this process; and flicking back to the point where the thumb was placed. And once they get to the end there is yet more: the raising of the hand then dropping it to indicate finality as the need to stop is asserted; the manipulation of the book to keep her place as the bookmark is reached for; the insertion of the bookmark; the closing of the book; the putting the book aside in an appropriate place e.g. on the chair as opposed to tossing it on the floor; and so on. Nor is all of the work here being done by the mother. Whilst being read to the daughter also moves her hands for the purposes of both ostension (e.g. showing her mother where she thinks she should read to), and for the manipulation of the pages. At the same time her hands demonstrate complicity with her mother by not trying to turn the pages instead, even though she is following the words on the page as well.

Even the position of their heads is a feature of the embodied practices of reading. The focus is the book and the words on the page. In this case, looking elsewhere becomes an accountable matter – as inattention or tiredness perhaps. The heads of each of them must be angled in just such a fashion as to accommodate the gaze and simultaneously demonstrate due attention. The direction of the gaze must accommodate the actual work of reading, the eyes tracking along lines in an appropriate fashion to preserve fluidity without losing one's place. As with the head the gaze is visible and diverting the gaze to some other object is accountable.

Similarly this isn't just any old reading, this is 'bedtime' reading and as such the child and parent are somewhere in the process of going or being out to bed. The child is ready for the bed, is physically tired and this can be seen in the yawns, the sucking of thumbs and the rubbing of eyes. The mother is alert to these signs – after all she has been doing this for some years and 'knows the signs' and responds in ways that are both comforting and rhythmical – she strokes the child's head as part of the 'cuddling'.

> S: MmHm MmHm
> *M Straightening out book and resting hand on top of S's head*
> M: 'Don't move' breathed a voice in Torak's ear (*stroking S's head*)
> (*Continuing to stroke S's head*)

He couldn't see anything. He was huddled in a rotten smelling blackness with a knife pressed at his throat. He gritted his teeth to stop them chattering. (*Shifting arm to put round S*)

Around him he sensed the chill weight of earth (*S puts her hand on M's*)

All of these embodied matters together make up both an appropriate positioning of the object for the ongoing work of reading aloud and being read to and make visible the orientation of the participants, with any variation being commonsensically readable as 'inattention', 'getting distracted', 'falling asleep', 'pausing for comment', 'about to ask a question', or whatever. The reading is jointly accomplished as a shared activity between parent and child. Subtle distinctions can arise with regard to how the book is held in relation to the and how it is manipulated as pages are turned etc. The following images capture some of the finesse of the matter:

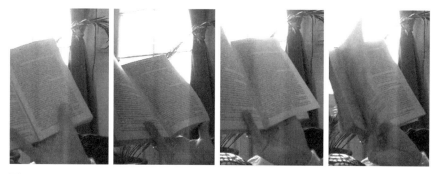

Figure 2.4   Holding the book and turning the pages

Nonetheless, matters of posture, direction of gaze, angle of head, grosser orders of keeping place and turning pages, the handling of bookmarks, and so on, are apparent whether reading to someone else or to yourself and many of these things are important for the economical and effective realization of seeing the words on the page and engaging with them in an appropriate order.

Book Reading is Manifest

Reading, by virtue of its embodied character, is also manifest to other people in a variety of ways. This makes it open to ordinary recognition and reasoning as a feature of the environment. The fact that someone is reading, just what they are reading, just where they are within the thing they are reading, how other things are organized around them, and so on, is all available to others in the setting, and carries a number of important implications for how others might orient to the reader. In this particular example any competent member of the setting can see, 'at-a-glance', that 'Mum is reading to Sarah' and this in turn has implications for matters such as: can I interrupt?, can I listen in?, can I put the TV on or some music? and so on.

Manifestness here is not necessarily a matter of what is visible but rather what is *audible*. Part of being a competent member of the setting is knowing, hearing, just what is being read as the current bedtime story to Sarah right now, and what other books might be likely candidates for bedtime reading. Thus, if the mother here was reading a book to her daughter in French, or it was the daughter herself who was reading to the mother, the scene could well be reasoned about as something else, such as Sarah doing her homework. And just how you interrupt that or orient to it as performance, etc. are quite distinct from if you had recognized it as the reading of a bedtime story. So, the very way in which the mother is reading the story, out loud, with appropriate voices, nuances of vocal timbre and attention to cadences at the close of paragraphs, etc. all make the reading of a story by Mum to Sarah a very evident matter.

Another thing that is readily available is just where they are in the book (beginning, end, in the middle, etc.) and, with only a little more inspection, perhaps even just where they are in a chapter in terms of 'just started', 'somewhere in the middle', or 'near the end', or even 'approaching the end of a section'. These are negotiable matters to the 'reader' and the 'read to' themselves. Here we see the mother and daughter actively engaging in just such a negotiation:

> M: ... He was caught between the living and the dead (*cat growling in background*). Something grabbed him from behind and dragged him down into the darkness (*end of chapter*).
> S: It was short.
> M: (*Shifting hold on book to close and turn page – looking down at S as doing so*) It was a whole chapter. (*Opening book out*)
> S: C'mon
> M: (*flicking to and fro*) Want more?
> S: More story
> M: (*flicking forward page by page – note finger still held in place at beginning of chapter*) Let me see how long it is (.) It's a lo:::ng o::ne
> S: Ple:::/ase
> M: (*Still flicking on*) it's a long one
> S: (*As M flicks back*) You could stop in the middle of it
> M: I could read up to (*pointing out section marker on page*) there
> S: No::::
> M: (*flicking on a page*) The next one
> S: (*flicking on a page*) Up to (.) there
> M: Up to that one (*pointing*)
> S: Yes (.) There (*pointing*)

For others this can provide affordances such as, is it worth me hanging around to talk to Mum or is she going to be reading to Sarah for a while? The fact the 'reading to' is happening at this time of day, in this place, and that Sarah is in her pyjamas, all contribute to a ready recognition of this as quite specifically 'reading to at bedtime'. That in turn makes available a body of other reasoning to those who know the household for they can presume that after this Sarah will be going to bed, she'll be in the bathroom for a while, mum will shortly be available or else mum will shortly be doing the washing up, and so on. Recognition of the bedtime reading in this way provides, for the competent member, for knowledgeable reasoning about its placement within the household routine.

Book Reading Has a Visible Order

Another important aspect that contributes to the manifest characteristics of reading is its very visible order. It has a beginning: books are located, picked up and brought to readiness for reading. There is a middle: books are ongoingly engaged with, with visible attention to the printed page, with the positioning of fingers just so for the fluid turning of the page, and so on. These things are only intelligible for what they are because of how they are ordered in relation to what has gone before. Then there is an end: books are closed, perhaps bookmarks inserted or pages turned down, they are put to one side so that their very placement speaks to how they are done with for the present. This ordering is visible in the bedtime reading in terms of: how the book is located by the child in the first instance, then passed over to the mother as she sits down; how the mother and the child together settle in readiness; the ways in which the book is opened out, the right place to continue reading from located, and the bookmark put to one side; how the pages are worked through; how a putative end is reached and negotiations ensue; how 'reading on' is brought about; and how a definitive end for this evening is accomplished, with the attendant putting in of a bookmark, the closing of the book, and the putting of the book to one side. All of this has a retrospective-prospective logic that cannot be simply put aside. These are presumptive resources rarely articulated and yet the possibility to reason about what is going on trades upon such assumptions. To see and recognize some course of action is to see what is happening just now as a feature of the unfolding of that complete course of action. So to see someone reading a bedtime story is to see all of these things as well and upon that rides other assumptions that render the doing of it naturally or openly accountable.

Book Reading Has Spatiotemporal Characteristics

As a reasoned activity within a household, bedtime reading has spatiotemporal characteristics. Notionally, of course, bedtime reading could happen anywhere. However, it doesn't tend to happen at the kitchen table, in the bathroom, on the stairs, or whatever. Each household may reason about these things differently but an important part of what is going on is the bodily contact, the 'snuggling up' so to speak, visible at the outset of the original example. Thus sofas, beds, large comfy armchairs, etc. afford for this kind of activity.

Temporally of course, 'bedtime reading' happens at bedtime: because that's the local locution for this thing. Bedtime, of course, has some degree of flexibility, but children go to bed *at some time* that is recognizable itself through accountable matters such as the child being in their bed, wearing their pyjamas or nightgowns (or whatever). Whether a bedtime story is appropriate on this particular occasion is always open to revision. However, to see a child in their pyjamas sat on the settee or in bed, snuggled up with a parent, being read to at any time where bedtime is an appropriate thing to reason then what is most likely seen to be going on is a bedtime story. Move it elsewhere or elsewhen and it will probably be reasoned about as something else – such as a child being ill. What is clear, though, is that this kind of reading has a particular time and place where members of the household will unproblematically see it for what it is in ways that would not work and would be called to account if it was shifted to a different location or a different time of day.

Book Reading Has a Place within the Household Routine

Bedtime has certain very definite characteristics and bedtime reading fits within that in ways that allow for those characteristics to be maintained: particular times of day, in particular places, in particular clothing, perhaps with particular accompaniments such as drinks, and with particular understandings that what will follow is the actual act of going to bed and that what should precede is whatever it takes for that to happen. This is not invented on the spur of the moment to be figured out on just this occasion but rather is something that is done recurrently in similar ways such that no-one might think to comment upon its regular, its ordinary character. In other words it is a routine and it has its place within other routines, and everyone understands that, once it is undertaken, there are other routines that will quite reasonably and ordinarily follow, like actually going to bed, for instance. This gives the enactment of bedtime reading as a routine a certain power for other things are expected to reasonably come next.

Furthermore, as this thing is a routine, a recurrent matter, it can be easily recognized for what it is and oriented to by others as well:

> If you're reading to Sarah and I'm washing up then I prefer the music off so I can hear too. And often, the other children, if they're doing crosswords or whatever, if they're down here, or even playing on the machine, they tend to lend an ear. So it isn't necessarily just Sarah being read to. But it is focused on Sarah so if none of the others are here she'd still get read to.

Clearly bedtime reading, by virtue of what it is called and how it is reasoned about, is centrally articulated around the routines of younger children and the work they and their parents do together to move towards a point where they are in bed and sleeping. However, other kinds of reading testify just as strongly in their accomplishment to various elements of how a household organizes its day and who is accountable to whom and for what.

Something else that is massively visible in the data is the extent to which aspects of the topology of the home are organized with the clear purpose of supporting various reading activities such that the very placement of books will speak volumes to a competent member regarding the book's status and how it might be appropriately engaged with. By very virtue of the placement of a particular book, competent members of the household will be able to say just who is probably reading that book. This is not a claim that specific people of a specific kind will always put their books in a place of this specific character, what it means is that members of the household will be able to reason about the placement of books in some fashion according to their understanding of the topology of that home. So the book for reading at bedtime will have some specific placement within the home's topology that allows for its recognizability as just that, bedtime reading, with a whole set of potential consequences should someone else claim it and wander off with it. Reading is then a way in which the rights and responsibilities of different members of the household are made manifest. Reading in domestic settings is organized in relation to the broader social organization of the home and thereby makes manifest the rights and responsibilities of different members of the household.

So, just prior to the data provided previously, the daughter is sat on the sofa, fidgeting around, waiting for someone to come and read her story. She asks her father to do it but he tells her it's going to be mum tonight so she continues to sit there, fidgeting. Her mother comes out of the garage where she has been getting the rubbish ready for taking out and the daughter calls out to her to remind her she's waiting:

M: Tr/is
S: /My story? Wolf Brother. A good story. Mummy? Ready?
M: Just get my hands washed
S: Okay
The daughter continues to sit for a while, then goes and gets the book from the cabinet where it is kept and puts it behind a cushion on the sofa. When the mother comes into view the daughter becomes more insistent:
S: Ahhem Ahem
M: (*to son*) Are you going to /go-
S: /Mum/mummumma
M: /Are you going to come back through the garage?
T: Hmm?
S: Allez au part=
M: =shut the garage up afterwards
S: Zitdownpa

M: Where's your book?

T: I usually /don't

S: /Sit! (*producing book*)

T: come back through the garage

M: Well come back through the garage coz/I've

S: /(*putting book on chair*) SIT!

M: left the door open for you

T: Why leave it open? I don't come through that way

M: The light! I thought you needed the light

S: hwer

M: Yup, yup

M picking up book to sit down as S reaches out to her

Once the mother is sat down and they've snuggled up together and the book is opened out, the mother asks her daughter what's been happening:

M: What happened in the last chapter d'you remember? Once the daughter has recounted what happened, the mother begins to read.

Notice here how a bunch of things are unremarkably (that is, they are not commented upon) presumed about what each of the parties to the reading should do and what each of them *can* do. The daughter can visibly wait for and expect to be read a story. She can remind her mother about the fact she is waiting for it, even nag, even order her mother to sit, because it is understood to be the responsibility of the mother to deliver just such a story and the mother is accountable for its delayed production, e.g. 'just get my hands washed'. Notice how, even though it is the mother who is expected to do the reading, the daughter has the right to pick up the book from its usual location in readiness, even play a joke with by hiding it behind a cushion. The picking up of the book does not make her a reader. It does make evident that she expects some business to unfold with that book and taking it into hand is another way of making visible her expectation. Once the mother arrives, of course, she has the right to demand the book of her daughter and the daughter readily complies. The presumed right to demand the book, however, makes visible her understanding of the fact that she is the one with the priority for actually physically handling the book and manipulating it. It is hard to see how the reading could be accomplished without this but it also makes visible the presumption that she is going to be the reader and others can see it that way too. This is a concomitant second part to the effective demand by her daughter that she fulfill her responsibility. The expectation provides for this in such a way that pretty well anything else is going to need accounting for.

Whilst they are reading the mother continues to keep hold of the book in various ways and do the reading out loud, occasionally resting her hand on her daughter's head or stroking her hair, and the daughter responds with occasional touching. This demonstrates the mother's differential rights to control and management of the book itself and the daughter's deference to this, though this does not deny the daughter the right to touch the book at all.

Where things get more interesting is when the mother arrives at the finish of the chapter. As we've already seen, what happens here is that there is a negotiation between them as to whether more reading should happen. The daughter has some claim for more because she suggests the chapter was 'a short one'. The mother resists reading the next chapter because 'it's long'. The daughter suggests she could stop in the middle of it, so the mother proposes a potential place to stop, physically showing it to her daughter. The daughter contests this and, interestingly, at this point is possessed of the rights to actually physically handle the book to show her mother where she thinks she should read up to. Only once this is agreed between them does the reading continue. All of this continues to attest to the overall right to handle the book and decide resting with the mother. But she has a responsibility to read 'for a reasonable period of time' and, clearly, what counts as reasonable is open to contestation.

Once the end of the chapter is reached, the mother is able to assert that she is stopping. The daughter checks this is where they agreed she'd be stopping and actively wants to see proof of the matter:

> M: She'd been useful for helping him evade the ravens but that didn't change the fact that she'd taken his weapons and called him a coward and she still had her knife pointed straight at him. (*M raises hand*) Right. That's where I'm stopping. (*M reaches over and gets bookmark from arm of the chair*)
> S: Is that the second /(…)?
> M: /That's the second one. That's the one we agreed on. Okay?
> (*M puts bookmark in book and goes to close it*)
> S: Is it? (*Pulling book back open*)
> M: It is
> S: Let's see. (*S flicks back through the pages of the book – pauses at a section mark, then flicks back to beginning of chapter – then flicks back to where she's kept the place with her other hand as M gets ready to put in bookmark*)
> *M puts bookmark in book, shuts it, and puts it over to her right*

Notice here how the daughter again asserts certain rights to manipulate the book. Once this is done the mother puts in the bookmark and puts the book over to the arm of the chair. She then asks her daughter for a kiss goodnight and the daughter goes off with her father to head upstairs to bed.

In this final part of the interaction the mother's right to terminate the reading is exercised, though it should be noted that the mother accepts the daughter's right to demand an account for this and to verify the accuracy of the account when it is given. This speaks volumes about how absolute her exercise of control might be. There are reasonable places where parents might effectively 'lay down the law', but this is not such an appropriate place and the very insistence upon it might itself be deemed accountable. The point to emphasize about this analysis is the way in which, at the point of reading a bedtime story, the playing out of these rights and responsibilities does not get worked up anew. Instead, the ordering of these concerns is accountable to the ongoing ordering of their relative rights and responsibilities within the household. Both mother and daughter have a commonsense understanding of what their rights and responsibilities are to each other and how these might play out in the case of reading a story at bedtime. This is not to say what they each should do and what they each have the right to do is not occasionally open to challenge, but the challenge itself then demands some kind of an account. In the above case, for instance, the daughter's account for challenging the mother's decision to stop is based upon a doubt she is honouring their agreement. Once it is clear the agreement *has* been honoured there is little else she has to say.

Reading is a Feature of How Social Relations within a Household are Accomplished

As we have seen above, reading practices can make visible the actual relations between the different members of the household. Indeed, ways of reading are an aspect of how those relations are ongoingly accomplished. The example of bedtime reading brings this home especially forcefully. In fact, it is an important aspect of how parent–child intimacy gets accomplished. The example we have presented is replete with these kinds of details, e.g.:

> *M picking up book to sit down as S reaches out to her ...*
> *M puts arm round S ...*
> *M Straightening out book and resting hand on top of S's head ...*
> M: 'Don't move' breathed a voice in Torak''s ear (*stroking S's head*) …
> M: Pardon me. (*Laughingly as continuing to stroke S's head*) He couldn't see anything. He was huddled in a rotten smelling blackness with a knife pressed at his throat. He gritted his teeth to stop them chattering. (*Shifting arm to put round S*)
> *S puts her hand on M's ...*
> *M strokes S's head and rests her hand on her head, holding the book with one hand, as she continues*
> *S raises her arms to take hold of M's hand ...*
> *M moves her hand down and puts it on S's knee*
> *S lifts her hand to hold M's hand on her knee and M glances down and strokes her knee ...*
> *Kisses her on top of her head*

Everyone, including the children who are parties to it, understand that this kind of reading, bedtime reading, is about something quite particular. And that particularity is not about the consumption of stories per se. The child in these examples is a highly accomplished reader and could, without any difficulty, be reading this story for herself. Why then should this reading matter so much to her? And it clearly does. The above observations of embodied and accomplished intimacy are core to the response to this. What the child and the parent, both, do get out of this is a degree of physical contact that can only be accountably demanded and provided in so many ways. Children can ask cuddles of their parents pretty well any time within reason (e.g. if the parent is visibly occupied or the child should be getting on with their homework). And those cuddles will usually be provided. However, to keep on asking for those things is to quickly start to become accountable for the recurrent request, e.g. they're obviously worrying about something, they're being clingy, or whatever (see Tolmie 2010). What things like bedtime reading do is they quite neatly provide licence for those kinds of contact to happen without fuss or account and on a regular basis. Thus bedtime reading is not just an opportunity for intimacy to occur or a place where, amongst other things, intimacy happens to be present. It is a *mechanism* for intimacy and, as concrete part of a day's routine, there aren't so many of those. It is not that the content of the book doesn't matter here. They clearly do care about the content and do engage with it, as to other members of the household as well. Furthermore, being read to out loud, with all of the voices, as a kind of performance, is a quite distinct thing from reading something to yourself. But the claim here is not that bedtime reading is all about intimacy. What is being proposed is that at least one extremely important aspect of bedtime reading is the fact that it quite systematically provides a mechanism for intimacy to occur and that this is something that matters to young children. And when children grow out of having stories read to them in this fashion is about the same time that they start to be held to account for their parents being seen to 'fuss' over them and where 'fussing over them' is something to which they may call their parents to account. Thus, all of the presumptions of touching rights and stroking rights and cuddling rights and kissing rights made visible above are things that make accountably visible very specific relations between these particular individuals such that, were the person being read to very much older, or patently of a similar age to the person doing the reading, different understandings of who they are and what they are up to would apply. It also provides for the subtle recognition of potential troubles. If one or other of the parties resists the intimacy or is patently unresponsive to it people may well figure there's some kind of trouble between them.

Book Reading: The Work of Reading

When we look at some of the 'work' of reading going on in this particular instance of bedtime reading, apart from its very ordinariness, one grossly observable aspect of the 'work' is the attempt to contextualize the reading to come in respect to what has already occurred in the story. Here the mother has used a bookmark to indicate how far she got in the story last time she read and before she reads on asks her child to recall aspects of the story:

M: You ready?

S: Yuh

M lifts out bookmark

M puts bookmark on arm of chair

M: Whe::re were we?

M settles back in place

S: Now then (.) …

M holding book in place as asking S to recall last part

M: What happened in the last chapter d'you remember?

S: Erm

M flicking back to prior chapter

S: Yesssum

M looking at prior chapter as S recounts what happened

S: They had to leave wolf behind. He got free.

M flicking back to current chapter

S: They tied him up and um:: Saeun told him that hm; about his father

M: MmHm

S: They knew the bear was going to kill him and um:: er then um:: .hh.h er;;they tied him Well then he um … managed to get free

M: Mmhm

S: And then he had to do something that he really didn't want to do umm … it was leaving wolf behind

M: Was it wolf who helped him to escape?

S: Yes

M: Ahh Okay (.)

M settling to begin reading

M: You ready?

S: Okay

M starting to read

Of course the story is brought to life in the telling and as part of the reading. Sometimes textual devices such as punctuation or short sentences need to be noticed by the reader and if used correctly act to help convey some sense of atmosphere in the story. In this next instance the mother is paying attention to the flow of the text and adapts her reading to incorporate the whispering that the text describes:

> … Sick with relief, Torak listened to them move away. After a while he tried to shift position but the knife-point stopped him. (*Whispering*) 'Stay still' hissed his captor. He recognised that voice. It was Ren. 'Ren?' 'You stink' she whispered. He tried to turn his head but again the knife stopped him. 'It's to keep the dogs away' he whispered back. 'They never come here anyway, they're not allowed'. Torak thought for a moment. 'How did you know I'd be coming this way? And why …?' 'I didn't. Now be quiet. They might be back.'

Paying careful attention to the text is clearly important since any error or omission is likely to be noticed by whoever is being read to, in this case a child, if they are following the story:

> M: She looked startled and then alarmed. 'You really can talk to him can't you?' She did not reply. He did /not
> S: /He!
> M: HE did not reply. (*S giggling*)

This final extract illustrates some elements of the embodiment of the reading, the evocation of aspects of the story and the atmosphere, the context, of the events being read and described. Here, for example, the reader shakes her head as an embodiment of distrust and then raises her hand exactly as if she was wielding the dagger being described in the story:

> He was tempted to tell her that wolf was his guide but checked himself. (*Shaking head slightly*) He didn't trust her. She'd been useful for helping him evade the ravens but that didn't change the fact that she'd taken his weapons and called him a coward and she still had her knife pointed straight at him. (*M raises hand*)

Figure 2.5   Wielding the dagger

Conclusion … And they all lived happily ever after …?

One interesting aspect of reading practices, and one of the ways in which, for example reading 'at work' sometimes differs from reading 'at play' (or in this case 'at bedtime') is their motivated character. Readings 'at work' are often 'directed readings' where the text will be read, not for its own sake, but for something that may turn out to be organizationally relevant. Reading bedtime stories, whilst clearly embedded in the organization of the household, rarely consists of stories that are organizationally relevant, though often, perhaps usually, they may have a moral component that has some resonance with the performance of everyday life. As the extracts show, readers, in this case the mother, employ a variety of techniques that enable them to work through (and occasionally point to) different 'orders of organisation' (such as by character, or by place or by time etc.) within the texts they read as bedtime stories – and that enhance their character as (bedtime) stories. These include, for example, following transitions from one topic to the next, or reading more deeply into particular topics or situations in order to make the story more understandable and 'readable'. These readings are 'accomplishments' and necessarily proceed on a provisional, 'wait-and-see' basis. In this chapter on reading bedtime stories we have taken the reader through some of the various ways in which reading, as an activity, is constituted by, and constitutive *of* the social organization of the home. Our discussion of intimacy is particularly pertinent in this respect. It is in just how a mother might read to her daughter, the tight specificity of their bodily orientations, how the book is held, who can touch what at what time, how the very words are enunciated, that the relations between that mother and child are made visible to others, not just worked up for themselves. One small change in any of these things can speak volumes about whether the mother and child have just been arguing, whether one or other of them is tired, that the child is in a sulk, or any number of other possible reasoned ascriptions that are themselves premised upon an understood and oriented to social organization of the home.

It is worth briefly concluding by noting that these observations exist within the larger canvas of familial concerns and predicates. The fact that reading is not outside of but rather an integral part of the social organization of the home makes it yet one more place where a whole range of considered activities may get accomplished that are understood to be something other than about reading for the pleasure of reading alone.

One such concern might be matters of recollection. Often stories may serve as prompts for particular kinds of recollections. This can turn upon the content of the book and what happens, but it can also be things such as the title, the author, where the book is set, even the picture on the cover, that might serve as an initial trigger. What is important about recollection is that it is always *somehow occasioned* and books are one of the ways in which such occasioning can occur. Another concern might be something like pedagogy. Thus, as we commented earlier, specific books may get chosen because they are seen to be somehow educational. However, pedagogy is also a situated and, once again, an occasioned matter. Thus, and for instance, children being read bedtime stories may pose questions about specific things within them. And this may be taken by those doing the reading as an opportunity to elaborate and instruct. Things arising may also be opened up for discussion at the conclusion of the reading. This is at least one way in which children can be understood to learn.

PART II
Having a Hobby

Chapter 3
Identifying Birds by their Song

Paul ten Have

Let me start with a story:

> Two friends are taking a walk in spring through a varied, park-like landscape:
> some small pieces of woodland, a few single trees, quite a lot of bushes, and open
> space in between. One of them (X for eXpert), makes a remark about a bird he
> hears singing: 'Hey! The Willow Warbler is back! That's the first one I've heard
> this year'. His companion (N for Novice) asks: 'How do you know? How can
> you recognize the song of this particular bird among all those different songs?'
> X says 'Well, I just know', he tries to vocalize the song, and he talks about some
> particular features of Willow Warbler singing, such as its stepwise downward
> melody. N makes an effort to remember this song and when they walk along,
> tries to catch another Willow Warbler singing. This is quite difficult for him, as
> he has to 'apply' X's descriptive efforts and his own memory of the first case with
> what he is hearing all around him. After some unsuccessful attempts, X comes
> in to explain that it is, at first, rather difficult to differentiate the various songs if
> you don't know almost any song. It's like listening to a symphony orchestra and
> trying to 'hear' the different instruments separately. You really have to 'know' the
> sound of these instruments in order to be able to do that. You have to learn that
> one-by-one. So it takes time, and patience! 'But why should one try to do that',
> N asks. 'Primarily for pleasure', X answers, 'it brings you closer to the birds, in a
> way'. Take the Willow Warbler I just heard for the first time this year. A tiny bird,
> 20 grams or so, flying in all the way from sub-Sahara Africa, losing about a third
> of his body weight on the way. And now he is singing, to attract a mate and ward
> off competitors. That's moving, isn't it?' N nods. 'And furthermore, you can use
> the ability to assist in a country-wide yearly inventory of birds. So it's also useful
> to support wildlife conservation policies.' N nods again and they go home, where
> X makes a note of his first Willow Warbler.

An episode like this might, for N, be a step in a process of 'becoming a member'
of a community of birders. One human being is trying to share with another his
acquired knowledge of some of the characteristics of a rather different animal such
as a Willow Warbler (*Phylloscopus trochilus*). As it happens, the vocal apparatus
of birds is completely different from that of humans, which makes a short-cut
like imitation rather difficult. So how can X and N solve their problem? How can
an eXpert's practical 'knowledge' of recognizing birds by their song be passed

on to a Novice? And how can a Novice learn by picking up various suggestions, examples, tricks, etc.? And, of course, N will often not have X around to help him, so instead he may turn to other resources: books, CDs or the Internet.[1]

I will, in this chapter, explore some of the ways in which a novice can become a member of the birder community by acquiring the ability to identify birds by their song.[2] This project is based on my own experience as a learner and teacher of bird song recognition, but I will use quotes from published and recorded suggestions to illustrate aspects of this process.

So while this chapter may seem to be about birds, its actual topic is the use by humans of a range of 'ethno methods' for recognizing bird songs. In other words, I am studying various practical tips and tricks that, in a way, are constitutive of what it is to be a 'birder', being able to identify birds just by their song, as X did in the opening story. These 'methods' function in two basic ways in birding practices, as teaching/training instruments, and as accounts for a particular hearing, for instance in a dispute among birders about which bird they hear singing. What I study, then, is the practical accountability of bird song identification, in the manner suggested in the following classical quote from Garfinkel:

> Ethnomethodological studies analyze everyday activities as members' methods for making those same activities visibly-rational-and-reportable-for-all- practical-purposes, i.e., 'accountable,' as organizations of commonplace everyday activities. (Garfinkel 1967: VII)

In his later work, he encouraged what has become known as 'ethnomethodological studies of work' (Garfinkel 1986). In such studies, the researcher should acquire a basic competence in the kind of work being studied ethnomethodologically, in order to satisfy what he called the 'unique adequacy requirements of methods' (Garfinkel and Wieder 1992). In this way, a series of 'hybrid disciplines' could emerge, a combination, of sorts, of the practical knowledge of a particular kind of disciplinary work and an ethnomethodological interest in the achievement of practical membership in that discipline (Garfinkel 2002: 100–103; cf. Lynch 1993: 271–5). The present chapter is, at least, 'inspired' by these notions.

---

1   With typing an item like 'Bird songs' in your search machine you will probably be able to find some good sources, but in any case I provide some suggestions on my website at: http://www.paultenhave.nl/birdsites.html.

2   Bird species are unevenly distributed across the globe; there is for instance a huge difference between Europe and the Americas as regards common birds. The examples I will discuss are based on my own experience and therefore limited to European birds. Kaufman (2011) is an excellent source on the art of identifying birds in America.

Songs and Calls

Ornithologists and birders commonly distinguish 'calls' and 'songs' when they talk about bird vocalizations. Calls are mostly short and serve a range of social functions, as in 'alarm calls' and 'contact calls' in a flock. Although they tend to be specific to a species, it is hard to use them for identification, both because of their shortness and for the fact that related species may have almost similar calls. Songs, on the other hand, are longer and more complex and clearly species specific. They mainly serve functions of 'self-presentation'. As such they are mostly used in the breeding season, in spring, by males to mark their claim to a breeding territory. By their song they try, on the one hand, to attract females, while also, on the other hand, to ward off other males. An exception to this characterization is the singing of Robins (*Erithacus rubecula*) during the winter season, which serves to mark a forage territory. It that case, both males and females sing. In this chapter, I will only discuss the recognition of 'songs', as you can hear them in spring.

Song Identification

The core problem in recognizing songbirds by their song is to 'connect' one's knowledge of a bird species' typical song with one's hearing of birds' singing. The preliminary problem, however, is how to get that knowledge. In the 'story' with which I started this chapter, the source is a friend with the relevant expertise, who, in turn, has the problem of how to instruct (teach, train) the novice. Although this kind of personal instruction in the field is probably the best way to learn how to recognize a bird's song as typical of a species, there are other sources which can be used by both learners and teachers to support or confirm one's learning or instruction. These include the descriptions and transcriptions given in field guides and specialized publications, recordings made available on CD, DVD and the Internet, and visualizations of these in the form of sonagrams. The task, then, is to mutually 'fit' these kinds of information with what one actually hears or heard in the field.

The best way to understand how this kind of 'recognition work' is done is by experiencing it yourself. I therefore will present a few exercises in which I invite you to engage in some particular learning activities, either by going out in the field or by relying on recordings. After each exercise, I will offer a sketch of what you may have experienced and how such experiences may be understood and extended.

Exercise 1

On a good day in spring, you should rise early, take a notebook with you and go to a nice setting outdoors. Select a park or a country site with a variety of bushes, trees and open spaces, preferably with some open water, a pond or a stream.

Sit down comfortably and listen, listen intensely to the birds around you. Try to distinguish the various songs that you hear and make notes on their characteristics, their rhythm, melody, overall sound quality; whatever seems characteristic. How many different songs can you distinguish?

It may be difficult to do this exercise if you are reading this chapter during another season than spring, and it is also difficult to simulate the intended 'total experience' by listening to a recording, as most of these are selected to feature one particular species. On some CDs there are tracks that offer an overall soundscape of a particular setting. If you can find something like that, use it for Exercise 1.

Let me guess at some of the sounds you may have heard and the song qualities you may have noted. One feature of the total soundscape you may have noted is the remarkable variety in terms of pitch, complexity and length of phrases. The higher pitches are often produced by smaller birds, while the larger ones tend to make lower sounding vocalizations. Some of the songs you hear may consist of 2 or 3 note phrases which are repeated a large number of times. Simple ones like these can be made by the Great Tit (*Parus major*). The Song Thrush (*Turdus philomelos*), on the other hand, repeats a short phrase several times, but then switches to a different phrase; its timbre is fuller than that of the Tit. If you listened carefully, you may have heard one song that consists of a single 'small' or 'thin' sound being rhythmically repeated about 10 times, with a slight suggestion of pitch variation. That's the Chiffchaff (*Phylloscopus collybita*), the one who marks the beat (to paraphrase the famous Dutch writer Jac. P. Thijsse's expression *het maatslagertje*). Note that in quite a few languages, such as Dutch (*Tjiftjaf*) and English, the name carries an onomatopoetic reference to the just noted pitch variation. And, finally, if you remember the characterization of the song of the Willow Warbler in the opening 'story' you may also have recognized his stepwise downward moving phrase, repeated time and again.

If you choose to do the exercise again, another early morning spring listening to the birds in a park-like landscape, the summary descriptions in the previous paragraph may already be helpful in getting a more diversified 'picture' of the dawn chorus produced by the birds (if you are using recordings, try another overall soundscape recording). What you are doing is a mental movement from the description to the sounds and back again, a mutual fitting, so to speak.

The following exercise invites you to concentrate on one of the moves mainly, the descriptive one.

Exercise 2

Get yourself an audio recording of the song of a Common Blackbird (*Turdus merula*), on a CD or from the internet. Play the recording several times and make an effort to describe the song at some length, say about 100 words.

Your description will probably cover at least the following properties:

1. the overall structure of the song can be depicted as: phrase-pause-phrase-pause, etc.
2. each next phrase is different from the previous ones, so the song is quite varied
3. the overall quality of the song is pleasant, relaxed and nice to the human ear.

In fact, the Blackbird is probably most people's favourite song bird.

For a third exercise you are invited to use descriptions of the songs of two related species of birds to recognize which of the two you are hearing.

Exercise 3

Here you need a friend who is willing to act as a quiz-master for you. He or she needs to get an audio record of the singing of two related birds, the Sedge Warbler (*Acrocephalus schoenobaenus*) and the Reed Warbler (*Acrocephalus scirpaceus*), which are hard to distinguish. Look-up the description of their song in a field guide. Let your friend play the recordings for you in a quiz-like manner, that is without you knowing which song is being played. Then try to identify the birds by their song using the field guide descriptions.

If you succeed in this identification task, you will probably have attended to the overall rhythmic quality and the amount of variation in the songs. If you failed in this task, be assured that for these two birds it is a rather difficult one. The songs of many others are easier to recognize. Now, with these experiences as a background, read some more on the ways in which song identification is supported in various ways by more experienced birders.

Transcription or Description

Until recently, writers of field guides used two distinguishable methods to characterize the songs of bird species. They could use the alphabet to evoke the song's characteristics in a kind of transcription as in *zitt-zitt-zitt-zitt-sett-sett-sett-tsjett-tsjitter-lEdia* (Mullarney et al.: 346), for the song of the Chaffinch (*Fringilla coelebs*). As birds don't produce vowels and consonants the way humans do such transcriptions remain a bit forced and are in my experience not very helpful. They are in any case hard to remember. An alternative is to imagine a verbal phrase in which words are put in the slots of the song, as in '*Come come come kiss me quick my pretty little dear*' (de Vos and de Meersman: 18), again for the song of the Chaffinch.

In more recent books, writers mostly abstain from efforts at transcription, limiting themselves to descriptions like 'Song is short, fast and rather dry. It is a descending series of trills that accelerates and ends with a flourish' (Holden and Cleeves: 280), Chaffinch again.

Here are some other examples from two major books: Holden and Cleeves'
RSPB Handbook of British Birds (2010) and Sample's *Collins Bird Songs & Calls*
(2010):
Blackbird:

> 'Noisy species with a beautiful, mellow song that is a slow, clear warble which
> "trails off" at the end.' (Holden and Cleeves: 225)

> 'The male's song is in well-defined verses, notable for the full, flute-like voicing
> and melodic lilt of the main phrase; the ending accelerates into higher-pitched,
> twittering phrases, of less immediate grasp to our ears. Not only does the main
> phrase have something that strikes us as a recognizable melody, birds vary it
> from verse to verse, generally with something that conveys a hint of thematic
> development for us.'(Sample: 170–71)

Willow warbler:

> 'The song is a pretty, liquid series of descending notes that starts softly and ends
> with a flourish.' (Holden and Cleeves: 249)

> 'Song is normally in verses of about 3 seconds, each a cascading, melodic
> sequence of slurred whistles, slightly sibilant, usually descending in pitch
> through the sequence. The first few notes build in volume to a peak, later
> declining again and slowing slightly towards the end.' (Sample: 191)

Note that the H&C-quotes are from descriptions in a field guide, with one page per
species, while the ones from Sample are taken from longer ones in a book purely
devoted to songs and calls.

Looking over these descriptions, one may note the use of a rather wide range
of descriptive categories, some having to do with 'voice quality' while others can
be grouped as 'structural' ones. Among the first, Sample (64) notes pitch, timbre,
pitch inflection, rhythm and tempo. Some major structures, relevant to songbirds,
which he identifies are 1) 'A simple motive that is looped', as in the song of the
Great Tit, 2) 'A formal pattern of distinct phrases, repeated at intervals', which
the Chaffinch exemplifies, 3) 'Verses of a set form, but varied in sequence', as
demonstrated by Blackbirds and Willow Warblers, and 4) 'Continuous warbling,
no obvious structure', as the Skylark (*Alauda arvensis*) or Sedge Warbler
(Sample: 66). But apart from such more or less objective categories, writers and
other birders often use more impressionistic and subjective ones, like 'beautiful'
or 'something that strikes us as a recognizable melody'.

A recent technical device of 'transcription' is the use of computer-generated
Sonograms or Sonagrams (Sound-spectrograms), which display frequency and/
or volume graphically. At present these depictions are mostly found in the more
specialized, professional literature (de Vos and de Meersman 2005; Constantine

et al. 2006). Apart from their use by professionals, an amateur birder can use sonagrams as an analysis of sorts of the structure of a song. Kaufman (2011: 133) suggest that one could as an aid to learning a song try to sketch sonagram-like depictions of a song one hears in the field, as he writes:

> …, I try to 'draw' a rough 'sonagram' of what it sounds like, showing where the pitch seems to rise, fall or remain steady. I try to fit letters to the syllables of the song; these are usually nonsense sounds, but if the song suggests actual words, I'll write them down …

As this quote illustrates, sonagrams (whether produced by a machine or by a human hand) and transcriptions can very well be, and often are, combined.[3]

In their efforts to communicate a bird's song characteristics some experts use special tricks. The Dutch expert Nico de Haan, for instance, sings and whistles, besides giving descriptions on some CDs. More often playful characterizations are given. The song of the Great Tit, for instance, is said to sound like a bicycle pump, while the rattle in the middle of the song of the Wren, in Dutch *Winterkoning*, can be evoked by saying *winterrrrrrkoning*. There have also been attempts to catch some of the details of bird song in musical notation (De Vos 2007), but this seems also to be of limited use.

Although descriptions, transcriptions, sonagrams and other tricks may be successful in catching a song's details that are useful in species recognition, the practical problem often remains one of 'finding' the relevant description when you hear a bird singing. Descriptions may be useful in remembering a song once you already have a 'label' for it, as it happened in the story with which I started. But when you hear a song for which you don't have a hunch about the species name, it is much more difficult. I will deal with this problem in a later section.

Context Information: Where and When

Apart from properties of the actual sound of a song, as can be caught on an audio recording, for recognition in the field various aspects of the singing bird's actual situation are also important. As birds have highly differentiated preferences as to where they breed and sing, each type of habitat has its own repertoire of locally breeding birds. So you have typical woodland birds, like the Chaffinch, ones that you can hear in half-open landscapes like Willow Warblers, and those that prefer wet areas like Reed Warblers. And within such areas there are even more finely differentiated preferences. Furthermore, the possibilities to hear birds sing are differentiated across time. Migrant birds are only present in their breeding areas in a particular season, spring, and even during that time they may be silent during certain periods of their stay. Nightingales (*Luscinia megarhynos*), for instance,

---

3   See De Vos and De Meersman (2005: 122) for an example of this.

will arrive around mid April and can be heard singing for about 6 to 8 weeks, less frequently towards the end. Their reputation, of course, is that they sing all night, but many people don't expect them to sing during the day, although they do quite enthusiastically. On the other hand they are very critical as to their breeding locations. They prefer woods, parks, and in Holland especially dunes with thick undergrowth, such as nettles, but in many areas that seem to fit their requirements they are absent. Their song is loud and clear, but they are hard to spot visually as their looks are rather unremarkable and they mostly sing hiding in the vegetation.

Knowing a bird's 'time schedule' in terms of season and daily cycle, as well as his locational preferences helps a lot in identification birds with more or less similar songs. Say that you want to distinguish the Sedge Warbler from the Reed Warbler (cf. Exercise 3). They both breed, and sing, in similar wet environments, such as reed land. It is helpful to know that the first arrives earlier in the year, mid-April, so you can first learn to recognize the Sedge Warbler. When some time later, late April and May, they are both active, you may note that the Sedge Warbler tends to sing from higher in the vegetation, while the Reed Warbler sings from a lower position, more in hiding.

In most sources, these differentiations in time and place are given verbally, but De Vos and De Meersman (2005) use very clever diagrams for the yearly and daily cycles (see Figure 3.1).[4]

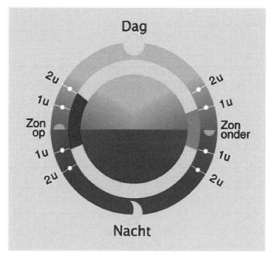

Figure 3.1   Daily cycle song of Whinchat[5]
Source: De Vos and De Meersman (2005: 122).

---

4   For an example of the yearly cycle, see De Vos and De Meersman (2005: 122).

5   This diagram is published with the kind permission of the publisher, KNNV Uitgeverij, Utrecht, the Netherlands ISBN 90 5011 195 5.

Learning as a Process

The ideal way to familiarize yourself with birdsongs is to go on field trips with an expert: getting the real sound in context with pointed instructions, descriptions, etc. When I take a group out on a field trip with a focus on bird songs, a common experience is that people express a kind of despair about ever being able to differentiate all those sounds and remember all those identifying details. My standard response is that if you succeed learning to recognize two birds each year, you will get to know twenty in a decade. A dedicated learner can do more than two a year, I think, but the major lesson is to learn songs one by one. Therefore, one should ideally start early in the season, say February or early March. When you go out then, in a park or woodland, you will probably hear just a few birds singing. A first differentiation you can make is between small birds that make a tiny sound, like Robin or Wren (*Troglodytes troglodytes*) and the various Tits, and the somewhat larger ones such as the Blackbird or the Song Thrush, who produce a fuller, rounder sound. Among the tiny sounds the Wren is distinctive in that it has a kind of rattle about half way through its song, so try to catch that one. You may already know the Blackbird, as it is very common and sings often exposed on a rooftop or in a large tree. The Song Thrush is very distinctive in its two to four times repetition of a phrase after which he switches to another one. So by mid-march you would already be able to identify these three birds. Then it's time for the Chiffchaff to arrive, one of the earliest returning migrant birds, with a very tiny sound repeated rhythmically. About two weeks later the Willow Warbler will start singing his one-phrase song, like descending a small staircase with irregularly placed steps. You might decide to say 'five is enough' and spend the rest of the season to recognize these birds again and again, firmly 'connecting' the various identifying details with the actual sounds as a whole.

What tends to evolve gradually when you go through a process as the one sketched in the previous paragraph, is that while at first you will have to consciously link sounds with descriptive details, in a later phase you will be able to recognize a song almost immediately. You then pass from a 'studied recognition' to an 'instant recognition'.[6] Descriptions never fully catch all of a song's characteristics, as some of these are hard or even impossible to describe. Such 'indescribable' properties do function in an observational *Gestalt*, a lived totality of perception and experience. It is such a Gestalt knowledge that seems to enable an 'instant recognition' by an experienced birder. For instance, having heard quite a lot of Nightingales one doesn't need a full performance of all the various phrases that Nightingales can produce. A single typical note in the right circumstances of time and place may suffice. This ability is especially important because birds at times produce less than full songs, make unexpected variations or in some cases insert

---

6   This is similar to 'Recognition at a glance', as described by Law and Lynch (1988: 296): 'Some birds in the field are "seen at a glance". Specimen and species identity are appropriated within the same instant'.

'imitations' of other bird songs or even mechanical sounds. It is, in any case, a common experience that each year one has to 'revive' one's acquired abilities. The first time one hears a particular bird in a new season, one often has to do a 'studied recognition', before one can rely on the ability to recognize a song instantly.

Contrasts

Probably the most difficult task in bird identification is to distinguish some almost similar sounding species, like Blackcap (*Sylvia atricapilla*) and Garden Warbler (*Sylvia borin*), or the Reed Warbler and Sedge Warbler, discussed before. It is in these 'confrontations' that teachers of bird song recognition have to really show the effectiveness of their art, and that novices find it most difficult to apply their suggestions. So let me explicate the delicacies of the Blackcap/Garden Warbler contrast, and my own experiences in the field.

Here are some quotes, first on the Blackcap:

> The sweet and melodic song is one of the most lovely sounds of summer. Similar to that of the Garden Warbler, but Blackcap has more obvious phrases, rich clear notes, varying tempo and generally ends with a flourish. (…) Sometimes individuals will mimic songs and calls of other birds. (Holden and Cleeves 2010: 244)

> Blackcap is a popular singer and a favourite for many. With a varied and melodically phrased song it provides a welcome lead-line in a woodland and scrubland chorus. I find Blackcap's voice a little shrill sometimes (…) and generally prefer the more mellow sound of the Garden Warbler, though a good singer is worth listening to for a long while. Nevertheless I often hear long passages birds singing rather tightly structures verses with no real sparkle in the phrasing. (Sample 2010: 186)

And a bit later in the description, elaborating the contrast:

> Compared with Garden Warbler, Blackcap song has more articulated and varied phrasing, with variations in pace and more broken rhythms. Verses end in a flourish, usually a recognizable motif. In the syllables of Blackcap song, purer tones and slightly shrill whistles predominate in comparison to Garden Warbler's bubbling 'burr'. (Sample 2010: 187)

You may note that in these passages on the song of the Blackcap, the authors note a rather varied set of features, both to characterize the singing itself and the obvious contrast with the Garden Warbler. Below are some quotes from their texts on the Garden Warbler:

(A)n attractive stream of sweet, musical phrases that is confusingly similar to that of a Blackcap. Tends to be more even, subdued and hurried in its delivery and carries on in the same way for a long time, often singing non-stop for a minute or more. (Holden and Cleeves 2010: 245)

Distinguishing between Garden Warbler and Blackcap song is something many, even experienced, birders find difficult. However, with practice, the difference is clear. (…) Full song is usually given in verses of around 3 to 5 seconds' length, occasionally extending into a more continuous warble. It is marked by the even, hurried tempo and rather even overall pitch, generally lower than Blackcap. There are few sustained notes and it's hard to pick out clear phrasing: it fair bubbles along. There is a slight burr to the voice and a general lack of the clear whistles that permeate Blackcap song. (Sample 2010: 185)

Again, these writers use quite a lot of words to focus on different aspects of these birds' songs (and the Sample quotes are just a part from longer texts). An Expert talking to a group of Novices in the field would probably need to be more selective. Furthermore, it is quite rare to hear these two birds singing at the same time and place. Earlier this year, 20th April 2011, I was lucky to hear these birds on two sides of a small road on which I was walking, so I could compare the two at ease. But when I heard just one a few days later, I was in doubt again. In my experience, it is easier to be sure about an identification of a Blackcap, with its stereotypical phrase, than a Garden Warbler which requires attention to more subtle features such as tempo, pitch and duration, if you don't have the alter's song 'at hand'. Some years ago I had a discussion with a fellow birder about a song we were hearing, whether it was a Blackcap, as I thought, or a Garden Warbler, which was his opinion. It became clear that we were using different properties of the song for our trial identifications. I was attending the 'melody' of the song, and he the pace of delivery. We could not resolve our dilemma.

Identifying a 'New' Bird

The information on bird songs provided by texts, CDs and on the internet is mostly organized by the bird's species. A field guide, for instance, mainly consists of a list of species in a conventional hierarchical order, by family and genus. This is not very helpful if you hear a song you don't recognize and there is no expert around. CDs, on the other hand, are often organized by biotope or habitat, like garden, woodland, march, etc. So you can listen to the songs of birds which are common in the particular type of environment in which you heard your mystery bird. In this way you get a repertoire of bird song for that particular setting, with the possibility that you recognize one of them; a kind of bingo game. Sample (2010) offers a collection of three CDs in combination with the book I already quoted from. On CDs #1 and #2 he gives an oral lecture with examples, by habitat, starting from his home and garden, and ending on a rocky coast, while on the 3rd CD he offers a lecture ordered by type of song in terms of structure and/or sound quality.

Some writers present a kind of decision tree structure to guide you in your search. De Vos and de Meersman (2005: 22–39) offer the most extensive example, starting with three main groupings: call songs, strophic songs, and continuous singing, with various subdivisions and a few extra groupings. The sub-keys for strophic songs are, for example: rolls, motive song, identical strophic song, half-free strophic song and free strophic song.

So there are some resources for an individual identification of a 'new' bird's song, but the company of a more experienced birder makes the task a lot easier.

Games

Identifying birds can be part of a range of organized activities or 'games'. The one that is most in focus in this chapter can be called 'enjoying nature', or 'enjoying wildlife'. This game is being played in an enormous variety of particularized forms, but the basic activity is going out, visiting wood lands, wetlands, parks, nature reserves, wherever one can perceive and experience landscapes, plants and wildlife, including birds. Within this enormous range of activities people can choose to develop one or more favourites, like birds. At first, that may take the form of just loose watching and listening, but quite soon one may want to be able to identify some of these birds. A next step can be to want to be able to do that for all the birds that one encounters. Then one is on one's way to become a birder.

When birders meet with others of the same interest, they will talk about birds, the ones they see or hear, and the ones they have spotted earlier, that day or season, in that area or elsewhere, or even during their lifetime. Some will talk about the number of different birds they have identified, the 'list' of their excursion, a particular day, or their lifetime. Then their game may take a competitive switch: who has spotted more different species, or seen more rare birds (cf. Law and Lynch 1988: 274). In fact when a rare bird is spotted, birders may alert one another, which may lead to a scene of one little but rare bird being surrounded by birders focussing their telescopes on the poor victim. There are specific organizations for these kinds of activities, called *twitching* or *chasing*, such as the *Dutch Birding Association*.

While the games discussed so far are part of an amateurish set of activities, some birders may go on to some sort of wildlife focused profession, such as a field ornithologist working for an organization like the RSPB (Royal Society for the Protection of Birds) or a biology department in a university.

The present chapter, however is focused on the early phases of becoming a birder, learning to identify at least some birds by their song.[7]

---

7   For this reason I do not discuss the use of various types of technological apps like the use of MP3-players in the field, etc.

To Conclude

I have, in this chapter, sketched some of the ways in which birders may try to share their abilities to identify birds by their song. A paramount, and probably the most effective way in which this is done is when a more proficient birder talks to a less proficient one about the typical characteristics of a bird song they are hearing, as exemplified in the opening story to this chapter. I have used my own experiences in such situations, supported by written simulacra of such situations, to explicate some of the main characteristics of the 'work' involved. In short, I have explored what birders do when they identify birds by their song.

As a first step, they differentiate songs from calls, concentrating mostly on the former, especially in spring. When hearing a bird singing, they listen to various aspects of the song itself, the various 'sound qualities' as well at the song's 'structure'. The more experienced birders will check their 'candidate identifications' with a repertoire of birds that can be expected to sing in the particular environment, at that particular moment in the year and day cycles. Or even before they hear a bird, they will have their expectations in terms of time and place already in their minds. With time and experience such identifications can be produced spontaneously or instantly, or – when doubted, contested, or when an account is requested – in a more explicit, what I have called 'studied' manner: detailing properties and conditions to support the hearing.

Such identification accounts can be based on a range of resources, of which I have discussed descriptions, transcriptions, sonograms, recordings, or combinations thereof. Two specially problematic situations are when one tries to distinguish birds having almost similar songs and when one hears an as yet unknown song without having any 'candidates' in mind.

My interest in this chapter was to explicate identification work in a leisure setting, as part of 'enjoying wildlife', but of course capacities acquired in such a setting can also be used a more 'applied' settings, for instance in voluntary work for inventory projects or as part of professional work.

Ethnomethodology is in the business of explicating the 'how' of socially organized ordinary activities. Birding is such an activity and this chapter is an exploration of the auditory part of how this is done.

Chapter 4

Seeing Fish

Michael Lynch

It should be clear from even a superficial acquaintance with ethnomethodological studies of work, that the approach applies no less to recreational pursuits than it does to remunerated jobs. Indeed, the 'discovery' that ordinary as well as professional activities are constituted through the artful production and coordination of embodied practices is one of the defining features of ethnomethodology. The skills and working lives of professional musicians, golfers, and chess players may differ significantly from those of the far more numerous amateurs, and one would not want to assume that a game played by novices is emblematic of what professionals do, but as long as the circumstances are specified there is no a priori reason to exclude the novices' efforts from analytical interest in the 'work' of playing the game – indeed, the novices' struggles may turn out to be revealing. Widespread recreational pursuits also can be particularly advantageous for analytical studies of practical actions. Not only can the study of such pursuits provide tentative insight into their professional counterparts, commonplace activities (whether done for recreation or simply as part of daily life) can be appropriate and highly accessible sites for investigating how coordinated practices constitute social order. For studies at the conjunction between ethnomethodology and science and technology studies (STS), it also can be similarly advantageous to study widespread and commonplace epistemic practices in addition to more specialized and demanding technical procedures. Studies of commonplace practices of reckoning with numbers, amateur forms of systematic observation and classification, elementary instances of following procedural rules and plans, and everyday routines of comparing and aligning procedural results can provide insight into more 'technical' and 'educated' variants of knowledge production and use. So, for example, in her critical analysis of the role of formal plans in cognitive science and artificial intelligence, Lucy Suchman (2007: 72) uses an example from recreational canoeing to elucidate the difference between planning a route through a series of rapids and actually navigating through it in a lively course of improvised actions and reactions. Harold Garfinkel (1996: 15) uses an exercise of describing in detail the 'troubles' encountered in attempting to follow a sketch map instructing a recipient on how to get from one locale to another (a variant of the 'occasion maps' drawn and used in ordinary situations, which Garfinkel describes as 'analytic cartography's stepchildren'). He used the exercise to demonstrate the contingencies involved in using formal instructions in the course of practical actions. Garfinkel (2002a: ch. 9) and Dusan Bjelic (2004) use attempts to re-enact Galileo's inclined plane and pendulum experiments, respectively, as a relatively simple and low cost way to examine the embodied work of experimentation and mathematization. In earlier studies, I have used exercises with popular field guides to explore the work of observation and visualization (Lynch 1988; Lynch and Law 1999). Eric Livingston (1999) uses simple Euclidean proofs as a way to introduce the local organization of mathematical proving. Although they involve elements of skill and organized practice, common and elementary pursuits also are familiar to many readers who have some acquaintance – direct or indirect – with the relevant practices and specialized language. Presenting and analysing examples from such pursuits runs less of a risk of leaving 'lay' readers bewildered by a barrage of technical terms, equations, and unfamiliar situations. Gardening is not botany, birdwatching is not ornithology, following a recipe differs from following a laboratory protocol, but the amateur pursuit is no less of a practice than the more 'educated' counterpart. And, in some cases, the amateur activity is itself rich with technical detail, and of interest in its own right (see, for example, Graham Button and Wes Sharrock's chapter on yachting in this volume).

The use of familiar examples has widespread use beyond ethnomethodology, though often, for example in philosophy of science, the examples often take the form of truncated illustrations used to introduce general ideas that apply to the more specialized and exacting tasks associated with the sciences. Thomas Kuhn (1974), for instance, uses an example of an adult instructing a child on how to distinguish between ducks, geese, and swans at a zoological garden. Kuhn uses that example to instruct his readers about how scientists working in specialized communities acquire and develop convergent perceptions that give empirical content and stability to their conceptual systems. Kuhn (1970), N.R. Hanson (1958), and Michael Polanyi (1958) make abundant use of familiar gestalt figures and social psychology experiments to open up questions about tacit knowledge and theory-laden observation. Such examples have proved to be highly effective for suggesting that science involves specialized and elaborate forms of cognitive practice, the cultivation of which can be witnessed in commonplace as well as technical situations. According to that picture, simple or common examples enable insight into the complex and rare skills of the scientist, and their use suggests that scientific observation is a matter of learning to see things under specialized circumstances.

Although ethnomethodologists' writings also trade on quickly presented illustrative examples, they also 'dig in' and devote an extraordinary level of analytical care to specific instances. In studies of work in the sciences (Garfinkel 1986), the aim not only is to present detailed descriptions of practices, it also can involve an effort to exhibit such practices in a way that readers can work through themselves, for example, by following the steps in a Euclidean proof (Livingston 1999) or reproducing an optical demonstration by inspecting a series of figures with a prism (Bjelic and Lynch 1992). Readily accessible instances, which a substantial number of readers are already prepared to follow with minimal instructions, have obvious advantages for such a demonstrative procedure.

The procedure of using everyday examples and familiar experiences to address topics associated with the sciences and professions has considerable appeal, but it also has limitations. Philosophers' examples often are notoriously 'thin' – concocted as vignettes or illustrative examples, with little concern for detailed organization or contextual variation. Ethnomethodologists take pride in going beyond potted examples to develop an extraordinary interest in the mundane details of actual practices, but we also recognize that simple modes of reckoning in daily life cannot stand proxy for the deep engagements in highly demanding practices that characterize advanced scientific and technical work. Although it may have tutorial value, a one-off field trip with a local plant society cannot provide deep access to contemporary practices in field ecology, and following the steps in a classical proof is far removed from cutting-edge mathematics. In any such case, there can be a question of how well an investigation of a more familiar activity can capture the practices that organize less accessible technical activities. Analogies with familiar activities can have pedagogical value as stepping-stones to more difficult and exacting practices, but that very advantage marks the limitations of their use and of the insight that can be gleaned from them.

The limitations are more than methodological, and in some respects they are intractable. If, as Garfinkel (2002a) has insisted, adequate descriptions of practical activities are embedded in, and constitutive of, those activities, then it becomes questionable to claim that a simple or common example of numerical reckoning, field observation, map reading, or cooking can be used to identify and elucidate basic methodological practices that come into play when measurements, systematic observations, cartography, or chemical analyses are performed under very different conditions. Distinctive sites, traditions, stocks of knowledge, sources of expertise, and many other matters are not simply contextual complications that surround basic competencies with using numbers, visualizing objects, interpreting traces, and so on.

Ethnomethodologists have long insisted that so-called 'cognitive' or 'perceptual' activities are organized in terms of interactionally organized practices rather individual perceptual and mental processes. Even something as basic as visual perception ('seeing'), for ethnomethodologists, is an irreducible social phenomenon that is distinctively organized in contexts of routine practice and social interaction (Coulter and Parsons 1991; Sharrock and Coulter 1998). The embodied organization, ecological settings, relevant verbal expressions and gesticulations are specific to different contexts of activity, and must be investigated in situ. Accordingly, an acquaintance with the literature on visual perception does not necessarily prepare one for investigating particular activities in which vision and visualization are accomplished, and descriptions of professional vision in the context of one activity do not necessarily transfer to studies of other activities. Surely, one may object, given the commonalities of bodies and languages, there must be *some* common grammatical or structural form to visual perception that underlies relevant activities in different practical contexts. Without denying such commonalities, I will suggest in this paper that visual perception – together with the use of expressions associated with looking for, looking at, seeing, and not-yet-seeing something of interest – is deeply embedded in organized practices. I shall use a recreational pursuit – fly fishing – to make the case. However, in this case, I shall not use the recreational activity as a proxy for a more technical activity, nor shall I treat it as a common activity through which to investigate visual perception *in general*. Instead, I shall use it to show that what is seen, how it is seen, and the very relevance of seeing is organized by distinctive situations of practice that arise in contexts of fly fishing.

Angling with the Fly

Fly fishing is a recreational pursuit, although it employs numerous people and companies as manufacturers and retailers of equipment, estate owners and agents who lease rights to fish on private property, and guides and ghillies who give on-site instruction to touring anglers. The activity itself is ostentatiously anti-commercial. The contemporary 'pure' form of dry fly fishing, with its restrictions on equipment and method, was largely designed by and for the Victorian estate owners and their guests from the leisure class who angled for salmon and trout on the famous chalk streams in the south of England and on the peat-stained freestone rivers of Scotland and the North of England. Although dry fly fishing for 'seen' and actively rising trout is a highly effective method in the clear, slowly flowing, and insect-rich waters of a chalk stream, it imposes restrictions on the efficient harvest of fish. The American (and increasingly international) practice of 'catch and release' underlines the Zen-like reputation for detachment from the apparent product of the activity. Currently, it has widespread and growing popularity, though still distanced (misleadingly in many cases) from the 'low' art of 'coarse fishing' (angling with baits and lures for warm-water fishes).

Fly fishing, like several other leisure pursuits, has an old and sizeable literature, dating back to a fifteenth-century *Treatyse of Fysshynge with an Angle*, attributed to Dame Juliana Berners. This treatise, like many that followed, contains practical information on the main species of interest to an angler, methods for catching them with baits or lures, and instructions on how to construct equipment. Fishing stories generally convey practical lessons, though occasional stories, such as Hemingway's 'Big two-hearted river', and Norman McLean's 'A river runs through it,' have become part of a more elevated order of literature.

By far the best-known item in the literature is Isaac Walton's seventeenth-century book, *The Compleat Angler*. Walton was far more eclectic than the 'purists' who revere his memory. Like Dame Berners' treatise, Walton's book provides a 'compleat' set of instructions for catching a wide variety of English fresh-water fishes with diverse techniques. A specialized section of the book devoted to angling for trout with the artificial fly was written by Charles Cotton, a younger friend and writer, whose estate encompassed a stretch of the River Dove in Dorsett. The part that Walton wrote takes the form of a dialogue between the protagonist of angling 'Piscator' and his companions, as they walk the banks of the River Lea, which is now largely buried under the pavements of the greater London metropolis, although the Amwell Magna Fishery has secured for the continued use of its members the stretch that Walton fished centuries ago. Piscator discourses on the merits of angling as a pursuit worthy of an English gentleman, while also delivering bits of lore about various fishes, and methods of catching and cooking them.

Seeing Fish as an Instance of Guided Perception

In this paper, I will draw upon my own experience with recreational angling to reflect on a general topic – seeing, or visual perception – that is of interest to scholars in a number of fields, including ethnomethodology and STS. The themes of 'guided projection' (Gombrich 1960), 'theory-laden perception' (Hanson 1958) and 'acquired sim*f*ilarity relations' (Kuhn 1974) are frequently mentioned in studies of the sciences to describe the cultivation of professional sensibility through organized practice. My remarks will 'bounce off' of an earlier study, 'Cultures of Seeing' by Eric Laurier and Barry Brown (2004), which also uses fly fishing as an occasion to examine 'the social organization of vision.' Laurier and Brown aim to demonstrate how 'seeing fish' is deeply embedded in the organized practices to fly fishing; an aim that I share in this paper. They also express the more general aim to elucidate 'seeing' as a general topic. Their approach is akin to that of Charles Goodwin (1994), who tacks between very different contexts of activity to develop an account of 'professional vision' that emphasizes how 'seeing' is bound up in organized cultures of language, practice and interaction, rather than being limited to the psycho-physiology of individual vision and cognition. Laurier and Brown also draw upon ethnomethodological studies of the systematic use of what Coulter and Parsons (1991) call 'verbs of visual orientation', in an effort to understand how recurrent methods of instruction and indication enable practices of 'looking' and 'seeing' in a specific context of activity. However, as I will suggest (if not demonstrate), in this paper, 'seeing fish' is so deeply embedded in the practice of fly fishing that previous work on the topic of observation and visualization (including my own work) yields limited insight into how fly fishermen rely on vision in the course of that practice. Although it is undeniable that fly fishing involves vision and visual acuity (aided by polarized sunglasses), it is not simply an instantiation of a general perceptual process in a specific context of activity. Numerous variants of fly fishing, and of the practical ecologies of the art, establish the occasional relevance of 'seeing fish' and of particular practices of looking and seeing.

There are several reasons for 'bouncing off' of Laurier and Brown's study. First, their study focuses on the embodied work of fly fishing as a perspicuous instance for examining visual perception – specifically, the skilled work of seeing an object (fish) as part of an organized social practice (fly fishing). Second, Laurier

and Brown relate their study to ethnomethodology and social studies of science –
specifically, studies of the practical production, disclosure, and display of material
objects featured in organized courses of work. Third, Laurier and Brown tie visual
acuity to practices of 'looking' and 'seeing', and they elucidate this relationship
by closely examining the embodied activity through which an expert shows a pair
of novices how to 'see' a specific object in ways that are bound up with a cultural
activity (in this case, the traditions and practices of angling for salmon and trout).
Fourth, Laurier and Brown's paper includes pictures, transcripts, and (through
web access) accompanying video clips; materials that can be re-examined and
re-analyzed by readers. (Their video is available at: http://www.geos.ed.ac.uk/
homes/elaurier/video/find_the_fish.mov [accessed 29 June 2012]). This is a
decisive advantage for understanding and criticizing conversation analytical
descriptions (Sacks 1984). Finally, their study provides an opportunity to develop
a contrast between practical situations of understanding and analysis. Laurier and
Brown write from the point of view of novices being instructed by an experienced
practitioner on how to see fish in terms of disturbances in the surface of a flowing
river. I am in a position to write from the vantage point of someone who has
enjoyed fly fishing for several decades. Though I would be the last to claim notable
expertise in the practice, I am not a novice. In addition to enjoying the pursuit as
often as possible (which is not nearly often enough), I have read a fair sampling
of the inexhaustible, though highly redundant, practical literature. I subscribe to
several fly fishing magazines, and I confess that I read them with more regularity
and interest than the several academic journals to which I also subscribe. This
difference in background makes a difference for understanding how 'seeing fish'
features in the activity – not only as an acquired perceptual skill associated with
angling but as a perceptual practice that is refined, made relevant, and often made
irrelevant, in the course of a day on the river with fly rod in hand. Whereas for
Laurier and Brown, 'seeing fish' is a contextually specific instance of socially
organized 'seeing', for me it is an occasional, often subordinate and sometimes
irrelevant, aspect of fly fishing.

     As Laurier and Brown make clear, the specific practice they observed is not
just one of endlessly many contexts of activity in which human visual organs
and cognitive capacities are deployed. Although there is no question that normal
perceptual capacities are a prerequisite for the practical and communicative
activities of fly fishing, what Laurier and Brown describe is not limited to the
physiology and psychology of vision. It cannot be encompassed even by a broad
'ecological' conception of visual perception (Gibson 1979). A hint of what is
involved is concisely expressed by Harold Garfinkel's (2002a: 240) dictum that
'looking's work' involves more than what is seen or done with the eyes. For
example, when I cannot find my keys or eyeglasses before leaving home for
the office, my work of *looking for* the missing thing involves going (and often
returning) to a series of places around the house where I might have left it; my
searching can involve looking under and behind a pile of recently delivered junk
mail on a table; or, when the object isn't in one of the 'usual places', looking under

furniture or turning over the cushions on a couch. My eyes are active through all of this work, but I am also rummaging around, trying to re-trace my recent pathways ('When was the last time I had them, and where was I?'), and also making use of my local history of losing-and-finding just this thing. I may discover that the lost object is in one of the places in which I looked-for but did not see it the first (or second) time through. My 'looking's work' is thus a whole-body activity, performed in a familiar environment, through which I reflexively stitch together temporal recurrences in my own biography.

An Instance

Laurier and Brown set up their paper by videotaping an on-site lesson for a novice delivered by an experienced (and, evidently, a highly skilled) angler: Laurier's father (whom I shall call 'the guide'). The site is a river inhabited by trout and salmon – evidently, a stretch of river with which the guide is intimately familiar. The guide's task documented on the video is to show the novice (his son, Eric Laurier) where fish are holding in the river and to teach him how to see them. The paper examines several episodes of seeing-showing in which the guide points to subtle features and changes in the conformation of the flowing surface of the river, and verbally instructs the novice on where particular fish are lying and moving. One sequence is transcribed in the article as follows (in the transcript, 'E' is Eric Laurier, co-author of the paper, and 'F' is Laurier's father, the guide):

> F: See look there's a big one rose right at the junction (5) there look! <he's still rising, He's feeding>
>
> E: So that's those ripples I can see in-between the
>
> F: Yeah they're intermittent [but]
>
> 1 →   +
>
> E: [That's] it! That's one. [There's another there]
>
> 2 →   +
>
> F: [That's it, you've] got it (*sniffs*)
>
> E: Okaaay.

                                              (Laurier and Brown 2004: 13–14)

During this brief exchange, guided by his father's excited indications and exclamations, Eric comes around from seeing 'ripples' on the surface to seeing 'one' and then 'another' fish then and there. Laurier and Brown then add the following commentary:

> If we go a little deeper into the wordings Eric's dad is using, he begins with 'see look' (or most often 'look') and this is then followed by a characterization of the fish's movement that will produce what Eric is still seeing as ripples amongst ripples – the 'rise' – and when these ripples are rapid & ongoing – 'he's feeding'. What is hopefully striking, as we have noted already, is that the ripples are not dealt with as ripples by the fisherman, they *are* a big fish. They are the actions that the big fish is doing – 'rising' & 'feeding'. It is the novice that deals with them as ripples since he still cannot see them with the skill of the fly fisher. (p. 14)

A key line in this analysis is that, for the guide, 'the ripples are not dealt with as ripples by the fisherman, they *are* a big fish.' This observation resonates with the theme of theory-laden observation (or, in this case, recreational-activity-laden perception): the guide does not see a disturbance of the river surface and *then* interpret it as an indication of a fish – a large one that happens to be feeding. In contrast, the novice sees 'ripples' – disturbances in the flow that have no immediate relation to fish, as opposed to rocks or other irregularities in the riverbed – and only after further prompting by the guide is he able to see *that* specific surface disturbances indicate fish. In brief, whereas the novice is brought to see 'the ripples' *as* [a sign of] the 'big fish', the guide's grammatical usage suggests that he sees the fish directly, with no delay or epistemic gap between seeing 'ripples' and inferring the presence of a large fish rising and feeding at the surface.

Laurier and Brown go on to invite readers to perform similar exercises with the video footage, and to follow up by going to a 'good salmon river on a warm summer's day with plenty of insects hatching …'. They note that the tutorial in this case is not a matter of being instructed in the arts of 'seeing' in a general sense, but is embedded specifically and deeply in a practice. They add that the lesson they explicate is but a beginning:

> And what happens here is only the very beginnings of entering seeing with fly fishers' eyes in the sense that the tutee is still struggling with the problem of seeing fish at all, while the expert sees fish catching flies, sees big ones and small ones. From these marks on the surface of the river she or he builds up to being able to make assessments of the intelligence of the fish that he might one day pursue with rod, line and waders in the midst of the river. (p. 18)

However, if we read this brief extract after already having acquired 'fly fishers' eyes', certain puzzles become notable about what is seen and how it is seen. An initial puzzle has to do with the *kind* of fish. Laurier and Brown do not identify the particular river at which the tutorial took place, but from the context of their discussion and the video, it appears to be one of the major rivers in the British

Isles. In a second paper in which the authors also present the same material, they use the word 'Tweed' in the titles of some of their transcripts and video clips (Laurier and Brown n.d.). I would guess that it is the River Tweed – a famous salmon river in the border region south of Edinburgh. The Tweed, like many other rivers in Scotland and England, supports (unfortunately declining) runs of Atlantic salmon (*Salmo salar*) and sea trout (*Salmo trutta* morpha *trutta*), and it also supports populations of 'resident' brown trout (*Salmo trutta*) which do not migrate to sea. Other species of fish also inhabit the river, but it is clear that the fish of interest are salmon or trout. One might imagine that the 'big one' the guide mentions would be a salmon, or perhaps a large sea trout, since the anadromous fish tend to grow larger than the residents, due to the richer diets available in the ocean and estuary environments in which they grow to maturity. Salmon and sea trout often move through a river in groups during their spawning migrations, and according to the guide, several fish are lined up in close proximity in this scene. However, the guide's reference to 'feeding', and the rise-forms and abundance of flying insects visible in the video, would strongly point to resident trout actively feeding during a hatch. Resident trout (even big ones at times) will rise to the surface to take a mayfly or other floating insect, but salmon and sea trout generally do not 'feed' after they move into the rivers on their spawning migrations, even though they may stay in the river for months before spawning. One source of continual discussion among anglers is how to induce a salmon to take a fly (which, depending on size, color, and design can evoke the appearance and movement of a small fish, a shrimp, or an aquatic insect), and there are numerous 'theories' of why salmon will chase and take a fly, even though they are in the stream to spawn and not to eat. It is generally agreed that fish fresh from the sea are more ready to take the fly; and they also are preferred for aesthetic reasons (they retain their silver sheen, are more robust when hooked, and they also taste better because of the high fat content that sustains them through the spawning migration). For a salmon to be seen 'rising' repeatedly to take insects off the surface would be remarkable indeed. Salmon and sea trout can be seen to splash at the surface, roll, and leap clear of the water, but they would not likely be seen to be 'feeding'.

A further puzzle arises from the guide's identification of the size of the fish. In some circumstances dry fly fishing for trout, when all that an angler sees is the rise and not the fish that made the disturbance, it can be difficult to tell the size of the fish from the rise form. Many anglers' tales begin by describing a cast to a small dimple at the surface; a delicate rise that surprisingly turns out to be a great fish that had been 'sipping' small flies from the surface. Small fish often make large splashy rises, and while it is often easy to tell from a rise-form that a fish is small or possibly large, it is a fallible indicator. The streambed is visible on the video through the glare on the surface, and the video is, of course, a degraded version of what a keen-eyed angler would be able to see from the riverbank. While I cannot see the profiles or shadows of the rising fish in question when I view the video clip, I can imagine that the guide may very well see them as they move to the surface. From the other descriptions and extracts in the paper, it seems that the guide is very skilled at spotting fish in the local stretch of river, so it is unclear whether he is seeing fish solely through their surface disturbances or seeing their forms beneath those disturbances as well. In other words, just how he is seeing fish, and just what he is seeing, remains unspecified in the novice's account.

Initially, we can characterize these as 'mundane' puzzles, which have little apparent connection to the 'deep' puzzles that preoccupy scholars who have one or another interest in 'vision' (professional or otherwise). However, they would be of interest to an angler: the kind of fish would be crucial, because traditional equipment and tactics differ greatly depending upon whether the fish is a salmon, sea trout, or resident trout. Moreover, equipment and tactics differ when the fish is seen to be feeding at the surface ('rising'), as opposed to feeding below the surface or simply holding in the stream. These practical contingencies of 'seeing' make all the difference for what one does next.

The Very Relevance of Seeing Fish

At the most general level, fly fishing is an angling technique in which a 'fly' (usually, but not always, a single hook on which feathers, furs, and artificial materials are wound and tied) is cast by means of a tapered line that is manipulated with a flexible rod in the manner of a whip. A skilled cast is beautiful to behold, as viewers of the film version of 'A River Runs Through It' may recall (the casts were made by a tournament caster doubling for actor Brad Pitt). Some flies are tied and dressed to float at the surface of the water (dry flies), while others are designed to sink to a variable depth (wet flies, nymphs, streamers). There are many variants of fly fishing, some of which are defined by the target species (trout, sea trout, salmon, bass, bonefish, tarpon, and many others), the type of water (large river, brook, lake, pond, estuary, coral flats, open sea, and many others), and terminal tackle (dry fly, streamer, wet fly, nymph). There are many further refinements of technique and equipment, depending on geography, local habits of targeted fish and their prey, tradition, and current fashion. In some variants of fly fishing 'seeing fish' is crucial, or even required by rule, whereas in others 'seeing fish' is unnecessary, and even a distraction.

In classic (i.e., Victorian-era) fly fishing on private estate and club waters in the south of England, strict rules about permissible technique were often specified for a controlled stretch of river: dry fly only, cast upstream, to 'seen' fish. Any other technique (downstream drift of wet fly or streamer; weighted nymph; downstream dry fly; tandem flies) was deemed unsporting when angling for resident trout (different rules applied for salmon or sea trout). Many clubs and estates have relaxed such rules in recent decades, but the technique of casting a dry fly upstream to seen fish is still often considered the technique of the 'purist'. The purist does not 'prospect' for fish by casting in hopes of inducing a take from an unseen fish, but only casts to an individual fish that is already visible. The fish can be 'seen' either directly as a shadowy form beneath the surface, or indirectly through the rise form or some other disturbance of the surface, such as the emergence of the tail as the fish tilts in shallow water to pick a morsel off the streambed, or a swirl at the surface and a scattering of small fish pursued by a predatory fish. The preferred technique when casting to a rising trout is to 'match the hatch' – to cast an artificial fly designed to imitate the size, colour, and profile of the insect on which the trout is feeding at the time. In order not to disturb the fish, a delicate cast must be placed upstream of the fish so that it drifts 'naturally' into the trout's feeding lane without drag from the line. Under the right conditions, this constrained approach also happens to be highly effective and a source of immense pleasure. The chalk streams are remarkably clear (the water having been arisen from springs in the chalk downs); the high alkaline content and even flow of the streams is conducive to abundant vegetation and regular hatches of the aquatic insects that draw feeding trout to the surface. In northern regions, where freestone streams arise from peat bogs and take on the color of tea, the water is more acid, insects are sparse, and the frothy waters flow rapidly over rocks, the rules and practices of sight fishing simply do not apply.

Another, quite different, variant of 'sight fishing' is practiced on 'bonefish flats' – shallow expanses of the Caribbean and other tropical waters, near reefs and mangrove islands, inhabited by a species commonly known as bonefish (*Albula vulpes*). Bonefish travel alone or in schools, and are difficult to see against the light sand and marl bottom of the flats. In a typical arrangement, the angler stands on a platform at the bow of a long boat, while a guide slowly moves the boat with a pole while also spotting target fish for the angler – instructing the angler on where to place the cast to an approaching fish or small school: 'Ten O'Clock [with the bow marking 12 O'Clock] 45 feet out!' Seeing fish is crucial, and based on my limited experience with this technique, very difficult. Bonefish blend in with the sandy bottom of the flats; the water surface is dappled with reflecting light (making polarized glasses a necessity), so that it is very difficult to see beneath the surface, especially at an oblique angle from the distance at which wary bonefish are likely to be spotted before they flee. For a novice, there often is a division of labour between the guide, who spots the fish, and the angler, who casts in the instructed direction. Not surprisingly, it is easier for an angler to place the cast effectively when he or she sees the target than it is when the guide indicates the target by distance and clock-face direction. But often it is the guide who sees and the angler who casts blindly. A crucial aspect of such a division of the labor of 'seeing' is the interactional coordination of the cast with the distance and direction of the movement of the target. If bonefish are approaching from a distance, a cast can be placed delicately in their path without disturbing them. Moving fish create a small window of opportunity to anticipate where they might be heading within the reach of the particular angler's ability to cast. Although pedagogy is involved as the guide tries to bring the angler also to see the fish, often the two of them settle for a coordinated barking of orders followed by an instant and dutiful reaction.

Fishing Blind

For many situations of trout and salmon fishing (indeed most, in my experience), 'seeing fish' is irrelevant. Or, rather, seeing fish is a consequence of, but not a prerequisite for, catching them. One finds the fish with the end of the line rather than with the eyes; what the angler looks for are places or 'lies' in which an undisturbed fish might be induced to take a fly. While angling for salmon with a ghillie on the Aberdeen Dee, I could see salmon occasionally splash and roll at the surface. After having noticed my intent interest in such fish, the ghillie instructed me not to bother with them – as he explained, what we were after were the few salmon in the pool that were fresh from the sea and willing to chase the fly. The target salmon were not necessarily visible, and the visible salmon often were 'red' (gravid, having lost the silver sheen of 'fresh' sea-run salmon) and 'dour' (in stream for weeks or months and less ready to chase the fly). The ghillie would indicate places where a fresh fish *might* be holding, and he also would indicate which 'lies' were more promising under different conditions of flow: particular exposed or submerged rocks and other obstructions; the head of the long pool in low water, or the tail of the pool in high water.

Seeing fish also can be a distraction in trout fishing. Even when large fish can easily be seen, and seen to be rising and feeding, sight fishing isn't necessarily called for. A common mistake is to spend an inordinate amount of time angling for a fish that one can see. A common maxim is that if you can see the fish, it can see you. In heavily fished water, the trout do not necessarily flee at the sight of the intruding angler; they may very well go on feeding, but with greater vigilance. A well-known stretch of the San Juan River a few hundred metres below a dam in New Mexico, which releases cold water into the desert surroundings, harbours a sizeable population of large trout that feed throughout the day on tiny insects. A park along the stream is open to the public, and the river is very heavily fished. Large trout can be seen in the slow-flowing shallower stretches, casually sipping insects at and beneath the surface, apparently undisturbed by the many humans nearby. They also are nearly impossible to catch. Presumably, they see the anglers nearby, and are on the alert, and they also have time to carefully inspect the food that floats by in the gentle current; sufficient opportunity to notice the difference between wiggling insects floating free in the current and small bundles of fur and feather wound on hooks and tied to lines. Experienced anglers often ignore these highly conspicuous trout in favor of unseen fish in the riffles, which can be approached and induced to take a skillfully presented fly that drifts more quickly in the swifter and more broken current. Novices are more liable to be hypnotized by the visible fish, and to exhaust their limited bags of tricks in a fruitless effort to move them to take the fraud.

In trout and salmon fishing, there is an entire lore of 'reading water': identifying promising lies (places where fish are likely to be found and ready to take a fly) from the way the water flows over and between obstructions. The challenge is not only to locate fish, but also to concentrate on lies where fish can be taken with a given technique: there is a conjunction of technique, place, and the practical significance of a seen or unseen fish. Some fish are effectively inaccessible for a given technique (a salmon holding near a rock at the bottom of a deep and swift run is rarely induced to take an unweighted salmon fly drifting near the surface as it is presented with a floating line). A novice who saw such a fish would be advised not to waste time trying to catch it; a more experienced angler, with sinking line and a fly tied on a heavy brass tube might try for it.

Singular Knowledge

Quite a lot can be learned from reading books about reading water, looking at illustrative drawings and photos, and gathering examples from personal experience. However, even the most skilled anglers often will hire a local guide when fishing in unfamiliar waters. The visiting angler may be practiced in the arts of casting the fly and well versed in the many complex aspects of the art. They may be skilled at 'reading water'. However, the guide can convey singular knowledge: up-to-date knowledge of which techniques and flies to deploy on this particular day, in this place, at this time of year, and under these particular conditions of river flow and clarity. Such singular knowledge often is conveyed by showing rather than telling, though spoken instructions are used as well: 'Try right here – stand upstream of the lie, cast over here, let the fly drift through the pocket. If you don't get a take after a couple of casts, try giving it a twitch, just as it reaches the lie.' Harold Garfinkel sometimes used the Latin term *haecceity* ('thisness') to refer to singular knowledge of 'just this' (see, for example, Garfinkel and Wieder 1992: 175). Philosophically, it is an interesting category – the gesture indicating 'just this' is not an ostensive definition of a *kind*; it is a singular indication of a thing at hand, in place, just here, just now. There is nothing particularly mysterious about such singular knowledge, but it can't possibly be conveyed in terms of generic instructions on tactics. *Just thisness* is not the same as *quiddity* (essence), because it is not an abstract basis of identity; instead, it is a way of speaking of the immediate, singular, concrete presence of a thing or place at hand: 'this is a good lie; several fish have been caught here recently.' Anglers who fish a stretch of water repeatedly tend to have very good memories of the fish they catch (especially notable fish), and of where and when they caught each one, and with which flies and tactics. The spatial 'art of memory' in this case operates not in terms of the *locus communes*, but rather in terms of the singular locus with a local history. They are places, often quite small, which have, for whatever reason, been discovered to be 'good' places that yield fish to the angler on a regular basis (or, maybe, just once – but it was a very memorable fish). Knowledge of such places is not necessarily private, although it is sometimes kept secret. Guides are indispensible for revealing such places to the visiting angler. On famous stretches of river, particular pools, runs, and other places often are given names to commemorate their histories as notably good places.

Haecceity is a fancy word, but it points to something extremely common. An understanding of the idea also allows us to dissolve some of the mystery surrounding the concept of tacit knowledge. Tacit knowledge is often defined as a mysterious knack – an incommunicable and even unconscious skill – but knowledge of singular places is no more (or less) mysterious than being able to recognize a familiar face. Singular knowledge can be, and frequently is, communicated, but only through descriptions and indications tied to specific locales. It can be extrapolated to other 'places like this', but anglers learn that there are many 'places like this', the vast majority of which just do not happen to be any good. 'Good' places aren't always good, just as 'good' tactics don't always work as well as they did under (apparently) 'the same' conditions, even the day before. An angler's paradox ensues from the tendency to concentrate on 'good' places and tactics, and the concentrated time and effort tends to raise the likelihood that they will be good again. There is mystery for the angler, but it is not a matter of an uncanny knack or unconscious knowledge.

Conclusion

I could go on. The subject is very deep and there is much more to say. What I have said should not be taken as a criticism of Laurier and Brown's paper, or of the perspective from which they wrote it. A novice's struggle to see what a guide instructs is a well-established and fruitful way to open up the analysis of a practice. The present chapter is more of a respecification than a criticism. Specifically, what I have respecified is the perspective from which 'seeing fish' is to be explicated. Laurier and Brown specify 'seeing fish' as an instance of socially organized vision. I have re-specified that topic in connection with occasional situations encountered in the course of angling. So, what is the difference? Can't 'seeing fish' be understood both as a perceptual practice and an aspect of angling? Yes and no. In situations of sight fishing, seeing fish can be crucial for competent action. Guided instructions, such as the instances that Laurier and Brown reproduce and describe, certainly come into play as part of the pedagogy of angling. However, when respecified as a highly variable and occasionally relevant aspect of angling, 'seeing fish' has less to do with 'seeing' as a general activity, and more to do with 'fish' – 'fish' construed as the intentional counterparts of specific techniques and circumstances through which, and in which, they can be located and caught. Even when 'seeing fish' is highly relevant, there is the question of the *point* of the activity. For the angler, unlike a train-spotter or birdwatcher, the point is not simply to 'spot' them and tick them off on a list. Careful watching may prove to be an enjoyable and instructive way to get to know fish and their habits, but seeing and identifying them is not the point of the activity. There also is the question of the kind of fish: not only the species and size, but its 'readiness' to be taken with a fly, under just these conditions right now, with just the equipment with which I can perform the relevant actions. These relevancies and *haecceities* are internal to fly fishing, and of little apparent interest for scholarship about 'vision' (cognitive, social, cultural, professional, or otherwise). And yet, approaching 'vision' from the perspective of a practice surely *is* about the social organization of visual perception. It is just that it seems virtually impossible to cut that topic free from its involvements with the recurrent situations, equipment, skills, and vocabularies of a particular practice, as well as highly specific refinements of that practice.

To appreciate the implications of this point, consider the pedagogical language game that Laurier and Brown describe. Their pedagogical exercise takes a recurrent form, which runs as follows:

> *Dad points at some ripples and says 'that's a fish.'*
> *Son looks around and points at some other ripples and says 'that's a fish?'*
> *Dad says 'that's a rock' and points at some other ripples, 'that's a fish.'*
> *(repeat this chorus at intervals during walk).* (Laurier and Brown n.d., 5; italics in original)

On the surface, this language game appears to be structured in a way akin to the pedagogical situation described in the quote from Augustine with which Wittgenstein begins the *Philosophical Investigations*:

> When they (my elders) named some object, and accordingly moved towards something, I saw this and I grasped that the thing was called by the sound they uttered when they meant to point it out. The intention was shown in their bodily movements, as it were the natural language of all peoples .... Thus, as I heard the words repeatedly used in their proper places in various sentences, I gradually learnt to understand what objects they signified; and after I had trained my mouth to form these signs, I used them to express my own desires. (Augustine, *Confessions* 1/8, English translation from the Latin, quoted in Wittgenstein 2001: 2e, n. 1)

Despite such resemblance, there is a profound difference between the two 'games', as Laurier and Brown make clear in their analysis. The Augustinian language game (which, as Wittgenstein points out, is often taken by philosophers to identify the essential referential function of language) is about learning the names of things. The language game between the guide and the novice that Laurier and Brown describe is not about learning to *name* the 'fish' that the guide indicates. The guide is not providing an ostensive definition. He is indicating where and how to *see* fish. We could liken the task of 'seeing fish in the rippled water' to a gestalt exercise of 'extracting the animal from the foliage' (Garfinkel et al. 1981: 132).

Wittgenstein (2001) doesn't refute Augustine; instead, he *respecifies* the classic philosophical 'picture' – which presents nominal reference as 'the essence of language' (p. 2e). Respecified in this way, *reference* is no longer the heart of all language, and various referential pedagogies become *particular* language games among innumerable others in the vast and complicated ecology of language use (see Lynch 1993b for a brief, satirical critique of a referential theory on the theme of 'fish'). Once this respecification is accomplished, we can begin to ask about the relevance of the Augustinian language game for understanding routine activities beyond the philosophy seminar: When is the language game relevant? How is it relevant? What else might be relevant in our practical activities? Although Laurier and Brown certainly do not use their particular language game to elucidate a conception of the 'essence of *seeing*', we also can ask what their game of 'seeing fish' has to do with the practice in question – fly fishing, in this case. In this paper I have suggested that seeing fish, and the particular pedagogical game that Laurier and Brown describe, may have *some* role in the ecological accomplishment of fly fishing, but that its role (or, rather, the various relevancies for and practices of seeing fish) is so heavily embedded in the practices and situations of fly fishing that we end up with very little to say about 'seeing' *as such*. Instead, we may be led to appreciate that the ethno-methodology of 'seeing' is bound up in the 'methodologies' in which 'seeing' has a role, and that this role may not trace back to *any* analytical conception of vision-in-general, whether individualistic *or* social in scope.

Chapter 5

All At Sea:
The Use of Practical Formalisms in Yachting

Graham Button and Wes Sharrock

Introduction

Yachting, while a leisure pursuit and a 'play' pastime, involves a lot of hard work, at least where the development of the skills required to safely and efficiently sail a yacht at sea are concerned. Leisure-time yachting is embedded in an environment of methods, practices and tools for working out – often by mathematical calculations – the means to ensure safe and effective sailing and in this respect it is a most thoroughly rationalised activity in the Weberian sense of the term. In addition, the yachtsperson is situated on a vessel which will embody numerous functional principles of design, embedded in an environment of technologies, instruments, and documentation, and, typically, working/playing with another or others on the yacht who will vary in their levels of competency. All of these matters are continuingly relevant, and deployable over the course of a sea voyage, of whatever length. The main aspects of rationalisation we will consider here are the *navigational* and *sailing* skills that come into play in yachting. These involve the mastery and application of formalisms. In the first instance to navigate a yacht *safely* from point to point, and in the second instance to maximise the *efficiency* of the yacht's performance as it moves from point to point. Thus the formalisms we consider are ones that are used to determine the sailing vessel's sea-going trajectories and efficient performance.[1]

Since Egon Bittner's 'The Concept of Organisation' was published in 1965, and Harold Garfinkel's study of researchers complying with coding rules for sociological data in 1967, ethnomethodologists have repeatedly demonstrated that understanding the meaning of rules and principles to be followed involves mastering their application in practice. This point is often made with respect to rules considered as formal algorithms, and it is made to establish that such constructions cannot operate as generative mechanisms for the production of situationally recognisable displays of competent conduct. In a way, this paper makes this same point for 'another first time', taking as its case the formalisms

---

1   This chapter only considers yachting under sail. While the principles of navigation that are considered here are common to motor yachting, the principles of sail management are, obviously, not applicable to motor sailing.

that are used in sea-going navigation and efficient sailing, identifying, some of, the practical vessel-familiar competences that are required for live-action application of those formalisms. Though illustrating the general point we attempt to do more than merely repeat it, and avoid what is perhaps a tendency in the ethnomethodological literature, namely, to treat the contrast as one between conduct as formally prescribed by formalisms and conduct as practically managed. This emphasis tends to underplay the fact that, in those environments in which they find their everyday use, those formalisms are themselves understood as practical constructions, which are, or can be, used as procedures for directing conduct but are understood by their users to be correctly implemented when they are deployed *in conjunction* with other formalisms and with unformalised understandings. Paul E. Meehl's (1957) methodological paper 'When shall we use our heads instead of the formula?' is memorable for its title and, thus, also for inviting what we think is the correct answer: always use your head, especially when using the formula.

We also wish to introduce into these discussions a distinction with respect to the understanding of what 'correctly following a formalism' involves. Formalisms are often means of making calculations. Certainly the *navigational* procedures we will be describing are commonly ways of calculating positions on the water relative to landmasses and sailing hazards.[2] In the case of calculations, correctly following the formalism is a matter of making appropriate transformations of the symbols making up the calculus. Thus, correctly following the rules of arithmetic is, in the first instance, a matter of grasping that the symbol 2+2 can be replaced by the symbol '4'. This applies very much to the on-land, school taught procedures of navigation. The correct application of such rules in practical circumstances depends not only upon being able to make the formal transformations, but also upon being able to correctly identify the inputs into the computation. In the case of elementary arithmetic, using addition in counting depends, of course, upon being able to identify the units that are to be added such that the transformation 2+2 is to be rewritten as 4 can be applied to them. The yachting case, as will be shown, involves a good deal of sea-going knowledge to determine the correct inputs into calculation of location, distance and direction whilst on the water in the yacht. One further point, whilst the formal calculus is to be employed in precise and determinate steps, it is understood by those using the calculus that its outputs reflect not only the precision and determinacy of the transformative procedures but also the rough and ready indeterminacy of many of the inputs.

---

2   This is most obviously the case with respect to navigational procedures. However, it is also true for the procedures involved in setting sails correctly because the yachtsperson is still involved in calculating the angle of the wind relative to the yacht's heading, using instrumentation that measures wind speed and direction, and drawing off formal calculations involved in aerodynamics in setting the shape of the sail in the most efficient way with respect to the angle of the wind across the yacht in the 'airs' in which the yacht is sailing.

The users understand that the result of applying the formal calculus is to be understood as supplying only estimates and approximations.

Yachting

Yachting is a popular recreational pastime in many countries. The Sport England Active People Survey reported on 16th June 2011 that 69,000 people in England sail once a week.[3] Given that most yachtsmen and women sail less frequently than this, the number of people participating in yachting activities during a year will be considerably higher. However, there are no legal requirements to be satisfied in order to sail a yacht in the UK. Quite simply, anyone can step onto a yacht and sail it even if it is their first time on a yacht. This is a principle up-held by the Royal Yachting Association (RYA), an association with over 102,000 members whose 'mission is to prompt enjoyable, safe and successful sailing and motor yachting' (RYA web site)[4]. The philosophy of the RYA is to keep yachting as free of legislation as possible by promoting safe and responsible yachting. To this end it has developed an extensive training program designed to instruct yachtsmen and women in the main *principles* of sailing, known as shore-based theory courses which are run after hours in schools, in peoples' homes, in colleges, in yacht clubs or the premises of yachting schools all over the UK. The program is delivered through a network of licensed instructors who are often enthusiastic amateurs or employees of yachting schools, which are run as commercial ventures. Although some of these schools amount to medium sized businesses, often employing professional sailors, more often than not they are run by individuals or as a family venture by enthusiastic yachtsmen and women as a way of making a living from their passion and paying for their yachting.

The shore-based courses incrementally elaborate the formal principles of safe yachting, and at the end of approximately 40 hours of learning per course, either in weekly doses or intensive sessions, there is an examination, and successful candidates received a certificate. These are amateur certificates[5] that do not certify that their holders can engage in yachting, though in the case of accidents the authorities might take into account that a person holds an RYA certificate, and some yacht charter firms might require persons chartering their yachts to hold one.

3　See www.sportengland.org (accessed January 2012).

4　www.rya.org.uk (accessed March 2013).

5　The Yachtmaster Ocean certificate of competence is, though, a pre-requisite for the first rung on the commercial certification ladder.

'Day skipper' teaches the principles of sailing a motor or sailing yacht that will provide people 'with enough knowledge to navigate around familiar waters by day. A basic knowledge of lights is also included to introduce you to night cruising.' The Coastal Skipper/Yacht master Offshore builds on the Day Skipper course and 'equips you to navigate on coastal and offshore passages.' The Yachtmaster Ocean course unravels 'the mysteries of astro navigation, using a sextant, ocean passage making, worldwide meteorology and electronic navigation aids.'[6]

However, the RYA understands the point we made in the introduction that the sailing formalisms are *practical constructions* that are to be put to use in live-action circumstances, requiring an interaction between those circumstances and the formalisms of sailing. In this respect, part of its training methodology is also to provide people with a series of practical water based courses in between the shore based theory courses in which they can experience what it is like to use the principles in actual circumstances, and familiarise them with the types of circumstances they may encounter within less controlled environments. In other words, the RYA recognises that formalisms are themselves understood as practical constructions, which are, or can be, used as procedures for directing conduct but which are understood by their users to do so by being correctly implemented when they are deployed *in conjunction* with other formalisms and with unformalised understandings.

These courses are not so much concerned with teaching people how to apply the principles in practices, but rather are designed to give them the hands on experience of applying them in practice *themselves* and having their application critiqued by an instructor.[7] In this way, yachtsmen and women start to build up their own stock of knowledge of the utility of the principles which they can draw off in subsequent applications, and this stock of knowledge continues to develop throughout their yachting lives. Figure 5.1 below displays the way in which the theory and sea based courses relate to one another:

---

6   All quotations are taken from the RYA website.

7   They will also start to hear, as they will continue to throughout their yachting lives, stories about yachting problems encountered and how they were or were not solved. Yarns and reminiscences become second hand experiences that can be added to a person's own experiences.

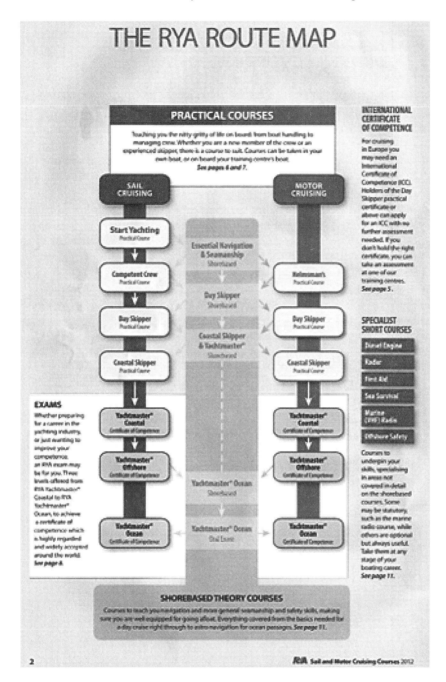

Figure 5.1   Taken from page 2 of *RYA Sail and Motor Cruising Courses* 2012

Navigation

The Formalisms of Navigation

There are three principles to navigation: 1) knowing where you were and how you got to where you are, 2) knowing where you are, 3) knowing how to get to where you want to be next.[8]

a) Knowing where you were and how you got to where you are. Knowing where you were is given by the principles involved in the second formalism 'knowing where you are'. Thus knowing where you were is given in previously working out where you are.

A first step in calculating where you are from knowing where you were is known as 'dead reckoning'. To work out, by dead reckoning, where you are it is necessary to know i) the constant 'heading' that has been followed, that is, the course through the water as given by following a constant ship board compass setting from a given starting point; ii) the constant speed of the yacht from the given point, and iii) the time taken from the given point. This information is then used to 'plot' on a 'chart' the course taken and the distance travelled from a given point. To do this it is necessary to correct the compass heading which is a 'magnetic' reading, to a 'true' reading that is used on charts. The magnetic pole varies with respect to true north, and the magnetic 'variation' is given by the chart. To move from magnetic to true the navigator must add the variation if it is to the east of true north, and subtract it if it is to the west.

However, compasses suffer inaccuracies due to their position on a yacht, and the construction of a yacht. Thus a compass is affected by metal such as the engine, and by electrical currents. Consequently, there can be a 'deviation' to the east or the west of a magnetic reading that is particular to the compass in use. This deviation has to be known. If the deviation is to the east then it must be subtracted from the magnetic reading, if it is to the west it must be added. Thus the magnetic reading that is 'corrected' to a true position first has to be corrected to take into account any deviation.

---

8   The discussion here will centre on navigating using paper-based charts. There are other tools and types of navigating; for example, astro-navigation and using electronic aids such as 'Global Positioning Systems' (GPS) based 'chart plotters'. The experienced yacht person will be well versed in at least paper based and electronically supported navigation, and the RYA provides instruction in both, as well as astro-navigation. However, it is important to stress that electronic based navigation, although extensively used at sea, and taught in the RYA shore based courses has not superseded paper based charts nor is it intended to. Rather, it is but another way of navigating. In addition, the principles of navigating using electronic aids also require the order of methods described here with respect to paper based navigation to be deployed to work them in actual circumstances. For the sake of brevity, however, this paper will just refer to chart work as it is a generic form of navigating, and one that is there to be used should navigating electronically fail because of fragile power supplies.

Having determined the true heading a yacht has been following it is then necessary to work out how far the yacht has travelled through using the equation: distance equals time traveled multiplied by the speed of the yacht: $D = T \times S$.

Thus, from a known point given by its latitude and its longitude on the chart a skipper can work out where they have traveled by plotting the heading and distanced traveled. This will inform the navigator as to where they are now.

However, dead reckoning does not take into account the influence of tides on a yacht, or the affect of wind on the yacht. Waters around the UK are tidal and therefore not only is the yacht moving across the water, but the water is also moving in relationship to the seabed, the ground, and thus the yacht is being carried across the ground as well as moving through the water. The 'course through the water' will not, consequently, be the same as the 'course over the ground', or the 'course made good', yet it is in relationship to the ground that a position is fixed, the given point provided. Therefore, a more accurate way of determining the course traveled, and obviously knowing more accurately where a yacht is, is to take account of the tide, knowing its direction and speed for the period of time that has been traveled. This can be determined by consulting a sailing almanac, or using specialised tidal information books, electronic aids or consulting the chart.

In addition to the effect of the tide on the yacht, a yacht can also be moved off its intended heading by the wind. Some yachts have high 'freeboard' which means that they have high sides, and also a lot of deck material, such as radar, 'doggers' life rafts and the like which can catch the wind. This means that such a yacht may be pushed to 'leeward' of its course more than a low slung uncluttered yacht. Of course, the strength of the wind must also be taken into account. Thus the leeward movement of a yacht in 'light airs' may be negligible whereas in a force 8 gale it may be 10 to 20 degrees. A navigator must take this into account. When the affects of the tide and the wide are applied to the dead reckoning plot, the navigator arrives at an 'estimated position' which, despite the name, is more accurate than 'dead reckoning'.

Thus to determine how a yacht got to where it, and thus determining where it is, is render through the following formalism:

1. Draw the heading followed on the chart from a known point having
    a. Corrected the magnetic heading for deviation
    b. Corrected the magnetic heading to a true heading
    c. Corrected the true heading for the affects of the wind
2. Calculate the 'distance run'
3. Measure the distance run along the line representing the heading since leaving the known point
4. From this dead reckoning position draw off a line or lines to reflect the effects of the tide (speed and direction) during the time taken to run the calculated distance.

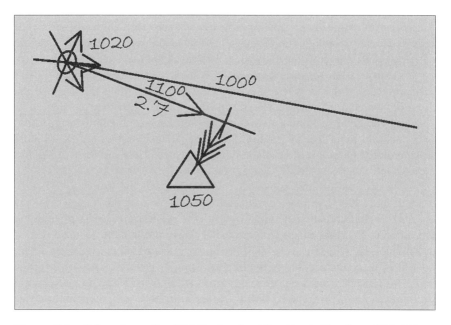

Figure 5.2   Taken from the *RYA Navigation Handbook* (Bartlett 2005: 98)

This will then provide the navigator with the course over the ground and the latitude/longitude position of the yacht. There are conventions for marking the lines: course through the water is market by >, the tide by >>> and the course made good >>. An isosceles triangle is marked around the point and is a universal symbol for indicating an estimated position.

b) *Knowing where you are*. Knowing how a yacht has travelled from a given point during a given time is obviously one way of knowing where you are. There are other ways. One is to take a 'sighting' on landmarks (such as conspicuous chimneys or headlands) or seamarks (such as buoys) that appear on a chart. Thus by taking a 'bearing' normally using a 'hand-held compass' (though there are other methods) from a land mark will allow the navigator to draw a line from that point on the chart; the yacht will be somewhere along that line. However the bearing measured by the compass is a magnetic one, so first it has to be corrected for variation and deviation for use on the chart. However the bearing is also measured from the yacht but since the point of the exercise is to find out where the yacht is, it is not possible to use the bearing from the yacht to draw off the line on the chart. Therefore the bearing from the yacht has, also, to be changed to the bearing of the yacht from the known land or seamark, which is simply done by adding or subtracting 180 degrees. The navigator then draws off a line on the chart from the know land or seamark.

However, the bearing only tells the navigator that they are somewhere along the drawn line on the chart and it is now necessary to calculate where along that line they are. To do this, the bearing from another charted land or seamark can be made and where the two lines intersect will 'fix' the position of the yacht. Usually, for the sake of accuracy, three bearings are calculated, ideally, spaced out.

Thus to determine where a yacht is using know land or seamarks the following formalism is used:

1. Identify charted land and seamarks from the chart
2. Identify those land or seamarks on the land or sea
3. Take a sighting from the yacht
    a. To the first land or seamark and record it
    b. To the second land or seamark and record it
    c. To the third land or seamark and record it
4. Correct the magnetic bearing of all three for variation and deviation to arrive at the true bearing
5. Correct the bearing from the yacht to the bearing from the land or seamark
6. Draw off the bearings on the chart and fix the position of the yacht where the lines intersect.

There are other ways of determining how far along a line from a given point a yacht is. One is to calculate the depth of water beneath the yacht at the time of the fix. This takes account of the fact that most yachts have depth gauges, which display the depth of water beneath the gauge's transponder, or the yacht's keel – though a hand held 'lead line' can also be 'swung' to gauge the depth. Charts also display what is know as 'charted depth' or 'soundings', that is, the death of water below a given data point, known as 'chart datum' which in the UK is the theoretically lowest possible tide, as provided by the 'United Kingdom Hydrographic Office'. Other organisations such the US' 'National Oceanic and Atmospheric Administration' uses the 'mean lower low water' (the average of the lowest tide recorded at a tide station). The point is to provide a fixed datum point to be used in tidal height calculations (though, of course, it is necessary to know which organisation's charts are being used if working across charts). Thus, if it is known how much water there is under the transponder, or the keel, that could be cross referenced to the data on the chart and if that corresponded to a point on the position line taken from a bearing, the position of the yacht would seem to be fixed.

We say 'seemed to be fixed' because chart datum does not actually inform the navigator how much water is beneath the transponder or the keel because it does not take into account 'the state of the tide'. That is, there will be water on top of the chart datum, or, if the land 'dry's out' there will be land above the chart datum - recorded on the chart in terms of its 'drying height'. Thus the depth of water is a function of the height of tide and the charted death or drying height. Information that can be used to calculate the height of tide can be gleaned from almanacs, which contain data on the predicted time and depth of high and low waters for every day of the year. Using 'the tidal curve' – a graph of the predicted height of tide of a port covering the hours either side of high water – of a relevant port to their approximate position, the navigator can then calculate the height of tide they can expect at the time they are establishing their position. Then, combining that calculation with chart datum would allow the navigator to calculate the depth beneath the transponder or keel, and correlate that to the position line of their sighting.

However, charts display chart datum irregularly across a chart, and therefore a calculation may not be possible because data is not available along the position line. Charts, though, do not just display charted depths, but like land maps they also display contour lines that link up similar charted depths, and thus contour lines for 5 metres, 10 metres, 20 metres and the rest are marked on the chart. Consequently, a yacht may be sailed along the position line until it intersects a relevant contour line and the estimated position of the yacht can be consequently fixed.

Tidal height calculations are also used to calculate the time a yacht might 'dry out' (ground) so that, for example, work on its keel may be done, or they may be calculated to know what 'height of tide' is needed to clear an obstacle such as a mud flat or sand bank that dries out at low tide, or the height of tide needed to 'go alongside' a harbour wall should that not be accessible at 'all states of tide'. When these calculations are done two further factors are introduced which is the draft of a yacht (the distance between the water line and the bottom of the keel) and the clearance between the keel and the sea bed so that a calculation is not made that rests the keel on the sea bed, but keeps it just above it. 0.5 metres is used as a standard clearance.

Thus to calculate a tidal height the following formalism is used:

1. For a given position (current or to be used in the future) record the charted depth
2. Consult the almanac and using the relevant data employ a tidal height graph to determine the height of tide at that time
3. Add the height of tide to the charted depth

To use this in determining a fix:

1. Read off the depth beneath the transponder (adjusting if the display is set for a keel reading) until a contour line that intersects the drawn position line is found

To use tidal heights to calculate what height of tide is needed to clear a drying out feature such as mud flats and sand banks:

1. Determine the drying height from the chart
2. Add to that the draft of the yacht and the clearance

To use tidal heights to calculate the height of tide needed to come along side:

1. Add the draft and the clearance together
2. Consult the charted depth
3. Subtract the charted depth from the results of 1

Tidal heights are also used in calculating the time at which obstacles can be cleared or yachts can go along side.

Another method for determining the position of a yacht if it is not possible to take more than one sighting or use contour lines is the 'running fix', and another is to use 'transfer position lines' which are also expressed as a formalism – though for the sake of space these will not be spelt out.

c) *Knowing how to get to where you want to be next.* In order to determine how to get from a current position, worked out using methods described above, to a destination, for example, it is necessary to calculate the heading that needs to be steered from the current position. To calculate this, a line is drawn on the chart from the current position to the destination point. However, the effects of the tide over the period of time that the passage will take need to be taken into account. To do this the average speed of the yacht is estimated and the time taken to cover the distance between the fixed point and the destination is given as a function of distance divided by speed. This will inform the navigator as to how many hours of tide need to be taken into account. The almanac is used to provide data on the speed and direction of the tide over the time that will be taken and that is then drawn off from the current position. The distance to be travelled from that point in the time period already calculated is worked out as a function of speed multiplied by time. That distance is then measured out on dividers (there is an easy way of doing this using the layout of a chart but which will not be described here) and an intersection from the tidal stream point is scribed on the original line drawn between the current position and the destination – interestingly this intersection may be past the destination point. The course to steer is then measured in degrees using one of a number of calculating tools such as a 'Portland' or 'Breton Plotter' (the use of which will also not be described here). This course to steer then needs to be corrected for the effects of wind, as above. However, because the course to steer has been calculated on the chart it is a true measurement and has to be corrected to a magnetic course to be followed using the ship's compass. To do this the reverse of the calculation used to correct magnetic to true is done: subtract the variation if it is east, add it if it is west. Any deviation must then be corrected for and the result is the compass heading to be followed to arrive at the destination, taking into account the time to be run and the effects of the tide. Lastly the course across the ground is carefully scrutinised on the chart to ensure that it does not take the yacht into any danger, such as passing over a wreck, rock, or sand bank for example.

Thus to determine 'the course to steer' a yacht from a current position is calculated using the following formalism:

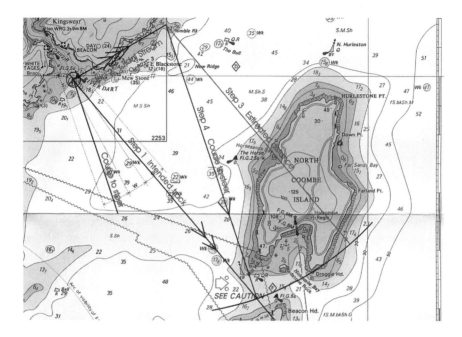

Figure 5.3   Taken from the *RYA Navigation Handbook* (Bartlett 2005: 93)

1. Determine current position
2. Draw a line on the chart between current position and destination (Step 1 in Figure 5.3)
3. Estimate duration of passage
4. Mark off on the chart from current position the effects of the tide for the duration of the passage (Step 2)
5. Set dividers or other measuring instrument to represent the distance to be travelled during the passage
6. From the position arrived at from the result of Step 2 scribe an arc to intersect the line drawn in Step 1 (Step 3)
7. Draw a line from the tidal point to the intersecting arc (Step 4)
8. Using an instrument to measure angles record the heading
9. Correct for leeway
10. Convert the true heading to a magnetic heading by correcting for variation
11. Correct for deviation

Using the Formalism at Sea

Of course just from reading these formalisms a person would not be fully able to calculate the position of a yacht, or the course to steer. For example, a person would have to know how to use a Breton plotter, and then having learnt that, they would need to practice with it and become proficient in it use. Applying the formalisms in the class room means learning how to use instruments but also how to deal with the ambiguities that surround following the instructions, becoming proficient in handling the 'tools of the trade', developing memory joggers to begin with to remember the steps and their order. There is, thus, a whole lot more to following the prescriptions than is contained in the prescriptions themselves. However, having learnt how to estimate a position, do tidal height calculations, develop a course to steer, and what that means in its embodied doing in the class room will enable a candidate to answer the questions posed in the RYA shore based theory courses.

However, the formalisms in themselves, and the developed ways of applying them will not enable a navigator to achieve their ends *at sea*, rather, to apply them within the practical circumstances of a voyage it is necessary to draw off a stock of yachting knowledge not covered by the formalisms nor by how to apply them in the class room (though some of that knowledge is relevant and deployable at sea), knowledge that is built up through the unfolding experiences of yachting. That is, the formalisms are practical constructs to be used in conjunction with other knowledge of 'being at sea' in order for a skipper to achieve their ends. That knowledge is developed through *being* at sea. So, what is it that a yachtsperson needs to know about being at sea in addition to the formalisms and how to apply them in the classroom that enables the formalisms to work at sea?

a) Yachts are not stable platforms. Yachts move around on the water. As a yacht breasts the crest of a wave it will, especially if it is, as most are, a modern, light, wide beamed production yacht, yaw to one side or the other, according to the affects of the water and the wind acting on the yacht. Yachts also 'heel' when sailing 'close to the wind', that is, as near to the direction of the wind as is possible. The angle of heel, however, can change moment to moment because the speed of the wind is not constant and will suddenly gust or moderate for short periods causing the yacht to further 'dig in' or move to a more upright angle.

Further, people on the helm have various abilities. Experienced helms people will easily put a yacht into its 'groove' – the ideal position to the wind – and anticipate changes in the wind by, for example, looking to the effects of the wind on the water in the direction the yacht is travelling, or observing the 'wave train' affecting the yacht. Inexperienced helms will be less likely to be able to anticipate wind changes, and the yacht is thus more likely to be blown around. Also the yacht will be twisting to the port and starboard of its course to steer as it crests a wave, especially if the conditions are rough. Inexperienced helms often over correct to bring the yacht back on course by swinging the yacht in the opposite direction and causing the yacht to go seriously off course in the opposite direction. Experienced helms are able to keep the yacht on course through slight adjustments.

Familiar instruments used and mastered in the classroom can behave in unfamiliar ways at sea. For example, reading a hand held compass is not a given matter, it has to be held correctly so as to be as horizontal and vertical as possible, and looking through the prism takes experience to ensure the correct marks on the compass are aligned to the land or seamarks, and to make the judgement when that alignment has occurred, all done as the platform on which the readings are being taken lurches and twists. It also requires the navigator to monitor the person on the helm, are they suddenly going to swing around, and the affects of the wind and sea on the yacht, is it suddenly going to lurch or sink into the bottom of a wave or rise up onto a crest? The navigator also has to have an appreciation of the yacht, is it a light bouncy one that will dance about on the crest of a wave or is it a long heavy keeled yacht that will just plough through the wave. The navigator has to think ahead, they are unlikely to remember the bearings so have they brought pencil and paper with them, or better still have prepared someone else to take down the readings as they sing them out? Complications can develop such as finding that what looked like a good land mark on the chart turns out not to be so good when actually viewed, or cannot be seen at all because it is obscured by a feature not marked on the chart. There can also be large discrepancies between the visualisation of the shore from the chart and actual viewing of the shore as moderated by stinging rain driven into the eyes. If one sighting is to be a headland, where on that rolling wide actual headland is the sighting going to be taken. In addition, time is of the essence, the sightings need to be taken quickly and then quickly transferred to the chart because the yacht is travelling and as soon at the reading is taken it will be incorrect because the yacht will have moved, and the amount of movement it has made from taking the sights and making the estimated position calculation needs to be minimised.

Thus, in following the instruction 'take a sight on known landmarks' the navigator will be drawing on their knowledge of what makes a good sighting in practice; the characteristics of the yacht; the experience of the helm; their handiness in manipulating the compass; the effects of the wind and the tide on the yacht; how to prepare for taking a sighting, amongst other matters that can arise.

Navigators also have to know that however good their sightings are they do not, in practice, do what they do in the classroom, which is intersect. Rather, in practice, the lines will intersect to form a triangle, known as a 'cocked hat' and the estimated position of the yacht lies somewhere in that cocked hat. Although they may have been told this, the question at sea becomes not one of recognising a cocked hat, but of deciding if its size is acceptable in the conditions, and in the proximity to danger. Some cocked hats will be larger than others because the sighted bearings have been less accurate, and navigators need to make a judgement as to what is acceptable and what is not. They need to take account of matters such as distance to shore, the presence of sand and mud banks, or if they are likely, given the weather conditions, to get a better sighting. Thus, in practice, the navigator may not so much be fixing the position of the yacht on the chart but rather identifying an area within which the yacht lies and in effect is not navigating the yacht on the chart, but navigating the area defined within a cocked hat around the chart so as to best take account of potential dangers by navigating the nearest part of that area to a danger away from it.

Thus in following the formalisms the navigator has to build into them their handiness with instruments in varying sea and weather conditions, their judgements about crews, and their sailing abilities, and judgments as to what is or is not acceptable.

b) Knowledge of yachts and instruments. Although there are rules to be followed and mathematical principles to be applied, which suggests that navigation is embedded within a system of mathematical certainty, nevertheless, navigation involves much *estimation*, indeed this is recognised in the phrase 'estimated position'. Thus for example, the seemingly simple instruction to take account of leeway will involve a judgment on the part of the skipper as to what leeway, in this sea, with these wind conditions a yacht is making. Leeway is a judgmental matter not something read off an instrument. Some sailors will, however, say otherwise, and it is possible to hear sailors dispute the matter with one another. For example, it is suggested that, using a hand-bearing compass, a bearing is taken on the 'wake' produced by the yacht as it travels through water. That is, how far off a straight line from behind the yacht the wake is. However, some will argue that this cannot be done as the wake itself will be moved by the tide, or is not practical because the wake is indistinct, or readings from different parts of the wake will differ. In practice a skipper has to really *know the yacht*, through their built up experience of sailing it in various sea states and wind conditions, and develop an understanding of what their affects on their yacht will be.

Yachts vary tremendously in their design. They can be built for racing, for cruising, for racing-cruising or cruising-racing. They can be narrow beamed for sailing efficiency or wide beamed for marina comfort. They can have deep long heavy keels running the length of the yacht in a traditional mode for rigidity and stability, or fin keels, short and long, pivoting around which makes them more manoeuvrable and agile than a long keeled yacht. They can have lead or iron keels, imparting more or less stability, bulb keels which are short keels with added weight to compromise between depth and weight. They can have bilge keels, which provide two short keels that will enable a yacht to dry out without falling to one side or the other, and the like. They can have different rudders: single rudders position in the centre of the yacht, or twin rudders, at each side of the stern, spade rudders operating independent of the keel, or skeg hung rudders which are integrated into the keel.

Yachts can have different sail configurations with varying amounts of sail, differently positioned and catching the wind in different ways. Thus there can be traditional Bermuda rigged sails with a foresail and a main sail at the same height, or they can have a Günter sail, a gaff sail, a lugsail or a spritsail. They can employ cruising shoots or spinnakers. They can have different rigs which hang the sails in different ways: a common sloop rig which has one headsail and a main sail, or a cutter rig with two headsails, or a yawl or a ketch which have two masts, the 'mizzen mast' being differently positioned with respect to the 'steering post'. They can be centre cockpits, which give high freeboard, and headroom below decks, or cockpits with less visibility and headroom but less freeboard and more protection.

The different keel, rudder, sail, rig and cockpit configurations are juggled by designers to optimise the performance of a yacht for the type of sailing and different sailing conditions they are designing for. However, owners then add items to their yachts such as radar, wind turbines, life rafts, spray hoods, sunshades, dodgers and the like, all of which, as noted above, can catch the wind. Owners may keep their yachts up to different standards. Some owners may be meticulous, their yachts having 'clean bottoms' with their hull free of weeds and barnacles, and tight sails, but others may be less meticulous having baggy sails and 'dirty bottoms'. The combinations of yacht design and owner configuration and maintenance will thus determine how '*this*' yacht will perform in '*these*' wind and sea conditions. Given this, the determination of the amount of leeway a yacht may make is the result of the situated judgment a skipper makes in the light of their *knowledge of the yacht*.

However, what does someone do if they do not know the yacht? In practice they might just ignore the affects of leeway and wait and see what happens. For example, the average time recommended for fixing the position of a yacht is every hour. After an hour they could employ multiple methods for fixing a position, cross check an estimated position with the position produced by taking sightings and if there is a discrepancy (and they feel confident about the sightings) then that will be the effect that the wind has had, but also, perhaps the tide, is currently having upon their estimations. That at least will give then a *sense* of correction they need to make. If they are worried or if they are sailing in potentially hazardous waters they could increase the frequency of their position calculations.

Consequently, the instruction in the navigating formalism, 'correct for leeway', requires knowledge of the yacht and the effects of wind and sea have on the yacht which is the result of developing experience of the behaviour of the yacht in various conditions, or is one that is set aside according to the judgment of the skipper as to its relevant applicability in these conditions, or is a calculation that is postponed until it turns out to be relevant. The application of the formalisms is thus very yacht dependent, requiring a developed or developing knowledge of how 'this' yacht performs in different sea and weather states. While the formalisms are universal, and while they would enable a navigator to navigate any yacht they become applicable in 'this' yacht, which has to be built into their use.

In addition to developing knowledge of yachts a navigator also needs to develop knowledge of instruments. As noticed above, it takes experience to use a hand-bearing compass in difficult seas, but different hand bearing compasses have their own characteristics, an understanding of which can aid in their use. Ships' compasses are interesting in this respect. It is rare to find that a skipper has actually produced a 'deviation card' for their compass. Doing so is demanding. It requires, for example, towing another person in a dingy who has a hand bearing compass and taking simultaneous readings on the ships' and the hand bearing compasses at different points of the compass and comparing them. Or it is necessary to find two land marks that are in transit, that is, line up with one another, and positioning a point of the yacht in line with these marks on different points of the compass and taking a reading from the ship's compass, then comparing that with the chart (adjusting for the difference between true and magnetic). In actual practice skippers often let deviation 'pass', or 'explain it away', for example, 'modern compasses are very accurate', or 'justify ignoring it' – 'I've checked it and its ok' or 'normalise it' – some yachts, especially performance yachts can have two compasses for reading on different 'tacks', and if they show, as many do, different readings of a few degrees, skippers may just average them.

With respect to tidal heights, almanacs embody detailed information needed to engage in a particular calculation. Thus, for example, in tidal height calculations aimed at determining when it is safe to enter a particular harbour or marina, the almanac will contain all of the information that a person will need to make the necessary computation. However, engaging in the computation requires making that information have traction upon the particular problem to be solved. For example, the times and the depth of high and low water in an Almanac are given for 'primary ports'. For 'secondary ports', the only information given is how they vary from the information supplied for the primary ports. Therefore, it is necessary to 'interpolate' the information from the primary to the secondary port. There are various devices that a skipper can use, to help them do that which involves constructing a grid on a separate piece of paper, or using a pre-printed grid, transferring the information from the almanac to the grid and matching the information. However, again this may be done in less than favourable conditions, and may be fiddly in the circumstances. Therefore, many skippers will do the interpolation 'by eye', using the information to make an estimation of depth and time. In the navigation theory courses this is referred to, but actually doing the interpolation by eye involves what is, by it nature, not something that can be taught according to a formalism, it is something that is done in the manner of estimating the distance of an object, it is 'eyed up'. People can get better at it the more they do it, but how they do it is not a matter of perfecting the application of a calculus, it is a matter of perfecting 'the eye'. In this respect, skippers may well build in a margin of error to be on the safe side.

Tidal height calculations are not done as ends in themselves, but to support activity, such as safely crossing a marina bar. The primacy is to cross the bar without hitting it with the keel, and in that respect the precise moment it is safe to cross is not as important as understanding what the window of opportunity to cross it is. In any case, the information in the almanac, while having the appearance of detail, is itself actually, and irretrievably, short of detail, for the actual height of tide, as opposed to its predicted height in the almanac, will be subject to influences that almanacs cannot take account of before the actual event, such as wind strength which may keep a tide in, or atmospheric pressure which may flatten the water.

All in all then, navigation is often a matter of what is acceptable inaccuracy for the sailing being done. If it is in home, familiar, waters, a large level of inaccuracy may be tolerated; navigation may be done by eye rather than by the chart. If it is unfamiliar waters with known hazards, then more levels of instrument accuracy may be needed. In any case, as with the developing knowledge of a yacht, skippers develop through use and understanding of how finely accurate or not their instruments may be.

Thus applying the formalisms becomes one of judging situationaly tolerable inaccuracy.

c) Knowledge of people. Yachts obviously involve people, and a skipper does not just have to use the characteristic of a yacht in order to navigate it safely, they also have to use the characteristics the people, the crew, to sail the yacht, even, if as is often the case, the crew is just one person, often a spouse or partner. Matching crew to tasks, or when a skipper undertakes task themselves in front of a crew, is involved in applying the formalism of navigating in practice, and knowing ones' own abilities and that of the crew is part of the situated application of the formalisms.

For example, people can be just as affected by sea conditions as yachts can be. The sea can affect different people differently and seasickness can occur in whatever conditions. Thus, for instance, sailing a yacht from Roscoff to Plymouth in rough sea conditions and force 7 to 8 winds overnight with a novice crew, a skipper might simply suspend developing an estimated position and course to steer as provided for by the formalisms. Keeping the confidence of the crew high, being cheerful and making tea, not showing any worry, keeping an eye on the crew, being in the cockpit or in view, giving the crew simple and clear instructions as to what to do, letting them know that the skipper is confident in their own abilities and also has confidence in the crew when he/she has to sleep, may all be matters that outweigh regularly plotting and estimating positions.

The skipper will know that once Roscoff harbour is cleared that the only danger (apart from shipping, and the skipper will have forcefully emphasised that if a crew member spots a light to tell them or wake them) is the Eddystone, but also that the light of the Eddystone light house will be a very useful navigation aid. The skipper will, before departure, have worked out the course to steer to Plymouth from Roscoff by simply reading off the heading by placing their Bretton Plotter on a line they will have drawn from Roscoff to just North West of the Eddystone. In all practicality, in these circumstances, the skipper might well ignore the tide because the passage will cover a number of tides, which, for practical purposes, might cancel each other out. In any case, the skipper will know that the novice crew might have difficulty in holding the course in the conditions and their inaccuracy might lead to more error than the effects of the tide. Thus the skipper may well give the course to steer, knowing that a correction can be made once the effects of the light of the Eddystone lighthouse can be perceived. The light can only be seen at a distance of about twenty miles, but the loom of the light, that is its reflection off the sky, can be seen for many more miles away. Thus the simple instruction, steer a particular compass heading until the loom is seen (if the skipper is off watch and asleep) and if it is to port, steer to port until it is on the starboard side of the yacht, and keep it on starboard, or if it is to starboard, keeping it to starboard will suffice. Keeping the Eddystone to the starboard will keep the yacht in deep water without the risk of land, and gives the helm a point of reference in addition to the compass to use. The skipper will know the time of departure, know the speed of the yacht and will have a rough idea of how far has been travelled. Thus, in these conditions, with this crew, and in these waters, the skipper might well suspend the application of the formalisms, rather preferring a rule of thumb method. Once the Eddystone is cleared, and the proximity of land might begin to moderate the affects of the wind, and light might well have appeared, then a more accurate course to steer and position keeping can be developed to safely reach Plymouth Sound.

This is an extreme, but actual, case of navigating from Roscoff to Plymouth. Of course, conditions might be such that it is daylight, not night, or foggy, which might require different decisions to be made. But, whatever the actual conditions, knowing the people on board, or making judgements about them is part and parcel of applying the formalisms. Does a skipper trust the readings produced by one crewmember? Is the skipper going to ask someone else to re-do it, or do it themselves, with the potential of demoralising that person, or is it better, for the sake of crew morale, to let it pass, knowing that it can be put right at a later date without any danger?

A skipper's knowledge of himself or herself is also important. Can 'I' remember if it is add East or subtract East if moving from magnetic to true? There are memory aids such as CADET – Compass, **Ad**d **E**ast, **T**rue – or 'Error west compass best, error east compass least. But these might seem tortured and confuse 'me', so do 'I' need to construct a crib sheet and tape it above the chart table? Also, navigating is often done at a chart table, but all the fun of sailing is in the cockpit, and that is also where danger can be seen and assessed. Novice skippers may often spend too much time at the chart table and not enough time in the cockpit. So what is the point of knowing, precisely, where a yacht is, if there are no immediate dangers that are being navigated around, when the real danger exists in hitting another yacht or yacht because no one has noticed it and the skipper is buried in the chart. The degree of precision needs to be weighed against other factors in order to make the situated judgement of what is good enough in the circumstances.

d) In the end. People new to yachting will often religiously attempt to apply the formalisms, but in the end, a good accomplished skipper should always know where they are without having to actually making the calculations on paper. They should, for example always, at any notice, be able to 'put their finger' on the spot on the chart where the yacht is. They should be able to do this by knowing the waters, land marks, and buoys they are sailing though and 'by eye' judging their relationship to those, or how far they are from them given the sailing direction, if they cannot see them. They can do this by either knowing their sailing area by having sailed it many times, or by having thoroughly familiarised themselves with the chart if it is a new sailing area, and drawing off their experience of what charted marks actually look like in practice. Also they should be able to judge the actual affects of tide and wind on the yacht, not just by consulting the almanacs and making their formal calculations and the like, they should also be able to judge the effects by noticing how other yachts are performing, how seamarks such as buoys are moving.

This understanding is developed in the activity of actually sailing and is all part and parcel of yachting. It amounts to the order of knowledge that yachts people develop in the course of yachting that cannot be captured in the formalisms of how to yacht, which in themselves are integral to yachting safely, and play a crucial role in making those formalisms actually work. As experience builds, the formalisms may be less and less referred to, or partially referred to. The experienced skipper who has not sailed in their home waters for a few weeks, may just look up the times of high and low waters for a day's sailing and may only do that, drawing off other matters that achieve the intended outcome of the formalisms.

The formalisms then become matters that are used to make people aware of the need to know where they are and their relationship to danger, and how they can get to a particular point. They are used in combination with the stock of knowledge of being at sea that a yachtsperson has built up, being more relied upon in the first flush of yachting, and less as that knowledge builds, but are always there to be fallen back upon if necessary and should particular circumstances dictate. Thus while the experienced skipper might confidently sail out of Harwich Harbour, tacking across the deep water shipping lane and not keeping to the small vessel route which would keep them away from the large container ships that constantly sail in and out of the harbour, in good visibility, without reference to the chart, it is a different matter in fog. In fog, the experienced skipper would find a safe contour line on the chart, position their yacht on it and sail along it by timed criss-crosses over it, thus keeping them away from the large yachts. And because they are experienced and know that other experienced skippers will be doing that as well, they will have their crews' eyes peeled for other yachts doing the same thing. The formalisms then, are practical constructs the use of which are knowingly entwined within the use of other matters and which determine what their application in the circumstances they cover actually amount to.

Sailing a Yacht

This chapter is only considering *sail* driven yachting and while sailyachts have auxiliary engines, which are a very important component of most sail driven yachts, the purpose, for most yachtspersons, in having sails is to actually manoeuvre and navigate their yachts under sail. Thus the formalisms of navigation are used by most yachtpersons, under sail, and there are formalisms also involved in 'setting' and 'trimming' sails so that the yacht is the most efficient platform to navigate around the seas. They involve three maters: yacht sectors, forces, sail shape.

The Formalisms of Sailing

a) Yacht sectors. There is a universal, formal, classification of sectors of a yacht and the aspect of a yacht with respect to the direction of wind. A yacht is broken up into eight sectors, the front part, 'the bow', to the right of that is the 'starboard bow' which stretches to the widest point of the yacht, its 'beam' and to the left is the 'port bow', similarly extending on the port side. The two adjacent widest parts of the yacht are the 'starboard, and port beams'. The rear of the yacht is 'the stern', and the 'starboard and port quarters' extend between the stern and the beam. Sailing a yacht involves putting the wind across these various parts of the yacht, knowing what the consequences of that is on the yacht and how to adjust the sails to maximise these consequences with respect to yacht performance. To understand what is involved, formalisms of sailing theory have been developed.

b) Forces. When the wind is passing over the sectors of the yacht that are before (in front) the beam the sails of a yacht act like the wings of an aeroplane and are subject to aerodynamic forces. The curved structure of the sail acts as an aerofoil and causes air that passes over their leeward side has to accelerate because it has further to travel than the air passing on the windward side. This causes low pressure to form on the leeward side and higher pressure to form on the windward side. This in turn causes the yacht to move, or 'lift', in the direction of the low pressure as does a plane start to lift as wind passes over its wings. The yacht is thus 'sucked' in the direction of the low pressure. There is a caveat which is that the aerodynamic effect of the sail disappears when a yacht is dead, or 'head', into the wind, or within about 20 to 30 degrees of the direction of the wind, when the aerodynamic effect is lost and the sails will either flap (sometimes violently) or hang limp, depending on the strength of the wind.

A sail needs to 'fill' with air to adopt an aerofoil shape and it cannot start to fill until it is at a certain angle to the wind. However, while the aerodynamic shape of the foyle produces lift, it also produces 'drag' which is resistance to being lifted. The more lift, the more drag. This is because the curve, or 'camber' of the sail is inevitably moving against the wind and consequently there is resistance to the movement, which increases the faster the yacht moves against the wind –this is 'form drag'. 'Friction drag' refers to the drag produced by the material the sail is made from; smoother cloth has less drag because the wind slides off it more easily than tufted material, which will hold the wind. There is of course drag to a forward movement that comes from the 'wetted area' of the yacht, that is, the part of the yacht passing through the water, as well as the weight of the yacht. Different yacht design will result in more or less wetted area and thus more or less resistance, as will different designs result in heavier and more resistant yachts than others.

Yachts, however, have more than one sail (unless they are junk rigged) and the gap between them is known as 'the slot'. How the air passes over successive sails to the 'fore sail' is, in part, dependent upon the slot, different slots can cause the wind to pass smoothly over the successive sails(s) or turbulently.

'Wind force' is also inevitably a force that acts upon a yacht. There is gradient pressure which means that the wind in contact with the sea is slower than wind higher up, and it is possible to see that the speed of the air passing over the bottom – 'the foot' – of a sail might be slower than air passing over the top – 'the head' – of the sail – hand held wind speed instruments used on deck produce different readings from fixed ones at the top of the mast. A last force worth mentioning is that of 'heeling'. As the wind passes over the sails, not only is a forward movement produced but also a sideways movement, which tips the yacht to leeward. This is why yachts have keels which together with the buoyancy of the immersed hull and the fact that wind 'spills' from the sail as it tips, prevent a yacht – except in most unusual and extreme conditions – from tipping over. The keel also restricts the degree of sideways movement.

The forces described so far are those affecting a yacht when the wind passes over the sectors of a yacht before the beam. When the wind is behind the beam – 'abaft the beam' – an aerofoil shape will not form. Rather, the yacht is pushed along by the wind, instead of being lifted.

Thus the main forces operating on a yacht involved in its movement through the waters are: lift, drag, pressure, airflow, heeling, gravity, weight and resistance. There are mathematical formulations that express their relationship to one another and enable them to be individually calculated.

c) Sail shape. The yachtsperson can control where the wind passes over the yacht and the shape of the sail in order to maximise the effect of wind on the yacht, and to maximise lift/push and minimise drag. They can steer the ship so as to have the wind pass over any sector of the yacht, though of course the sector they will normally chose is that presented by the course they have to sail to get to where they want or need to be. Thus although most yachts will sail faster with the wind passing over the port or starboard beam and the helmsperson might position the yacht with respect to the wind to achieve this, for example, for exhilaration or fun, the direction in which the destination lies may require that the wind is positioned over the starboard or port bow – 'close hauled' – which will usually result in a slower speed than a 'beam reach' with the same wind strength.

A skipper can also control the shape of the sail and change this with relationship to the part of the yacht that the wind is passing over. To maximise the effects of the forces that play on a yacht and thus maximise the speed of the yacht they can change the shape of the sail using a number of tools. 'Halyards' are ropes (or wire) that haul the sails up the mast. They can be slackened or tightened so that the edge of the sail closest to the wind – the 'luff' – is tight or baggy: a tight sail will more cleanly pass through the air producing less turbulence and enabling a better aerofoil to form than a baggy sail, but if too tight will stretch and deform the sail. 'The sheets' are ropes attached to the bottom of the sail – the 'foot' – at a point furthest away from the halyard – the 'clew'. The edge of the sail that is furthest from the wind and which runs from the top of the sail – the 'head' – to the foot is known as the 'leech' and the sheets are used to change the curve of the 'leech', its 'roach'. This is because sails are made or 'cut' so as to have a curve to them. Lay out a sail on the floor and it is not flat, there is extra material that catches the wind. The curve of the sail accommodates this and so by tightening the sheets the curve will be reduced and the sail will be 'flattened'. Thus sheets are used to flatten the sail or make them fuller. This curve of the roach is called its 'twist'. Thus, in effect, its camber can be changed.

With respect to the sail nearest the wind – 'the fore sail' – the sheets pass through 'a side car', which can be adjusted, to change the angle at which the sheet exerts a downward force on the sail. On the 'main sail', which is the sail that is hoisted up the mast, tightening the main sheet will cause the 'boom', a metal or wooden pole extending from the mast to which the sail's foot is attached to, to lift, thus distorting the shape aimed for by tightening the main sheet. To counteract this, the 'kicking strap' is used to pull down on the boom. The angle at which the main sail enters the wind can also be controlled by the 'traveller', which controls the amount of movement made by the bottom of the main sheet from a centre position. Thus the main sheet can be tightening or loosened and the twist controlled, from different positions relative to the centre point. The foot of the main sheet can also be tightened or loosened in the manner of the luff. This is done by the 'outhaul', a rope attached to the clew. Lastly, on some yachts, particularly those that are 'fractionally rigged', and performance oriented, the shape of the mast can be changed by tightening or loosening the 'back stay' – a wire running from the top (or, in the case of a fractional rig, 1/8th of the height of the mast from its top) of the mast to the stern of the yacht and which forms part of 'the standing rigging', a system of wires that stabilises the mast. Bending the mast can be used to tighten the sails.

d) Bringing sectors, forces and sail shape together in the formalisms of sailing. The shape of the sails can be changed – 'trimmed' – in order to maximise the prevailing force of the wind over any sector of the yacht. There are formalisms, which are intended to guide trimming so that following them will result in the most efficient sail shape for the force and direction of the wind. Thus for the most common sail combination, a sloop with a Bermudian rig, when *close hauled* in *strong winds* the main sail profile should be flat with an open leech, and the foresail should be flat. This allows the wind to fill the sails about two-thirds in from the luff which will minimise turbulence and maximises lift. To achieve the correct profile for the main sail, the main sheet should be tight, the traveller to leeward, the kicking strap loose, the luff at maximum tension and the backstay tight (on a fractional rig it should be very tight). For the foresail the sheet should be very tight, the sheeting position midway, and the luff tight. In *light winds* and *close hauled* the profile of the mainsail should be round with the leech tightly closed, and the foresail should be round with a slight closed leech. To achieve this in light winds the mainsheet should be loose, the traveller slightly to windward, the kicking strap should be loose, the luff should be smooth, the backstay loose. For the foresail the sheet should be loose, the sheeting position slightly forward, the luff should be slightly creased.

There are similar formalisms with respect to *reaching* and *running* and moderate winds which are designed to progressively change the profile of the sails from one that is aerodynamic to one that projects the maximum surface area of the sail so as to catch as much wind as possible to push the yacht along. For brevity, these will not be stated.

Using the Formalisms at Sea

Watching the behaviour of other yachts' sails at sea is a favourite pastime of experienced sailors and the source of judgements being passed on their skippers. A flapping sail, a fluttering leech, a yacht too far off the wind for its obvious course, a slow yacht, will all be used as evidence of a sloppy skipper, whereas the skipper who breezes past without hand on the wheel or tiller because the yacht is perfectly balanced because it has been perfectly trimmed will be given a begrudging wave. This is because although the formalisms are intended to provide the means for achieving maximum efficiency, they, as for the navigating formalisms, are put into practice by drawing off the stock of sailing knowledge built up by experience. With respect to the use of sails, that stock of knowledge encompasses various matters.

a) Marrying the description to what can be seen. It is a relatively easy matter to learn the names for the different sectors of a yacht and parts of the sail, but descriptions such as twist, fullness, moving the wind back along the sail, leach flutter, and the like really need to be seen to fully understood. This is also true with respect to the changes in performance that manipulating the sails through the various ropes and mechanisms available can make. In a strong wind when sailing close to the wind, if the foresail is loose then 'hardening' it by 'sheeting it in', that is pulling hard on the foresail and main sail sheets, will bring about a noticeable affect: the yacht will quickly pick up speed, and the angle of heel will increase, and, depending upon other circumstance, the wheel, or the rudder may start to feel heavier. However, while this is a universal matter, its particular affect is moderated or exaggerated by the particular yacht. Thus some yachts can fly more sails for longer as the wind increases than other yachts can, and some can sail closer to the wind than others. Therefore understanding the terms is developed within the locality of 'this' yacht, which then becomes available for comparing to other yachts.

For example, if the skipper has trimmed the yacht for strong winds and is sailing close to the wind as described above, and is sailing a heavy long keeled yacht then all might be well, and the description of the abstract shape of the sails may be given a concrete understanding by relating the description to these sails. However, should the same person now be sailing a light yacht, built to take advantage of light airs, then conditions that brought about the shape of the sail on the heavier yacht might change the shape of the sail on the light yacht. For instance, as the air passes over the sails the aerodynamic force encourages the yacht to head straight into the wind. If it did that then the wind would spill out of the sails, they would lose their aerodynamic force and start to flap around, and the yacht would move to an upright position. The rudder counteracts that tendency. However, as wind force builds it can overwhelm the effects of the rudder, and the yacht will 'round up' into the wind. This can be a frightening experience the first time it occurs because the yacht feels out of control – it is actually quite safe because all the 'drive' has gone out of the sails and the yacht will quickly 'lose way'. Thus the instruction 'sheet-in hard when going to windward in strong winds' can produce different effects on the sail depending on the yacht, and thus what hardening up and flattening the sails means becomes intelligible not from the description of what it does but from the experience of the effect it has on 'this' yacht. In this way hardening and flattening become handy-work matters, what is hard for one yacht can be too hard for another, and the heave om the rope needs to be moderated or exaggerated in the light of its effects on the yacht. Eventually any yacht may become 'over-pressed' as wind builds and yachtspeople learn, through experiencing the feel of the yacht, how to minimise this or put off the time when it becomes necessary to reduce the amount of sail by 'reefing'. Thus a skipper sailing with their family nearing their berth may be reluctant to put the crew through the rigours of reefing. Thus instead of hardening the sail as instructed by the formalism, the skipper might actually 'spill' wind from the sail by loosening the sheets, or setting the traveller further leeward, or sail 'large' by sailing more off the wind.

Sailing a yacht thus also involves 'feeling' the yacht. As the wind acts on the sails in different ways the yacht will start to feel different. It is by relating that feel to sail shape that an understanding of how to work the formalisms of sail shape develops. Thus, as mentioned, hardening the sheets, for example, can change the feel of the helm, which might become heavier. As wind increases 'weather helm' can build up to a point where the helmsperson can no longer steer the yacht. Although weather helm is found in sailing theory, just what it means as a lived matter, is settled in how the tiller or wheel actually feels in the hand. There is no hard and fast rule as to whether or not a yacht uses a wheel or a tiller, but most yacht designers will employ a tiller up to about 34 foot, though there are many yacht-building companies that will put a wheel on a 31-foot yacht. Experienced sailors can move from tiller to wheel and back again without matter, though many will, if pushed, confess a preference for a tiller, for the precise reason that they can gauge the feel of the yacht more accurately. With a wheel, the play of the water over the rudder is moderated by a system of wires; bearings and pulleys whereas with a tiller, changes in sea state and the interaction of the yacht with the water can be more finely felt and more quickly responded to. Conversely, less experienced yachtspersons are often more comfortable with a wheel, because it more closely resembles driving a car, and moving it in the right direction comes more naturally, whereas a tiller involves pushing or pulling it away from the direction the helmsperson wants the yacht to point to.

The formalisms of sailing theory thus prescribe how the sails should be set for different points of sail, flatter close hauled, open and fuller when the wind is across the beam and the yacht is on a broad reach, and very full when the wind is to the stern of the yacht. However, 'feeling a yacht', understanding how the wind and sea are acting on a yacht, becomes all-important in setting and trimming sails to fit the particular conditions being experienced. The correct angle of attack of the sails to the wind is gauged by changing it and feeling the effects on the yacht. The formalisms, then, become practical guides to trimming actions, giving a rough understanding of the sail shape to be produced, which then is honed through the feel of the yacht. For most cruising sailors this will be done occasionally, after a course change or if the wind and sea conditions change significantly, but for a racing or an enyhusiastic skipper, trimming the sails becomes a continual activity.

It should be held in mind that trimming and setting sails involves, as mentioned above, 'handy-work'; people pulling, tightening and slackening ropes. For example, let them go too fast, and rope burn can ensue; jerk them tight and a back can be put out. Also, knowing what the prescription 'tighten the sail' is, is not defined in the word 'tight', for example, how tight is tight, is this tight enough? Sails can be trimmed using a winch, but even using a winch is not just a matter of rotating the winch handle – a novice sailor provides others with entertainment as they fail to engage the cog wheels with the crank and go spinning to one side as they start to 'grind', or peer into the winch to understand why the handle will not fit, or ask if they have the correct handle if its not fitting, or unduly exert themselves because they do not realise that a winch has two speeds, involving pulling on the handle as well as pushing it away.

Thus *how* a sail shape is achieved can be as important as the sail shape itself. For example, if a change of course requires the yacht to move off the wind and onto a broad reach questions such as when the sail is re-trimmed, and how it is re-trimmed come into play, answers not provided for by the formalisms of the theory. Supposedly, the sail could be re-trimmed at different stages in the change of heading: it could be done before the change of course takes place, after it takes place, or as it takes place. But each will have different consequences for the yacht, and it is in the light of experiencing different eventualities that an understanding of how to make that manoeuvre develops. Thus, should the yacht be re-trimmed in anticipation of the manoeuvre, then wind would spill from the sails, yacht speed would drop and time and distance would be lost. Should the trimming take place after the manoeuvre, then, as the yacht made the manoeuvre, it would become over pressed, it would heel more and attempt to round up and hamper the success of the change of course. Therefore, as the helm 'comes over' to affect the course change, the sheets are progressively slackened to maximise their shape as the manoeuvre takes place, and final trimming then smoothly takes place as the course is taken up. This way the yacht maximises its speed and composure. The formalisms of sailing say nothing about this, and doing it this way develops as the best way in the course of the developing experiences of sailing.

b) Real yachts. The formalisms of sailing are developed without regard for the yacht on which they are performed. Though it is understood that different yacht configurations must be taken into account, the actual yacht itself does not figure. Yet it is on an actual yacht that they are indeed performed. Some yachts have heavy use, and someone new to sailing may not be sailing their own yacht, but perhaps a charter yacht or a yacht school one. Heavily sailed yachts especially charter yachts, can have old sails and 'dirty bottoms', both of which will affect the way a yacht behaves. It just may not be possible to properly set old stretched, patched sails. In these circumstances, a skipper must compromise, setting the sails inappropriately for the point of sail, but appropriately to coax the best out of these sails.

In this respect, yacht maintenance is important for the achievement of sail shape. The mast of a yacht is held in place by fixed rigging (standing rigging) which if properly set will hold the mast true. But if the rigging is not properly set up, the mast may go slack on one 'tack' meaning that it might be bent out of true. Not only can this result in the mast coming down, it will also mean that a proper sail shape cannot be achieved. So matters such as taking care of the sails, scrubbing the bottom of the yacht and applying anti-fouling, properly 'stepping' the mast and adjusting the rigging all become part of what needs to be done in order to ensure that the results the formalisms involved in sail setting and shape are intended to produce are achieved. People pick up tips on yacht maintenance from others, can experience the differences between sailing a well or poorly maintained yacht read books on sails and rigging, but relating that to the formalisms is something that is done *through the yacht* which becomes not just something that is acted upon by the application of formalisms, but becomes a 'vessel' through which the formalisms become accountable.

c) It's only for fun. It needs to be remembered that yachting is a 'play' activity; people do it to enjoy themselves and have fun. Naturally, anything involving the elements can be exacting, so the weather can change and what was enjoyable can become something to be endured, and anything involving other people can be enhanced or diminished by their behaviour – many a novice crew member has been put off sailing or enthused by the actions of their skipper. In that respect the formalisms are not of the same order of stipulation as those involved in, for example, the safe running of a nuclear power station. Exactness in following the formalisms in setting a sail shape may or may not matter. Someone who is very keen about their passtime, sailing their own yacht regularly with their spouse who is just as keen, may gain enjoyment through their precision and exactness. Someone who sails with their young children may think that it is more important to ensure that they are having an enjoyable time and learning to love the sea rather than constantly barking orders at them or criticising them for not pulling the rope tight enough. And, of course, how someone considers the matter of sailing can vary from one occasion to another, one time considering sail trim to be something to constantly tinker with because they want to beat their rival back to the berth and boast about it in the yacht club afterwards, and at another time, sail trim being a take it or leave it matter, even putting the engine on to 'get a move on' if wind direction is not favourable.

This means that the formalisms involved in sailing theory become frameworks to be used in accomplishing the ends of the moment. At one extreme they provide a supporting structure that will enable the yachtsperson at play to move in the desired direction under sail, wherever the wind is coming from. At the other extreme they can support the yachtsperson in achieving the maximum efficacy of a yacht under sail in particular circumstances. How they are implemented, together with all the other matters involved, is done as part of engaging in the leisure, hobby, pursuit of sailing, and what someone is wanting from that (which can change from episode to episode) conditions their use of the formalisms and the frameworks they build from out of them. As for navigating, the formalisms are treated as practical constructions used in the actual course of the live circumstances at sea which are responded to within a framework of differing interests and experiences.

Conclusion

Not surprisingly, given the historical and practical significance of sailing on oceans in the development of human civilisation, yachting is embedded in a rationalised system. All the parts of a yacht have technical terms that are used as practical matters of instruction and communication at sea, the wind passes over named sections of the yacht, sail shapes and parts are named as is the effect of the wind on sails, best sail shape and set is determined within the laws of aerodynamics, and headings are described within the terms of geometrical formalisations and calculated within a system of mathematical conventions. Thus sailing a yacht for leisure purposes is circumscribed by a highly rationalised formal system, and it would be an irresponsible and foolhardy person who went to sea without either having a yachtsperson on board who has experience of working and playing within this system, or who had not taken a RYA training course in which the basics of the system are taught. The RYA shore based theory courses equip yachtsmen and women with, amongst other matters such as knowledge of lights and signals, weather forecasting, anchoring, rope work and close quarter maneuvering, with the principles of navigating and sailing.[9] These involve learning the formalisms of both, and working out answers to questions, such as what heading do I take to reach my destination, and what sail shape do I deploy to propel the yacht along that trajectory, by applying the formalisms.

However, as noticed in many ethnomethodological studies, the use of formalisms is done in actual circumstances and involves matters not covered by the formalisms themselves, and these studies have described the interaction between the formalisms and the context of their application in describing their circumstantial improvisation. This interaction can be certainly seen in the case of yachting and part of this chapter has described the circumstantial particulars that interact with the formalisms. However, while it may be news for others, such as those professionally interested in the description of human action and interaction, just what the sorts of matters involved are for a particular undertaking, knowledge of these matters, is not news for those involved, they know what they are in the course of making the formalisms work.

---

9   The RYA courses are recognised world-wide for their excellence, and are a model for how to effectively transmit the major components of knowledge about an area that has been built up over centuries in an economical and engaging way.

In this respect, it is not just a matter of there being an inevitable disjuncture between formalisms and the contingent character of the circumstances in which they are to be applied, necessitating the deployment of situationally ad hoc methods to make the formalisms work. The relationship between the formalisms and the context of their deployment involves more than just this, though it does involve this. This is because the development of the experiences of yachting, the development of a stock of practical yachting knowledge, which is the resource that is drawn upon in bridging between the formalisms and the situations of their application, is itself predicated by and anchored in the formalisms themselves. That stock of practical yachting knowledge is itself, in large part, generated through the formalisms. Thus, we have also been interested in describing how knowing that formalisms have to be applied in practice is used by the RYA as part of instructing people in safe and efficient yachting. Thus instructing people in the formalism is only one part of the instruction process, the other is to provide them with the opportunity to learn what using them at sea is, in other words providing them with the opportunity to use their heads in applying the formalisms, and to begin to build their stock of practical knowledge of yachting. Using their heads is a matter of developing a stock of knowledge by being at sea and how to use this stock of knowledge to apply the formalisms. In many respects, as this stock of knowledge develops, the yachtsperson will more and more rely upon their experiences rather than the formalisms. The formalisms will, over time, fade away as everyday yachting matters, as the yachtsperson use of their 'head' and 'eye' with respect to the wind, tide, and obstacles, and use of Global Positioning technologies to work out directions and headings. The formalisms are there to be fallen back on when necessary. Yet, at the same time it is the formalisms that underpin the development of the practical experience of yachting, and which underpin the GPS systems, and without those formalisms themselves, the practical experience of yachting and the development of the practical knowledge of yachting could not be anchored. The formalisms are then knowingly treated, as practical, not abstract constructs, to be applied, not followed, within a developing stock of knowledge built up through the experiences of yachting as they unfold for any person. The sea-based courses start to provide an opportunity to encounter live-at-sea experiences that play upon the formalisms, which, in themselves, actually underpin the development of those experiences and organise them as practically usable knowledge. Without those formalisms the experiences could not, themselves, be rationally organised and used; yet in those experiences the formalisms become less intense and vivid in the course of everyday yachting.

Acknowledgements

The authors and editors wish to express their thanks to the Royal Yachting Association for their kind assistance in the preparation of this chapter for publication.

Chapter 6

Remixing Music Together:
The Use and Abuse of
Virtual Studio Software as a Hobby

Phillip Brooker and Wes Sharrock

Introduction

Remixing and producing music in a virtual (digital) music studio is, for some people, a career (i.e. writing a jingle for an advertisement, a film score, or similar), and for others, it is a hobby with no such defined goals and no defined methods with which to undertake it. For hobbyists, there is a notable lack of dependency on being able to produce a finalised end-result, and a notable lack of tried and tested routines for producing results. This chapter presents various aspects of 'constructing a remix' as a leisure activity, where there are no guidelines or restrictions on the ultimate outcome (i.e. there is no 'ideal song' to orient the day's efforts towards), few abiding standards on either what a desired end-result may sound like or the methods by which such a remix may be generated. This analysis concerns how an activity in which those involved have no real dependency on the outcome (other than their own enjoyment) is ordered and organised through the use of available technologies and the management of creative ideas.

Hobbyist remixers and music producers may: collaborate remotely as well as in person; use piano-keyboard instruments to input musical ideas as well as programming them in with computer mice and QWERTY keyboards; take samples of existing audio pieces as well as composing their own; utilise software that enables them to play at performing and recording music as well as producing, mixing and mastering it; focus intently on one piece or less intently on a broad array of half-ideas; and so on. Hence, the activities collected under the term 'remixing music' are legion, and the activities themselves may be very broadly defined. Yet somehow, despite the limitless horizons where no defined end-product is set apart as the-thing-to-be-achieved, hobbyist remixers are able to produce *a* song. In this remixing, limitless possibilities are honed down to concrete details, and aims to examine some of the practices through which the end-result of 'a completed remix' is achieved.

We focus on the activities and practices in a collaborative musical project involving constructing a suitable entry for submission to a remix competition, which is achieved through using various software packages to manipulate and reformulate an original piece of music into a further original audio creation. These activities involve the principal author (PB) and a friend (LC), whose shared (and collaborative) hobby is designing virtual instruments and using those to assemble pieces of music.[1]

Two software packages form the basic tools through which this is achieved. The primary tool (program #1) is a virtual music studio package, which provides, amongst other things: a selection of digital 'synthesisers' (some designed to emulate analog sound synthesis and some more unashamedly digital); rhythm sequencers for drum and loop programming; sampling units for playback of audio files from outside of the software package itself; a variety of sound effects units (including reverb, distortion, phasing, delay, etc), and; auxiliary 'equipment' such as mixing desks, merger/splitters, equalisers, compressors and stereo imagers.[2] This package also facilitates the generation of musical arrangements, and users can input musical phrases (through either the computer's mouse and QWERTY keyboard, or a MIDI-enabled piano keyboard controller connected to the computer) into the program and structure them into whatever arrangement they choose. Having done so, structured 'songs' can be played back, listened to and analysed within the package, and can be converted to Waveform Audio File Format (.wav) files that can be treated as any other digital music file (i.e. they can be listened to, loaded onto portable music players, shared online, etc.).

The second package (program #2) is for editing audio samples and loops to be used in the first. It is the use of this package particularly that forms the basis of the activities under investigation in this chapter.

The principal author and LC entered a remix competition hosted by a band, wherein competitors were to download 'stems' of an original song by that band, and reformulate them, tweak them, add effects to them, re-structure them, incorporate their own audio additions and so on. Here, the term 'stems' refers to audio files of an original track, broken up into its component instrumental tracks. Hence, the 'stems' being dealt with in this activity were six different files, each containing the recorded audio of separate instruments (i.e. bass guitar, drums, lead guitar, rhythm guitar and two vocal tracks). The ultimate aim here was to create a new version of the original song that is sufficiently audibly distinct from it, yet retains identifiable features of it. The competitive element is that the stems of this original song had been made publicly available, and the band who initially

---

1   The end-product of this activity is available to interested readers online, at: http://snd.sc/ztxWHe (accessed 18 December 2012).

2   We apologise for the possibly gratuitous use of technical terms, although we feel this brevity necessary in the interest of providing an account of the activities and practices involved in collaborative remixing as opposed to a lengthy description of the functions available in a virtual music studio software package. Readers wishing to learn more about some of the more esoteric items listed above would do well to refer to Izhaki (2008) *Mixing Audio: Concepts, Practices and Tools*, and Owsinski (2008) *The Mastering Engineer's Handbook* (2nd edn.).

recorded it had offered to pick their favourite remix entry to feature as a B-side on the officially released single version of that track. The 'play' here then is in the competitive nature of the task, and in the creative re-working of an original song out of its component parts. The fun is in the manipulating of old material into something creatively 'new' (and traversing the technical difficulties involved in doing so – literally, coercing the software into processing the given audio inputs in the ways desired), and in the addition of personal stylistic 'flourishes'. Although the audio stems were to some extent 'untreatable', in that it was impossible to create sounds from those stems that were not present in some form in the original audio files, much could be done to them to make them sonically distinct from the original song they came from. For instance, the remix in question ultimately featured, amongst other things: layered stems with new melodic and rhythmic ideas arising from the counterbalance of re-structured original material; the loading of stems with 'digital-sounding' effects so as to distance the remix from the original conventional band setup recordings (which featured a singer, two guitarists, bass guitarist and a drummer); loops and samples taken from guitar parts and vocals, both sped up and slowed down to create cross-rhythms between stems that differed from the original; the more prominent use of less identifiable guitar sections (i.e. textural sounds) as achieved through altering the overall mix of amplitudes of individual tracks, and so on.

Though this remixing enterprise was competitive, this particular activity was treated as 'low stakes' – though the drive to produce something of 'winning quality' (an endeavour which required the technical know-how of how to use the two software packages as well as the musical creativity necessary to produce something audibly appealing) and an idea of what such a thing might be was a goal to bear in mind throughout, the principal author and LC did not depend on their entry being chosen as the winner. Indeed, the principal author and LC have previously on several occasions downloaded stems from other remix competitions and worked them up into half-songs with unfinished ideas. As such, the main aspect of play was simply in the making of the song itself.

We turn now to some features of the practices involved in collaborative remixing descriptions and to do so we draw on ideas from video data collected by the principal author, capturing both the action and interaction occurring before the screen (i.e. between the principal author and LC) as well as on-screen (through use of video screen capture software).[3] Firstly, we look at how creative ideas are (and can be) gradually honed down from a vast array of possibilities, which is an activity made feasible through building up a familiarity with the catalogue of available components. Secondly, we analyse how the activity is shaped by the

---

3   It should be noted that the transcriptions we present are not to be read as exercises in Conversation Analysis. Rather, we have simply aimed to review and represent the practices and activities discussed with as much reference to the actual goings-on of the setting as possible, and this is reflected in the loose (although we hope informative) transcripts provided.

definition of the music-to-be as specifically 'a remix', and what that means for the practices that are undertaken in light of that definition. Finally, we present a more fundamental problem for the study of members dealing with sound – how specific audio ideas and concepts are communicated between members who have no standard techniques for reproducing exact sounds vocally or otherwise. Through analysis of these three features, we hope to come closer to an understanding of 1) some of the defining aspects of 'a remix' and how these aspects inform the practical collaboration of the activity, 2) how the activity is gradually made more and more 'realisable' through the iterative developing of approaches to it, and 3) some features of the collaborative talk surrounding the activity that contribute positively to its completion.

Managing the Preservation of 'Identifiability' with the Display of Creativity

To return briefly to the underlying motives to the participants' remixing activities, one salient feature of a remixed version of a song is that the remix should be a creatively and structurally new piece but one that retains elements of the original song in some form – either literally sampling the original song itself, or 're-composing' identifiable features of it (a melody, a bass line, a drumbeat, etc.) with different instrumentation, or both. Hence, the activity is oriented to the re-use of old materials in creatively new ways, and this objective is reflected in the remixing. For instance, although the principal author and LC did not use the original drums or bass guitar, the constant endeavour was to keep the original song recognisable through use of other elements, such as a melodic guitar riff, or a sung vocal line. There is an ever-present objective of making the remix sound sufficiently different from the original song (otherwise, why bother?), yet not so different that it is unrecognisable as a remix (otherwise, the activity would have to be reframed as 'composing original music'). Aside from their audible appeal to the principal author and LC (as discussed in the following section), part of the motivation to choose which parts to keep and which to discard was centred on the issue of what makes the new composition recognisable as a re-working of the original song. The constant questions throughout were: will listeners (and the band themselves, as judges of the competition) be able to recognise the original song through our reformulation of its component parts? And how can the sounds of these original elements be altered to mark them out as creatively new, while still retaining a sufficient degree of recognisability in the overall composition? The activity at hand was not to create entirely new music but to create a remix of a band's song that is of high enough quality to be suitable for submission, high enough possibly even to win, in a remix competition, and this fact gave direction to the participants' approach.

It is useful at this point to outline some features of how exactly this space between the 'identifying details' (Garfinkel 2002: 222) of parts and the creative aspects of remixing is achieved in practice. Key to the activity is that the song –

any song – features certain recurring motifs prominently, which count as the most identifying details of that song. This is to say that had you heard the song yourself and someone asked you to sing 'how it goes' (inclusive of how, say, a guitar riff sounds as well as vocal melodies and lyrics), these are the essential parts that you would choose to sing – it is this fact that makes such details identifiable to remixers and ethnomethodologists (and anyone else) alike. Hence, part of the activity of remixing is to listen to the original song *as a song*, to identify these details and take those as a basis for reconstructing the song into a new piece. For the principal author and LC, such a listening to the song provided a sense of the places of individual components in the wider structure (i.e. the guitar line in the verse, the textural noise in the intro, and so on) and as they occurred in relation to other components (such that it is recognised that the guitar riff might be the most easily identified detail of the song, or that the snare hits of the drumbeat are what gives the song its particular swing). Thus, a listener's perspective is required to provide remixers with an initial set of guidelines from which to continue their remixing, setting the context and conditions of the overall recognisability to be preserved. Additionally, listening this way draws attention to those details of the song that *aren't* immediately identifiable (say, an introductory texture that is not repeated throughout). These non-immediate details themselves may also hold some interest for remixers, in that they make up the *underplayed* elements of the original song, less identifiable but which may be interesting to turn into something that holds a more prominent focus in the remix.

However, taking such identifiable (and perhaps also overtly less identifiable) details is not quite enough for a remix – if the remix is to be more than a simple looping of particular identifying details, these elements must be creatively *changed*, and can be done so in countless ways. This could be achieved, for instance, through layering them with sound effects (chorus, delay, reverb, distortion, etc.), or stretching them out or over longer periods of time (or shortening them), or changing their pitch, or panning them (i.e. changing the extent to which the sound plays through either the left or right speaker or headphone), or filtering out specific frequencies (i.e. bass, mid, treble), or playing them backwards, and so on. Additionally, the choice of tool – a digital music studio – provides the most striking means of differencing the remix from the original band recording, allowing for the making of stylistic decisions to emphasise and give prominence to the 'digital' or 'glitchy' sounds that can be produced by such software but *not* by the band's original setup of guitars, bass guitar, drums and vocals. However, such creative changes must be balanced against how much of the identifiability of the original material is preserved, in that it is possible to disfigure samples to such an extent that they are no longer identifiable as anything other than newly produced material. For instance, imagine a sample of a sung chorus so saturated with distortion (literally, the controllable degradation of sound through 'overdriving' analog equipment, or through digital signal processing to emulate analog distortion) that it is impossible to discern any remnants of the original melody, words or tonality of the voice. Hence, remixers have to identify various details of the original song which they might want to include, whilst being careful to adapt and modify their sound in ways that ensure they stay identifiable.

Identifying details and creativity also become apparent when structuring a remix into a cohesive song. It is not a stipulation of remixes that they must feature an identical structure (made up from elements such as intros, verses, choruses, bridges, outros, etc.) and as such, remixers can create new structural arrangements of songs so as to distance their own output from the original song. In this case, the participants built up an arrangement that differed greatly from the original song, but in such a way as to ensure its identifiability through more than just the careful re-use of stems. Taking one identifying detail, a guitar motif, as a basis, its melodic and rhythmic ideas were programmed and played through an original synthesised instrument designed by the principal author and LC in program #1, so as to recycle this particular motif on a different instrument. However, to make this more recognisable as a remix, the principal author and LC positioned the inputted motif as a 'build-up' to a final section, as an attempt to create a different 'feel' out of the re-use of these original materials. In this section, the melody played is an identifying detail of the original song (although the instrumentation it was recreated on is, notably, not), but as opposed to positioning this piece as in the original recording (where it was used to draw the main riff to a close), it was repeated in a loop, gradually including more and more instrumentation – some from stems, some newly composed – thereby creating the effect of a more gradual build-up to a finish. Again, this serves to retain an identifying detail of the original song – a melodic line – whilst changing other details – chiefly, this melodic line's structural role and its instrumentation. Hence, the effect is to produce something that can be recognised as specifically a *remix* of the original song and not some other type of composition (say, a new song, a cover version, a promotional 'teaser', etc.). It is through the careful management of these audio classifications (i.e. original identifying details vs. new creative details) that the remix gradually begins to take shape, and the original stems start to sound recognisably different as part of the remixing of them, to (what is hoped will be) pleasing effect.

The Remix as a 'Potter's Object'[4]

Figure 6.1   Listening to, selecting and writing an index to a catalogue of sampled sounds

To begin the remixing activity, the first thing the principal author and LC turned to was a discussion of how best to approach the material at hand, and it was agreed that a better understanding of where to begin could be achieved through listening to each of the available stems and reconstructing the original song from them.[5] This in itself prompted a discussion of how the available software packages might be used to achieve the desired result:

---

4   Garfinkel, Lynch and Livingston 1981: 137.

5   Although there is undoubtedly much to say on the matter, this chapter will not attempt to broach many of the more fundamental agreements surrounding music-making that the principal author and LC share. For example it is taken for granted by both remixers that the remix should: be based around assonant compliances with Western major and minor scales; feature specific kinds of structural arrangement; represent a broad range of frequencies (i.e. with some instruments focussing on bass frequencies, some on treble, and some in between) and that these frequencies should be mixed accordingly; have a tempo set to a 'listenable' pace (and what exactly 'listenable' might mean) and so on. All of these things are agreed on by the principal author and LC without any explicit acknowledgement. How this is done is very much relevant to the activity at hand, but will require a different approach based on more than the few hours of video of two members in one setting that we have at our disposal.

Excerpt 1

LC: I think … a *good* thing to do might be to … erm … if you cut the start off
the drums, yeah? And then note where- exactly what time that is, and then cut
everything else at the same point.

PB: … yeah.

LC: Then it'll all be in time then.

PB: Weren't we going to … fuck the drums off altogether?

LC: Yeah I know, but, the drums are obviously in time aren't they?

PB: Yeah.

LC: At *all* times … d'you know what I mean? It's a nice … like … sharp peak
of a sound that (program #2) would pick up nice and easily.

PB: Yeah, it will … So, do the drums first …

Here, LC's suggestion of cutting out elements of the drum stem was regarded
by the principal author as a possible waste of time, relating to a previous day's
discussion about programming a creatively new drum sequence against other
stems, since a programmed beat would be more malleable than one derived from
an audio sample (in terms of making variations on it). However, in the interest
of generating some creative momentum – to keep the task moving in some way
or other – and given the principal author and LC's belief that program #2 could
accomplish this task with little fuss, the practical activity of reconstructing the
original song became the first task at hand, despite having already agreed not to
make use of each of the individual components being dealt with.

Having then edited the drum stem, the principal author and LC moved on to
listening to and reviewing the stems of one guitar part. This revealed a multitude
of possible exciting ways in which to manipulate the source material, heralded by
the activity of listening to the guitar part and making use of program #2's ability
to automatically detect component 'slices'[6] in audio files given a user-inputted
level of sensitivity. This function of the program facilitated a collaborative
listening to individual sections of audio, which are contained in groups of slices
(see Figure 6.2). At this point, the talk turned to how appealing (or not) certain
sections of stems were, in terms of what could be done to and with them as part
of a broader remix:

---

6   Program #2 allows users to chop audio files up into individual 'slices', which can
then be arranged to preserve the original temporal order or otherwise in program #1's
looping device. Hence, a slice refers to the level of granularity of an individual drum hit in
a 4-bar drumbeat, or an individual guitar chord in a longer chord sequence, or an individual
word in a vocal chorus, and so on.

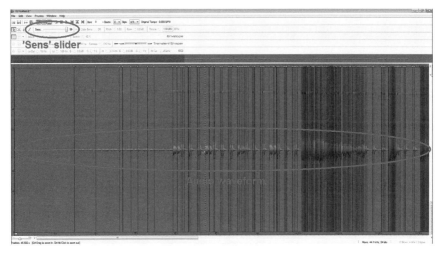

Figure 6.2 A guitar track in program #2. The black lines intersecting the blue audio waveform are 'slices', which can be placed manually with the cursor or automatically using the slice sensitivity slider ('sens') near the top left of the screen

Excerpt 2

PB: Do we want this? [*Plays a series of slices*] I want that as well.

LC: Like, chops[7] of that?

PB: Yeah, yeah.

LC: Yeah, I'd like that.

Excerpt 3

LC: [*Plays a long slice*] [*Commenting on the guitar playing evident in the slice*] That was a strange drop wasn't it?

PB: Hmm?

LC: I don't think I want any of that.

PB: I don't.

At this point, the principal author and LC scrapped the idea of listening to stems for which a representation in the ultimate remix was not intended – for instance, the drum and bass guitar stems, on the dual grounds that retaining these elements would restrict the vista of what could possibly be done with the structure of the

---

7 'Chops' is a term sometimes used interchangeably with 'slices', and sometimes used to refer to a level of granularity above 'slices' but below 'stems' (for instance, a whole guitar riff, or a sung verse). Confused (with good cause!) readers should refer to the later section of this chapter that deals with the development and usage of such impressionistic impromptu slang in order to see what sense, if any, can be made from it.

remix, and that it would be more audibly interesting to program in creatively new and different bass and drum patterns. Reassembling the track from the available array of component stems in the hope that this would generate ideas was already being achieved, more easily and quickly, through focussing on only those stems that were actually planned for usage. Moreover, though reconstructing the song as originally planned would serve as perhaps the most systematic way of preparing to assemble a catalogue of candidate sounds, this was nonetheless a laborious task which was ultimately abandoned for this less rigorous, but more fun, way of doing things:

Excerpt 4
[*Listening to slices*]
PB: I-I reckon we just get these as chops and not bother about reconstructing the song.
LC: Yeah, I reckon as well.
PB: We got ideas already.
LC: We probably won't need to reconstruct any of it, actually …
PB: No.
LC: … thinking about it, so … which is *good*, I'm glad we've listened to it through now.
PB: Yeah, yeah.

At this point, the principal author and LC began to write down which sections were most audibly appealing in terms of generating creatively new material, so as to be able to quickly refer back to these sections and 'rip' (i.e. extract) them from their parent audio files after the listening activity was over. These short episodes of talk and activity, spanning roughly ten minutes in total, see a movement towards reconstructing a song from stem components, which necessitates a closer listening to them, and playing with them, and ultimately moving 'off-task' when the talk turns more towards which parts to take from one of the guitar stems. In diverting from the original task onto a more fun collaborative activity – a discussion of which elements of the stems are most audibly appealing – a new focus is developed that both counts as a positive contribution towards the assembling of a catalogue of sounds from which to construct a remix, as well as being more enjoyable than the technical task of reconstructing the original song.

What the presentation of this ten minutes or so of plan-formulation and first-steps is intended to demonstrate is despite having absolutely no guidelines – no clue even! – as to how the eventual remix might or should sound, the principal author and LC can methodically begin to hone down the limitless possibilities into something that will contribute positively to the activity. Whereas the stem tracks are, as yet, unfamiliar fragments of audio (making it difficult to choose exactly which parts are or are not appealing), it is possible for the principal author and LC to rely on a shared prior knowledge of the virtual studio as a tool. The principal author and LC have collaboratively made music with these software packages since 2010, and in doing so, have learned how to make use of the devices and functions it offers. Having built a repertoire of 50 or so songs using these software packages – some finished, many not – the principal author and LC consequently have a good idea of how to use each piece of software to make the kinds of music that hold personal (and shared) audible appeal. This practice at the craft of the hobby strikes an obvious similarity to Sudnow's development as a jazz pianist:

> I recall playing one day and finding as I set out into a next course of notes … that I was expressly aiming for the sound of those particular notes … that I had gone to *do* them, as when walking you bring 'attention' to the sounds of your steps and thereby, by the same token and with that very 'act,' you begin to expressly do the soundedness of your walk. (1978: 37)

This familiarity with the tools of the principal author and LC's music-making brings about 'A different sort of directionality of purpose' (Sudnow 1978: 38), and a 'melodic [and rhythmic, and structural, and tonal, and so on] intentionality' (Sudnow 1978: 41), which serves to helpfully constrain the ways in which the activity (might) be approached. Given this, repeated listenings to and commenting on the stems and the instrumental sections within is part of an iterative process to come up with ideas of what this remix should sound like, in the name of generating a catalogue of candidate slices with which to achieve that sound. Although not *all* candidate slices were used, assembling the catalogue allowed for the development of a clearer sense of the musical ideas the remix could feature, and this was a positive step in moving towards a finished piece of music. However, this is not a step in the sense that having assembled a catalogue it can be confidently claimed to be finalised – the principal author and LC might at any point find need for slices that had not yet been ripped from the stems (as they did), necessitating a return to the original stem to add to the catalogue retrospectively. However, the fact that assembling such a catalogue of pieces relies on vaguely 'feeling out' the way towards possible ideas and sounds through playing with them does not make the activity redundant. Rather, the activity is a musical version of the 'potter's object' (Garfinkel, Lynch and Livingston 1981: 137), which refers to how a potter might embark upon creating an object from a lump of clay without being sure of what is to be made from it. A potter can start the wheel and begin shaping the clay while unsure as to what the result will be, but having started working the clay, the potter can begin to 'feel' an object residing somewhere within the raw material. As the shaping gradually unfolds, so does the object itself, and the potter can come to an understanding of what-is-to-be-made from simply starting to make *something* and using his hands in the familiar ways of 'making'. In much the same way, the principal author and LC are able to work up a finished remix out of the collected elements of an original song, by beginning to assemble a catalogue of sounds to use as an initial 'jumping-off point' from which to start thinking and talking increasingly clearly about the kinds of thing that could be done with the burgeoning collection of slices.

Assembling the catalogue, then, is simultaneously a 'finding out' activity (in terms of the principal author and LC finding out what exactly what could be done) and a 'generating materials' activity, where the two proceed in tandem and refer to each other constantly. This is achieved through first listening to stems, then writing down which elements hold some audible appeal, and then finally ripping these elements from their parent audio tracks. The reformulation of the ever-provisional plan from reconstructing the original song to taking candidate slices is not simply a choice between two possible-though-arbitrary starting points. For the principal author and LC, the immediate goals of the plan, at first, extend no further than being able to reconstruct the song – a strategy which is not followed to completion. The decisive move is when the listening to and playing with guitar sounds becomes more productive (in terms of the grander goal of creating a remix) than the original plan to reconstruct the song, and this avenue becomes the one on which to focus in order to move towards achieving this goal. Moreover, each of the choices being made has important limiting implications for how the remix is ultimately to be done. For instance, a decision is made not to work with the drum stem provided *and this has the consequence* that it will be necessary to input a creatively new drumbeat, giving the principal author and LC the choice as to whether or not to feature a different beat to the original (perhaps emphasising a different 'swing' or perhaps in a different time signature). It is also decided that the bass guitar stem will be disregarded *and this has the consequence* that the bass frequencies will be under-represented unless new creative ideas are generated in that specific frequency range, perhaps not following the original melodic and rhythmic ideas featured in the bass-line, and perhaps making more use of the synthesiser tools that are available when creating synthesised bass instruments. A decision is made instead to take elements of guitar and vocal tracks only *and this has the consequence* that those elements can be turned into looped sections (literally, looping them at specific points so as to create an interesting 'stop-start' feel to them), or layering them with sound effects, or altering their pitch and speed in audibly appealing ways. For the principal author and LC, merely playing with the available sounds and deciding which parts of a song are of most audible appeal (and which might be happily disposed of) makes early decisions as to how the wider activity of remixing a song might be approached. Although these decisions are far from concrete at this stage, they nevertheless tighten the boundaries within which the rest of the remixing can take place, in such a way as to render the task actually achievable against its background as a daunting, limitless field of activity.

Talking About (and With) Audio Ideas

When developing, trying out and playing with musical ideas for the remix the principal author and LC are inevitably drawn into communicating these ideas to each other. Indeed, the 'doing together' of collaborative music-making and the sharing of a common interest in making music (both of which feature talking as a necessary though enjoyable element) is part of the fun of the activity. However, given that all of these ideas ultimately refer to a specific sound to be achieved, it becomes necessary for the principal author and LC to develop pieces of 'impromptu slang' to facilitate communication. There is no ready-made vocabulary at hand, and hence the principal author and LC have fun playing at developing an impromptu slang out of various audible identifying details of the sounds at hand:[8]

Excerpt 5
[*Playing through slices to identify candidate 'chops'*]
LC: *dwerrrr* (*high, rising pitch, mirroring the slice just played*) [*slices continue playing*]
LC: I quite *liked* that bit. [*Goes to replay slice. Replays wrong slice*]. Oops.
PB: *We* could do that.
LC: This? Not that. [*Plays slice*]. *Tcka-tck*
PB: Yeah.
LC: Sounding quite percussive.

Excerpt five demonstrates some of the features of how the principal author and LC develop impromptu slang terms and incorporate them into any discussions that may follow. Here, the activity is one of listening back to a stem track to identify candidate slices to take from it, and LC interjects with the noise *dwerrrr*, which refers to the slice just heard. In replaying the slices through the computer speakers, both the principal author and LC can hear the same thing. As such, the sequentiality of the event – the hearing of a noise *and then* LC's vocal repeating of it – marks it as one to direct the principal author's attention to the slice containing the noise just played (although notably, *not* the noise just vocalised by LC). As the sequence of slices continues to play, LC interjects again, referring to one of the panorama of noises just heard by both members (the 'that' of LC's 'I quite *liked* that bit'). As yet, the exact noise to which LC refers is not known by the principal author, in that it could be the *dwerrrr* which LC chose to emulate or some other noise following it. At this point, LC pauses the playback of the sequence and selects a single slice for a more focussed repeated listening. The principal author then adds to the discussion with a claim as to the possibility of synthesising the noise just heard ('*We* could do that'), although exactly which 'that' that could be done, is not clear from the video data alone. This brings up the possibility that the principal author and LC may in fact be talking about different noises, and LC reorients the conversation to the noise to which he is actually referring by replaying the slice itself, and repeating the noise vocally (*Tcka-tck*). His talk here – 'This? Not that.' – is a question designed to reorient the principal

---

8   The elements of talk parenthesised with asterisks are to indicate where the speaker has made a noise outside of standard English language usage. This is to say that these utterances are unlikely to be understood outside of the context of their utterance, which hopefully will not present too much of a difficulty for readers.

author to his 'this', assuming that it is the *wrong* 'that' to which is being referred (i.e. another noise, perhaps the previously heard actual and vocalised *dwerrrr*). Having heard the noise as played in the slice, and as confirmed as the-noise-to-be-heard through LC's vocalisation of it, the principal author concurs with LC's liking of the noise, and LC offers a further confirmatory description demonstrating that the topic of discussion is now, conclusively, shared – the topic is the noise that is 'Sounding quite percussive'. What this shows is how the principal author and LC begin to express ideas to each other that exist, for their simplest referrals, in an audio realm (as opposed to being 'easily spotted' on-screen visually). Here, the principal author and LC draw on such resources as vocally reproducing identifying details of sounds, as well as relying on features such as the sequential unfolding of events coupled with the use of grammatical indexicals (i.e. when LC asserts that he likes 'that', the 'that' to which he refers is to be taken as having only just been heard) and with resources provided by program #2 itself (i.e. the ability to replay individual slices for repeated listening).

Two notable 'types' of talk about audio ideas can be drawn from the analysis of the collected video data. Whilst all the talk presented here involves the discussion of audio ideas and things that the principal author and LC can hear, clearly such talk takes contextual cues as to what resources are available to facilitate discussion. For instance, there is both talk about noises which have identifying details that allow them to easily be vocalised, and talk about noises which do not so readily support such reproductions. With the former, the principal author and LC can rely on features of the noises themselves (and their accompanying vocal emulations) to support the discussion, whereas with the latter, other resources must be drawn upon. To further elaborate, two excerpts are presented:

Excerpt 6 – Using impromptu slang

[*PB plays through a series of slices as identified by program #2's automatic finding function*]

PB: I'm happy with *chocks* like that [*Replays the first set of two slices that program #2 has divided the *chocks* into*]

LC: Yeah, don't cut that [*points to second set of *chocks*, which are undivided*] any further.

PB: [*Moves cursor over the first – divided – set of *chocks**] So, you happy with that?

LC: That's fine.

PB: Do you want me to delete this?

LC: Er, no? … Cos … play the- play the two separate ones … like …

[*PB Plays the two divided *chocks**]

LC: *T'p. b'p.*

[*PB replays the two divided *chocks**]

LC: I dunno.

[*PB continues replaying each of the divided *chocks**]

LC: Doesn't ma-. We won't use that. I can't imagine it.

Excerpt 7 – The availability of on-screen resources for clarifying grammatical indexicals

PB: [*Moving slice dividers around the screen*] Are they about … even?

[*PB replaying slices in background*]

LC: Actually, yeah, go on, do that again.

PB: What, just backwards?

LC: No, just th- play- play those *two* again.

PB: Which two sorry?

LC: The two you just played. They're the same.

PB: I- I don't know.

LC: Oh right. [*Pointing to last slice then first slice*] L- I *think* it was the first one last one.

[*PB plays the slices LC pointed to*]

LC: [*Pointing to last slice then second slice*] No, first one second one.

[*PB replays last slice and second slice repeatedly*]

LC: [*Pointing to last then second slice*] That's like a more in tune version of that one.

There are significant contextual differences between the talk in the two excerpts above which frame how each instance of talk unfolds, such that what is being talked about dictates (to a large extent) the available resources for talking about it. Excerpt 6 deals with an instance of talk about a noise with an easily identifiable detail (*chock* – a percussive noise produced by a guitar when the strings are muted then struck). This particular noise – the *chock* – is easily talked about precisely *because* it is easily picked out from the other surrounding noises. Hence, the principal author is able to vaguely vocally reproduce the noise for LC to orient the talk to the topic of the only recent occurrence of the *chock* in the current playback activity. By contrast, Excerpt 7 (which could be characterised as a 'trying' sequence featuring multiple 'tries') is not so easily talked about by reference to the audio qualities of the noise in question. This is because each individual noise in this sequence is, broadly speaking, similar to the last, and this presents a difficulty in LC's attempt to orient the principal author towards the two particular slices he wants to have replayed. The topic of talk here is about an eight-slice sequence of a vocal melody, and although the melodic features of the slices show changes in pitch (i.e. the note being sung) over the course of the sequence, some slices play sounds that are in fact at the same pitch. Hence, the major audible differences between these slices are more to do with the lead-ins and tail-offs from and to the preceding and following notes, which may feature quick transitions (rises and falls) between pitches. It is these lead-ins and tail-offs that identify each slice as unique. For the reasons outlined above, the origins of this eight-slice sequence as a sung piece do not make it any easier for LC to vocally reproduce the desired noises for the purposes of an explanation. In this case, simply singing the notes of the two slices is not enough to cause the principal author to understand exactly *which* two of the note-bearing slices is meant, since any attempted reproduction of the very subtle identifying details of slices – the lead-ins and tail-offs – might go unnoticed. Hence, given the unavailability of a definitive vocal reproduction as an explanatory resource, LC coerces the principal author into an understanding step-by-step (see Figure 6.3). First, he relies on an indexical term ('play those *two* again'), then refines this with a temporal attachment ('The two you just played'), then directs the principal author's gaze towards the relevant slices through pointing and referring to their position in the whole sequence ('first one last one' and 'No, first one second one').[9] The decisive move in the explanation is LC's visible pointing to the two desired slices, which results in the principal author's successful understanding of which ones to repeat. At this point, a comment on them is made ('That's like a more in tune version of that one.'), drawing the activity of 'communicating which two slices are the topic' to a close.

Figure 6.3a   PB: 'Are they about … even?'

---

9   It is interesting to note that LC's pointing and talk about which slices he means does not seem to tally up on first glance in the video data, in that he refers to the order of slices in reverse. The principal author's replaying of slices follows LC's order of pointing rather than the order suggested by his talk (which is the reverse of what might be expected, in that it plays out as a right-to-left reading of the slices as they appear on-screen). This reversal, where a said first is a visual last and vice versa, is a possible result of the principal author's last action prior to the talk having been to play the sequence of slices in reverse, in which case LC may be referring to a sequential order not based on a visual reading of on-screen slices, but on a temporal understanding of the actions the principal author has just performed (i.e. playing the slices in reverse). However, this posited explanation is not drawn entirely from the video available.

Figure 6.3b   PB: 'Which two sorry?'

Figure 6.3c   PB: 'I- I don't know'

Figure 6.3d   LC: 'Oh right. L- I *think* it was the first one last one'

What the presentation of these excerpts (and the accompanying storyboard of Excerpt 7, presented as Figures 6.3a–6.3d) is intended to show are some of the different features by which the principal author and LC communicate audio-based ideas to each other (which itself is a practice that informs the kinds of collaboration that produces musical compositions of varying kinds, including remixes). In Excerpt 6, it is, in principle, possible for the principal author and LC to refer to the properties of the noise in question through use of the technical language relating to music composition. Here, the principal author and LC could rely on purely technical verbal description, calling that noise 'a sequence of two muted percussive semi-quavers', and from thereon use those descriptive properties in the discussion. But such a protracted description is not considered for use, despite both the principal author and LC being capable of sharing an understanding of what those technical terms might refer to. Rather, the principal author and LC pick out the salient audio features from the surrounding audio 'mess' (where lots of other audio things are going on simultaneously) and put *those* into words. The 'sequence of two muted percussive semi-quavers' (or any other such description) becomes a more palatable '*chock*', and it is the '*chock*' which is referred to from that point on. However, not all of the talk is so easily boiled down to identifiable details of various noises, and in cases where it is more difficult to differentiate between a corpus of noises to find specific ones, other resources must be referred to in order to facilitate any discussion. These include visually-directing gestures (i.e. pointing at 'those *two*') and the temporal history of events (i.e. 'The two you just played'). Here, the principal author's confusion is resolved through a gradual refining of terms, until there comes a point where an understanding is achieved. LC attempts an explanation based on one set of resources, then evaluates whether the principal author has understood or not. When it's clear that no such understanding is achieved, he calls upon another set of resources to try another and then yet another (ultimately successful) means of explanation.

The point to be drawn here is that for remixers (*and* ethnomethodologists) it is not so easy to talk about or understand ideas and concepts that take their ultimate shape in a purely audio field, and the principal author and LC rely on a 'mutual tuning-in relationship' (Schutz 1976: 161), whereby one of two people recognises and situates the actions of the other to frame their own. In much the same way, the principal author and LC are able to collaborate, drawing on an existing set of shared knowledges – what Schutz calls a 'preknowledge' (1976: 168) – which is used to structure the unfolding interactions. Hence, what each of the three presented excerpts demonstrate is how the practices of listening to stem tracks as part of constructing a remix involves a reliance on various shared knowledges, using both common features of ordinary language (i.e. indexicals, temporality, sequentiality, etc.) and various 'technical' terms, some of which may be developed on-the-spot and embedded episodically for the purposes of facilitating discussion. The fact that this is achieved naturally and easily highlights what might be taken as one of Garfinkel's fundamental 'preposterous problems' (Lynch 2006: 487) – given the uncertainty of the possibility of a definitive agreement on the noises being talked about, there is nothing to say that when LC refers to a noise, the principal author understands that reference as referring to the same noise. Put simply, LC's '*Tcka-tck*' might not be the same as the principal author's. Yet somehow, the principal author and LC have always found that such agreements on which noise is being referring to are easily achieved, and this is largely because these noises may be considered as the 'technical terms' which, when used in conjunction with ordinary language, imbue the hobbyist activity of remixing with a shared and shareable order and organisation.

Although it may at first glance (to non-remixers at least) appear to be a potential source of problems for the activities that principal author and LC involve themselves in, in that these impromptu terms are fleeting and are in no way established prior to being drawn on in conversations, these on-the-spot technical terms are embedded in an ongoing course of action which has its basis in the audio (audible) properties of a given set of tracks. Hence, the use of these terms addresses the problem of having only a limited pre-established vocabulary with which to discuss musical ideas, through utilising the identifying details of relevant audio topics and making onomatopoeic vocal representations of them. How any sensible meaning might be drawn out of the kinds of nonsensical nomenclature that the remixers put to use is in large part due to the fact that the principal author and LC are playing on assumptions about what each other might *be able to* make sense of. LC is aware of the range of things that the principal author might understand and can appeal to them to communicate ideas, and vice versa. From this point, an impromptu slang is consolidated such that it can even become a topic itself – for instance, should the principal author talk about a '*Tcka-tck*', LC might ask 'do you mean a *Tocka-tock* or a T*a*cka-t*a*ck*?*', with the answer to that question made possible through the ordinary language of question-answer sequences as well as the technical language of the noises to which we are referring. As Caton notes, an essential element of hobbyists' activities is the usage of these kinds of 'technical language', which may seem esoteric (i.e. talk about the finer detail of virtual music studio equipment) and bizarre (i.e. the noises we make at each other as part of our talk) to a casual listener. However, in the episodes of talk and interaction presented here, hobbyists such as the principal author and LC 'do not find it necessary to devise new kinds of questions in order to cause their colleagues [or collaborators] to explain what they are saying: new questions to be sure, but not new *kinds* of questions' (1963: ix). As Caton notes, 'technical language is always an *adjunct* of ordinary language' (1963: viii), and it is this framing of technical terms (which includes both the shared technical vocabulary and any impromptu noises or slang developed throughout the talk) within the broader structure of ordinary language use that ultimately makes sensible meaning of them.

Concluding Remarks

The aim of this chapter has been to present and unpack some of the features of the order and organisation of a play activity, namely, producing a remix for a competition. Broadly speaking, for the principal author and LC one possible difference between the music-making activities outlined here and music-making as work is perhaps that if the principal author's and LC's music was being produced as work, the end result would be the deciding factor as to whether the efforts made had satisfied some set of pre-established objectives. For example, such an objective might be to produce an advertising jingle that could be sold, or even just to produce something that would count as a winning entry in the remix competition. This is to say that should the end result not meet the expectations made of it, the work would not be satisfactorily complete. However, since the activity is one of play, to a large extent the satisfaction with the activity determines the end result – the principal author and LC have had several collaborations not resulting in a finished song – the fun has run its course in the time spent tinkering with fragmentary musical ideas. The principal author and LC may or may not return to these fragments in the future, but the output is, in a significant sense, not the only motivation for these music-making activities. This emphasis on the activity as 'not-work' also facilitates the taking of diversions from the music-making activity. At any point, talk could turn in any direction and participants' activities can step outside those related to music-making. Framing the activity in this way, the practices presented here are 'low stakes' – like Sudnow, the remixers are 'not tied to the occupation and a need to make a living at it' (1978: 34) – and are treated as such. Nothing would have been lost had the principal author and LC not been able to submit an entry to the competition, and there was no dependence on winning it.

Yet despite this relaxed attitude towards music-making, it is clear that there is a solid organisational basis to it, grounded in the ordinary and technical knowledges shared by the principal author and LC. The motivations of the practical and technical usage of the two software packages outlined above is, ultimately, purely for the fun of it. The fun is in both the creation of a piece of music built up from selected elements of source materials and the problem-solving required to manipulate those materials into audibly appealing (to the principal author and LC at least) sounds and musical structures. The playful collaboration and the various features therein (i.e. the not-so-systematic approach to the task, the talking about possible things to do with audio files, and so on) is organised around the enactment of various practices relying on all manner of features of shared knowledge, all of which are performed in the name of playfully constructing a remix.

PART III
'Getting Out of the House'

Chapter 7

A Day Out in the Country

Peter Tolmie and Andy Crabtree

Introduction

It is now commonplace to make strong distinctions between tourism and visiting practices in city environments and rural environments (see LAgroup and Interarts 2005), with significantly different motivations presumed to pertain to the two kinds of activity. This being given, a whole segment of social scientific study over recent decades has taken as its interest the re-invention of the rural environment as a place not of work but of leisure (Agyeman and Neal 2006). In company with this interest, a wide variety of different theoretical perspectives have evolved. Thus one body of literature sees the push towards outdoors activities as a direct response to the ways in which modern living conditions numb sensorial experiences, leading to a need to re-engage with such experiences in some way (e.g. Le Breton 2000). This train of thought has been carried further in some quarters with the suggestion that visits to nature reserves and national parks are about attempts fill a void in people's spiritual lives by seeking less formalized methods of spiritual engagement (e.g. Allcock 1988; Cohen 1998). Others, however, question whether this is really about spirituality or more about taking pleasure in a direct sensorial experience of place (e.g. Sharpley and Jepson 2010). A different strand of interest is dedicated not to the benefit of such activities for individuals so much as their potential benefit to rural communities, leading to a variety of discussions regarding the relative merits of responsible engagement with the natural world, commonly referred to as 'ecotourism' (e.g. Neth 2008). Not all analyses of such 'responsible' management of the natural world in response to an upsurge in visitors with widely differing interests are so sanguine. In some cases the stress upon environmental management is seen to have negative social and economic consequences because of the constraints it places upon visitors (see Paget and Mounet 2009). However, there is a body of analysis that also seeks to find ways in which a balance between these distinct concerns can be brought about (e.g. Revermann and Petermann 2002; UNEP 2011). Other works again try to situate these kinds of activities in the broader pattern of global tourism, with discussions about differing levels of active sensory engagement and interaction with these environments and the kinds of 'gaze' they are subjected to (e.g. Urry 2001). In these kinds of discussions the importance of natural phenomena is the extent to which they can be marked out as different from the other things with which people might ordinarily engage (Hetherington 1997), with differing kinds of value being placed upon them according to both this and the context in which they are consumed, for instance in the company of (or absence of) others (Walter 1982). In this vein certain analyses have sought to explore how people proceed throughout different features of visiting practice in terms of 'touristic performance', where even just exploring places online counts as a 'virtual' performance, whilst the taking of family photographs can count as a 'family performance' where sites photographed become generic because the photograph is what is deemed important, not the site (Baerenholdt et al. 2004). Postmodern and critical theoretical treatments, meanwhile, have focused their interest upon how places visited and things seen might be considered to be 'texts' that are 're-made' by those consuming them through the 'lens' of tourism (e.g. Hollinshead 2004).

In this chapter we set aside these various theoretical concerns and focus instead upon what enjoyment of the countryside might involve as a practical matter that takes work and organization. We do this by using a recently accumulated body of data that focuses upon the observation of families and individuals undertaking trips into the countryside, notably to national parks and nature reserves, to pursue a range of different leisure activities. The advantage of proceeding in this fashion is that we take as our starting point a recognition that, for the parties involved, going out for the day is already an orderly phenomenon, replete with ordinary everyday but nonetheless methodical practices. By taking these methodical practices as a topic rather than a resource for analysis we discard a perceived notion, central to the practices of theorizing, that order has to be imposed from the outside rather than as something that is locally produced. We also thereby set aside the risk of 'ironicizing' the member's point of view (Button 1991; Garfinkel 1967) by giving priority to the external topics imposed by the analyst.

Whilst some ethnomethodological work has been undertaken previously with regard to visiting and wayfinding practices and certain aspects of tourism, investigation of family visits in this way is new. As such it should be set against studies such as Brown and Chalmers 2003 discussion of the use of mobile technologies to support tourism in city environments, as a complementary body of work that exhibits parallel concerns and explores some of the same themes but in the context quite particularly of how family days out make visible the ongoing work of *being a family* and managing family relations. An important part of this, as we shall be exploring in more detail, is the way in which there is a tight sequential organization to these kinds of activities. Thus we will be examining along the way topics such as: the planning of an outing; the equipping oneself appropriately for such an outing; the actual work of getting there with its own attendant concerns regarding planning and equipment; the numerous ways in which the trip is actualized once on site including practices of wayfaring, observing, recording, managing mundane matters such as food, drink and toilet stops, and so on; the work of return; and the work of explication to others through both talk and artifact. This is a rich assembly of practices, loosely termed leisure-making, approached here as anything but loose in its oriented to coherence as 'a day out in the country' and with all due emphasis being placed upon how these outings are actually accomplished, or 'made', as a practical and highly ordered job of work. This assembly of practices is not somehow separate to the business of being members of a shared household and all of the relationships that pertain to that but is rather embedded within and constitutive of those relationships and, as we shall see, it is the just-hows and just whats of the day-today realization of the relationships that animates these practices and makes them *meaningful* as a sequence that unfolds.

The Study

The study we shall be drawing upon in this chapter is one of a series of studies that were undertaken and as a part of a UK EPSRC-funded project geared towards developing technology to support community-based activities in rural settings (EPSRC Grant EP/I001816/1 'Bridging the Rural Divide'). The particular study chosen is of no greater intrinsic merit than any of the others. It does, however, offer itself up as an especially perspicuous example by virtue of having been tracked across all parts of the process, making it relatively complete.

The objective of the study we shall be looking at here was to record in detail the planning, realization and follow-up activities for a family trip to the countryside with the specific intention of uncovering ethnographically the order, practices and reasoning involved. The specific trip observed was that of a family of six to the 'Parc Naturel Regional de Chartreuse' (http://www.parc-chartreuse.net/) in South-Eastern France, about an hour's drive away from where the family lived, in November 2010. The family itself was composed of Dave (50), Chloe (42), Paul (20), Jane (16), Marcus (14), and Sarah (8). The visit took place at a weekend and the nature reserve in question had recently experienced one of the first major snowfalls of the year (much of the reserve is above 1,000 metres). All of the data was gathered through natural, in situ observation and took the form of a mixture of video and audio recordings, photographs, and handwritten notes. Data collection started several weeks before the trip, when the idea of the visit was first occasioned, and continued through until after the trip when photographs were downloaded and shared with family and friends.

Making a Day Out in the Country

Something that quickly becomes apparent when one looks at the overall organizational features of family days out like this, is that they are possessed of an extremely tightly interwoven order, with each part riding somehow upon the accomplishment of the preceding part. We will therefore track this order through, from beginning to end, in order to explicate in more detail each of the constitutive parts. It is the ensemble of these parts and their accomplishment that together amounts to how this particular 'day out in the country' was made. However, the order uncovered here is an order descriptive of the accomplishment of many other similar endeavours and is therefore of import for how we might understand other such things, including family days out across a wide variety of possible destinations, shorter group trips out for a variety of reasons, and much longer trips such as holidays. It should be noted that our primary goal here is to provide a concrete sense of the overall order to be found in such endeavours. The examples provided here are therefore to be seen as illustrative snapshots rather than exhaustive descriptions of each component part, all of which could merit chapters in their own right.

A Visit is Occasioned

Before any other matter can be pursued, the first step towards a trip happening is the occasioning of it as a possibility. There a variety of ways in which such occasioning might take place:

1. So at least one way is that the proposition of a trip as a possibility might arise apparently a propos of nothing. This is not to say that it's *actually* nothing, but rather in a form that members might describe along the lines of 'nothing much in particular'. Accounts for why a trip might happen will still be available, but they will be of the order of 'because we were bored', 'because the weather is nice', 'because we need to get out of the house for while', 'because the kids are driving us crazy', and so on.
2. Another kind of occasioning can be through reminders and temptations. For instance, some member of the party might mention that a trip was promised some time ago and it hasn't yet happened, and isn't it time it did? Or it could be that a trip is specifically offered as a way of encouraging someone to do something else, such as a particularly onerous project for homework.
3. A very commonplace way in which occasioning can take place is through recollections of places already visited, either in the course of some specific reminding, or as an outcome of happening across photographs, someone mentioning someone else is going to a place you've already been to and liked, and so on.
4. Some trips have the character of being recurrent things that are done at certain times in the year or with a certain frequency, such as each year when the swans are nesting, or getting out to the woods at least once a month. Here the occasioning is the arrival of a time when the local inhabitants might recognize that such a trip is 'due'.
5. Perhaps the most commonplace occasioning of all is the occurrence of some special event, such as Mum's birthday, or it being Easter Monday, or an anniversary, and so on.

This is far from being an exhaustive list of potential ways in which trips out might be occasioned, but something to note is that each of these occasionings carries with it certain kinds of accountabilities and rights. This is something to which we shall return shortly. And, in relation to this, it is worth pointing out that the principal example to which we shall be referring here was not occasioned in any of these ways. Rather, what happened was that a decision was made that the whole family should go out for a day to the country so that a record of the visit could be made. This distinct form of occasioning had notable consequences and this, too is something to which we shall return.

Deciding Where to Go

When discussing places to go there are really three inter-related issues on the table to be spoken about. One of these is 'when' to go, another other is 'where' to go, and a third is 'what to do' when you get there. Let us take each of these in turn:

When   Family routines rarely allow for total spontaneity – decisions about when to go on a trip have to accommodate these routines, and involve the following kind of reasoning: Are the kids at school? What about work? What other commitments have been made? What else might be happening that day? What time does the routine say you can leave? And what time must you be back? Aside from questions of schooling, work, and prior commitments decisions may also turn upon matters such as what the weather is likely to be like on the day, whether the place might be heaving with people (for instance on a bank holiday), and whether there are things to be done the next day that might be impacted.

> Dave: I'm thinking to do this on Saturday two weeks from now, The constraint is it has to be somewhere we can get to within a day, and it has to be rural. I think it has to be a Saturday, with Jane being at Lycée during the week. And on Sunday we have to be back by a certain time because of school and everything and getting up the next day. If we do it on a Saturday we can take as long as we want and get back when we like.

At the same time, decisions also have to be made by a certain time. Depending on the undertaking, the reasoning here might include matters such as: what pre-planning and preparation must be done, what purchases need to be made (and, if you have to shop before you go, will there still be time to do it?), what kind of warning needs to be given to others, and so on.

Where to go, what to do   For all of the complexity outlined above, decisions regarding when to go out for a day are still often, depending upon the original proposition, much more speedily resolved than decisions regarding where, as the example we are examining here illustrates. Short trips, with just a few members of the family, to specifically proposed places can involve little in the way of planning, and discussion can be little more than ratification of the proposal (e.g. 'let's go to the river this afternoon'). What one finds is that the people involved in deciding where to go depends upon the proposition and the potential cohort.

Not all days out will necessarily encompass everyone in a household. Some members of the household have limited discussion rights (young children and babies) and can therefore be largely ignored. Depending on the occasioning there may also be strongly differential rights regarding who gets to decide (e.g. if it's your birthday, you decide). For a whole family day out for a special occasion, such as the one we are looking at here, everyone is potentially involved and this can lead to lengthier discussions. Furthermore, when the reason for the day out gives no-one particular rights of choice, it can become especially hard to arrive at group ratification. Figure 7.1 shows how the discussion in this family unfolded and the amount of frustration provoked by no-one having priority in the decision-making process. Something else we can also see here is the extent to which discussions of where to go and what to do elide into one another such that divorcing the two would be artificial. Indeed, where to go is often an implicit decision about what to do and vice versa.

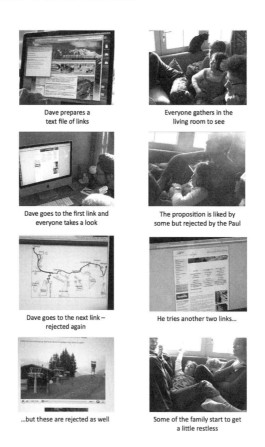

Figure 7.1   Deciding Where to Go and What to Do

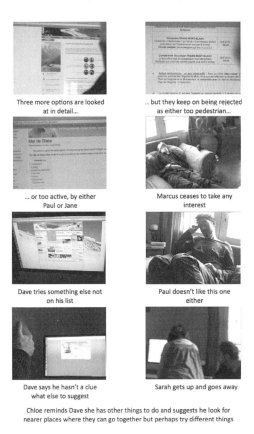

Three more options are looked at in detail...

... but they keep on being rejected as either too pedestrian...

... or too active, by either Paul or Jane

Marcus ceases to take any interest

Dave tries something else not on his list

Paul doesn't like this one either

Dave says he hasn't a clue what else to suggest

Sarah gets up and goes away

Chloe reminds Dave she has other things to do and suggests he look for nearer places where they can go together but perhaps try different things

Figure 7.1   Continued

Looking at the mechanics of deciding where to go, there are some things to point out. Just as with the very first occasioning of a possibility a proposition of a place to go is necessarily tentative rather than prescriptive. So it's not a case of saying 'right, we're going hang-gliding' but rather 'shall we go hang-gliding?' which can then implicate either acceptance or rejection. However, there is subtlety at play here because it's not, in any family cohort, quite as black and white as this. Instead it proves to be differentially organized. So, it turns out for instance that there *are* those in a family to whom it might be said 'we're going hang-gliding' as a statement (e.g. younger kids). It can also be that decisions are to be made between a sub-set of the total cohort (e.g. the parents), with the decision then being reportable to others in the family in exactly these declarative terms (e.g. as news). At the same time, those who have similar rights to decide (e.g. parents, older adolescents, etc.) do not have the right to frame a projected trip to one another as a statement in this way. For them it has to be worked up as a proposition.

Once an initial proposition has been floored, subsequent suggestions may be considered iteratively. Consider, for instance, the following:

> Chloe: Dad suggested visiting a glacier. A guided walk up into the mountains.
> Jane: Yeah, that sounds good.
> Dave: That's what I was thinking because the alps are within striking distance and we could do that within a day trip
> Paul: (*dubiously*) Mmm
> Chloe: What else could we do up in the mountains?
> Dave: I don't know
> Chloe: Bobsleighing
> Dave: It depends whether there's snow
> Paul: I'd like to do that
> Jane: I'd be happy to go up into the alps just to take photos
> Paul: Go skiing? Family skiing trip
> Chloe: Well I like skiing
> Paul: I haven't tried yet
> Chloe: And if we go to a centre there's not just skiing. (…) Iceskating! There could be iceskating
> Jane: I don't like iceskating any more
> Chloe: No?
> Jane: Well every time I do it I keep getting knocked down.

What can be seen here is that an initial proposal provides for the subsequent utterances to be equally ratifications or counter-proposals. Furthermore, two or more suggestions open the floodgates because apparent uncertainty provides the rights for proposal across a broader cohort.

There are numerous grounds upon which the appropriateness of a suggestion may be considered. This can depend upon the original proposition and the character of the day out that has been proposed. With this in mind, time, cost, distance, weather, relative interest, majority and minority interest, novelty, risk, excitement, intelligibility, informability, proximity (for itineraried trips), adherence to the original proposition, and so on, can all enter into the discussion. All proposals are potentially accountable to these considerations and rejections can be articulated on the same grounds.

Arriving at suggestions at all can take work, depending upon the generality of the original proposition and the character of the day out being proposed. This being the case, suggestions can take prior research to amount to more than 'shall we all go out somewhere on Saturday', which is easily ratified but proposes nothing more than the possibility of a trip. In Figure 7.1 above we see Dave working outwards from a list of links he has prepared in a text file. Arriving at this list of links took substantial prior work on his part, with a range of Google searches, examination of specific websites, and copying over of links from the browser to the text file so that they could be quickly transported to the machine in the living room and thus made visible to everyone at the same time. In this way group discussion can revolve around physical presentation and display of a range of different resources associated with the possibility, some technologically grounded, some not, including: websites; search results; brochures; newspapers; flyers; maps; recollections; advertised or known about events; habits and routines; recommendations; and so on.

Planning the Trip

The work of planning for a trip pulls upon the competent use of a range of both physical and digital resources, with some aspects being directly collaborative (e.g. what to do about food), whilst other aspects may be undertaken by dedicated individuals (e.g. online searches). A number of considerations are potentially relevant here, including: how to get there; exactly what route to follow; what to take; when to leave; what to do once you are there; financing; fuelling; who to tell; contingencies to cover; and who should do what and when. Figure 7.2 provides an overview of some of the work Dave was involved in on this occasion:

Keying in a search for activite chartreuse

Locating a site with walking routes

Copying the link to a text file

Going to the main site for the parc

Copying more links to the text file

Going to another site listing activities

Checking what some of the activities listed involve

Saving text file to copy to other machine for discussion

Figure 7.2   The work of planning

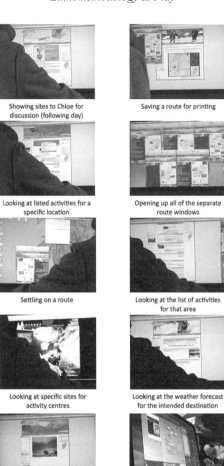

Showing sites to Chloe for discussion (following day)

Saving a route for printing

Looking at listed activities for a specific location

Opening up all of the separate route windows

Settling on a route

Looking at the list of activities for that area

Looking at specific sites for activity centres

Looking at the weather forecast for the intended destination

Opening live webcam to see what it's like

Printing stuff off for taking

Checking the route

Figure 7.2   Continued

Making Ready to Depart

Families do not just go out on day trips by walking out of the door. There is a whole range of work implicated in *getting* out of the door. Things of relevance, things to be taken, have to be brought together, as is illustrated in Figure 7.3:

Buying in snacks for the day

Finding hats and gloves

Finding ski jackets and salopettes

Checking stuff still fits

Getting map books and directions ready

Getting cameras ready

Putting everything together on the table nearest the door

Lining up the boots on the floor

Bringing stuff together involves verifying and assembling a variety of potentially required items in locations convenient for packing in the car

Figure 7.3   Bring stuff together

However, much of this cannot be done days ahead of departure. Often it is work that has to be done just before you go. So, people have to be got up and organized in readiness for this, and this itself may have to be discussed the day before. In this case they decided an exact order of who would get up and wake who in turn in the morning. Things to be taken – especially food and drink – may take active preparation no sooner than the night before, perhaps even on the day itself. And then things have to be loaded into cars:

Dave goes out to car with coat and boots – Opens the boot and puts them in – Goes back into house and gathers up all the other coats and brings them out to put in the boot as well

Figure 7.4   Loading the car

Goes back into house and brings out another pair of boots and a rucksack and plastic bag to pack – goes back into house and gets stuff on table (batteries, cameras, wallet, phone, etc.) pulled together in one bag – others getting coats and scarves on – Dave checking with Chloe whether there was anything else that needed to go in the car – Chloe comes over to look – Jane's stuff but she'll sort for herself – other boots are going to stay there

Houses may have to be prepared for a day of absence by locking doors, shutting windows, changing the heating, and so on. Verification may happen at a number of places that the right things are being brought together and prepared, as we can see in the above interaction between Dave and Chloe. And, beyond all of this, *people* have to be loaded into cars, which can itself involve extensive negotiation as family members vie for what hey consider to be preferred positions within the car.

It can be seen from all of the above that the work of making ready is distributed, collaborative work that may implicate and render accountable anyone in the household, yet only certain individuals may initiate certain activities (e.g. not just anyone decides it's time to load the car), and this, too, falls within the larger organization of relationships within the household and just who may appropriately ask what of someone else.

The Journey to the Site

The next principal phase, once everyone is out of the door and into the car, is the actual journey to where it has been decided the family will go. This journey can itself involve a number of competences and considerations, some of which may be planned for in advance, such as resources for wayfinding and in-car entertainments, as we saw above.

Journeys themselves can become a feature of the day out and may involve the remarking upon and recording of passed environments and scenes of interest, especially where the destination involves travelling a route that has not been followed before.

> *Passing sign saying 'Detecteur d'Avalanches – Arret Imperatif au feu rouge clignotant' (see picture)*
> Dave: If anyone sees a flashing red light, panic

Figure 7.5   Noticing an 'interesting' sign

There may be a need to accommodate toilet stops and other interruptions. It can also be the case that the exact proposition and details of the plan will get fine-tuned once the trip is already under way, especially if delays, diversions or other unexpected contingencies arise along the way. In this particular case the priorities were fine-tuned en route as they decided that they'd go for a walk first of all, then eat, then do other things as they came across them.

Thus, as was so famously articulated by Suchman (1987), it can be seen that these kinds of plans, whilst being a vital part of how the overall endeavour is accomplished, provide nothing more in themselves than a set of orientations and provisions that are negotiated into actual practice along the way as they are made to fit with the in situ and contingent organization of the real world. This proved to be recurrently the case as the day out was seen to unfold in practice.

Arriving at One's Destination

Arriving, especially when it's a visit to somewhere you've never been before can itself involve a measure of work. Some of the attendant problems here are: recognizing you're there; deciding it is where you actually want to be; knowing where to stop; and ascertaining whether it's the right place to stop, e.g. if you are walking, where will you be setting out from, will you need to intermittently revisit the car? Consider the following:

> Dave: Right, this is Saint Hillaire. Next question is where to stop. Just stop in the centre and hope we find it?
> Sarah: I'd like to get out and stretch my legs
> (*Carry on driving through village*)
> …
> Chloe: Now we're coming out of town
> (*Carrying on driving*)
> *Chloe commenting on coming into next village*
> *Dave saying looking for signposts*
> *Chloe noticing signpost for station de ski*
> Dave: Yeah, I think stop somewhere around here and see
> Chloe: What about going up to the ski station?
> Dave: What I want to do is make sure we park where we're not too far from where we can eat – Like near an auberge. I'm not going to be doing too much driving because I don't want to drive up into the high Chartreuse where we'd need snow tyres
> (*Slowing down*)
> Dave: How about there?
> Chloe: There's a cafe restaurant
> Dave: Shall I park up here somewhere?
> Chloe: Yeah
> *Dave turning off road into parking area. Pulls into parking space next to other cars and stops.*
> *Near tourist information office and just after cafe-restaurant Chloe pointed out.*

Note here how there had been no prior decision made about an exact place to stop and it takes work in the course of driving just to figure out what an appropriate place might be. It starts with a vague effort to locate relevant signposts, but concretizes around the spotting of a café restaurant by Chloe, which will facilitate part of the plan in view of providing somewhere to go and eat as well. However, parking near the restaurant had not been formulated as a part of the plan. Rather, it presented itself as an appropriate proposition in situ.

Of course, once you have come to a stop there are still things to be done. The bringing together before setting off is essentially a provisional and contingent bringing together of possibly required things. There is now the work of ascertaining

what should actually come along. Here, too, there are those who have the right
to decide and do the actual apportioning, and others who are expected to do what
is asked of them. A detail here is that it is snowy outside and everyone needs to
don certain appropriate pieces of apparel. Thus there is a rather long-winded but
necessary procedure adopted whereby Dave passes things into the car from the
boot so that people can put them on before getting out, which then becomes a
business of getting out and dressed one at a time.

Once everybody is out of the car and ready there is still work involved in seeing
what it will take to begin the visit: Just where do you go? Just what signs do you
follow? In this particular case the work involved is extensive. It involves decisions
about whether to eat first or walk first, research regarding what information is
available in situ, the work of locating meaningful signs, the work of ascertaining
what routes might be followed and what grounds would make them appropriate
(e.g. duration), and, preliminary to all of this, the work of uncovering just exactly
where you are in relation to everything else that might be of interest.

> *Walk across car park together to look at tourist information office*
> *Get to map on board showing footpaths around the area*
> *Chloe and Dave work out together which car park (marked P) they are at on*
> *the map*
> Chloe: OK, so there's a sentier [footpath] (*pointing to map*) just here
> Dave: Just there, yes. Towards the parapente.
> Chloe: (*tracing path around in a circle and back to P sign*)

Figure 7.6   Tracing a possible route

Chloe: Perhaps we can do that. (*Looking up at tourist information office*) It looks shut to me up there, but I'll go and look anyway

Dave: It is shut, yeah. There's no lights on or anything

(…)

Chloe: So, if we're here (*pointing to map again*) La Chappelle is there.

Dave: We're at the tourist information anyway, aren't we. We're on the main road. I think we're here (*pointing to map where there's an 'i' symbol*)

Chloe: Which way are we facing then?

Dave: Errm, well we know that the er-

Chloe: The parapente is up that way

Dave: Yeah

Chloe: So if we head out-

Dave: So that's looking that direction, yeah (*pointing to map and then pointing towards bank behind them*)

Chloe: I'll go and see if there's anything up here

Chloe goes up steps to tourist information office. Dave follows.

Walk around the outside and browse through some brochure they find next to the door, then discuss what to do

…

Chloe: There's a footpath thing marked up there

…

Chloe walking further up beside office

Chloe: Just up there a ways is the sentier- path marked

Dave: Is there? Oh yeah.

Chloe: So we'll go and see, er- I'd like these (*leaflets she picked up*) put in the car

Dave: Okay (*takes the leaflets back to the car*)

…

Chloe: (*as Dave walks back towards them*) I think we ought to go and eat first.

Dave: What time is it?

Chloe: It's twenty to twelve

Dave: Is it!?

Chloe: If we go for a two hour walk everything will be shut by the time we get back

Discussing whether they're hungry enough to eat yet

Chloe: The footpath thingy is very informative. It tells you walks and how long they take.

Dave: Right, okay. That's good.

…

Chloe saying she really thinks they should eat before they go

Dave goes up steps to look at signpost as Chloe takes picture of information board

(Kids playing making snowballs during all this time)

Dave gets to signpost and studies it

Figure 7.7   Signpost with timings

Walks back to join others

Dave: Do you not want to do one of the forty minute ones before we eat, just to work up a bit of an appetite, because there a moulin whatisface that takes forty minutes going that way (*pointing*)

Chloe: Okay lets go up and decide together

Dave: There's several forty minute ones

All walk back up to signposts, Chloe calling them to come along as they depart

Dave: So there's the signpost. What d'you fancy?

Chloe: We'll head for the Moulin de Porte Traine, and we'll decide where it branches I suppose, whether we want to carry on to do the slightly longer one

Dave: Yeah

Chloe: If we only do the forty minute one we'll be back in time

Dave: And we'll build up more of an appetite because I'm really not hungry yet

All start to head off together along path indicated by the signpost

Conducting the Visit

We have already revealed in the preceding discussion a wealth of practices involved in families going out for a day in the country that have done nothing more than get the family to the point where they can begin their visit. In this next section we take a look at some of the various practices involved in visiting itself. Some of these continue to be tightly ordered and dependent upon one another's realization. Others are much more contingent but nonetheless central to how specific visits are accomplished in the way they are. The actual doing of the visit is most particularly contingent upon the decisions made, the nature of the visit, and the character of the locale.

There are, however, some notably robust features that can be seen to resonate across many such undertakings and these are the features upon which we shall concentrate.

Revising the plan   It is in the way of visits to these kinds of settings that exactly what route is to be followed is something that is under constant potential revision, adaptation and elaboration. Almost straight away this becomes a feature of this family's visit as the prospect of visiting a waterfall presents itself to them:

> *Chloe brushing snow off of signs as Dave comes up*
> Chloe: This is where it branches apparently
> Dave: Okay
> Chloe: So it's a one hour route that way (*pointing to right*).
> Dave: Okay
> Chloe: A forty minute route to the left
> Dave: Okay, we're probably taking the shorter one aren't we? In view of the fact they're fretting already
> Chloe: It says there's cascades as well
> Dave: Oooh!
> Chloe: I wonder if it's on the way? A frozen waterfall would be fantastic.
> Dave: It would

The art of wayfinding   Another implicit but vital part of visiting sites such as nature reserves is the work involved in actually finding one's way around. A particularly striking feature here is how much of the wayfinding is both collaborative across the whole of the family and actively negotiated and made explicitly visible, e.g. 'there's a sign over there'. Note also the part that can come to be played by the traces left by other people.

> Chloe: There's a sign over by that tree (*pointing to a tree in middle of large expanse of snow*).

Figure 7.8   Signpost off the path

Paul: We're not going to be able to read it from here are we?

…

Dave tries zooming in with his camera

Dave: I can't quite get a focus on it because my hands moving too much. Somebody want to come and hold it steady?

Jane comes and takes camera and tries zooming in instead

Jane can't get a focus either. She suggests getting out her tripod but they decide it would be too much effort.

Carry on following the tracks left by other people

Chloe, Paul, Marcus and Sarah have come to a halt up ahead

As Dave and Jane reach them Dave reports on problem of getting a focus on the sign

Chloe: (*Pointing to a post with two arrows on it pointing different directions*) I think we have to turn right. That's our most informative post there.

Figure 7.9   The second signpost

Dave: Right
Chloe: We must be heading towards that signpost there
Dave: We must be
Sarah: Mum, there are footmarks leading that way
Chloe: There are. We'll go that way. There's one leading that way too, but we don't know where it goes.
Dave: No

The remarkable and the mundane   The preceding points are tightly bound up with how the family goes about managing the fashion in which it traverses the landscape. However, there are also a number of recurrently visible features that relate to what the family *does* as it is traversing the landscape. Something that particularly provides for the character of a specific visit is just what comes to be taken note of along the way. This is, after all, an implicit or even overt element of rationales for visiting nature reserves: going to see what's there and making visible you *have* seen it when you've seen it.

What all this amounts to is that there are things to be attended to and things that are passed by without remark, being oriented to as utterly mundane features of the environment in some way. It is also worth noting that it is not solely a case of people remarking for their own benefit. Much of what happens amongst groups is 'callings to attention' where some feature is explicitly pointed out to some or all of the other members in your party:

> *Paul suddenly runs ahead and stops a little further up, looking to the right.*
> Paul: Everybody come here!
> *Everyone walks up to join him.*
> Dave: Oh wow, yeah, I see. The mountains.
> (*spectacular view of the mountains with clouds banking up around them*)
> Paul: A nice shot.

Some aspects of what might count as remarkable or mundane fall out of the above observations. So one thing that makes a difference is the understood objectives of the visit. What one sees of a snow-filled landscape as a skier is not necessarily what one sees as someone there to walk or to observe wildlife. The sheer legibility of the environment can also matter. Being unable to recognize what it is you are seeing can make it an explicit object of reference as part of the work of trying to figure out just what it is. At the same time, certain plants or animals can be passed over by some as 'just another bird' or whatever, whilst for others the fact it is a specific bird is exactly what will make it worthy of remark. Some things are recurrently presented within landscapes as objects of anticipated interest (e.g. viewing points), and other things are clearly almost impossible to be appropriately made an object of interest without subsequent account (e.g. paths themselves, which might be an object of interest to those managing the site or other similar sites, but where 'oh look, it's a path' would be a strange utterance for most people). This latter point emphasizes something else about all of this: differing cohorts have an important impact upon what might count as interesting in any particular case. Nothing is intrinsically interesting in and as of itself

Making a record   Something that can feature strongly in family visits to nature reserves is the making of a record of various aspects of the visit, usually by means of cameras. Much of this is once again premised around what is worthy of interest and capture, with the added element that family members themselves and their actions can count as part of this. Here are some ways in which this concern was made manifest during the specific visit we followed:

Example A:
Dave and Chloe wait at the displays for everyone to catch up
When Jane arrives she gets out the family camera and takes a photograph of the view across the valley to the mountains

Example B:
Chloe breaks icicles off of house eaves as passing and hands them to the children
As walking back to car they fight with them like swords and some break in two
A little further along Paul positions two halves so that it looks as though he has been impaled on one from his back through to his front
Then he does the same on either side of his head
Jane takes a photo

Figure 7.10   An icicle through the head

Example C:

Jane decides to take some photos of the cascade
Chloe gets tripod out of her backpack for her
Jane sets up the tripod and attaches her camera
Chloe heads off with Marcus and Sarah
Jane peers through viewfinder, adjusts angle of camera and adjusts focus
Starts to take photos
Chloe calls back and says there's a place where they can get a shot of the middle
of the cascade
Jane, Paul and Dave walk up path
Chloe tells her to follow the animal tracks
Walk through trees following tracks
Dave goes to join Jane as she sets up camera in new place looking straight
across to the cascade
Takes several photos then moves upstream a short distance to take more
Then comes back again and takes another lot with a different ISO

Figure 7.11   Photographing the cascade

Then detaches camera from tripod and takes more shots just holding the camera
Folds the tripod down and then they head back to join Paul who is waiting for
them
Then the three of them follow the path back up to join the others

The above examples illustrate a number of discrete orientations to photography it is worth noting. In Example A it is all about capturing things of interest within the landscape, such as views. Example B is about capturing the presence and deeds of specific people within the group. In Example C the interest is overtly artistic.

Notice how these differing orientations impact upon what might count as being both worthy of capture and as appropriate work and effort, with 'art photography' being unproblematically allowed to call upon significant amounts of investment, whilst the same amount of investment attached to 'family snaps' would require significant account.

Reading displays, reading the landscape Another part of the business of uncovering aspects of the environment worthy of attention or otherwise is the work that can happen with situated displays, i.e. noticeboards or information panels of various kinds inserted in the landscape. Consider the following:

> *Sarah, Chloe and Dave arrive at a viewing point looking across to mountains*
> *with two boards laid across the top of posts*
> *Chloe walks up to one and starts to sweep the snow off of it*
> *When snow is swept off it's just a blank board underneath*

Figure 7.12   Working with situated displays

Chloe: There's not actually anything on them right now
Chloe walks over to the other board – sweeps off snow
Chloe: Nothing either
…
Dave tries to lift board and finds it is hinged so that you can raise it up
Dave: Ah, no no no no, No no. It doesn't work like that, look.
Sarah: Mum!
P: It is actually a workable display that knows that it gets snowy
S: Mum!
Dave: Because it opens up (see Figure 7.12)
Chloe: Ah!
Dave: See
Chloe: For clever people.
Dave: Yes, for clever people. So they've thought about the snow

Clearly such displays are positioned by those managing the site in an effort to explicate certain aspects of the locale in some way. A couple of things fall out of this, however. First of all something has to be recognized as a display to that purpose and this is not always straightforward. Secondly, the explication turns upon the recognizability of the things being explicated in situ and this, too, can prove problematic.

What the work of trying to disambiguate a situated display reveals is that there are ways in which it forms a part of a larger enterprise of trying to make the landscape one is passing through legible. This is not simply another aspect of wayfinding. It is, once again, as much about trying to locate within the environment what should and could be worthy of your interest.

Being together, being apart Something of particular moment for how family days out unfold, especially in open environments such as nature reserves, is the work various members of the family undertake to preserve proximity and contact with one another, or the opposite. Evidently, for a family of six to retain tight proximity to one another throughout the course of a lengthy walk around a nature reserve is improbable. Rather, what happens is that various members of the group break off together to form sub-groups: various numbers of siblings together, or individual parents with certain siblings, or even, occasionally, certain individuals on their own. All of the sub-groups engage in work to retain some kind of degree of proximity to one another, usually on the grounds of lines of sight, occasionally by calling out. These sub-groups can form apparently spontaneously around a number of different orientations and are hugely flexible over the course of the visit. Individuals on their own can be understood to be going about their ordinary business (e.g. taking photos, finding a place to go to the toilet, taking in the view, and so on). Going off on your own, however, can also be understood to be problematic for the rest of the group in some way and called to account accordingly. What is clear is that all members of the group are continually engaged in the business of monitoring where one another are and proceeding on the basis of this. To 'not notice' that you have fallen behind, or left everyone else behind, or gone a different way, etc. happens on a regular basis, but it is also routinely called to account by others in the group.

> *Chloe and Dave set off down path, then stop and turn round to wait for others to catch up*
> *Jane turns round and calls out: Sarah, come on!*
> *Sarah is only just visible behind them on the path*
> Dave: Come on sweetie!
> *Jane, Paul and Marcus walk along the path towards Chloe and Dave as Sarah slowly trudges up the slope behind them*

Figure 7.13   Falling behind

The art of enjoyment and the accountability of pleasure   Days out in the country are also very much about enjoyment and the ways in which members of the group work to make that enjoyment manifest to one another. You are not there to do workaday stuff and if you seem to be (e.g. by walking too purposefully, taking things too seriously, obsessing about the schedule, and so on) the others in your group will want to know why.

Enjoyment (or at least a willingness to be diverted and entertained) can be made manifest in a variety of ways: through laughter; jokes; clowning around; bothering to look; bothering to pay attention; exhibiting curiosity; taking up features as worthy of recounting and talking about; and so on. Here is a case in point:

Paul balances a snowball on Sarah's head as she stops beside him.
Then Chloe leans over and wrestles Paul down so that he falls in the snow

Figure 7.14   Clowning around

They both roll over in the snow
Paul: (*standing up*) She used a wrestling move but I knew one too
Chloe stands up as well and both brush themselves down, laughing
Chloe tries to charge at Paul but he backs away and she falls over
She reaches out and grabs his leg so that he can't move without falling over
Then Chloe tries to pull him down to the ground but doesn't fall
Then Sarah throws herself down on top of Chloe
Chloe turns her over onto her back in the snow

At the same time as all of this, family groups also clearly work to monitor these things in various ways. Pleasure, in these circumstances, is accountable and if pleasure is not what you see, you have, as a family member, generally the right to ask why. This is somewhat differential with parents clearly most engaged in this kind of work, but others in the group can take it up as well. So things that can definitely lead to concern amongst others can be seen to include: being sulky; being snappish; refusing obligations; looking glum; etc. As the following example demonstrates, in this group there was problem with one of the members whose camera was not working properly, and 'because her camera isn't working properly' became a regular account for her not displaying pleasure appropriately. An additional twist here is that such accounts have a certain duration such that they don't continually need to be reiterated. However, they also have a time limit and if they continue to act in the same way for too long they will start to be called to account instead for 'making too much of it':

> *Jane comes up and asks Chloe to take back family camera*
> Chloe: You don't want it?
> Jane: No
> Chloe: At all?
> Jane: No.
> Chloe: You've got your other lens out. You're going to have a go with that are you? (*zipping up Jane's backpack as asking*)
> Chloe: But please, don't- every time it has a problem, please don't witter

Calling it a Day

Days out like this do not typically come with a set end time, but of course, a stage is reached, especially where people are walking or otherwise exerting themselves in some way, where various members of the group start to voice a wish to 'call it a day'. Sometimes it is first voiced by children who are getting tired, sometimes it's voiced by teenagers who are getting bored, sometimes it's more immediately universal (for instance when the heavens open and everyone is getting cold or wet). However, it is important to note that bringing the visit to a close doesn't just happen by magic. This too involves work. Propositions or requests are made. Various people with various rights and responsibilities will ratify or otherwise, just as we have seen with regard to other matters along the way. This business of negotiation is an essential preliminary to the actual business of heading back. To ignore these interactional niceties and to just make a unilateral decision that you are heading back regardless would have powerful consequences, with others in the group immediately seeking out some kind of account. Here's how the visit was brought to a close in our principal example. Note in particular how the proposition of calling it a day is not just made on its own but also accounted for in various ways: initially it's about fatigue; then it also comes to be about the need to get back in time to eat:

> Chloe: I'm tired now, let's go back.
> Dave: But we haven't seen the waterfalls yet
> (*decide to go and look at waterfall first*)
> …
> *Try to follow path down to waterfall but can't get close and path heads parallel to watercourse instead of descending.*
> *Chloe and Dave go ahead but it carries on the same way*
> Chloe: Let's go back. I want to be back in time for lunch
> Dave: Yes
> Chloe: It's one o'clock. It'll take us an hour to get back. So we could – could go up by the village

Dave: Yep
Chloe: And on the road
Dave: Yep
Chloe: Perhaps back in half an hour and things might still be open
Dave: I hope so
Both walk back up the path to rejoin the children

Getting Ready to Go Home

There comes a point where everyone in the group is back at the car (or other point of departure) and getting ready to go home. Note here how departing retains some characteristics of both making ready and arriving. However, it is typically more constrained. The primary aspects here are: the relocation of the car; unburdening of individuals and replacement of things in the car; the redistribution of its occupants (which does not have to be exactly as it was before and can still be an object of negotiation); and the work involved in figuring out how to physically regain the route and head for home.

The Journey Home

The actual journey home from the site that has been visited is possessed of many similar characteristics to the journey there such as matters of wayfinding, toilet stops, and in-car entertainments. However, there are some distinctive features as well. In particular these involve working up through talk certain aspects of the visit that captured people somehow. This is not just a general discussion of what took place but rather specific recountings, discussions of the order of 'what bit did you like', and post-mortems regarding bits that didn't go so well. Thus the journey home becomes one of the principal relevant occasions for the mutual working up, as a family group, of what was 'interesting' about the day and thus 'storyable' in some way. The journey home is also a prime occasion for future planning. Visits beget visits and in the car on the way home is at least one appropriate place for a next visit to be discussed. In the case of this particular visit discussion in the car on the way home returned several times to the topic of what it might be like up there in the summer and this, in turn, led to the proposition of going back to visit again the following summer and see.

Arriving Home

Something else our study revealed that should not be discounted is that a family doesn't just arrive home and that is it. Instead it takes work to get back into the house after a visit. Some of this work is obvious but nonetheless an important aspect of the overall sequence that cannot be set aside without ramifications of some kind. Thus there is work involved in physically getting out of the car and regaining entry to the home, with various people having various rights of precedence regarding entry. Then people will re-distribute themselves around the home in accountably appropriate ways. In this case Chloe started to get herself and Sarah out of their outdoor clothes whilst Paul took himself off upstairs and Marcus doodled on the guitar. Jane, meanwhile, was co-opted into assisting Dave with unloading the car. The actual unloading of the car can itself involve significant labour. On this occasion Dave systematically ferried everything into the living room first of all. Only after this did they begin to then re-locate various things to various locations, kitchen things (cups etc.) and rubbish to the kitchen, cameras etc to the living room table, coats and boots by the door, and so on.

Beyond these moments of first entry the immediate post-visit phase can be seen to involve the rapid re-occupancy of the home and the re-constitution of the household routine. One of the first topics of discussion in this case, for instance, was what to do about supper. Arriving home can also involve the recognition and handling of the house's own contingencies (e.g. matters of heating and hot water, animals and their whereabouts, what would normally have been done during the day and hasn't been, who may have called, and so on).

After the Visit Has Taken Place

After a day out in the country has taken place the relevance of the visit to other matters becomes rapidly diffuse. Talk about the visit amongst the family mostly takes place in the car or immediately afterwards. Indeed, we should note that it would become accountably odd to continue to talk about it much beyond this. Instead one finds that talk about it amongst the family from here on in will address specific features as they are occasioned, for instance by other possibilities of trips, topics of interest, or looking through the photographs.

Conclusion

To conclude this analysis of family days out to nature reserves we want to concentrate in particular upon two aspects that sing loud and clear throughout all of the data. The first of these is the profoundly sequential character of such trips: the order of realization is almost impossible to overturn without it becoming something else entirely. The other is the extent to which the activities involved become an important canvas for the ongoing accomplishment of family relations.

Family Days Out – A Sequential Accomplishment

What is evident in our analysis of a family day out is the fact that the accomplishment consists of a series of remarkably consistent paired activities. You can't decide where to go for the day if it's never been occasioned in the first place, but at the same time the occasioning immediately implicates negotiation regarding where to go. Decisions about where to go themselves implicate various kinds of planning.

You can't go on the trip without bringing relevant materials together or without doing the work of putting those things in the car. At the same time, to fill the car with stuff and then *not* go on the visit is implicative of all kinds of troubles and disappointments to come. The sheer activity implicates the trip ahead. The journey itself projects a moment of arrival and, as we have seen, arrival itself is not something that just happens by beaming in. Actions taken upon arrival themselves implicate how the day might unfold. The trip itself does not unfold without a projected end and the end itself implicates the work of getting back to the car, loading it up again, and driving home. Arriving home, too, is not a simple matter of getting back but rather replete with ordinary labour regarding reconstitution of the household routine.

What needs to be said about all of this is that this intensely sequential accomplishment is no kind of mystery to the parties involved. All of the practices of realization and orientations to 'what comes next' are things that members of households find utterly familiar and just anyone knows that this is what it takes to go out for the day as a family and what the whole affair turns upon. We need to reconsider, in that case, the status of the numerous theoretical accounts we mentioned in the introduction regarding what is going on when people go out for the day in this way. What seems apparent here is that there is no mystery for the people involved. They know exactly what they are up to and can account for it in all of the ways we have been outlining here (and more besides). Theoretical treatments of visiting practices regarding matters such as catharsis, or the adoption of a gaze, or the seeking out of difference, or whatever, completely overlook the mundane but essential work that is involved. Instead they project a view of what is going on that is, necessarily, partial to the analyst and therefore of no truly special privilege. It is just another account, another member's perspective, that rides upon an unspoken presumption of all the practices we've been looking at here, but with the added ill that it *does* attempt to claim privilege even though it sits outside of any one specific happening and the actual in situ reasoning that such a happening would involve.

Family Days Out and the Accomplishment of Family Relations – Once Again

The other matter we want to emphasize here is that families do not get together like this so very much. There are numerous ways in which families do the ongoing work of making visible their relationships with one another, their concomitant rights and responsibilities, and the whole moral order of the home. Several other chapters in this book also take a look at this topic (see, for instance, Rouncefield and Tolmie on reading and Crabtree et al. on cooking). What is of value in this case is the sheer intensity of exposure the family have to one another's presence in cases like this. Thus all of the work, all of the negotiation, all of the practices regarding proximity, pleasure, pain and playing, are situations where the specific relationships between people are inevitably made visible through what they take for granted and what they choose to call to account. Whilst certain meals, or living room encounters, or arguments about the bathroom, etc., provide another canvas for the working up of the moral order of the home, in the case of days out in the country as a family, this work is going on *all of the time*. If ever a youngest child should wonder what she might be able to get away with, a day out with her family like this provides a salutary lesson. And the same goes for everyone else. These are the potential stresses of going out together in this way, but they are also the source of important updating regarding what is going on in each other's lives and what you are really like here-and-now, not as an abstract proposition or character assessment, but rather as a matter of just what you do or do not do in practice with the rest of your family around you and what you do or do not orient to as of interest in some way.

Acknowledgements

The research on which this chapter is based was funded by EPSRC Grant EP/I001816/1 'Bridging the Rural Divide' and EP/J000604/1. Our thanks to the family who allowed the whole of their trip, from conception to finish, to be observed throughout, warts and all.

Chapter 8

Playing Dangerously: An Ethnomethodological View upon Rock-Climbing

K. Neil Jenkings

Rock climbing is an increasingly popular recreational sport and as a recreational activity it is historically closely linked with romanticism (and colonialism and nationalism). From the early mountaineers onwards it has drawn people to mountains and crags in a quest for adventure and risk, and increasingly, although not for the first time, seen as an escape from the mundane and safe world of contemporary *western society*. Two key features are seen to define rock climbing. The first is its idealistic origins in romanticism and the quest for sublime experiences via 'wilderness' and nature as both beautiful and dangerous: a romanticism still alive today (De Leseleuc et al. 2002). The second is the sub-cultural and locally specific experience of climbing as a practical sports activity where the focus is on skill, fitness and completion of increasingly difficult grades and routes (with names often reflecting their difficulty e.g., 'Where Angels Fear to Tread' or pain e.g., 'Weeping Fingers'). In climbing, routes completed and their difficulty (and danger) – which have official grades – are markers of the individual climber's ability, for both themselves and others, and their 'standing' as climbers. Although these two features are not necessarily mutually exclusive, this chapter will focus the later activities, i.e. the practical activities of rock climbing 'games'.

Climbing 'games' (Tejada-Flores 1986), whether indoor, outdoor, traditional or sports (Donnelly 1994), while popular recreational sports activities are also potentially dangerous activities. Climbing has always been associated with risk, although right from the initial popularity of the sport technological developments, now seen as inseparable from climbing to one's limits (Lyng 1990) and even making climbing possible (Rossiter 2007: 301), have attempted to mitigate certain aspects of that risk (Heywood 1994). At the same time, certain types of climbing have been 'standardized' and formalized, e.g. subcultures 'restricting' the use of assistive technologies (Schuster et al. 2001), to retain difficulty and risk in the face of these technological developments. Although inevitably 'standards' and boundaries are not 'fixed' but are part of an interactional nexus (Fuller 2003) and are also locally negotiated practices.

This chapter with reference to two types of rock climbing 'games', 'The Crag Climbing Game' and 'The Bouldering Game' describes some of these physical, practical, technical and interactional geographical phenomenologies of rock climbing through an ethnomethodological description of the situated practices of climbers. The explication of rock climbing will be described through the description of 'generic', but locally contingent practical contexts where the constant relations of modification and reciprocity by, and between, climbers, their equipment and their environs occurs (Anderson and Harrison 2010). In other words it will be treated as a praxiological phenomenon. Specifically, it will look at the range of verbal and non-verbal interactional practices and processes that shape the organization, initiation, production, and completion (or termination) of climbing activities. What this chapter will do is: look at members practices and how climbs emerge as interactional phenomena. Interactional practices and phenomena that are not just verbal, or ocular centric, but are also those involving tacticity and haptic phenomena (Allen-Collinson and Hockey 2011). Drawing attention to these haptic, as well as verbal and ocular activities, is a key aim of the description (a description which is not meant to illustrate ethnomethodological practice but rock climbing practices*[1]). To 'bastardize' David Sudnow's (1978) introduction to his 'Ways of the Hand', his influential account of the haptic and tactile practices of playing jazz piano, for my own purposes I would say the aim here is, like his then, was description and not explanation (although that too is present), an ethnomethodological inquiry into the body work and interaction (with human and non-human participants) of rock climbers. A description of, at least broadly so, from the perspective of the climber of the orderly activity of improvised interaction in rock climbing: at least the initiation of that project! A project, which apart from a very few studies, the exceptions being those of John Hockey and Jacqui Allen-Collinson on running (Allen-Collinson and Hockey 2009, 2011; Hockey and Allen-Collinson 2007a, 2007b, 2009), studies of sport have yet to undertake.

Introduction

As Lito Tejada-Flores (1978) has noted in the seminal essay 'Games Climbers Play': 'Climbing is not a homogenous sport but rather a collection of differing (though related) activities, each with its own adepts, distinctive terrain, problems and satisfactions, and perhaps most important, its own rules' (p. 19). Tejada-Flores lists these 'games', or 'styles', as: The Bouldering Game; The Crag Climbing Game; The Continuous Rock-Climbing Game; The Big Wall Game; The Alpine Climbing Game; The Super-Alpine Climbing Game; and,

---

1   Practices* with the * is used to indicate that these practices explication are in need of further ethnomethodological studies – but the * will not be adopted throughout the chapter with the use of 'practices' although it is applicable.

The Expedition Game. This list would now be supplemented with at least one other 'game', 'The Indoor Climbing Game'. In this chapter what I present is an attempt at an ethnomethodological description of aspects of the first two of these games. Firstly, 'The Crag Climbing Game' often referred to as 'traditional', or 'trad' climbing (climbing in pairs with ropes and equipment without the use of fixed protection, e.g. bolts to secure the rope to the rock); and secondly, 'The Bouldering Game' (climbing without ropes or protection on often technically very difficult 'problems' relatively close to the ground). These descriptions are not intended as complete descriptions, or even outlines of 'the rules' of each, neither are these descriptions aimed at the climbing fraternity, indeed hopefully everything I describe below is regarded by anyone who actually climbs as patently obvious. This is not a flaw since what studies of workplaces, and the climbing venue is in many way a workplace, is all about '... what is it that that those party to a workplace understand themselves to be doing and how do *they* find the orderly organization of their – and their associates' – work from *within* the workplace? Finding this out is a matter of letting the members teach the ethnomethodologist how to understand – which in many ways, is the same as *recognize* – the features of the workplace' (Randall and Sharrock 2011: 16). So what I describe should hopefully be obvious to those who taught me rock climbing, although there is no doubt also the potential for a 'constitutive ethnography' (Mehan 1979) in which the descriptions describe what participants 'know' but which they do not, for whatever reason, articulate. Rather it is for those, especially ethnomethodologists, who don't 'climb' but wonder what people, often seemingly precariously and very static, are doing (in a practical sense) on cliff faces and how they managed to get there. Of course, for the academic reader hopefully there is an interest in the various practices, which may also be illuminating for their own studies, of the production of another area of 'social order' through members' practices. The choice of 'Crag' and 'Bouldering' as the two climbing 'games', or 'styles, is in the hope that they mutually elaborate each other and facilitate the description of members' practices that produce a 'rock climb'. What climbers themselves will realize is how little I have been able to cover and how much more there is to describe, hopefully experienced climbers will take up that challenge and put my efforts to shame. Following these descriptions of practice we shall talk about some of the more generic issues of relevance to the themes of this book.

Background

The following is an account of some aspects of the recreational activity of 'rock climbing', it is certainly not intended as standing on-behalf of 'rock climbing' as a whole. Rather it is *an* account of how some people I have had the pleasure of spending time with have 'climbed'. I have climbed with them, but more often been an observer of others – which is itself a mundane, but crucial, activity for climbers in their situated learning practices. Initially this larger participation of both climbing and watching was motivated purely by my friendship with people who climbed and with whom I accompanied on some of their days 'having some sport', often climbing but also engaging other activities such as fell running, wild swimming (as it is now fashionably called), cycling and walking mountains of various types and in various conditions. Eventually the climbing activities, where I participated or observed, became what are often referred to as 'busman's holidays' in that I would happily enjoy applying my 'sociological eye', or more specifically my 'ethnomethodological being', in participating and watching people climb at various 'venues' in the North of England. My friends got used to me having a notebook with my climbing kit and eventually my lugging audio video equipment with me to various climbing venues where, in response to the questioning looks of other climbers at the venue, it would be explained that I was 'from the University doing a project' which, in the end, became the truth. While I am not an experienced climber, I am an experienced researcher, and so knew when the seriousness of the activities required the 'ethnomethodological mouth' to be kept shut and the 'ethnomethodological eyes, ears and other senses' to pay attention. On the occasions when I climbed the whole of one's senses would become engaged in the activity of climbing and, since we often 'free soloed', i.e. climbed without protection high enough off the ground to kill oneself, not falling became the paramount reality (the ethnomethodologically reflexive self having suitably disappeared for a moment).

Over the years I have collected various forms of rock climbing data in the formal methodological sense – but much has accumulated from just going to climbing venues and 'hanging around' with climbers socially. This is important since being 'a climber' and associated climbing activities occur well beyond the rock face, even if, fortunately, much of the talk is about what happened on the rock face. The aim is to produce a description of members practices that they engage in whilst rock climbing utilizing this 'knowledge', the way this is attempted is via an ethnomethodological ethnographic description of two types of 'climbing games' – The Bouldering Game and The Crag Climbing Game – which the 'data' has come from participant and non-participant observation, which is used to describe the activities in videos of examples of each type of climb. However, though the descriptions are grounded in the explication of specific videoed climbing practices, the aim of the description is the highlighting of generic aspects of locally accomplished and specific practices by climbers. The reason for this approach is to facilitate a description of rock climbing that, while necessarily incomplete, allows a description of members' methods but one that is not just a description of two specific cases but brings in knowledge from the analysis of the whole corpus of my rock climbing data.

Rock Climbing Games

1. The Crag Climbing Game

When we think of rock climbing we think of people up a rock face climbing with ropes attaching them to the rock, often, but not always, following a route which we can pick out with the naked eye. However, before a climber gets to even start the climb there is a lot of work they have to undertake first, so what is that work?

Rock in its 'natural state' may have all sorts of plants and growths on it, it may have loose rock and finer debris all on its surface, of which are usually cleaned away by the people setting the 'problem' or 'route' – this material may return over time if the route is not used on a regular basis. So the rock is not climbed in its 'natural state' it has been 'prepared'.[2] When climbers approach a 'route' to be climbed, i.e. not virgin rock which few climbers climb, they invariably do so with reference to some information they have either looked at previously and/or currently have with them. Once they locate the crag that they are hoping to climb, itself not always a straight forward task, the information about the 'route(s)' will be consulted either from memory and/or by reading the guide(book) material they have with them. They will look at the rock to make a fit between the guidebook material[3] and what they see before them. They do this to locate actual climbing routes up the rock face and to decide upon potential future action, this includes what route(s) they are going to climb, how they are going to climb it, then who is going to lead (go first), and what equipment they are going to require. Amongst the decision making issues they face are whether it is actually feasible to climb any of the particular routes available? The guidebook may have stated the various grades allocated to each route to describe their degree of difficulty – which the climbers can measure against their own abilities – but there are also local factors that need to be taken into account that are not in the guidebooks:[4] what are the weather conditions and forecast for that day? In particular, is it going to rain? What is the condition of the rock? In particular is it wet? Most climbers will not climb on wet rock as the water acts as a lubricant and thus makes it slippy and the climbing dangerous. What is the texture of the rock? Climbers will know in advance what type of rock the crag is made from, e.g. granite, gritstone, slate etc. and what direction it faces,[5] but they may not know the condition of that rock as local variations occur and all rock gets weathered differently, impacted

---

2   The UK term for this is to 'clean' the rock, but to 'clean' the rock in the USA is to remove climbing aids, so I have used the term 'prepare' instead.

3   Pictorial representations vary in style and form with the increasing use of photographs.

4   Climbs may be temporarily out-of-bounds due to nesting birds of prey, farming requirements, even quarantine, e.g. Foot and Mouth disease.

5   South facing rock dries quicker, North facing dies slower may have been climbed less, have vegetation on it and be colder place to climb. Direction may influence the time of

upon by local vegetation and effected by years of use by other climbers.[6] All of these factors are taken into consideration when assessing routes to see if they are climbable, whether they are too hard, too easy or 'worth doing' (grade, exposure or aesthetics[7]). Also to be taken into consideration at this stage is what 'mood' the climbers themselves are in, whether they are 'up for it' or not in the right frame of mind. Part of the process of deciding on routes to climb is about understanding the potential mental and physical readiness of oneself and one's climbing partner (if climbing with another) to undertake mentally and physically strenuous activity (which may change throughout the day). The pre-climb activities and talk are an opportunity to assess these – in light of an assessment of the difficulties of the climb, including talking to and watching other climbers – and to also psyche oneself, and each other, up. Climbing can be a very dangerous activity and climbers need to know their, and their partners, potential capabilities for the trials that lie ahead and spend time at the rock face assessing them.

Climbing 'Problems'

What we can see so far is that unless a climber is undertaking a climbing route 'free soloing' i.e. on their own with no ropes or equipment other than climbing shoes and a bag of 'chalk' to keep their fingers dry (magnesium carbonate the same compound gymnasts use), they are doing so in collaboration with another climber.[8] Even those 'free soloing' are likely to have other climbers either with them, or near by, with whom they may have discussed some of the issues mentioned above, even if they are not going to technically assist in the climbing itself. What climbers talk about are 'problems' or the 'crux' of a climb (i.e. the most difficult part) and often referred to as 'a problem'[9] in climbing language games. 'Problems' are discussed and analysed (and written about) by climbers in terms of how to overcome them, indeed climbing can be seen as a 'game' of problem solving. 'Problems' are to be overcome 'mentally and physically', and of course these two aspects are not separate but 'of a whole'.

So how do climbers 'see' a problem, how do they anticipate and see it in advance of their physical encounter with it, see the dangers that might be in store for them – and mitigate them? From the bottom of a crag there is much of the details of the rock that they can not see, and what they can see may be at such

---

day for climbing a particular route, and this may depend on time of year and other weather conditions.

6   Years of use will often polish the surface and make it more difficult to climb.

7   There is not room to discuss climbing aesthetics here but it is a important aspect of climbing and are described and grade in light of this.

8   Climbers may solo easy route as warm-ups for a difficult two-person roped climb.

9   'Problems' were originally part of the 'bouldering language game' but usage seems to have moved into other climbing games' language games.

an angle as to not allow an appreciation of its detail, they have to take this into account in their decision making, but how? They know that there is much they can't see and that which they can see they will encounter from a different angle from their present view,[10] it is implicit in their knowledge of rock and may be both implicit and explicit in their discussions of that rock and the impact it will have on climbing the route. It seems that the work being done at this point is 'defining the situation', where their understanding of 'problem' is not abstract, but 'occasioned' and 'emergent' upon the various factors mentioned above. There is much that is 'unknown' but they are working towards a point where their knowledge of the 'problem' is 'good enough for all practical purposes', to make a decision on whether to climb or not, and if they are, how they are going to set about that. Much appears implicit, their ways of seeing the rock and the route – and anticipating the potential 'moves' required to overcome the problems – are implicit, only key moves are discussed in detail. But how do they do this, what is the expertise, what are the ways of seeing, what are the ways of touching, how are the assessments made, and what is the nature of the negotiation that occurs, what constitutes the 'assessment of the other'?

Climbers often, but not always, know each other well, how well they can climb, what sort of 'problems' they are good or bad at, what sort of 'moves' they excel at and which are their weaknesses, e.g. 'hand jamming' or foot 'smearing', they know what type of rock they prefer to climb on and which they find more difficult. However, just as the ecology of the rock is dependent of the daily fluctuations of the weather, so is the ability of each climber dependent on their current 'form', i.e. how well they have been climbing lately, and their physical and mental condition on the day (which can often be related to their general 'form'). These assessments are being done prior to getting on the rock, although they will continue once the climbing has started and seeing 'how well' a climber is climbing – or not!

Pre-climbing Anticipation of 'Problems'

Once climbers get on the rock they find that 'things' emerge that they have to deal with, however, as much of this that can be anticipated in advance the better although climbers vary in their attitude to this. This is not just an oral and visual activity, as noted climbers will touch the rock to get a 'feel' for it, to feel what sort of friction it is giving the hand, and also the feet – although they will not have their climbing shoes on at this point. They will search to see where the start of the route is, and what line up the rock it follows, they will also look to see where safety equipment can be placed and will discuss what possibilities there are and what the options are on the various 'problems'. This leads us to another aspect of the pre-climbing activities, this can be seen as preparation of equipment. Climbers will

---

10   What can't be seen may make the route harder, or easier, but anticipation of the former is usually the main concern, although the latter may aesthetically disappoint the climber.

turn up at a rock climbing venue with a varied amount of equipment, shoes and 'chalk' have been mentioned but it may also include ropes, climbing harnesses, helmets, and racks of 'gear'. Gear is best described as the metal climbing aids which can be 'placed' in the rock and made secure so as to prevent the climber hitting the ground should they fall. The types of gear are numerous and most climbers will have a large selection which they take to the day's climbing venue. They do not usually climb with all of this equipment, which can be very heavy, but make a selection from their main rack of climbing aids, 'gear', which they will attach to their climbing harnesses for use on the climb.

One of the decisions that the lead climber has to make is what pieces they might need, as mentioned above, this is one of the activities they do when looking at the rock face. However, while they are doing this they will also visually and physically check the condition of each piece of 'gear' before adding it to their harness. Also, it is very common for climbers climbing in pairs to share or 'borrow' bits of gear for the climb from their climbing partner if they do not have a piece of 'gear' they anticipate using. Thus, the preparation for the climb includes assessing what 'gear' might be needed and whether they have it in their 'communal racks'. Climbers usually colour code their gear so that they can both identify the individual types of 'gear' and also the ownership of that piece of equipment. This is important since the 'second', the climber following the lead climber, has the responsibility of collecting all the pieces of gear out of the rock[11] as they follow the lead climber once the lead climber has got to the top and secured themselves by constructing a belay. Once the climbing is over at the end of a route or end of the day the climbers need to sort out their racks, to check they have all their gear and that they have not left any behind, the colour coding helps distinguish who owns what after the communal usage.

When the lead climber selects the gear that they want to take with them they will place it on their harnesses in the sequential order that they anticipate using it, they will also place it on the left or right-hand side of the harness in anticipation of which side will be the easier side to access it from in their anticipated position on the rock. This rarely works out exactly as planned and climbers will take more 'gear' than they anticipate using since they know it will be unlikely they have made the exact and correct choices from they view of the rock from the ground, but attempting to do so is likely to save them precious time in putting in the correct 'gear' when on the rock face. Time is important since putting in 'gear' in natural rock can be an awkward activity, as much tactile as visual (of both the rock and equipment), and all the time the climber may be using up energy 'placing gear', energy that they will need for actually climbing the route. The 'second' climber has the same problems in reverse getting the 'gear' out, this is often very difficult as the 'lead' climber will have tried to 'place' the gear as securely as possible, often wedging it tightly into a crack in the rock. Each climber carries a 'nut key/ tool', a metal stick or blade, on their climbing harness whose purpose is precisely

---

11   As noted this is 'cleaning' in US the climbing language game.

for 'knocking out' the 'gear' from the rock, but this can still be a time, and energy, consuming task. On a multi-pitch climb the second is likely to be the lead on the next pitch, in which case they will also need to carry some 'gear' up with them, but they will bear in mind the gear which they will remove and add to their 'rack' on the way up the first pitch – obviously, the more 'pitches' in a route the more complex the 'gear' choices and amount of 'gear' that might be required. Also they can exchange 'gear' with the leader of the first (or last completed) pitch when they are both at the top of it before initiating the second (or next) pitch. Extra 'gear' of course means extra weight and climbers have to build this into their assessments of the climb and how this will impact on their climbing. Climbers who solo a climb without any gear do not have to make such decisions, although they are obviously unprotected against a fall and will build this as a factor into their assessment of the route and the plans to climb it.

Tacticity

This tactile aspect of climbing activities, e.g. checking and selecting 'gear', not just physically touching the rock itself, is a key feature of climbing preparation. For example the climbing harness, which will be used to attach the climber to the end of the rope, while pre-adjusted to a certain extent, will be adjusted and positioned on the body carefully so as to be tight-fitting but not so tight as to prevent movement or blood circulation. This is a physical knowledge rather than just a visual one, although both are used, the harness may be checked for wear and tear before being put on,[12] but its sense of fitting correctly is a physical one. The same is true of the climbing shoes which most climbers buy several sizes too small and squeeze their feet into, this makes them painful to put on and wear, but the benefits being that that it gives the climber a better feeling for the rock and a better 'edge' or and secure 'foothold' when climbing. The actual pain of wearing shoes too small is largely forgotten when climbing, but not when the climb is finished and walking in the shoes is undertaken. The same physicality applies also to the clothing that a climber wears, there is much 'technical clothing' on the market designed for climbers, but while it is an option for many, a significant number of climbers will have favoured clothing that they feel comfortable in when climbing. Of course clothing is seasonal, rock type and weather dependent, but most climbers will have their climbing clothes on underneath other warmer clothing and will take this off to climb. If doing 'warm-up' routes prior to harder routes, clothing will be kept on to keep warm and help prevent muscle damage. The choice of clothing is also dependant upon the amount of time the route is likely to take and the number of pitches, although even with a single pitch the lead climber could be belaying the second climber from the top of the route for a significant amount of time, especially if the 'second' is not climbing well. If dressed only in what they climbed in, and

---

12   Many harnesses now have a 'wear tag' which indicates when a harness needs replacing.

on exposed sites open to the elements, they could quickly loose body capacities vital to their climbing e.g. feeling and flexibility, so clothing choices are important not just for the amount of movement they allow the climber (even if attached in a stuff sack to a harness), but to allow them to function in all aspects of the climbing activity. This is less a problem for the 'second' who belays from the ground as they can remain in their warm clothing until the 'lead' has reached the top of the 'pitch' and it is their turn to climb, although the same problem may face them if on a multi-pitch route and they are to climb the second pitch.

The decisions on what to wear and how they fit (harness, shoes and clothes) are a personal matter; to an extent the gear that the 'lead climber' will take is too. However, the discussion of the climb is a collaborative activity and when looking at the route and discussing the 'problems', issues of 'gear' naturally arise. Assessments of climbing aid use such as 'you might get "a friend" in there', i.e. cramming device that secures into the rock, while pointing to a rock feature are common practical activities in assessment of the route and how to climb it in preparatory activities. Climbers who are familiar with each other will have a lot of implicit understanding in their discussions, indeed one feature of 'expertise', at least the 'display of expertise' (which may on occasion be the same thing) is through a lack of conversation, certainly topics that a novice may raise are eschewed by more experienced climbers and inter-personal communication can often be minimal. Of course, this is a generalization and when 'expert' climbers discuss a route they can enter into expansive displays of expertise in terms of routes, features, problems, solutions and 'gear' requirements – but the less difficult the route, the less this may be engaged in.

Seeing and Finding a Route

When climbing the rock, the lead climber is usually following a named and described route with various technical grades and a basic guidebook description. They will have also viewed the route from the ground below the route. As noted they will have planned what equipment they may need and built in scope for unseen difficulties and 'problems'. In finding the route the climber is facilitated by the fact that the rock is not 'virgin rock', it has been climbed before. The 'lead' will possibly be able to see 'chalk' marks on hand-holds used by previous climbers, there may be hand and foot-holds indicated by their polished smoothness through use by climbers, on some routes a lack of vegetation can be a good indication of the route and foot and hand placements, there may even be old 'gear' left in the rock or at least marks on the rock indicating where it has been previously placed. However, on many routes there is always more than one option as to where to place hands, feet and 'gear'. Just because there are chalk marks on a rock does not mean that there is a definite 'hold' there. When climbers climb they do not rely on sight alone, not necessarily even primarily, once on the rock climbers start to read the rock with their hands and feet. Assessing a hold by looking at it is not as good as actually placing your hands in it and 'testing the hold' via touch and even applying some body weight to it. It must also be remembered that, when climbing, the climber's face may be very close to the rock not affording them much of a view of anything – although they invariably move their head and torso around as much as possible to facilitate a visual assessment, even leaning back off the rock if they have a secure hold. So it is through the hands that the climber finds the route in the main, they literally feel their way up the rock reading the rock like Braille rather than a visual text. A further key aspect in reading the route, and the 'holds' to allow the climb, is body position and to an extent, the difficulty of the climb itself. Climbers as they have gained more and more experience will be able to anticipate where a climb should be in relation to their body position, climbs are like physical puzzles in respect that they have a 'certain' logic to them, there are likely to be a certain number of 'candidate', if not always optimal, areas where the next hold will be. This is most easily seen when someone is climbing for the first time and they cannot 'read' the rock, they will not have a sense of where the next hold will be in relation to their current body position, and their untrained body will not be telling them where the next likely and optimal move will be, their hand may flail all over the rock trying to find the next hold (this aspect will become more obvious in the 'Bouldering Game' below).

Starting to Climb

Climbers feel the rock not just to test for its solidity, but for the texture and 'grain' of the rock, so as to understand its affordance for 'holds' and when using 'gear' its ability to 'take and hold' climbing aids. Different types of rock, even of similar format shapes and angles, have different properties key to its climbing affordances. This is not just applicable to types of rock, as the same types of rock have different affordance relating to whether they are coastal or inland, the weather they have been subject to (over time and recently), and even whether they face North, East, South or West. Additionally all these factors combine and need to be understood, to some degree, when deciding on when and how to climb a 'route' as they will inform the assessment of 'holds' and the 'limits of practical risk taking'.

When starting to climb a route in a pair, the 'lead' climber is attached to the end of a rope via their harness and attached to the 'second' who belays the rope out to the lead. The 'second' runs the rope through a belay device on their harness which can be used as a 'lock' preventing any more rope going through if the climber falls (they may supplement this by stepping away from the rock and thus shortening the amount of slack rope between the two climbers). This only works once the 'lead' has put the first bit of 'gear' into the rock and secured the rope to a point on the rock face – unless climbing the second or more pitch on a multi-pitch climb where the belayer will be secured to the rock face (which also ensure that both do not come off if the 'lead' falls). This ensures that the 'lead' climber on a tight rope falls only the distance they are above the 'gear' plus that same distance below, as long as the 'gear' holds. As long as this is less than the distance from the 'lead' to the ground they should be safe, although they may swing into the rock face like a pendulum, but that is dependant on factors such as the shape of the rock face, angle of body to 'gear', the distance fallen and the placement of the 'gear' in relation the above factors. If the 'gear' 'fails' the equation is the distance to the next piece of 'gear' and same below – hence the importance of not leaving too big a distance between placing 'gear' in the rock (route grades are harder, for equivalent technically difficult climbs the less places there are to place 'gear').

This draws our attention to one of the key skills of the 'belayer', as the other factor influencing the distance of the fall is the amount of rope that has been fed out to the 'lead' climber, if the distance above the gear is two metres then the climber will fall four metres, but only if there is no slack rope (which there usually is). Consequently, one of the skills of the 'belayer' is to feed enough slack rope out to allow the lead to move freely, but not have any more slack in the ropes than necessary. Thus the 'belayer' has to be able to judge what the 'lead' climber requires and they can do this by reading what the lead is doing and what the requirements of the rock and the 'moves' are at all stages of the 'lead' climber's assent. It is not uncommon for the 'lead' climbers to shout to the 'belayer' to give them 'more slack' on the rope when it has become too tight and hampering their freedom of movement. They also may shout for the 'belayer' to 'take in the slack' on the rope when they are about to make a move, or are in a precarious position, where there is a chance of them falling. This is especially the case when the 'lead' climber has moved out of the direct line of sight of the 'belayer', although experienced climbers when 'belaying' can 'read the ropes' by their movement and tension, Taking-in the 'slack' and 'giving slack' more appropriately than more inexperienced climbers, even when out of direct line of sight of the 'lead' climber, thus cutting down of the verbal communication between climbers. Although they may well be shouting up words of encouragement throughout the climb, and the lead shouting down advice on difficulties the 'second' may encounter on their assent up the same route. This information exchange can be seen as an on-going activity of mutual co-ordination of activity and understanding of the problem in specific, and the route in general.

When the 'second' is watching the 'lead' climber, they are also engaged in judging whether, and how, the lead is climbing well or badly which their belaying activities reflect. The 'second' will also potentially see the 'lead' climber come across problems that were not visible from the ground when they made a joint assessment of the rock. The 'second' will also, depending on visibility, also be able to see how the 'lead' undertakes overcoming the problems that were visible from the ground. Hence the 'second' will be taking a keen interest in the actions of the 'lead' climber not just for safety reasons, but because they can learn from them in seeing what 'moves' were successful, and from their mistakes what were possible alternatives, and thus be in a better position to know what they have to, and can do, when it is their turn. So the 'second' has the advantage of getting a 'reading' of the rock with a climber on it, this not only shows them where the route is, and how it was climbed, but also a 'human-scale' view of the shape of the rock and distances between 'holds' and 'moves'. The 'lead' climber will also make visible the potential difficulty of the climb ahead for them which thus far had been potentially only a textual description in a guidebook (and assigned 'grades'), and from the visible reading of the rock from the ground (and what tactile information can be felt at ground level about the rock). Communication may be verbal but less so with experienced climbers. The 'second' may be able to see the on-going physical reading of the rock made by the hands and feet of the 'lead' climber, to the experienced climber this can be seen as almost the equivalent of an 'oral reading' by the lead in terms of its presentation of information to the second and is a key aspect of interaction and information sharing. Indeed, often the 'lead' climbers will exaggerate aspects of their tactile explorations and route finding for the benefit of the 'second', these may or may not be accompanied by oral accounts of their activities. This is especially the case when the 'lead' climber comes across loose rock which will not support a climbers weight, or a particularly hard to find hold or difficult move. This is all information the 'second' will 'absorb' and potentially utilize when they come to climb. Another key piece of information they will be able to glean from the first climb's assent is the location of potential resting places on the way up, this is important in that it allows the second to better judge their energy expenditure on the various moves and also avoiding 'burning out' in inadequate rest places when better ones are available (rest place on climbs may nevertheless still require the use of energy if they are not good). So the 'second' will potentially have a lot more information when they come to climb than the 'lead' climber had, the route will have been 'picked out', with a physical and oral reading of the route for them by the 'lead' climber and they will use this information as they ascend the route themselves. It is not surprising then that it is the 'lead' climber that gets the 'glory' for the assent of a particular pitch, although they are facilitated by the 'second' in terms of discussion of the rock and route, the safety of the 'lead' climbers is facilitated through good belaying, and through verbal encouragement and information giving. As well as shouting up encouragement to the 'lead' climber, the 'second' may also shout out instructions to the 'lead' should they get 'into difficulty' and the 'second' can be in a position to see where a potential solution to the problem may lie. Although on the whole shouting is seen as a dis-preferred activity at the rock face especially by experienced climbers.

2. The Bouldering Game

Bouldering, is a climbing game in which the only technology used to climb is that of shoes, chalk and clothing choice (although small brushes may be used for cleaning excess chalk before climbing). Frequently climbing mats are used, these are placed underneath the area where the climber is climbing, because although the climber in bouldering is, by definition, not very high off the ground, they may be horizontal across the rock and even facing head-down to some degree. The mats are used to allow such manoeuvres while minimizing the impact of landing badly, especially as the ground around the boulder may be strewn with rocks and associated sharp debris. Bouldering, because it is a sport about problems, rather than routes as such (although routes are involved they are usually short) allows us to see some practices of climbing close up – often not possible on crag routes where climbers may be tens, or hundreds of feet off the ground.

Preparation for bouldering is much like that for climbing crags, and guide books are increasingly available for initial orientation and referencing, what is different is that most of the route is likely to be visible, and much of it even touchable, from ground level. This allows a great deal more inspection of the problems to be encountered by the climber and if they are climbing with another the discussion of the route and the problems more amenable to detailed discussion and the 'seeing' of them facilitated by the touch and tactile engagement of a 'Braille-like' reading. This allows a greater discussion of the actual feel of the rock and the affordances of the various holds themselves. As mentioned above, bouldering does not require a 'belayer' instead a climbing partner, when not climbing alone, may be used as a 'spotter'. A spotter's role is to closely watch the climber and to move the climbing mat so that it is underneath the climber at all times. In addition to this the spotter will position themselves underneath, or some other suitable position, so that they can support the climber should they fall or guide their falling body feet downwards and towards the mat so they are less likely to injure themselves. This close collaboration of the spotter also allows them a close view of the actual moves and choices of the climber, since the climber may be in touching distance for much, if not all, of the route. This close viewing can allow them to gain a reading of the rock with the climber on which will facilitate their attempt should they be attempting the same route, which they are likely to be doing so.

Sequences of Action

What becomes clear when watching climbers on boulders, and applicable to other types of climbing, are the sequences of action. Climbers 'envision' a move and then move, then 'envision' and move. A 'move' may be of just one limb at a time or a set of body movements before the body comes to a rest, if momentarily, this is then repeated until the 'problem' or route is completed (or one fails the route, i.e. comes off the rock or touches the ground in some fashion). It could also be described as see-touch-move, although that is a 'gloss' of the details of the actual practice and locally situated details of each of those elements. This moving is not just about the next move, and this is especially so in bouldering, the moves must be thought about in terms of two or three or more moves ahead, somewhat like in chess or snooker, but the moves are not of inanimate objects but the climbers own body. Boulders will often shut their eyes and envision the moves required as preparation prior to actually climbing. The 'problem' is how to move across the rock in a sequential order, while staying on the rock usually with only the most tenuous 'holds' for feet and hands, and in often contorted positions. The task is to get one's body in a certain position so as to move across the rock using difficult holds requiring great skill, agility and athleticism, to do so using as little energy as possibly (bouldering usually involves bursts of intense energy use), this usually requires a smooth series of movements – a fluidity of motions – which is aesthetically pleasing both to the climber and any observer of the 'moves'. This produces a kinesthetic which is embodied in the actions of the climber and felt as an aesthetic by them, it is seen as aesthetic by the viewer, but the climber themselves will usually never see the visual aspect unless they are being videoed.

Tacticity and Body Position

We have mentioned the envisioning of the 'next move' in the sequential progression of 'moves', this envisioning is not just a visual activity, but a tactile and physical envisioning. This is especially the case when 'holds' have been felt previously, either when examining the rock prior to the 'climb' itself or on previous attempts at boulder 'problem'. Boulder problems are usually difficult and involve frequent failures and require a number of further attempts, indeed this is one of the reasons they are rarely high off the ground. Rarely are they achieved on the first attempt, or 'flashed' as a successful first attempt is known, unless one is climbing at grades below what one can climb at when pushing one's limits.

Climbers may spend some time warming up on easier graded problems before tackling a harder or higher graded problem, but these 'lesser' routes or 'problems' are not really significant as the climber is usually trying to 'push' themselves to higher grades of route – higher-grade routes mean not only that the climber feels their abilities are progressing but especially in the 'Bouldering Game' there are also high kudos and status values attached to the ability to climb higher grades. The smoothness of movement, or 'style' of the climber (not to be confused with 'styles of climbing' as the various climbing games e.g. traditional, bouldering, sport and mountaineering etc. are often termed) involves not just the actual move itself, but the preparation when the climber may be static on the rock in terms of their hand and foot positions, but moving their head and torso so as to gain various views and perspectives on the next, or following moves and the position of hand and footholds. Reaching for new holds, whether with the hand or foot, is not just about 'grasping' the rock firmly or securely as possible. The touching of rock when 'feeling a hold' involves moving the body in accordance with the amount of grip or purchase that that hold allows, judging the amount of weight that can be put on it (and personally how much weight the climber's own muscle and tendon strength allows), how many fingers or amount of foothold the 'hold' allows to be used. All of this is in constant negotiation with the position of the body and affordance of the other 'holds' being used at the same time and how these develop or change as new moves are made and body position alters.

All the time the climber is trying to maintain their balance on the rock and fight against gravity, which in bouldering especially is a key aspect of the difficulty of many of the moves and requires both strength and stamina as well as agility and flexibility of the body. The climber is continually negotiating these aspects with respect to the affordances of the rock and requirements of the 'problem' or 'route'. Although only one hand may have moved position it will have usually required a redistribution of body weight across the rock and on the holds being currently used, this will be done tentatively to assess not just the new hold, but also the viability of the existing holds and a decision made as whether to stick with that move or to return to the previous position (if still possible).

How much strain is used to maintain a hold will depend upon the 'strength' of the climber at that time, the amount of time to be in that position, and the requirement of being in that position to progress through the 'problem' and move on through the route. Once in a position the body weight and stress may be able to be redistributed without any moving of the hand and foot holds, and thus gaining more stability and less stress on the body (with a resulting saving of energy and ability to hold the position longer). This may, or may not, involve some minor adjustments to the hand and foot positions to get into the best stable position, what may be termed 'micro' adjustment which may involve little more than pressure shifts from finger to finger. The climber will not keep this stable position for long, unless they are taking a rest, otherwise it is just to prepare for the next move.

The preparation for the next move, will likely require a certain amount of body shifting including some degree of destabilizing of the body as weight and relative 'grip' on 'holds' are realigned to allow the release of one of the limbs from its current 'hold' to search for the next 'hold' in the sequence of 'moves'. As suggested, while this is partly visual and partly from a memory of what the rock looked like when it was read from the ground, the limb itself will feel the rock for a 'hold', that is then checked for 'grip' and 'support' that will facilitate the rest of the body in the stabilization of body weight and progress to the following 'move' on the 'problem' or 'route'.

So there are a lot of practical sensorial activities and continual monitoring of both touch and bodily position on the rock, as well as on-going issues of 'grip' or 'hold' on the rock. These are in turn continually monitored in terms of gravitational forces of the body and the amount of pain from maintaining the 'holds' and the abrasion on the body, both of which are sources of pain. There is a lot of muscular tension when 'holding' a position and the less time doing so the better as climbers can 'pump out' as the lactic acid builds up in the muscles and muscles start 'cramping up' and ceasing to function. Holding a position is best done from a less stressful 'resting' position (the possibilities for which are less common in bouldering than in crag climbing) if the route allows it. 'Resting' positions while potentially less stressful on the body rarely entail actual 'rest', but are positions creating relatively less lactic acid and potentially allowing some movement of the limbs to counteract the build of the lactic acid that has already occurred. Continual movement on a boulder climb is usually preferred if possible, and when achieved gives the climb its smooth flow and aesthetic sense. Of course there are some moves, principally dynamic 'leaps' for 'holds', that require a pause to prepare the body for the 'whole body' action of the move – in contrast to the movement of predominantly one limb and readjustment of others. Nevertheless, depending on the severity and nature of the route, and the fitness and skill of the climber, there is only a certain amount of time to do a 'problem' or 'route' before the climber has to 'drop off' due to exhaustion and inability to 'hold' onto the rock: it is at this point the 'spotter' is required to minimalize the consequences of the 'drop off'.

'Spotting'

Although arguably the most important role of the 'spotter' is to do this task when the 'climber' drops off suddenly in mid move, this requires the 'spotter' paying keen attention to the progress of the climb and seeing where the difficulties and potential falls may occur. This requires not just a reading of the rock, but the continual monitoring of the climbers physical signs of stress and loss of strength. This may be through verbal interaction but is usually through monitoring general body movement and muscle 'tremors', so the 'spotter' is reading the rock and the climber for signs of a 'fall'. The climber themselves will be monitoring their own body for signs of loss of strength, ability to grip and the effects of lactic acid build up. It is better for them to do a controlled 'drop off' than it is to fail mid-move and risk potential harm. (They can rest and recuperate until their strength is back and try again, potentially only a few minutes later. So they have to make a judgement about where to keep going, which they may do if they are close to finishing, or to try again getting to the same position while retaining more energy and strength so as to have a greater chance of success on the 'problem' or 'route', i.e., having learnt from their attempts thus far, and to attempt to get to the same position again but with better 'style' and thus retaining more strength for the next 'move'.) Alternatively climbers may retrace their route backwards to get to a position where they can rest, before attempting to re-climb a 'move' or 'problem' they have not been able to negotiate. Although retracing is more likely in crag climbing as 'bouldering problems' are usually so short and low off the ground it is easier to do a controlled 'drop off' and start again. Although this option also allows a better recovery, a renewed analysis of the 'problem' from the ground and a discussion with the 'spotter' (and other climbers, as more than one 'spotter' may be being used) as to the nature of the problem, it is not always taken. When they do this another climber, often the 'spotter', may attempt the same 'problem' or 'route', and hence roles swapped, as the first climber will have been seen to have had 'their go' – one competitive reason for not 'dropping off'. Of course such turn-taking is locally negotiated and the 'problem' may be beyond the 'grade' of the other climber(s) and thus not attempted, although even if this is the case they will usually be inspecting the rock from a climber's perspective and discussing its 'features' and 'moves' with the other climber. Finally, as with the 'second' on crag routes, the 'spotter' gives verbal encouragement to the climber and may also direct them as to the position of potential holds, which they can see from their position slightly back from the rock and the climber cannot see due to their closeness to it.

Tactile Envisioning

We have stated that the climbers view the rock from the ground, and in bouldering especially, they can physically touch many of the potential 'holds' that they will be required to use to complete the 'problem' or 'route'. They may, from the ground, 'envision' the climb and not just visually but by feeling the 'holds' they will use sequentially. Thus, the envisioning is a tactile and haptic exercise, as well as a visual one. One of the reasons for this is that when they are actually climbing, and they cannot see a hold, they can feel for it with their hands or feet and recognize it as the 'hold' they are 'looking' for. This is the 'Braille' reading of the rock mentioned above. Of course, on the rock they may be at a different angle to the 'hold' than they were on the ground, but on the ground as part of their envisioning the experienced climber will anticipated the angle their body will be at on the climb and try to simulate that from the ground by angling their body to that anticipated in the climb. Climbers see the rock and see potential 'holds' which may give them 'purchase' on the rock to allow them to climb. However, it is only by actually touching the rock and testing its 'features' physically that the climber will 'know' if they can potentially use it. They need to 'put some weight on it' to test its robustness, i.e. that it will not dislodge from the rest of the rock when used, and also that it allows sufficient 'grip'. A hold may allow 'grip' but if it does not do so in the context of a sequence of moves, in combination with the position of other limbs and their 'holds', at a certain body angle, and with the potential dynamic movement, it may not be useful and an alternative may have to be sought. Often a 'hold' with lesser 'grip' but in a better position may be preferable, it is the skill of the climber to make these judgements and they can only be done through a combination of visual, tactile, haptic and kinesthetic judgements. It must be remembered holds are tested to see what effect they have on the muscles and tendons of the body, as related to the position of the rest of the body and their 'holds' (as noted above).

Individual Considerations

Climbers have to 'understand' the rock that they are going to be climbing on. Different climbers prefer climbing on different types of rock, this preference may be due to factors such as their 'skill-set' and their body 'structure', e.g., climbers are of different 'builds', and some types of rock (and specific rock formations) favour one 'build' over another. On such a site a less capable climber may out perform a more gifted one due to their build and type of body strength, or climbers capable of the same technical grades may have different difficulties on the same 'route'. A simple example is the advantage of being tall and being able to make long reaches for 'holds' on slabs of rock with few features, yet this tallness can be a disadvantage for 'problems' and 'routes' in cramped spaces where moves are closer together. Consequently when climbers of different builds are climbing together they may encounter and resolve 'problems' differently on a route, issues which are key in deciding what routes to climb, and who should lead each pitch – obviously one choice (but only one factor in the decision-making) is to let the climber best suited to lead each pitch (where possible).

By Way of a Discussion

This chapter on the 'Games of Rock Climbing' while entitled 'Playing Dangerously' has attempted to describe rock climbing members' practices which are about mitigating risk while achieving the goals of climbing 'routes' and overcoming 'problems' in a quite literal sense. The focus has not been on explicating ethnomethodology but describing practices of climbers and hopefully encouraging others to do so too. While attempting to give a description of rock climbing and some small description of practices, I have been interested in these activities and attempted to articulate their relationship to the perceptual modalities involved. This has been done cautiously since 'for ethnomethodologists there is a very, very serious question to be asked about the warrant for using any concepts at all apart from those which are familiar to, and understandable by, those people subjected to study' (Randall and Sharrock 2011: 18). Coulter and Parsons (1991) have noted the limitations of theories of visual perception to one or two modalities: 'seeing', 'looking' and 'scanning'. They focus on the logic of perceptual grammar critiquing the homogenizing of visual orientation and of the human ecological environment, critiquing on the way some aspects of the work of Harvey Sacks and Charles Goodwin. This chapter has no theoretical critique to make and certainly has not addressed the theoretical (or otherwise) literature on perception, but while it has been concerned with describing the practices of rock climbing it is evident that there are a number of praxiological activities involved. What is evident is that the perceptual activities are multiple, varied and embodied in the on-going and emergent order of climbing activities of a situated ecology (environmental, technical, social, communicative and perceptual etc.) of practice. Like Coulter and Parsons I would therefore advocate perception as being grounded in the practice of human activity, and that those perceptual practices explicated not as theoretical constructs, the weaknesses of which as isolated senses Coulter and Parsons clearly expose. Rock climbing is one, and in my view a very good one, practical accomplishment (Garfinkel and Sacks 1970) which would allow further ethnomethodological explication of 'perception in practice' as advocated by Coulter and Parsons (1991). Readers will have noticed parallels in this description of rock climbing to the 'professional vision' Goodwin (1994) describes, and indeed one of my ways into this study was originally by considering rock climbing as involving a 'professional vision' of sorts, which indeed I would argue it does. However, in many ways the actual climbing of the rock involves practices which are more akin to those described by David Sudnow (1978) in his 'Ways of the hand'. I was amazed on returning to Sudnow, after having described rock climbing above, at the similarities between learning to rock climb and learning to play the piano as Sudnow describes it, indeed at times his description could be of learning to climb when he talks of 'modalities of reaching' and how 'looking's workload progressively lightens for finding distances ... as places gradually become places towards which appreciative fingers, hand and arm are aimed' (p. 12), and that 'I was gaining a sense of their location by going to them, experiencing a rate of movement and distance required at varying tempos, and developing thereby, an embodied way of accomplishing distances' (p. 12).

To conclude, rock climbing, as I hope I have in some way described, is a complex practical accomplishment with numerous facets that need further investigation. Previous studies of 'work' and 'play' can be drawn upon to facilitate this by way of 'generic' practices and inspiring studies, although in the end it is the practice of climbing rock that is the phenomenon which should be their source and as is yet, only understood by the climbers themselves. Hopefully, while the specific climbs on which the description is based are not focused upon but back-grounded and their details used to provide a description, this description will be in some sense programmatic and provoke interest in these topics to be followed up by more focused research.

Chapter 9

Distance Running as Play/Work: Training-Together as a Joint Accomplishment

John Hockey and Jacquelyn Allen-Collinson

Introduction

This chapter considers a mundane activity that can be characterized as both hard (physical) work and 'play' of a certain kind, in that it can be undertaken as a pleasurable, playful and relaxing leisure activity. For us as 'veteran' runners, apart from in the early days of our youthful running biographies, when first introduced to running as a 'fun' leisure activity, running constitutes an activity we define as mundane, but 'serious leisure' (Stebbins 1993, 2011), immersing us in a culture of commitment in leisure (Tomlinson 1993). We briefly describe below our running biographies in order to situate the ethnomethodological analysis of our 'running-together' as a crafted co-production, accomplished on a quasi daily basis over many years. Whilst running is therefore defined as a 'serious' activity for us, it also constitutes outdoors 'play' when juxtaposed against the long hours of arduous 'headwork' indoors, as required by our paid jobs as academics. In order to address our topic of running-together (specifically in training, rather than in racing), this chapter is structured as follows. We first examine the general theoretical framework of ethnomethodology, and consider the literature that utilizes an ethnomethodological approach to sports and physical activity participation, as this body of work relates more directly to our own lived experience of running than does literature examining other forms of 'play', such as the game of chequers/ checkers (Livingston 2006), for example. We then proceed to describe briefly the collaborative autoethnographical/autophenomenographical research project from which our illustrative data are drawn, before portraying these data via an ethnomethodological analytic lens.

Ethnomethodological Groundings

Four recent literature reviews (Allen-Collinson 2009; Haldrup and Larsen 2006; Hockey and Allen-Collinson 2007; Sparkes 2009) indicate that research into the phenomenological ground of actually 'doing sport' is currently underdeveloped.

Whilst there is a substantial literature focused upon more abstract theorizations of sport (e.g., Maguire and Young 2002) there has been relatively little linkage between this level of analysis and the phenomenological ground of the activities themselves, although there are some exceptions with regard to phenomenological investigations rather than ethnomethodological analyses specifically (see for example, Merleau-Pontian perspectives on football/soccer (Hemphill 2005; Hughson and Inglis 2002); yoga practice (Morley 2001), female distance running (Allen-Collinson 2011a) and sporting embodiment more generally (Hockey and Allen-Collinson 2007a). Without a 'grounded' analytic connection, it can be argued, the foundational adequacy of theories about sport remains open to question. So the challenge is not so much to establish the theoretical problem of order, which allows sporting activities to be accomplished, but rather to establish analytically the empirical production of order on singular occasions, as Lynch (2001) highlights; a production which is repeated each time the sport is practised. This chapter seeks to subject to analysis and to interrogate such a production, in this case a co-production: the routine, mundane, practical activity of running-together in training, as accomplished by two distance runners.

The theoretical perspective employed here derives primarily from the phenomenology of Alfred Schutz (1967), elements of which focus upon the ways in which individuals construct and manage routine social life using a 'stock of knowledge at hand', constituted of sedimentations of previous experience, permitting them to make sense of particular contexts. The great epistemological problem for Schutz was discovering *how* such common-sense understanding is possible. In his formulation, common-sense knowledge is constituted of *typifications*, the common-sense constructs which individuals use to order the social world on a moment-to-moment basis, and which: 'organize our impressions, at the start, into objects, events, and categories and so structure our experience' (Benson and Hughes 1983: 53). In applying Schutzian insights to the study of members' methods for producing everyday social order, Harold Garfinkel (1967) developed ethnomethodology, the study of 'the common-sense reasoning skills and abilities through which ordinary members of a culture produce and recognise intelligible courses of action' (Heritage 1989: 21); succinctly put: the processes 'members use to do "going about knowing the world"' (Benson and Hughes 1983: 56). Ethnomethodological research practice therefore focuses upon the detailed analysis of the precise ways in which social order is constructed and maintained at the micro-level of social interaction, and consequently demands the close empirical examination of the 'detailed and observable practices which make up the incarnate production of ordinary social facts' (Lynch et al. 1983: 206). Such practices are generally taken for granted in the routine, everyday scheme of things; for the most part they are based on tacitly held and operationalized assumptions, and so 'bracketing' and 'marking' them for analytic attention is one of the key tasks facing researchers within the phenomenological and ethnomethodological traditions (see Allen-Collinson 2011b, for a discussion of the challenges of epochē/ bracketing in relation to sporting activity).

Researchers employing ethnomethodological approaches have in general tended to focus predominantly on linguistic communication and conversational analysis, with a relative paucity of literature that addresses more 'bodyful' embodied practices (Goodwin 2003: 162), such as the art of walking (Ryave and Schenkein 1975), including walking the beat (Bittner 1967). Other embodied experiences that have been subjected to ethnomethodological attention include Sudnow's studies (1972, 1978) of looking and the gaze, and of piano playing, Sharrock and Anderson's (1979) examination of the use of hospital signs, and Lee and Watson's (1993) consideration of interaction in public spaces. Ethnomethodological analyses have also addressed bodily and sensory impairments, such as Goode's (1994) in-depth study of blind and deaf children, and Robillard's (1999) autobiographical analysis of the lived experience of Motor Neurone Disease. Ethnomethodologically grounded literature, which focuses on embodied action remains, however, relatively sparse. More specifically in relation to the field of sport, ethnomethodologists and ethnomethodologically-inspired work have paid scant attention to sporting practices generally and even less attention to addressing the more corporeally-grounded, embodied aspects of sporting practice (for example, Burke et al. 2008; Fele 2008; Kew 1986; Miller 1998), with a few exceptions (for example, Coates 1999; Hockey and Allen-Collinson 2006). Despite this relative lacuna vis-à-vis sport and embodiment, the ethnomethodological approach offers a potent and insightful perspective, given its analytic focus upon precisely *how* people go about doing things; highly apposite for the case at hand, namely investigating *how* distance runners go about the accomplishment of running-together in training. We now proceed briefly to portray a collaborative autoethnographic/autophenomenographic research project from which our illustrative data are drawn.

The Autoethnographic/Autophenomenographic Production

Whilst undoubtedly still having its critics (see for example, Atkinson and Delamont 2006) autoethnography is an autobiographical research genre that has in recent years developed a substantial corpus of work, and a number of proponents have posited powerful justifications for its use, including in relation to researching sporting activity (e.g., Allen-Collinson and Hockey 2005; Sparkes 2000). Autoethnography emphasizes the linkage between themes within the researcher/ author's own lived experience and broader cultural and subcultural processes, and analytic forms of autoethnography seek to situate these themes within a theoretical framework. In order to contextualize the context and events described below, and the collaborative autoethnographic project in which we engaged, it is first of all necessary to make visible some 'accountable' knowledge in terms of our individual and collective athletic biographies. We both have been involved in distance running for several decades and now, in our 60s and 50s respectively, are categorized as 'veteran runners' within the UK classification system. We ran and trained together habitually for 19 years, and raced over distances ranging from 5 miles to marathons. This required a commitment to training together 6 or 7 days a week, on occasion twice a day. In effect we are experienced, committed, 'serious' distance runners and fulfil Garfinkel's (2002: 175) 'unique adequacy requirement', namely that of possessing in-depth, insider knowledge of doing distance running. Coincidentally, during one stormy, wind-swept November week some years ago, we both suffered quite severe knee injuries. Almost from the onset of these injuries, we came to define the situation as substantially worse than the usual 'bodily niggles' which plague the habitual runner.

    We quite rapidly arrived at a collective decision systematically to document our lived experience of the injury and rehabilitation process, which, together with its detailed documentation, took a full two years before, with relief, we were able to return to full running fitness. With regard to the data collection process, as runners we were well used to the habitual maintenance of running logs detailing daily training performance, and thus the discipline of daily recording of information was already in situ. Rather than compiling just our usual individual training logs, we instead constructed logs on the process of injury-rehabilitation, which also encompassed our collective and individual endeavours to return to the status of fully functioning athletes. Each of us constructed a personal log (indicated as Log 1 and Log 2 respectively in the extracts from field notes provided below) which was individually and jointly interrogated for emerging themes using a form of the constant comparative method (Charmaz 2006). We then created a third collaborative log detailing these joint themes. Micro tape recorders and notebooks constituted the means of recording our daily experiences; tape recordings were transcribed and the collaborative log constructed within a day or two of events occurring. We subsequently analysed and re-analysed our log entries, employing processes of re-memory (Sanders-Bustle and Oliver 2001) to send ourselves back in time to try evocatively to recapture the lived experience.

    Commensurate with the phenomenological bracketing practice of *epochē* (from the Greek: to abstain, or keep a distance from), where the researcher aims temporarily to set aside her/his pre-suppositions about what is claimed to be 'known' about a phenomenon in order to approach it freshly, without prejudgment, we undertook a rigorous and detailed questioning of the previously held tacit assumptions surrounding our accomplishment of running and running-together. Via this bracketing process, we also became aware of a substantial, shared 'stock of knowledge' (Benson and Hughes 1983: 52) that we had previously taken for granted when engaged in the everyday practice of running. The detailed documentation of this stock of 'tacit knowledge' (Watson 2006) was added to our initial analytical task, that of recording our responses to the injury and rehabilitation process. A further key bracketing practice in relation to running-together has been, due to the vagaries of life circumstances, enforced running-apart for the past six years when one of us moved in order to take up a job elsewhere. Solo running has, for us both, highlighted many of our prior assumptions and suppositions surrounding training for distance running and more significantly for the purposes of this chapter, regarding running-together. It also became apparent during the data analysis process that many of our experiences had a phenomenological grounding, and so the collaborative project could be deemed autophenomenographic (see Allen-Collinson 2011b for a detailed discussion) as well as autoethnographic. In autophenomenographic studies, the researcher analyses her/his own experiences of a phenomenon rather than of a 'cultural place' (as would be the case in an autoethnographic study). Autophenomenography is thus an autobiographical genre in which the phenomenological researcher is both researcher and participant in her/study of a particular phenomenon or phenomena, rather than of a particular *ethnós* (social group sharing a common (sub)culture), and subjects her/his own lived experience to sustained, rigorous sociological-phenomenological analysis.

The analysis that follows is based on the running project data and constitutes an example of what Kew (1986: 308) has termed 'ethnomethodological ethnography', a tradition that focuses upon the 'accounting practices' that social actors use to manage social order; accountable in that they are also observable and reportable (Sharrock and Anderson 1986: 56). In the case at hand, the practices are those which sustain the routine, daily training regime of distance runners, which we next describe in relation to doing training.

Training as a Joint Production

For almost 20 years we regularly trained together, often six or seven days a week. One of us (male) has over 40 years' experience of distance running, whilst the other (female) has 25 years' experience of middle/long-distance running. Nowadays, we do not undertake running training in order to win races, and although acknowledging that in common with many serious runners, we 'regularly (run) further and faster than fitness for health would demand' (Smith 2000: 190), nevertheless we run primarily for the physical and psychological health benefits afforded and as a serious leisure activity. In Stebbins' (1993: 23) definition, serious leisure is the: 'systematic pursuit of an amateur, hobbyist, or volunteer activity sufficiently substantial and interesting for the participant to find a career there in the acquisition and expression of a combination of its special skills, knowledge and experience'.

Collaborative training for distance running involves joint ongoing practices by both athletes so as to sustain the activity in its 'distinctive orderliness' (Weeks 1996b: 205). This requires of participants considerable attention and effort so as to sustain a mutually but usually tacitly agreed pace together, given that runners are 'naturally', left to their own preferences, unlikely to run at the same pace when training alone. The key state which needs to be jointly produced is that of running-together in a condition of physical co-presence, one that is mutually recognizable as 'proper togethering' (Ryave and Schenkein 1975: 271). For if co-runners lose too great a degree of proximity, they cease to be co-runners and revert to a state of running-alone. With a background of running together habitually for nearly two decades we both possessed a stock of knowledge about how to do distance running personally, and also about each other as runners; knowledge which was utilized to maintain a mutual pace via the interrogation of a number of different mundane indicators, which we now proceed to portray.

Listening for the Other

A key way in which runners arrive at the judgment of pace – both their own and that of others with whom they are running (and racing) – is via an acute attentiveness to breathing patterns. When the running pace is tolerable there is an ease, a fluidity and stability to breathing patterns, which remains in operation, or is quickly re-established, even when there are changes in the terrain traversed demanding harder work, such as moving from flat ground to ascending a hill. Runners often become highly sensitized and attuned to the breathing patterns of their training partner(s) and, in the case of maintaining running-together, arrive at definitions of whether the pace has been set too high for the running partnership, and consequently requires adjustment, as one of our Log entries reveals:

> A bit of a rough session for J. this evening. Lots of heat all day and the humidity just builds relentlessly, and lots of pollen too, so pretty tough conditions for distance running – particularly for someone with asthma. Up the slope by the tennis courts she was labouring hard, and I could hear her breathing much more heavily than normal when she usually just floats up quietly. By the time we got to the bottom of the park she was sucking in the oxygen desperately like she was racing, so I dropped the pace and she gave me a little smile and grateful nod. (Log 1)

As well as breathing patterns, other auditory indicators were routinely used by us to assess toleration of pace. These were comprised of a gamut of grunting, blowing, sighing and groaning noises, providing the experienced practitioner with an indication of the degree of ease or discomfort experienced at different kinds of pace. In addition, when pace levels proved hard for us to maintain, one of us had a propensity to indulge in profuse, virulent and colourful swearing, a practice which the other used regularly to gauge the degree of physical difficulty her training partner was experiencing and so adjust her behaviour accordingly:

> Saturday morning and a well duff run for J. That good old Anglo Saxon F word erupted with passion every hundred metres or so. Still, it got him around 7 miles effectively enough, especially as he swore profusely about the cursed work leaving his legs dead for the running. We're both exhausted from the overwork at the moment, fed up of how it leaves us with nothing for the running. I know well by now that it's best for me at such junctures to leave him to his own devices, whilst I hang just behind his shoulder and let him set the pace. (Log 2)

A further, seasonally-specific auditory means for checking the proximity of our training partner came into play during the autumn months when running through paths strewn with fallen leaves provided a platform of sound indicating the closeness of the other runner. Interestingly, data analysis revealed that whilst directly questioning each other about tolerating the pace did occur, this was rare, as other aural indicators could be relied upon to provide the necessary information. On occasion, however, advance verbal warnings of likely 'form' were signalled immediately prior to training sessions, via vocabularic indicators that the running-body was not feeling particularly energetic or enthusiastic on that particular day. These usually took the form of utterances of the order of: 'this body/tracksuit or these/shoes/shorts sure don't want to get going tonight!'

Seeing the Other

When training habitually with another runner, one begins to accumulate and then utilize knowledge of her/his visible corporeal signals in order to maintain proximity via mutual pace. So, it gradually becomes apparent to the attentive observer exactly what constitutes a co-runner's 'normal' form when s/he is running with some degree of ease. This requires close attention and attentiveness to her/his routine postural and facial expressions, often via 'the glance' (Sudnow 1972). Given the importance for runners of ceaselessly scanning the terrain they are traversing, more prolonged visual checking of one's training partner is usually impossible. Thus, brief glances constitute an effective means of evaluating visible signs of the other's bodily experience of the training session. When facial indicators such as frowning, sunken eyes, tightened jaw or even grimacing are observed, these provide the considerate co-runner with 'intelligence' that can then be taken into account to achieve pace moderation in the light of the other's perceived difficulties in maintaining the pace. In a similar fashion, bodily posture is also visually checked and monitored. A partner's stride length, arm swing, angle of torso, degree of neck and shoulder tension are all taken into account. The interrogative glance also notes any repeated tripping, stumbling, general lateral movement, shuffling the feet, low gait, and generally looking 'disjointed'; all indicators that the pace of the session needs to be reduced for a while:

> When J. is running well, he is usually very compact, very neat, very efficient; he doesn't waste any energy in unnecessary movement. Conversely, when he's struggling, not running well, the contrast is immediately apparent. This morning was our last session of the week. He was really tired and his left arm, which normally swings straight front to back, started to swing across his body, trying to propel him forward against the fatigue. That always happens when he gets knackered, I've noticed (and remarked on it) over the years; it's like a red flag, because I know other 'symptoms' will usually follow: his stride length shortening, he begins to stumble and sway around, then I know I really do have

to ease off the pace a bit. Today, though, I was exhausted too, it's been a long hard haul at the office and chalk face, we need some chill-down time … (Log 2)

Not only are a running partner's physical bodily indicators used in order to gauge form, but even the form and movements of her/his shadow can, if falling in a certain way, provide useful visual indicators to the well-trained runner's eye.

Thus far, we have considered how an attentiveness to mundane aural and visual indicators is utilized in order to achieve a mutually acceptable pace, necessary to accomplish running-together; we now move on to address the ways in which we physically accomplished running-together when traversing the terrain of our specific training routes.

Choosing the Path and Leading the Way

Distance runners often train over routes that become well-known to them in terms of distance and the nature of the terrain, such as flat, gentle, hilly, smooth, uneven, rugged, and so on, selecting a route as appropriate to seasonal and meteorological conditions. Within each route there are a myriad of possibilities for selecting paths or 'ways', and when running together, these have to be jointly negotiated and navigated. It is beyond the scope of this particular chapter to interrogate a whole multiplicity of 'ways', so we will confine ourselves to examining some convergences and divergences or 'meeting' and 'parting' points on the run; points which demand mutual interpretation and anticipation so as to achieve 'synchrony' (Weeks 1996b). Our co-experience and stock of knowledge, developed and refined over years of co-running of certain routes, meant we achieved a high degree of familiarity vis-à-vis favoured paths, ways of traversing routes and our own running preferences. Habitually this resulted in a personal favouring of specific pathways across particular sections of particular routes; these personal preferences and also particular abilities were well-known to each other. So for example, one of us was usually a more sure-footed runner on precipitous or friable downhill sections and was liable to run away from the other over such terrain. The following field note illustrates how we negotiated such differences and divergences, and then met again to re-establish running-together:

> It's noticeable how we move apart and come back together again. J. has always been better than me at downhill running, she's more agile, supple and sure footed. It reminded me today when we were out running on the hills – she will go away from me in terms of pace, and plunge down (somewhat recklessly at times; but then she hasn't had so many fell-running injuries!) regardless of how rough the ground is. I'm slower, more cautious, considered, in terms of descending and I always try to choose a path as smooth as possible. So, at the bottom, she will usually run a little circle or run on the spot whilst looking at the view, so as to meet up with me again. (Log 1)

The reverse applied with regard to uphill running where the other partner, with stronger quadriceps, generally had a greater ability to ascend rapidly. When ascending steep hills, therefore, somewhere near the bottom of the hill constituted a parting point, whilst the summit constituted a meeting point. The habituated practice was for the individual in the lead briefly to circle around waiting for the other partner at meeting points, before proceeding on to the next section of the route. Parting and meeting points were many and varied over our running routes, mainly comprised of 'natural boundaries' (Ryave and Schenkein 1975: 266) such as changes in terrain where woods gave way to ploughed fields, or where there were 'man-made' boundaries such as roundabouts, road intersections, underpasses, and so on. All such points required ongoing attentiveness, and mutual recognition and anticipation in order for running-together to be accomplished. If one of us 'switched off' mentally for even a short period of time, running-together fragmented into running-alone, sometimes to the consternation of the partner who was, temporarily, left behind. Focused convergence activity was an ongoing process, requiring constant attention, given our individual differences across a whole range of factors, such as agility, sure-footedness, hill climbing/descending ability, leg speed and power, as well as day to day variations in individual 'form':

> I am hyper conscious of J.'s form on particular occasions. She can suffer from exercise-induced asthma, which is an absolute drag and means that pollen and pollution levels can impact on her running day to day. She can be having a good week of training generally, and then suddenly, for example if we're running in a traffic-heavy area with lots of exhaust fumes, she's having a really bad time. That happened today and she 'came off the back' all of a sudden – drifting well behind me. I think it was probably all the thick pollen through the fields. I was particularly aware of it when we hit any hills, even small ones, where I am normally stronger. Once I realized she was struggling, I eased the pace a bit, making sure she could still run fairly close behind. (Log 1)

Taking Precedence

Where training routes permitted, our normal practice was to run alongside each other, rather than in file. Sometimes, however, the path or terrain precluded this practice and single file running proved necessary. In such instances, convention concerning precedence was long established; the rule of thumb being that the more sure-footed partner led, so that she could, if necessary, shout back information about potential obstacles – human, animal and other (stones, rocks, pot holes, branches, pine cones, dog excrement, etc.) en route. On rare occasions, however, particularly when there was a degree of ambiguity as to whether single file running was necessary, 'disputes' over precedence did occur. These instances, our data analysis revealed, were often linked to recent changes in conditions, such as having suddenly to revert to more seasonally-appropriate routes, for example, a route that had not been used since the previous winter. Such instances generated the rare use of what might be termed 'performative utterances' (see Turner 1975 for a detailed discussion) where the talk – for someone with a member's knowledge – also referred to a specific action, for example:

> Running the park route during the long winter nights mostly depends on enough light filtering over to our route from the floodlights of the nearby athletics stadium. Usually it's fine when athletics training is scheduled, but occasionally for some unknown reason the lights are not on at the allotted hour or they go off suddenly. When that happens we are unexpectedly plunged into darkness. Usually we run side by side where the route around the park edge is barely lit by adjacent street lamps, the arcs of which provide just enough illumination for us to be able to make out a faint pathway over the grass. That's fine unless the floodlights go out suddenly, and we find ourselves at the section where the local mini golf course begins, with its deep, potentially ankle-twisting/breaking holes. Without the lighting, and without the summer flags in place to warn the unwary runner, the holes can be distinctly hazardous. My myopic eyes are pretty poor in the gloom, even in the twilight, so as we approach the golf hazard zone, J. often grunts, 'On me!' – meaning he should take the lead for that particular section and I must follow 'obediently' in his wake. Inevitably, that sometimes leads to a few strides of discontent, dispute and jostling, more often than not ritualised, sometimes jocular, together with pointed comments about my (woefully short of) 20/20 vision! (Log 2)

Accomplishing Training in Public Spaces

As Smith (1997: 60) has noted, the vast majority of UK distance runners' training is undertaken not in purpose-built athletic stadia but in the 'normatively ordered spaces' of 'public space', in which conduct is largely regulated via tacit, implicit conventions, approximating an informal 'code of the street' (Jimerson and Oware 2006). The 'public' is not of course a homogenous body with equal access rights, and the 'gendered' nature of such space has been signalled by many, including those utilizing a feminist framework (see for example, Allen-Collinson 2010; Wesely and Gaarder 2004). Given the largely indeterminate nature of conventions regulating behaviour in public places, walking pedestrians, cyclists and runners can constitute a 'navigational problem' (Ryave and Schenkein 1975) for each other, as do other creatures, such as pet dogs, sharing the same space but not the same 'rules' of conduct.

Researching the perceptions of pedestrians who habitually occupied the same public spaces as we did was beyond the remit of this particular research project, but the data did reveal a persistent patterned response by pedestrians to being confronted by speeding (on good days!) runners. In contrast to Ryave and Schenkein's (1975: 267–8) findings that solo walkers were expected to do walking-around those decidedly doing walking-together, we noted that whether running-alone or running-together through public space, it appeared that as runners *we* were generally deemed responsible for avoiding pedestrians, and not vice versa. So the particular, local social order seemed to be predicated on the assumption that doing walking was 'normal', 'unmarked' (Brekhus 1998) majority behaviour, whilst doing running was 'deviant', 'marked', minority behaviour. The attitude of the general walking public therefore appeared to be that runners should make every effort to take avoidance action with regard to walkers. If this navigational problem was not managed effectively and collision, or more likely near-collision occurred, walkers' responses ranged from indignant or angry shouts and pushing to disconcerted grumblings and utterances of irritation such as 'tut-tutting' (see also Smith 1997: 64). A possible rationale for the assumption that pedestrians should take precedence is that the public understanding of the 'official' use of public ways such as footpaths and pavements is that they are to be used primarily for *walking*. And/or it might be that walking pedestrians perceive runners as moving with greater velocity and therefore obliged to make allowance for walkers on the grounds of the latter's slower speed of movement, rather than the actual action of running *per se*. With regard to Ryave and Schenkein's (1975) observation that solo pedestrians are expected to do walking-around those doing walking-together, it could be that our running-together was not recognized as a proper togethering and so we were not accorded the usual courtesy of being walked-around. But these are speculative notions, our ethnomethodological analysis must remain with the observation of the repeated and patterned behaviour.

Whatever the social constructions and rationalizations held by walking pedestrians, in terms of their actual practices, they certainly adhered strongly to their perceived *right* of way:

> A tarmac path leads to the narrow, dark, dank underpass and on either side there is soft ground, often muddy and slippery, and also quite steeply angled and rough, difficult to run on. Normally we both run on the path. Often, however, there are individuals, linked couples or small groups of people walking there, strung right across our path. The usual behaviour, observed over many years, is for people to keep walking towards us either singly or in group formation, so that we are then forced to stride on to the soft, slippery ground on either side of them. It's not as if we are unseen, or come across these people unexpectedly, because we have monitored their eye contact regularly. It seems clear that they are doggedly determined to plod on regardless, and not cede space to us. So we are now well used to predicting their behaviour and therefore move on to the soft ground. Sometimes, though, we direct a quizzical look in their direction, just to challenge gently their presumptions! (Log 2)

One exception to the above routinized, patterned behaviour was the occasional case where (usually) middle-aged or older adults would graciously cede passage to us, and sometimes simultaneously make encouraging comments about our running performance. In addition it was also apparent from scrutinizing the data that another quite different informal rule of conduct pertained to very young children and human-accompanied dogs. It became clear to us that adult pedestrians perceived the latter categories of social actor as having little or no responsibility for taking avoidance action in the form of walking-around, and would on occasion command them to stand aside or would physically restrain them as runners approached. On the basis of careful and long-term observation, in the main, adult walkers expected runners to cede passage to them.

Doing serious distance running is an activity replete with injury potential due to the repetitive nature, high volume and considerable intensity of the training needed to sustain and improve running performance, and to compete in races. Runners not surprisingly become sensitized to injury as an ever present possibility (Howe 2004: 145–60); a threat which, if fulfilled, can ruin hundreds of miles of training in an instance, and abruptly end a whole competitive season. Threats of injury from the public via collision – accidental or deliberate – reinforce and heighten this sensitivity, particularly as the majority of serious distance runners are relatively slight in physique and liable to come off second best in such collisions! The problem of managing 'the public' and its 'auxiliaries', ranging from dogs, bicycles, skate boards, prams and pushchairs, to small children, constitutes an ongoing task when seeking to accomplish training in shared spaces. Hence, doing training-together often requires that each training partner be aware, sometimes acutely, of the safety of the other when doing running-together:

> Thinking about what happens when training, it's become apparent that part of training together is being aware of what's going on out there on the route. That awareness is for myself and also for J. We both have a litany of incidents when negative things have happened 'out there', so we monitor what is happening for each other. Sometimes she sees dodgy things developing faster than I do, and vice versa. I, for example, in my running time have had half a house brick dropped on my head from a railway bridge by a couple of under 10-year-olds, been attacked by a young Doberman Pincher in a Nottingham park and been hit in the left ear by a heavy handbag swung by a female teenager – 19 miles into a 20 mile training session on a summer Saturday afternoon, crossing the George Street bridge in Newport! All occasions when I was not aware enough. J. has been grabbed at, lunged at, bitten by a dog that sneaked up behind her, hit accidentally but very hard with a cricket bat wielded by a young lad ... That's been hammered home, so there is now a perpetual surveillance by both of us, of what is approaching down the road ... (Log 1)

Examining the data, it became clear that the most challenging and potentially threatening navigational problem we came to define as groups of adolescents and teenagers, who fit Smith's (1997: 61) Goffmanesque category of an 'idling congregation', often stumbled across in the environs of particular pubs or bars, known to be notoriously difficult to navigate when out running, and thus to be avoided if at all possible. Training 'out there' in public space, however, there was inevitably the possibility that such groups would be encountered unexpectedly.

Again, the local public golf course proved to be an area we defined as a potential danger zone, particularly when inhabited by troupes of teenagers:

> On the park in the spring and golf is in 'full swing'! Most of the time that's fine as it's families or adults participating. Sometimes though, like yesterday you get groups of teenagers playing. What they do, when the mood takes them, is to hit the ball directly at us or very near, often calling out 'fore' [meaning 'watch out afore'] at the last minute and then breaking into collective sniggers if they detect any reaction at all from us, the more anxious we look, the better, it seems! So we watch, we monitor, we periodically look ahead when out training, particular along certain routes. It's like a film unfolding, watching what's building up; often you've seen the same scenario play in front of you countless times before, so you know what action is likely to occur … Whichever of us sees that kind of troublesome group first will then mutter: 'idiots/dickheads to left/right/over there!', indicating to the other that it's definitely advisable to follow a different trajectory. Avoidance is the usual favoured strategy as there is no point in confronting the kids if they start that kind of rubbish. Anyway, confrontation requires stopping the training and the momentum of the run, and also, more seriously, might mean being hit by a stingingly hard golf ball in the quads or somewhere even more vulnerable, with consequent time off training if the bruising is very severe. In sum: not worth the hassle! (Log 2)

Once again, the combined interactional devices of the 'glance' (Sudnow 1972) and the 'performative utterance' (Turner 1975) came into play, to help us manage doing running-together, as safely as possible, in public places.

Concluding Comments

As Brekhus (1998: 36) has observed, the routine and mundane practices of everyday life are frequently left 'unmarked' and 'unaccented'. Thus, all too often the concrete practices of everyday life are unquestioningly taken for granted by sociologists, without being subjected to detailed analysis; sometimes unreflectively used as a resource for theory construction. The sociology of sport and 'play' is no exception, for at present there exist very few studies of a phenomenological or ethnomethodological persuasion, which examine *how* play, and more specifically in our case, how sport is actually done (Sparkes 2009). As Francis and Hester (2004: 26) note, following the ethnomethodological tradition demands that the researcher explicate 'the practitioner's knowledge and competence' and this chapter has attempted that task by portraying one example of 'members' methods' (Sacks 1992: 10–111) for doing running-together for distance running training. Despite the mundanity of this activity, the effort and concentration required to produce running-together should not be underestimated; this production work is complicated, embodied, interactional and social. Just how much concentration and practical work is required to accomplish running-together was regularly highlighted to both of us when contrasted with the demands of running-alone; the latter being a relatively easy solo production in comparison. It is hoped that this brief analysis has started to unveil and to provide some insight into the routine, mundane, but also complex and intricate practices involved in accomplishing running-together; a 'playtime' activity that also demands both hard body work and ongoing interactional achievement.

PART IV
Doing Stuff Together

Chapter 10

Playing in Irish Music Sessions

Peter Tolmie, Steve Benford and Mark Rouncefield

Introduction

Traditional Irish music sessions are a very distinctive form of social music making that have spread worldwide. Most major cities in Europe, North America and Australasia have at least one traditional session where Irish musicians gather to play together, almost always in pubs and bars, and, as such, they have become an important part of pub culture. Although Irish sessions can involve both music and musicians that are not Irish, the majority of the music played at such sessions is of Irish origin and competent musicians in the genre have a fairly clear idea of what 'counts' as being part of the 'Irish session' corpus, though this is of varying degrees of flexibility according to the venue.

The repertoire in these sessions includes thousands of tunes, with many being derived from folk dances such as reels, hornpipes, jigs, waltzes and polkas. The keys in which tunes are played are relatively limited, mostly G Major and D Major, and most of the instruments involved will play in unison with one another, with very little in the way of harmonization. Improvisation is typically about embellishment of the melodic line rather than free breaks such as might be encountered in other genres such as jazz. Usually one player starts off playing a tune, apparently unprompted, with others joining in. Tunes tend to be played a standard number of times and in a standard set. In addition there is a particular body of instruments likely to be involved, including fiddles, flutes, pennywhistles, melodeons, accordions, concertinas, and bodhrans (a kind of drum), guitars, banjos and mandolins, with some other instruments such as uilleann pipes (rather like bagpipes) appearing occasionally. Electronic instruments are frowned upon at most sessions.

Sessions are, on the one hand, hugely informal with the players typically sitting in a circle and coming and going as they please, with other activities in the pub going on around them. On the other hand, the musicians involved adhere to some surprisingly tight matters of etiquette and protocol, bound up with a strong rhetoric of tradition. This includes a whole body of other potential injunctions such as no written music, no breaks in style to other related folk genres, no overt indications of being rehearsed, no repetition of what has already been played that evening and, in some sessions at least, a reluctance to allow the intrusion of technology for activities such as recording. The writer and musician Barry Foy offers up the following characterizations of Irish music sessions:

'There's no "jamming" in Irish traditional music. Irish music is very specific: specific tunes in specific rhythms, played in specific ways in specific keys on specific instruments. You can't walk in to a session unprepared and unschooled and expect to bluff your way through it.'

'… a session is not an occasion for trotting out carefully wrought arrangements, stunts such as following a hornpipe with a reel and then back into another hornpipe, or breaking from a jig into a slipjig … Those kinds of things fall into the category of show biz …'. (Foy 2009)

In this chapter we take the apparently perverse route of insisting in particular upon the extent to which Irish music sessions are informed by the fact that they take place in public houses to underscore how the musical practices are *a part of* the way in which pub-going as an activity is constituted by those who are involved. Thus the study of session practices will reveal by turns how pub-going for Irish session musicians extends far beyond just the matter of them drinking a beer and socializing. It is found to ramify at the level of specific musical practices and how turn-taking mechanisms are organized amongst the musicians. Thus the ongoing constitution of a 'traditional' set of practices, the ordinary organization of an evening out with friends, and their orientations to a pub setting are found to be tightly interwoven in numerous different ways.

Prior Work

There is a relative paucity of ethnomethodological studies of music-making. This seems rather surprising given the centrality of Garfinkel's notion of the 'missing interactional what' (Garfinkel, unpublished manuscript 2) in ethnomethodological studies and its provenance. Here is Garfinkel making direct reference to observations by Sudnow to illuminate the matter:

> … David Sudnow epitomizes the issue as follows. On the basis of his studies of the gestural organization of ensemble musical play he speaks of the 'Howard Becker phenomenon' in sociologists' studies of jazz. To take Becker's studies for example we learn that there are jazz musicians, where they work, who they work with, what they earn, how they get their jobs, or what the audience will request of them. But … a curiosity of the reportage, Sudnow points out is that Becker's articles speak of musicians' work and do so by omitting entirely and exactly the practices that for those engaged in them makes of what they are doing …: making music … In that musicians are together in that place for the so-and-what they are doing, Becker's account takes on its character as the thing it **can** be about. But it can be about that in a singular way. Sudnow points out that even though it was written by a jazz musician, it is an **appreciation** of the work of jazz musicians. … (Garfinkel op cit.)

This chapter is not, however, the first ethnomethodological piece to tackle the practices of music-making. Sudnow (1978), for instance, provides a seminal account of the embodied practices of playing the piano in his book entitled *Ways of the Hand*. He made use of his own competence as a jazz pianist to systematically unravel and describe the embodied ways in which he accomplished the work of jazz improvisation. Peter Weeks produced a series of papers over the years looking at matters such as: the work of coordination amongst amateur musicians playing in a septet in order to regain and preserve temporal 'synchrony' (Weeks 1996b); the collective practices musicians use when playing together to accomplish *changes* in tempo (Weeks 1990); and the ways in which members of orchestras use both embodied practices and talk in order to work up how a piece of serious music should be performed (Weeks 1996a). Much of Weeks' work can be seen to be a working out of earlier observations by Alfred Schutz (1976) on the phenomenology of music. Schutz makes a couple of core observations that have proved influential for the more detailed examination of musical practice as an accomplished aspect of social interaction. One of these relates to the notion of all communicative practice, including musical practice, hinging upon what he calls a 'mutual tuning-in relationship'[1] whereby a 'vividly present *we*' can be experienced as part of the ongoing activities you are engaged in together. The other observation of moment is that 'the system of musical notation is merely a technical device and accidental to the social relationship prevailing among the performers'. It is the situated practices through which that social relationship unfolds in time that is core to how people 'make music together'.

Looking at Irish music sessions in particular, there are a number of texts, notably ethnomusicological ones, that explore aspects of them from a variety of perspectives. One of the core concerns amongst these works is the rising popularity of Irish music in recent years and the consequent 'commodification' of Irish music and its working up for tourists in Ireland (Kaul 1997, 2007). Other texts delve into the dynamics of various relationships within sessions themselves, hinging upon issues such as status (Hamilton 1999), gender (O'Shea 2008a, 2008b), the construction of community (O'Shea 2008b, Thurston 2010), and conflict (O'Shea 2006–2007). Other texts again seek only to paint a picture of sessions and their surrounding environment (Carson 1998), and others again focus upon the technical aspects of how the music is structured and instrumentalized (Carson 1986). To criticize ethnomusicological texts for having omitted to take on board the need to provide a *sociologically* adequate description of their phenomena would be inappropriate and unjust. However, a worry from an ethnomethodological point of view is that, whilst these studies can be found to exhibit certain merits, there are ways in which many of these too allow the very phenomenon of which they purport to be speaking – music-making – to slip away from them by focusing on

---

1 Brooker and Sharrock's chapter regarding 'remixing music together' in this volume can be seen to also be influenced by this concept.

other kinds of issues. Thus this chapter can be seen to fill a gap in just how these kinds of activities are currently being described and understood.

As a final caveat, Garfinkel and Sudnow's critiques of Becker's work (see Becker 1963) are, of course, both foundational and appropriate and have underpinned ethnomethodological discussions across any number of domains. However, what this chapter sets out to do is to demonstrate that, whilst Becker's approach was clearly lacking, there is an equivalent danger that it is important to offset. Whilst it was certainly not intended by Garfinkel that one should unduly focus upon the embodied practices of music-making as a wholly detachable and free-standing mechanism for the production of music, or anything else for that matter, there is a certain risk that the injunction against Becker and other conventional accounts might be read this way. What this chapter seeks to emphasize is that an exclusive focus upon the actual mechanics of making music to the exclusion of all else risks missing instead the critical ways in which machineries of interaction are made use of by members as machineries for the purposes of accomplishing highly specific things in highly specific settings, and it is only through this that such machineries come to have any sense at all. Thus this chapter will aim to unravel not just the work of musicians as musicians, but as musicians who are also actively engaged in the work of going to the pub and hanging out with friends, where the very nature of the particular pub and particular people hanging out there can come to have import for how the actual production of the music gets accomplished.

The Study

The data being used in this chapter relates to four different Irish music sessions, each with a markedly different character. All four sessions took place in pubs in cities in the midlands and north of the UK. One of them, the Vat and Fiddle, was very much focused upon playing traditional Irish music repertoire, but with some degree of tolerance for other genres. Another, the Hop Pole, displayed acceptance of a much broader range of genres and songs. Another session, the King Billy, was what was deemed locally to be one of the most expert sessions, with strict adherence to Irish repertoire and the level of playing tending to preclude the involvement of less experienced players. Finally, another fairly demanding session, the Oak Tree, was observed where, once again, most of the repertoire was Irish with some small tolerance for local Northumbrian music. The actual approach to gathering data during the sessions was for one person to actually participate in the session whilst another made video and audio recordings and took detailed notes. The primary goal was to understand how session participants organize and reason about their affairs. In particular, in view of the focus of this chapter, it is important note that, to uncover how Irish music sessions are an orderly local production of all those who are a party to them, one has to pay close attention to the organization of all of the local ecology i.e. the fact they are happening in a pub. After the sessions both researchers also reviewed the video and audio together, thereby enabling the participating member to explicate the finer nuances of situated reasoning as they were unfolding.

The Work of Playing In Irish Music Sessions

The Turn-taking Mechanism

At first sight the actual ways in which tunes get played in Irish music sessions appear to be tremendously informal and unstructured, with the production of music seeming to be wholly spontaneous and uncontrolled. However, for all of this apparent informality, there are ways in which Irish music sessions have a range of highly ordered characteristics, characteristics that are tightly bound up with how sessions unfold in a pub environment where the job in hand is as much about socializing with friends as it is about making music. This is not to relegate the music to something epiphenomenal to the social characteristics of the musicians involved (alla Becker). Rather it is to recognize that these two things go hand in hand and to ignore one or the other is to arrive at only a partial understanding of what is going on.

In the long-standing tradition of creative misreadings in ethnomethodology,[2] we make use of a well-known 'machinery' described in conversation analysis as 'the turn-taking mechanism'(Sacks et al. 1974). For Sacks, the elaboration of the turn-taking mechanism was not simply about explicating how members do talk but rather about how the methodic characteristics of talk provided for them doing the ordinary business of producing situatedly intelligible and account-ably ordinary orderly phenomena. It was, at heart, a mechanism for getting the job of ordinary everyday doings done. It provided, in its enactment, a *solution* for how to get those ordinary everyday doings done. And it did that in a wonderfully economic yet powerful way. It is in this spirit of solving the ordinary problems of producing ordinary orderliness that we are borrowing upon the turn-taking mechanism in this chapter. We are *not* suggesting that the production of talk and the production of music are just the same at the end of the day and subject to the same over-arching forces. We *are* saying that there are certain turn-taking akin phenomena at play in Irish music sessions, that these too offer up powerful and economic ways of getting the job done, given the nature of Irish music sessions and the environment in which they are seen to unfold, and that borrowing upon

---

2   Garfinkel (unpublished manuscript 1) suggested that the whole programme of ethnomethodology was, in a sense, a creative misreading of Wittgenstein. This is not an idle practice or just to be bloody-minded (though others might wish to ascribe this to us). It is rather to be productive because the misreading (or what is really more of an unanticipated application) leads to useful insights into the ways in which the local production of order is brought about.

some of Sacks' propositions gives us insight into how Irish music sessions are also orderly and coherent affairs. In subsequent parts of this chapter we shall seek to demonstrate just what we mean by this.

Before we explicate in greater detail what happens in sessions it is worth briefly glossing for the reader certain aspects of the turn-taking mechanism that were outlined in Sacks, Schegloff and Jefferson's seminal *A Simplest Systematics for Turn-Taking in Conversation* (Sacks et al. 1974). These are the features we want to focus upon and why they might be of interest:

1. Foundationally, and if chaos is not to ensue, *only one speaker may speak at once* (Sacks et al. 1974: 705–8). Much of the simplest systematics falls out of how the ordering of conversation serves to solve this fundamental problem so that orderly communication can take place. Clearly more than one musician can play at once so this is not, at first sight, a problem for Irish music sessions. However, Sacks et al. stress this to be about accomplishing the effective sequencing of talk, and effective sequencing of tunes most certainly *is* a problem in Irish music sessions.

2. Given the foundational concern with only having one speaker talking at any time, the next organizational problem becomes '*whose turn is it to speak next?*' (Sacks et al. 1974: 708). This associates closely with the problem in Irish music sessions of 'who is going to play next?' The thing here is that, although everyone *does* end up playing together, they *do not* start out playing together. Someone has to start the tune, and then they can all pile in.

3. There are two basic solutions to the organizational problem of who should speak next: a) *the next speaker is somehow selected* (Sacks et al. 1974: 703, 716–18), or b) *someone self-selects* (Sacks et al. 1974: 703, 718–20), i.e. chooses himself or herself to be the person who should be speaking. Both of these happen in Irish music sessions, but self-selection is by far the more common route.

4. Once selection has occurred there is a general orientation towards it being the person now speaking's right to *continue to talk until the 'first possible completion point* or *transition-relevance place'* (Sacks et al. 1974: 707–8, 720–23). That is, as soon as a natural pause within the speech occurs, others may jump in, but not before. Speaking prior to this is understood to be an interruption. Clearly, players are not left alone to play until they have finished in sessions. Indeed, others not joining in is considered a potential source of trouble. Rather, opening up playing is an *invitation* or *offer* to others to join in. However, there are other rights that *do* accrue to the opening player: the selection of other tunes within the same set. Thus, just as the current speaker 'owns' the current turn of speech for its duration, the selected player in an Irish music session 'owns' the current set of tunes for its duration, though they can cede those rights in various ways. What commonly unfolds in Irish music sessions is an orientation

to the conclusion of a tune as a potential first completion point. Thus, at the beginning of each new tune within the set the problem arises anew of 'whose turn is it to begin a tune next?' if the playing is to continue. The rights of the initiating player solve this in principle but, if there is any hesitation on the part of the initiating player to continue straight on into another tune, another player may self-select instead. This can lead to brief moments of competition at the beginnings of second and subsequent tunes as several players choose different tunes with which to continue. Nonetheless, players, when self-selecting with a tune are embarking upon a putative *set* or *sequence* of tunes rather than just the tune they are playing at present and prepare themselves accordingly.

Over the course of the rest of this chapter we explore a range of matters that fall out of the above gloss of the turn-taking mechanism in much greater detail in order to explicate what the production of sets in Irish music sessions turns upon, what it consists in, and what, in its own right, it manages to accomplish, given that the production takes place in a particular kind of setting, namely a pub.

What is Going to Be Played?

We remarked above that players 'when self-selecting with a tune are embarking upon a putative *set* or *sequence* of tunes rather than just the tune they are playing at present and prepare themselves accordingly'. This sentence glosses a world of work and potential pain, work that players often go to great lengths to disguise in the course of sessions themselves (Benford et al. 2012). Put quite simply, Irish music sessions rely upon people being able to turn up with their instruments and play tunes. But those tunes have to come from somewhere, players have to learn how to play them somehow. And more than that, players do not just work up any old tune that happens their way. Appropriate tunes for learning have to be somehow selected. More than this, sessions are so organized that knowing each tune as simply a free-standing tune is not enough, players have to prepare for the production of sets. And, beyond even this, they have to somehow provide for their capacity to produce that, not sat comfortably at home in their living-rooms or bedrooms, but in pubs, amongst other musicians, musicians who may hold them accountable for their production of sets in a variety of ways. What is being indexed here is a vast enterprise that cannot be given full justice within this chapter. It should not be forgotten, however, that the production of music we are addressing here turns itself upon this vast body of pre-existing work.

Who is Going to Play It?

Having somehow undertaken the work of preparation it should be stressed at this point that this is not enough on its own to solve the problem of collaboratively bringing tunes and sets of tunes into being in an actual session. What now needs to be recognized is that nothing gets played without the player to play it and just whom that player might be is not readily open to prescription. Any adequate system for providing for players of tunes in an environment where just who might make up the available cohort of players is inevitably unpredictable, will have to allow that it is *some group of players* (where 'some' is to be read as any available body of competent players) that manage the inception of tunes, rather than *just this group of players* (where they are open to precise identification in advance of the playing happening). This simple prerequisite has significant implications for how the playing might unfold.

Player selection   Given the above constraint, one possible way in which player selection might get done is for some responsible person present to look around the room and say, 'you', 'you', or 'you ... it's your turn to kick off a tune for us'. Certainly this overt allocation of turns to play is something one can witness in folk clubs but, for most sessions this is not the case and having it like that might prove to be a risky venture because it all hinges upon the efforts of just one or two people, who *must* be present for it to work and who *must* have significant knowledge of the capabilities of the cohort they are calling upon for the production of tunes.

A more random way of solving the problem might be to have the musicians present sit down together and openly discuss just what tune they should play next. Once again this kind of thing does happen. However, it has some evident weaknesses. First of all it has, once again, a strong dependency upon mutual familiarity with one another's repertoires. Secondly, it lacks economy because it necessitates pre-proposition and pre-ratification before a single note gets played. Sessions run in this way would risk quickly devolving into a continual round of propositions and counter-propositions with sets only happening after extensive verbal interchange. Worse than this, if the playing is not going to cease after every single tune, the proposition is going to have to incorporate the ratification of not just one tune but several.

What one finds, then, in the majority of sessions is a system that neatly solves the problem of allowing for an unspecified cohort whilst not being overly dependent upon shared knowledge of one another's repertoires and not being unduly bound up with elaborate sequences of negotiation.

Player self-selection   One of the primary organizational features of turn-taking in Irish sessions is that players self-select, i.e. they opt to kick off tunes and sets for themselves without being invited to do so. Because of the unpredictability of potential participants, it is not the specific right or turn of any particular person within the session to start off a whole new set. Instead, anybody may reasonably select themselves as the person to start a new tune, without anyone present taking them to task for having done that or treating it as in any way unremarkable. The player *may* be taken to task for doing that using sheet music, for selecting a tune that has already been played, for opting to play bluegrass, or any number of other things to do with *just what they have selected to play*, but the principal right of self-selection is never challenged.

The following presents an example of situated player self-selection as it happened in one particular session in the Vat and Fiddle:[3]

The players have all just finished the preceding set of tunes and are laughing about the way it fizzled out. Several of the participants pick up their drinks and the **Bhodran drummer**, who sat out of the previous set, pushes his way through to get back to his seat in the corner.

Violinist B kicks off a tune, and shortly afterwards the **Banjo**, **Mandolin** and one of the **Flute** players put down their drinks and try to join in.

---

3   Note that the groups of 5 lines upon which music is conventionally written are called staves. Where two or more staves are bracketed together, as in Example 10.1 here, one is meant to read the bracketed staves as one lump with all notes above or below one another vertically being played at the same time. Thus the last note of the violin part in Example 10.1 happens at the same time as the first note of the flute part.

After a while the other players give up. **Violinist B** stops a few notes afterwards and says 'why wasn't anyone joining in?'

Violinist B and the **Banjo player** then discuss the tune for a while and the banjo player tries to pick out how the tune continues on his banjo.

Whilst they are doing this **Violinist A** doodles a short sequence of notes then stops, and as he finishes a flautist doodles a different tune for a short while before petering out again (see Example 10.1[4]).

---

4   Throughout this paper the production of music will be rendered in standard musical notation. Whilst it is unlikely that all or even most of the readers of this chapter will be able to follow this in fine detail and reproduce the music for themselves, standard musical notation has the virtue of having been refined over a long period of time exactly in order to capture as much as possible of some musical phenomenon so that it can be recreated. The point here, however, is that the precise competence needed to read music is not required to grasp the aspects of the phenomena we are pointing to. It is sufficient to be able to track the shapes, trajectories and patterns within the notation to be able to see the phenomena at a gross level. For those who wish to get at the real richness of the phenomena the authors are able to offer up recordings that were actually collected in situ.

As he stops the **Mandolin player** starts to doodle something different again. Everyone else continues to drink and chat.

Shortly after the **Flautist** stops but whilst the **Mandolin player** is still doodling, **Violinist A** kicks off a tune in earnest (see Example 10.2).

At point (**a**) on Example 10.2 (second-half of the first phrase) **Violinist C** and the **Bhodran** join in. At point (**b**) (beginning of second, answering phrase) a **Double Bass player**, two **Guitarists**, **Violin B**, two **Flautists**, the **Banjo**, and the **Mandolin** all join in together, most playing the melody in unison with **Violin A**, but with the guitarists playing chords and the bass player playing longer bass notes. During the course of the second part of the overall tune **Violin B** changes to playing guitar as well.

In the above example we see one abortive attempt at self-selection, followed by several other brief tentative openings that are also aborted, and then a more determined effort that is quickly taken up by the other musicians. Note here how Violinist B starts off a tune and is then joined by three other players, all of whom drop out after a few bars. Violinist B's opening counts as a proper case of self-selection: no-one else is playing and he starts up a tune. He is then joined by others. However, the rapid breaking off by the others amounts to a rejection of his proposal and it shortly becomes clear that the reason for this is that no-one really knows the tune. This leaves the way clear for further cases of self-selection, Violinist B having lost all rights to a continuing set. Violinist A now tries out a few notes but stops before having got going and a flautist has a go instead. Note that Violinist A's opening here presages his bolder essay a little later: the case of self-selection that finally works. Comparison of Examples 10.1 and 10.2 will show that the first four notes of his two attempts are identical. The flautist's short effort is effectively discontinued by him before others make any attempt to join in.

This reveals something important about how self-selection works within the overall sequencing of play. Self-selection is not enough on its own for play to be sustained, as Violinist B's first opening here reveals. Self-selection is, instead, the first part of an adjacency pair (see Sacks 1992): it requires others to join in as a second part for it to become implicative for the continuation of the sequence of play. Now joining in, for musicians, is not just a case of starting off the moment the notes fall beneath your fingers. Rather, what happens is that musicians await what one might term *the first eligible entry point* to start playing. 'Eligible entry points' typically include things such as the beginnings of musical phrases or repeat points within tunes. To musicians these are not just abstract entities but rather hearable phenomena that are announced by other hearable phenomena such as a counted out number of measures or clear harmonic cadences. If musicians miss such a point, they wait for the next. That's just what happens here in Example 10.2. At point (a) (following on from the first cadence) only two players are ready to join in, so all the others wait until the next phrase beginning at point (b) before they come in. What all of this goes to say is that, as well as self-selecting, you can also effectively de-select if you decide to stop before any eligible entry point is reached. And that's just what happens with the flautist here. Shortly after the flautist drops out, Violinist A comes in with his now recalled tune and it is duly taken up.

The business of 'knowing' or 'recognizing' a tune well enough to join in here is far from simple. There are different orders of knowing a tune. One particular brand of joining in is recognizing enough of a tune to 'busk along'. This is not a neat business of saying 'I recognize such and such a sequence of notes and it's called McGuire's jig'. Music is made up of many different parts that can each be subject to recognition in different ways. This is nothing to do with some bunch of cognitive processes you might want to call recognition. It is about the availability of a set of embodied configurations of fingers, physical postures, blowing, and so on that can produce something that is an adequate fit to the circumstances. In short it's about being able to do enough to participate without getting called to account for one's inadequacies. So one thing music is made up of is a set of linearly produced pitches of varying duration usually glossed as a tune or a melody. Being able to participate in the production of that involves you in particular set of competences that may not be anything to do with being able to say that's such-and-such a tune, but rather to do with your capacity to translate a bunch of pitches you are hearing to finger positions on your instrument such that you, too, can produce them. Irish music is enormously repetitive and skilled musicians who have a lot of experience of playing different tunes can become very adept at this kind of thing such that they can join in a song and play along with it without having the foggiest idea what its called or ever having previously knowingly played it. Then another thing that music is made up of is a series of vertically related pitches called harmony. Once again the harmonies underlying Irish tunes can be relatively basic and repetitive and those who are playing harmonizing instruments such as guitars can often pretty quickly spot what the chords are in relation to the tune. Armed with this, they too can participate even if they, too, have no idea what tune this is we are playing. And once you get down into matters of beat and measure and tempo, these are things that can be spotted very readily within a small number of musical phrases, making it possible to join in with percussion instruments quite rapidly and, once again, without any particular recognition of the tune as one might formally term recognition.

So something important we have here is that formal recognition of a tune is in no way directly related to adequate performance. What the above speaks to is the fact that being armed with enough to join in is sometimes not very much so we need to be clear what we mean when we say musicians do not join in with a tune 'because they do not know it'. Clearly 'not knowing' is about a lot more than whether you have it in your repertoire. It is about not having any hooks upon which you may hang enough participation for it to seem adequate in situ.

It should be stressed that there is no need for everyone to join in for a tune to continue. Even one other participant is often enough for at least the current tune to be pursued to its conclusion. In fact, other participants in the session can join in straight off, late, or not at all without ever being called to account. Instead they may talk over the music, mess with their instruments, get up to go to the bar or the toilet, drink and eat, clown around, and all manner of routine pub behaviours without a murmur from those who are still playing, and without a hint of reasoning that these things might be problematic. This emphasizes the extent to which the pub setting shapes the accountable production of music, otherwise the overt *disregard* of music-making would be oriented to as something problematic and in breach of what the business in hand is understood to be about.

What does matter here is that once a new tune has begun, certain rights remain with the person who began it. It is not for anyone else (without good account) to then choose to strike up a completely different tune and play that directly over the person who has already started. Instead, the offered up beginning has to fizzle away and die before someone else can self-select and begin a different tune. That is, just as with the one speaker at a time maxim uncovered in the *Simplest Systematics* (Sacks et al. 1974) for conversation, once some particular player has begun, they have the floor. The rights of other players at this point extend to being able to complement, reinforce and support the initial tune proposition by joining in and playing *the same tune*, not to being able to self-select and *play some other tune instead*.

Of course, quite frequently players begin tunes and get no takers. This leaves the initiator with two stark choices: to continue regardless and call it a solo performance; or to stop playing. Given that the scenario of 'no-takers' is a common one, it is not altogether surprising that one can also see subtle refinements in the ways in which tune introduction is managed, refinements that in some respects resemble once again the solutions native speakers have evolved for managing orderly characteristics of conversation.

Offers and pre-sequences   Something already alluded to in our description of tune-openings is their potential characterization as 'offers'. This can be seen to carry through in a number of respects, most particularly with regard to what, in conversational terms, is often called pre-sequences (Schegloff 1988). Something one can readily see in any number of sessions is that an integral part of starting up a tune is that it is not, at the outset, automatically to be taken as an inevitable playing out of that tune. Players may or may not join in. The player who kicked it off may continue or they may drop out. At a tune's inception none of these things are predictable. So, as any tune opening runs the risk of non-acceptance it is initially only putative, lending it the character of an 'offer'. This is not to say that tune-openings are literally offers but rather that they share some structural similarities. The following observation pertains to both phenomena: offers have a very particular two-part form – the offer is made and then, adjacently, the offer is accepted or turned down. So, for an offer such as 'Do you want me to carry that for you?', acceptance looks something like an immediately adjacent 'Yes, thank you, that would be great'. An acceptance-type phenomenon, in the context of an Irish music session, can be said to be an adjacent and ensuing joining in by other people.

Now, there's a thing about adjacency pairs such as offers and acceptances/ rejections in conversation that is also important for our considerations here. It is not some kind of cosmic accident that the two halves of an adjacency pair come together. It is rather the case that the production of the first part actively *implicates* the production of the second part and any failure to produce a second part of some kind is itself accountable. So what we are saying here is that the production of a tune-opening by one particular player implicates something: the acceptance of it by joining in or the rejection of it by not. This business of accountable second parts has some interesting consequences when it comes to certain kinds of things like offers and invitations. Particularly note that the second part of an adjacency pair in these cases has an asymmetrical bias about it, what has previously been termed a 'preferred' and 'dispreferred' response (Pomerantz 1984). Acceptance demands no further account, but rejection *does*. This being the case what one finds is that offers and invitations do not always get stated outright in their first articulation, instead you get what has been termed a 'pre-sequence' (Schegloff 1988) that helps the initiator to avoid getting locked into being rejected, for instance:

'What are you doing on Saturday?'
'Oh, we've been invited to my sister's'
'Really, how's she doing anyway?'

Here the response indicating prior commitment enables the initiator to avoid having to make the invitation and get rejected in the first place. In Irish music sessions the scenario musicians dread is kicking off a tune and having no-one join in. So it's hardly surprising that ways have evolved whereby musicians can, using something akin to a pre-sequence, float tunes in ways that similarly avoid rejection. The following excerpts provide a sample of the kind of thing we're discussing:

Player A plays a snippet of a tune on his pennywhistle. **Player B** is drinking beer and has his flute wedged between his legs [Figure 10.13]. **Player C** has put down his mandolin completely and is scratching his head, staring across the room, whilst holding a list of tunes in his right hand. All the other musicians also have their instruments at rest and are engaged in various conversations.

After a very short pause, pennywhistle still to his mouth, **Player A** plays another snippet. At point (a) **Player B** puts down his beer and picks up his

flute.

Over a period of 3.5 seconds **Player A** changes from a 'D' pitched pennywhistle to a 'G' pitched pennywhistle. He then plays another snippet (x). Whilst he is playing this **Player B** wipes his mouth with a tissue.

After another very short pause **Player A** plays some more. Note the slightly muffed 4th note as he works to bring the tune 'to mind' and to his fingers.

There is a pause of 3 seconds then **Player B** starts to play his flute. This phrase is directly related to the tune at (x). Note the 2nd, 3rd, 4th, 5th and 6th notes are all identical (if one takes the first note 'G' in (x) to be held rather than repeated), with just the first note being added as a lead in and the ending being changed. As he is concluding this short fragment, **Player A**, partially overlapping with the conclusion [point (b)] plays a re-articulation of the same phrase as at (x).

Player A waits half a second then repeats and extends the same tune (y).

One and a half seconds later **Player B** plays a more florid triplet figure on his flute that proves subsequently to be an embellishment of the second part of the tune **Player A** has just been playing on his pennywhistle. At point (c) **Player C** picks up his mandolin.

Player B pauses very briefly then plays the same tune that **Player A** was playing at (y) but sees the tune through to its end (see Example 10.10). At point (d) **Player A** visibly draws in breath ready to play.

Player B immediately repeats the same tune and is joined this time by **Player A** (see Example 10.11). Throughout the course of this **Player C** is tuning his mandolin. At point (e) **Players D and E** get ready to play and at point (f), where the second half of the first tune begins, **Player D** joins in on a low whistle, playing the same tune, and **Player E** joins in, strumming the guitar. At point (g), just before the conclusion of the second time around the tune, **Player C** and **Player F** get ready to join in with the mandolin and another pennywhistle respectively, both with fingers physically placed over the positions on their instruments where they will play the first notes.

Guitar continues to play chords against the rest

Players B, A, D and E continue immediately onto yet another repeat of the same tune, this time joined by **Players C and F** (see Example 10.12) and the tune is properly underway with all of the players playing.

Now what you'll see here is that the whole thing kicks off with a pennywhistle player (Player A) doodling a tune on a D pitched whistle. He has another quick go at something, but in both cases he never reaches a definitive eligible completion point and sets the D whistle aside in favour of a G whistle. The tune he picks up here is fateful for what then unfolds. On this first iteration he doesn't get far with it, and, after a pause, muffs part of the next phrase and thereafter briefly sets it aside. At this point there's nothing much to differentiate what's going on here from the failed self-selection examples we looked at in the last section. However, these kinds of floated, incomplete doodlings sometimes get oriented to by other players in a different way. Instead of being simply dismissed when the first eligible entry point never arrives, they are taken to be *offers* or proposals of tunes that might be played. And that is how Player B orients to this tune here. After a short pause he plays something musically similar to the phrase Player A was trying to play. This amounts to a preliminary acceptance of Player A's proposal for a tune who can now see that there is at least one other player who might buy in to the tune. Player A therefore goes for another try at the same tune, and then does it again in a more extended fashion. What comes next is Player B playing an embellished version of the second part of this tune. We, as outsiders, might not recognize the two parts as being related, but competent players who know the tune in its entirety would see this readily. Player B then launches into a definitive version of the tune, complete with a proper eligible entry point which Player A duly orients to so that he too is playing the tune as it goes round again. By half way through this next iteration other players are also joining in.

What we can see here is that the rudimentary structure of a pre-sequence provides in the context of Irish music sessions a non-committal way of proposing a tune by enabling you to see both acceptance and rejection in the offing and, if necessary, to take further remedial action by just letting it drop when no-one takes it up. Thus a shared understanding of how the sequencing of tunes gets done amongst the musicians in Irish music sessions provides not just for self-selection but for the recognizability of what counts as a proper tune under way and, more importantly, for the potential to propose tunes without being obliged to commit to them for others to indicate acceptance before a full playing out is under way.

First possible completion point: next player up and the production of sets   Let us now return to our discussion of the turn-taking system. We made two important observations earlier. The first of these is that musicians, both in the course of the session itself and in their work of preparation, are oriented to not just the production of single tunes but *sets of tunes*. The other observation we made is that there is a strong orientation to the person who starts off one tune having continuing rights to select the next tune within a set. With regard to these two points we want to remind the reader of another aspect of the *Simplest Systematics* (Sacks et al. 1974): namely that once someone is speaking there is a general orientation towards it being the person now speaking's right to *continue to talk until the 'first possible completion point'*. Now, at first sight the first possible completion point in an Irish music set is at the end of a tune and one does, indeed, get some shift in leadership of tunes here from time to time. However, the maxim discussed in the *Simplest Systematics* (ibid.) is, at heart, about *ownership* of a turn at speech, and the set-based organization of music in Irish sessions is similarly about ownership of a turn at choosing the tunes. So, self-selecting to play at the moment a tune ends in a set that someone else has initiated amounts to butting in and can, on occasion be oriented to quite visibly in this way. However, the shift to a new tune is nonetheless a vulnerable moment. Once again the matter of what to play is on the table. One particular player may have more rights than the others to propose just what the tune should be, but the selection sill requires the ratification of others by means of them joining in and this cannot be presumed. What one therefore sees is a bunch of phenomena arising as a tune end approaches and a new tune begins that both echoes and extends beyond the organizational features of a first tune beginning.

Members of the cohort of speakers of some natural language evidence phenomenally fine-tuned capacity to anticipate the end of a turn of speech. Resources that assist here are the workings of a grammar known in common, cadences of speech, demeanour, the drawing in of breath, direction of gaze, and so on. All of this works towards the production of an ongoing flow of conversation that is not eternally punctuated by pauses as listeners discover someone has stopped speaking and it is time to figure out who is going to speak next. In Irish music sessions there is a similar goal: to produce an unbroken set of tunes that flow easily into one another. This being the case potential 'tune completion points' become an object of focus for three related problematics: i) What is going to happen next? Carrying on with the same tune? Starting a different tune? Stopping?; ii) Whose turn is it going to be next?; and iii) What is going to be played next? (If anything at all). So here too one sees the exploitation of commonly understood structures expression, gaze and posture, as everyone gets ready to handle the moment of transition.

Each main part in a traditional Irish tune is usually repeated, and then the whole lot is subject to one or two repetitions. The common practice is to play the whole thing three times, but this is open to variation. Understanding of this structure and a potential up-and-coming transition point is made visible in various ways. For a start, having noted that the player who first started off the tune is given first preference as the 'leader' of the set, people may show some careful attention to the leader at the end of the second and third repetitions onwards, anticipating a possible completion and looking for any sign as to what the leader is going to do next. There are various ways in which leaders may signal their intentions to the other musicians who are playing, for instance by physically looking at the other musicians as the end approaches and somewhat elaborating the movements they are making to play their instruments. Sometimes there are such standard segues between pieces and this basic signaling is all that is required for people to smoothly transition together from one tune to the next.

However, standard segues are relatively rare, so everyone neatly turning the corner into the next tune together is also a rarity, regardless of the ideals of smooth continuity everyone aspires to. Instead what usually happens is, as soon as one tune ends and whilst the set leader or someone else sets about introducing another tune, the other players will fall silent and go through the same mechanics of either choosing to join in or not, according to their capacity.

In the next slightly simplified[5] example we see the way in which such transitions get handled. It demonstrates a number of the features we have discussed above.

---

5   Simplified in the following ways: a) despite multiple instruments playing a single line is presented – this is because most of the instruments are playing more or less in unison; b) those instruments playing rhythm rather than the tune are repeating over the rhythmic figure shown in the example (note how this figure matches the basic rhythm of the tune – one long and two short notes); c) some of the more fluid melodic ornamentations have been removed to keep the pattern clear.

First of all, notice how the mandolin player begins the first tune and is then able to assume the right to kick off the next tune as well, and note how this right is ceded to him unchallenged by the other players. This neatly shows the orientation to *set ownership* we mentioned previously. More than this, note how the presumption of carrying the next tune enables the mandolin player to already have a next tune 'in mind' and to segue into that tune in such a fashion that an unbroken flow of music is preserved.

There is not perfection in the realization of tune transition here. A number of the musicians start to play another repeat of the first tune. Two things are particularly noteworthy about this, however. 1) They all stop within a note or two, leaving the mandolin player unchallenged and reinforcing the point we have made about who is treated as having ownership of the set. 2) They all look specifically to the mandolin player at this point, rendering their expectation of leadership openly visible. There is no exchange of glances between each other, they only look at him.

Another feature worth inspecting is the fact that the mandolin player also engages in what might be termed 'tune transition management'. He actively looks to the banjo player, one of the few players still following him, putting the tune to him as the banjo player stumbles for a moment then catches up. Critically there is an *exchange* of gaze here, with the banjo player looking back to the mandolin player as he regains his step. The others (except for the rhythm instruments) have stopped by this point and it is quite specifically for the mandolin player to bring the banjo player along. Other players look to him, but are not playing, so do not require the same immediate level of engagement on his part. Nor does tune transition management stop at this. Note also how the first melody of the second tune gets played four times (rather than twice) before moving on to the second part of the tune, thus allowing for others to join in as well.

The first tune of a set is begun by the **Mandolin player**, following on from a short conversational interchange with the **Flautist**. At the first possible entry point the **Mandolin player** is joined by a **Banjo**, a **Violin** and the **Flute**. At the very next possible entry point a guitar and the **Bodhran** also join in. At the next possible entry point after that all of the other players join in as well. People playing at this point are (clockwise round the room): **Guitar 1**, **Violin 1**, **Violin 2**, **Banjo 1**, **Accordion**, **Banjo 2**, **Guitar 2**, **Mandolin**, **Pennywhistle**, **Flute**, **Violin 3**, **Bodhran**.

As the tune comes to an end the **Mandolin player** continues straight on to play a different tune (see Point **(a)** in Example 10.13). **Banjo player 1** and the **Bodhran** continue with the **Mandolin player** into the new tune.

There is the briefest of fumbles from the **Banjo player** and the mandolin player looks directly at him and the banjo player returns his gaze as he picks up the tune properly.

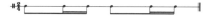

The **Bodhran player** maintains the same rhythmic figure he was using in the previous tune (see adjacent Example 10.14). All of the other players go to play yet another repeat of the first tune but within a note or two have stopped and are looking directly at the mandolin player. At the first possible entry point (**b**) in Example 10.13 a guitar joins in strumming chords to the rhythm.

At the next possible entry point (**c**) **Violinists 1 and 2** join in but stop again after a couple of notes. The accordion joins in here as well and keeps going.

At the next possible entry point (**d**) the **Flute** joins in and the accordion drops out (**Banjo player 2** is tuning her instrument here in the background)

At the next possible entry point (**e**) **Violinists 1 and 2** join back in and keep going this time.

These are then the players who keep going for the rest of the tune, being joined subsequently by the accordion player who changes his instrument for a violin.

Of course, specific sets must ultimately come to an end, with tunes being typically played in groups of two or three. So any potential tune completion point is also a potential set completion point, with this becoming increasingly likely as the number of tunes played increases. As with individual tunes, musicians are generally oriented to looking for a potential stopping place at the end of the second complete tune onwards and will look to the other musicians and the leader for cues to this effect. The way in which this is actually brought about is subject to some variation. Thus some tunes will slowly peter out with more and more musicians dropping out of them, whilst on other occasions musicians will work together through a series of visual and aural cues to try and bring the tune to a conclusion together.

Once a set has been brought to some kind of adequate conclusion the rights for continued tune selection that resided with the leader of the set are effectively rescinded and once again the session returns to a state where anyone present has, in principle, the right to self-select.

The Pub Setting as an Organizational Problem

At this point we need to enter into a somewhat broader set of considerations. Let us begin by once again reminding readers that Irish music sessions are situated in pubs and, this being the case, many ordinary pub-going features are preserved. This is evident straight away in how musicians, upon arrival and before setting up to play, will often go to the bar and order drinks. They are also quite routinely involved in buying rounds for other musicians they know, just as they would be if they were visiting the pub for other social activities. Engagement with the actual business of the session therefore wavers amongst the participants as they orient to other ordinary pub business such as chatting and catching up with people. In relation to this, the making of music becomes something of an organizational problem because being utterly single-minded about the playing, to the exclusion of the surrounding social milieu, being dictatorial about how the session is structured and just who should be playing, would itself become accountable for its impact upon these other matters, so it is hardly surprising that musicians do not typically orient to sessions in this way. This inevitably contributes to some of what are considered to be the more 'informal' characteristics of sessions.

Of course, what might be called formal or informal in any circumstance is open to all sorts of situated considerations. However, when Irish sessions are spoken of as being 'informal' this is usually a way of expressing how they are seen to be different from other more performative or rehearsal situations, with little accountability to the more usual niceties one might expect to hold when it is all about playing the music together. In the sessions we observed this became manifest in a number of ways. So one way it became apparent is the extent to which the musicians were inclined to pay attention to other things than what was going on with the music, even when musicians were currently playing. This is clearly not something you would encounter where musicians are understood to be performing. An even more forceful way in which this becomes apparent is in how the session is itself oriented to by other people in the pub apart from the musicians. In the below images, for instance, one sees a spectator who knows some of the musicians but who is not involved in playing in the session, wending his way amongst the musicians, distributing leaflets for another event, and chatting to some of them as they play:

Figure 10.29   Moving amongst the musicians to distribute leaflets during a set

The significance of this example with regard to how music gets played, performed and rehearsed in other settings is the orientation it exhibits towards the interruptibility of the musicians and the extent to which other pub business and social business may breach the zone of musical activity without any evident sense of accountability on the part of the perpetrator, or any effort to call him to account on the part of the musicians. This is relatively unique to sessions of this kind. Pub-bands performing are provided a stage of sorts and everyone else constitutes themselves as an audience around it, with concomitant orientations to the preservation of that space for the musicians and their activities. Even in rehearsals the interruption of ongoingly played songs by others outside of the musicians themselves is treated as a genuine interruption and called to account accordingly. Thus the spontaneous production of music in this kind of setting is understood by both musicians and non-playing pub-goers to be quite distinct from the business of 'serious' music-making that should be respected and applauded as something outside of the other business in the pub.

Sometimes this understood informality is also made visible in how people (musicians and non-musicians) position themselves within the space notionally devoted to the session, and the kinds of activities they engage in when doing so.

So one thing you regularly witness, for instance, is non-musicians (frequently family and friends) sitting down amongst the musicians and chatting with one another and with the musicians themselves as other musicians are playing. This understood informality can also be noted in the kinds of things musicians will do quite unreflectively right in the middle of a tune being played, for instance, taking off a pullover, getting stuff out of a handbag, sending text messages on a mobile phone, eating a sandwich, getting up and going to the toilet or the bar, and so on. Nor does it stop at the matter of comportment. It is also visible in how the musicians handle the actual playing of the music, especially with regard to how they start or stop playing, often simply dropping out in the middle of tunes: matters for which they could well be accountable in other musical settings. In relation to this, we emphasized earlier the ways in which complete non-participation can also escape accountability in ways that would prove problematic in other more strictly musically-focused settings.

However, what is perhaps most important of all for our discussion is the way people drift into the session in dribs and drabs rather than all arriving together, and then depart in a similar fashion. It is unimaginable that in a properly constituted performance the musicians would just turn up when they felt like it and take their place amongst the other performers at their leisure. Nor would they take their place whilst the other musicians were actually playing, physically getting out their instruments right adjacent to someone playing a tune at that moment. It is as though Irish sessions are oriented to on the one hand as being endlessly interruptible, whilst simultaneously not taking these potential disruptions as an excuse to stop. Indeed, if everyone stopped playing each time another musician turned up and took their place amongst their ranks it is easy to see that Irish sessions would quickly become unworkable. And, as departures are similarly likely to occur whilst others are playing, it can be seen that these too are oriented to in this highly permissive fashion.

Of course, a particular consequence of this trickle in and trickle out of players is that it is hugely difficult to predict who might actually be there and playing at any one moment in time. Whilst players do turn up in groups and do occasionally work out set lists, for the larger part, as we have already noted, Irish sessions do not exhibit any pre-programmed order. Just what might be open to being played is dependent upon who is present and their own particular repertoire. Yet it is impossible to say just who might be present at any moment in time. Instead, then, a characteristic feature of Irish music sessions that has co-evolved with an allowably flexible cohort is the practice of musicians who are present being left to make the choice as to just what they are going to play now, though this is not simply a matter of anything goes. At the same time we can see how this orientation to flexible cohorts would be highly disruptive for the organization of other things such as rehearsals. How can you plan to rehearse specific pieces together when you never know who might or might not be there? But what you do get instead here are the same kinds of organizational concerns as you can find in other social events, such as going to the pub with friends without any particular interest in making music, where the *spontaneous* sequencing of interaction occurs.

Let us think about this for a moment: There are not many strictures upon who may or may not be present in a pub at any one time beyond the usual legal ones. Individual groups of people may make individual arrangements to turn up at a certain time and may be accountable to one another for these arrangements, but this arrangement is not constituted across the whole body of people within a pub and there are not, beyond standard opening and closing hours, set start and finish times that everyone must adhere to. Thus it is with Irish sessions as well and it can be seen that this is impactful for a number of the apparent informalities witnessed within them, such as their resistance to interruption, the way tunes are chosen, and in particular the way tunes get started up through self-selection.

Self-selection and Pre-sequences as a Solution to the Pub Setting as an Organizational Problem

So what we have got to, by way of the above considerations, is a realization that playing Irish music in pubs, as a part of a shifting and unpredictable cohort, where what you are as much about as anything else is going to the pub with friends (or to meet up with friends) constitutes, from the point of view of the effective production of music, a quite specific organizational problem. Now, in relation to such a problem, people could go about solving it methodically in any number of different possible ways. Yet what you find when you look at it is a rudimentary and economical turn-taking system that is massively redolent of other kinds of solutions people already use to manage other organizational issues, such as how to manage having no more than one speaker speaking at once whilst allowing for the ongoing and unbroken flow of conversation. We have at no point suggested that the particularities of these two systems are identical. What we have taken note of is that they resemble one another in a number of ways, not least in the character of the fundamental problems they are enabling people to resolve, i.e. who to play? / who to speak? and how to keep the music-making / the conversation going (i.e. to provide for sequences of music or of talk that can be continuous or discontinuous with changing parties leading off (see again Sacks et al. 1974)? Sacks et al. (op cit.) propose that the turn-taking system that has evolved amongst natural language speakers across all kinds of speech-based activities is ultimately addressed to the problem of *sequencing* speech in an effective manner. Sequencing is just as much of a problem for those engaged in the production of music. And the fact that it arises as a problem in the way it does for Irish session musicians is completely bound up with how sessions occur within a pub setting. This being the routine environment for sessions, it has given birth to the need for some kind of solution to evolve. It is perhaps therefore not surprising, but nonetheless significant, that features that have evolved to handle the management of sequences of talk in the spontaneous production of speech have presented themselves as routine and to hand ways of solving the spontaneous production of music as well.

Conclusion

Earlier in this chapter we discussed how Harvey Sacks developed his analysis of the turn-taking mechanism in conversation as a vehicle, not for understanding specific properties of the natural production of speech as an end its own right, but rather as a means of grasping the methodic ways in which members accomplish the production of an ordinary society in a multitudinous variety of ways. So the turn-taking mechanism provides for a way of getting things done, and also for recognizing when those ways of getting things done are being breached, on purpose or otherwise. The mechanism we have outlined here for the production of music in Irish music sessions is a similarly methodic, accountable and generative mechanism whereby sets of music can be realized without too much fuss and bother, without too much overt and dedicated *management*, in the context of people going down the pub. It is that context of being musicians in pubs, with friends, buying rounds, chatting about any number of different things, arriving and going at times that suit the others you also associate with, and allowing for the fact that everyone else around you is working within those same concerns, that has provided for the evolution of this system of music-making. What the system solves is not something that is uniquely a musical concern but rather a sociological concern, not of analysts, but of members.

We started off this chapter expressing the view that, whilst Harold Garfinkel's critique of Howard Becker's discussion of jazz musicians was on the mark for its concern with the way it lost the very thing that might give their activities coherence, i.e. the production of music, his injunction to pay close attention to the work of producing the music itself runs a certain risk. This risk is the same as the risk that attaches to taking Sacks' interest in the ordered properties of conversation too literally. A great many endeavours in the world of conversation analysis have concentrated much of their effort upon the classifiable properties of speech whilst missing utterly the work those properties might, in situ, be accomplishing. This criticism is far from being my own (see Lynch 1993: 231–47) but it delineates an important difference between ethnomethodological treatments of phenomena and their conversation analytic counterparts. The risk with taking Garfinkel's injunction too literally, then, is that it will lead to a myopically reductive analysis of the different features of the production of music without seeing how that production works as a means of accomplishing the making of music, not as a technical but as a *sociological* problem. With regards to how music-making gets done in Irish sessions, one has to see the pub setting and its implications for player attendance, and the other things players do once they are there, to understand the character of that problem and what the organization of tune production in sessions is therefore solving as a sociological concern. Attending to the actual production of music is an essential part of this but to stop at that would never be enough to understand any production of music in its entirety because music never falls outside of it being about its social accountability, not its technical accountability alone.

Acknowledgements

The work undertaken in Irish music sessions that is discussed in this chapter could never have taken place without the support of the UK Engineering and Physical Research Council (EPSRC) platform grant 'Widespread Adoption of Ubiquitous Computing' (EP/F03038X/1) and the Horizon Centre for Doctoral Training (EP/G037574/1). More importantly, it could never have taken place without the dedicated efforts of the numerous different musicians who can be found enjoying the 'craic' as they say, in pubs and bars in numerous cities, towns and villages all around the world and most especially the musicians at The Vat and Fiddle, The Hop Pole, and The King Billy in Nottingham, and the Oak Tree in Durham.

Chapter 11

Vine Right, Shimmy, Shimmy! Accomplishing Order* in a Line Dancing Class

Russell Kelly

Introduction

What circumstances brought someone interested in Ethnomethodology to a Line Dancing Class? Like other ordinary folk, sociologists are not special, different, distinct. When they leave the office, the field, 'work', they engage in the same sorts of activities and leisure pursuits that other ordinary folk do; some drive and maintain classic cars, others design crossword puzzles. Some spend too long in the 'gym', watch The Simpsons on TV, others support their local soccer, hockey or football team – the list is as long as the roll-call of ethnomethodologists – and at least one accompanies his partner who likes to go Line Dancing. There is nothing special, outstanding, ironic, unusual, unique, or 'outside'[1] about these leisure pursuits. These are the kinds of activities that ordinary folk choose to engage in when they are doing 'leisure'.

So what is it about the Line Dancing Class that provoked the interest of this sociologist? First, it was just that (Garfinkel's quiddity), the doings of ordinary folk who come together repeatedly, for one hour, once or more per week, voluntarily, to engage with others in learning how to do line dancing. Line dancing involves the repetition of sequences of movements of the feet, body and, in some cases, the hands, in a relatively small space, in step with a tune selected from the discography known as 'Country Music' or in more traditional locations, 'Country and Western Music'.[2] The range of steps, moves and turns are choreographed into 32-step sequences, which are repeated for the duration of the tune, approximately

---

1 Sociologists have often been criticised for focussing their attention on the 'deviant' – from Georg Simmel through Alfred Schütz to Howard Becker, there has been reference to the 'Fremde', the 'Stranger' or the 'Outsider'. Becker (1973), for example, maintained this long tradition in Sociology writing about the marijuana user and the jazz musician. Ethnomethodology's radical approach is to focus on the routine, the ordinary, everyday, taken-for-granted activities of ordinary folk. See Liazos (1972).

2 Peterson (1997), pp. 194–201.

two to three minutes.[3] A 32-step sequence will involve at least one quarter turn such that the complete dance will involve at least four turns, leaving the dancer and the line facing the direction that they faced at the beginning, the so-called four wall dance. A class involves two sessions of up to an hour, interspersed with free dancing time where favourite tunes of the regular attenders become the basis for practiced dances or occasional displays of higher proficiency by the more accomplished dancers. The first session is devoted to demonstrating, rehearsing and performing one simpler sequence (often described as 'Beginners'). The later session involves learning a more complex sequence ('Intermediate/ Advanced'). Sometimes, the second complex sequence is a variation of the first sequence but including a wider range of steps, more turns, a faster pace, performed to a livelier, faster tune. Participants who find the first session challenging can opt out after the first sequences are performed, or can continue in a reformed line using the simpler sequence to dance to the quicker, more lively tune, or can risk trying the second advanced sequence only to find it, at this time, too demanding.

Dancers' spaces of about one square metre each, are arranged in rows, or lines, all dancers facing in the same direction, thus 'line dancing'. So, a critical question: 'Is there a minimum number necessary for a line to form?' and 'How many lines and participants-per-line would be too many for the space available?' The answers to these questions are not fixed, mathematical calculations as in number of dancers, in equal lines, per numbers of square metres of floor space.[4] These are ongoing calculations, based somehow in prior experiences, done by each member as they, along with others, approach the floor. That one, or a number of individuals, reach just this calculation, on this evening, with just this size of floor, and just this many potential dancers, is one of the myriad haecceities[5] accomplished to achieve the autochthonous order*[6] that is the Line Dancing Class.

---

3   Quinn (1997).
4   Livingston (1987), p. 6 for a representation of people forming orderly queues.
5   Haecceities – Garfinkel (2007).
6   Garfinkel (1988).

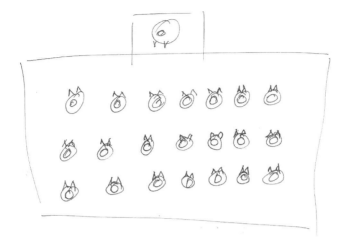

Figure 11.1 Facing teacher – lines facing the first wall[7]

Unlike many other ethnomethodological studies of the classroom, the laboratory, the workplace, a medical consultation or the courtroom, the Line Dancing Class is not a formalized, organized setting with a shared, extensive cultural history. Participants for the most part attend of their own volition. They may pay an entry fee or subscription. Their greatest 'power' in that situation is their decision 'not to go' this week, or not to exercise their freedom and the desire to go, this week, because something of greater attraction 'cropped up' or mere apathy overcame the desire to get ready and go. This is the second feature which attracted the interest of the ethnomethodologist, that members came together voluntarily, without pressure or demand, to create and enjoy with others an experience of their own making, in a setting provided for the purpose attended by a 'teacher'.

The problem for attenders at a Line Dancing Class is to 'attend' to the social order of what they are about to experience.[8] Attending for leisure and pleasure at an event such as this requires some form of acceptance of membership for the individual or couple to justify re-attending at some future time. Attending involves work in the form of preparation and, as we shall see, making decisions about dress, dress codes, footwear, head gear and so on. Prior decisions about purchasing these items, where to purchase them and whether to purchase hats, boots, shirts or skirts may all precede the decision to attend, or to attend again. The pleasure, satisfaction, enjoyment, skills acquisition, or whatever the motivations associated

---

7   With due credit to the style of Eric Livingston (1987), p. 6.

8   A different version of this paper appeared as One Step Forward and Two Steps Back: Woolgar, reflexivity, qualitative research and a Line Dancing Class (Kelly 1999: 1–13). That version was less detailed and focused on methodological issues associated with doing qualitative research.

with attending, will depend on acceptance by and into a group, or groups, experienced as a sequence of events. Identifying the groupings that the attenders might wish to, or be able to join, to identify their significations of membership, to understand the taken-for-granted rules involved in becoming a member of a group within a Line Dancing class are the primary challenges of the prospective Line Dancer and the concerns of this paper.

What is interesting, here, is that the act of presenting yourself for membership is voluntary. This is a leisure activity. Prospective members could equally well have stayed home and watched TV. Lives outside the class are somehow suspended on dressing in the attire most appropriate to how the individual sees themselves this evening, at just this class. The more 'dressed up' the attender is the more of any other life, or the status, power and responsibilities attending that life, are suspended. In the process of joining the class, one's categorial standing is both claimed and acknowledged in the way that interacting with others gets done, as we shall see. Any 'structures' of inequality, of class, or gender or of race, of the powerful against the powerless, are brought to the line-dancing class and created and sustained there by members, by participants.

> Under the attitude of everyday life … under the auspices of members' practical interests in the workings of the everyday world, the member's knowledge of the world is more or less ad hoc, more or less general, more or less fuzzy around the periphery. The member finds out what he needs to know; what he needs to know is relative to the practical requirements of his problem. His criteria of adequacy, rules of procedure, and strategies for achieving desired ends are for him only as good as they need to be.[9]

Members subject themselves to any structures of authority (e.g. teacher-pupil), to any operant system of rules, to processes of adjudication, rule enforcement, sanction and punishment, as and when they leave home, when they arrive at the venue and as they pay the entry fee. Any order viewed in old sociological ways is a self-imposed order, created and sustained by members as a practical accomplishment. Equally, participation in interaction within the venue serves to create, sustain, define and redefine the structures, rules and processes as an ongoing activity that is the Line Dancing Class. Members, in interaction, define their own requirements in relation to others, constantly define and re-define their expectations, persistently set and reset their expectations and to the extent to which they are being served and met, ultimately reach a decision whether or not to come 'next week'.

A matter of considerable interest is that irrespective of who the participants were from week to week, month to month, nightly from Wednesday through Sunday, a Line Dancing Class occurred and in much the same fashion that it had, does, would or will occur across the period of the eighteen months that the class was subject to participation and observation. Like Garfinkel's traffic flows

---

9   Zimmerman and Pollner (1971: 85).

or service queues, the Line Dancing Class happens just like that, there, then – and within it lies a template for looking at a host of other social interactions that routinely occur in the lives of ordinary folk (Garfinkel 2002).

Method

1. 'Participant as Observer' (Gold 1958) or 'Member-as-sociologist-doing-sociological-inquiries' (Garfinkel 1967).

2. Curiosity. Became bored watching the dancing at an early session and decided to scribble some notes on scraps of paper (Whyte 1943). Observations became more and more involved and new sessions involved looking at particulars. The research role shifted back and forth between participating and observing. Incidents occurred which led or directed the observation or participation from session to session, irrespective of the outline work-plan that might have been emerging as a new session approached. Planned observations rarely followed a pre-conceived programme but somehow the work got done either at that session or at either of the next one or two. This supports a key methodological realization for ethnomethodologists, that the order that is the Line Dancing Class is routinely reconstructed in different ways by members. Whoever the population cohort at a particular session might be an order was achieved and maintained – the 'autochthonous order properties' of a Line Dancing class (Garfinkel 2002: 45). Equally, the 'ethnomethodology' was redefined, redirected for the researcher-as-member by other members as interesting features emerged for examination in any session, irrespective of what the 'planned' observation might have intended.

3. As the fieldwork observations were on going and the first draft of a document was prepared, it was circulated generally to the owners of 'Fort San Antone' and to the various participant groups involved in the venue. There was no objection to the work or its publication and the response was generally one of curious appreciation for widening the audience and the range of possible participants. Suggestions that the report was to be submitted for publication were regarded much like free advertising and a draft copy of this paper was passed around among members. The draft paper was treated much like editions of Line Dancing magazines which contained reports of events at the venue or achievements by regular attenders who had entered competitions, created new dance-step combinations, or were otherwise the subject of reports. The paper was scanned rather than read for approval, then passed on. No one objected to this paper being written or to being the subjects of such a paper. Occasional references to the paper by the Line Dancing Class teacher during class passed without provoking any further interest. Her reference to the paper was probably the highest authority in the group necessary for common acceptance of it and its purposes.

Background

The popular fascination with 'Cowboys and Indians' in the United Kingdom probably dates back to the French and Indian Wars (1754–63) and the American Revolution (1775–83). Various stories were told and retold in a classic colonial style of the heroism and barbarism of the 'natives' as in James Fenimore Cooper's 1826 novel, *The Last of the Mohicans*. The fascination in popular culture was mirrored in more academic circles like the Royal Society and the Eugenics Society who published works of 'anthropology' like E.B. Tylor's *Anthropology of 1881* which included engravings made from 'ethnological photographs' of Colorado Indians and Caribs in a chapter on 'Races of Mankind'. The male Colorado Indian is pictured firing a flintlock rifle, suggesting a posed photograph.

This trend in popular culture was exploited by the European tour of Buffalo Bill's Wild West Show during the 1880s, starring Buffalo Bill (William Cody) and including 'Cowboy and Indian' displays and demonstrations of shooting skills, using rifles and the Colt revolver, which, we will see, still features at Line Dancing events. The coming of the cinema popularized the cowboy-as-hero, reaching its zenith of popularity in the 1950s and, in colour, in the 1960s, where the cowboy hero or law enforcer (the Sheriff) was portrayed by movie stars of the period, like Gene Autry or John Wayne.[10] The hero prevailed against overwhelming odds to save the 'community' of 'innocent' settlers, or to win the affections of the hard-done-by 'bar-girl', or of the distressed woman-farmer unable to work and protect her land against 'land-grabbers' or 'hostiles'. Out of this genre of movies comes the cast of characters who are to be found in and around the Line Dancing Class.

I first encountered the Country and Western scene in the late 1960s by visiting a series of 'theme pubs' where the entertainment, which accompanied a 'night out', was a performance by a popular UK Country and Western band supporting imported US C&W stars. There was some crossover between the emerging Liverpool scene that produced the Beatles and other to-be-internationally-famous Rock and Roll bands because the repertoire of many of these groups included one or more C&W ballads. Cowboy music, which had appeared in the popular Westerns of the black and white movies, has always circled the periphery of the music scene no matter the extremity of Punk Rock or Garage Music, which dominated youth culture. Latterly, the popular music scene across the world has seen a reverse cross fertilization with C&W stars like Garth Brooks, Reba MacEntire, the Dixie Chicks and Shania Twain joining the elites of popular music. What, however, distinguished the C&W pubs from others was the increasing tendency for the 'regulars' to appear

---

10   Interesting the 'singing cowboy' image associated with Gene Autry was the original role into which early John Wayne was cast. The tough cowboy hero (who didn't sing) was a later recreation of the movie studios (Peterson 1997). This later image still adorns the walls of San Antone, our venue, as a fresco, alongside Elvis Presley and Sioux Chief Sitting Bull. Dolly Parton is portrayed, representing the generations of women country singer-songwriters.

in 'Cowboy and Indian' attire, often homemade, and replicating the supposedly authentic dress seen at the cinema.[11] Other pubs, clubs and dance or music scenes had 'uniforms' or dress styles and codes but few, if any, had adopted the dress of a culture/subculture that was itself part myth and part fiction. The contrast with the dress style of Rastafarians, which was authentic, original and imported from Jamaica, or the original twentieth-century version of Goths, dressed in black with white make-up on the face and single colour, silver jewellery and metal adornments, distinguishes the Line Dancers by age and generation. Many were re-living some kind of fictional, escapist world that they remembered from an earlier time, which turned into a device determining qualification for membership in the subculture. The nearest parallel would be the recreation of the Rockers of the 1950s with their Brothel Creeper, crepe-soled shoes and brightly coloured suits with black felt collars and cuffs and, of course, the Elvis Presley greased quiff with DA ('Duck's arse') hairstyle.[12] The difference with youth trends or exclusive minority interests was that Line Dancing would become, if briefly, a national, mass leisure activity.

C&W venues can be found throughout the UK and across Europe, extending far into East Europe, especially the so-called former Communist states, where 'Cowboy' movies had been used to popularize themes of class oppression and capitalist (the railway baron) exploitation of the rural peasants (the dispossessed woman farmer). The venues, like the one we will examine later, often took on the character of a ranch or cavalry fort in the 'Wild West' with the bar and dance-floor in a central building and other buildings providing shops for C&W goods, horse riding, canoeing, archery and other C&W compatible sporting and leisure activities. Food was classically barbecued steaks, chicken or burgers with fried potatoes, garnished with gherkin and tomato ketchup, served from some kind of open-fired 'range' or grill.

The Line Dancing Class and the general popularity of dancing as a form of exercise emerged with the focus on fitness and individual self-reliance in the 1980s but Line Dancing in the United Kingdom only became a major national activity in the late 1990s. Line Dancing classes and sessions are now generally available in locals halls and social clubs and are offered at beginners', intermediate and advanced levels.

Dress at the more local 'exercise' Line Dancing classes is less likely to be the complete C&W authentic attire and might involve a Cowboy or Stetson hat and Cowboy boots, although many village halls discourage the wearing of these boots

---

11   Note that Peterson (1997) subtitles his book 'fabricating authenticity'. His theme, that country music culture has been a constant process of redefining the authentic-to-be-fabricated, has been mirrored in the phases of Line Dancing and associated trends in the UK and Europe. Peterson's point was that there never was a truly authentic 'country' or 'hillbilly' or 'country and western' persona or identity but that it was re-invented as different media imposed different demands on the visual or audio representation.

12   Cohen (1972).

and the more excessive foot tapping/scraping steps of accomplished dancers to protect their wooden floor for use by other sporting or exercise groups and for other social events. The more the venue is exclusively devoted to Line Dancing and associated C&W activities, the greater appears to be the tendency to pursue authenticity in the attire and dress of the different categories of participants.

The Place

The venue for the Line Dancing Class to be observed was in a long-standing, out of town, out of the way theme park ('Fort San Antone'). Rarely advertised outside of the regular Line Dancing magazines, it would only be known to afficionados or, as in my case, a random passer-by whose curiosity was pricked by a roadside signboard. The site comprises a number of buildings which include a store for buying specially imported, authentic, C&W clothing and attire (catalogues for mail-ordering were available), a stables and horse riding school, caravans and a caravan parking area, with toilet blocks and other facilities for campers, and chalets for weekenders in the form of log cabins, styled on those appearing in movies where they were usually burnt down by marauding Indians. The complex, like many others across Europe, is centred around a large building which houses the bars, restaurant, dance floors and stage.

This centre is an oblong building entered at one corner. The stage (as in performing) fills the opposite corner to the door at this end of the oblong. Across the far end of the oblong is a bar with a standing area with one of its corners given over to a food serving area (beef burgers, spare ribs, and all that). The dance floor (of wood) is at the centre of the oblong building and is surrounded on three sides by tables and bench seats or chairs, although one long side is raised to a mezzanine level overseeing the dance floor and on a level with the stage. On the opposite long side to the balcony is a walkway with access to toilets. This walkway is divided off from the dancing floor by an arrangement of wooden poles like ranch fencing but with a surface to rest elbows, ashtrays and drinking glasses. This 'fence' divides at its centre to provide the main entry to the dancing floor although access to the dance floor can be gained from the other two, non-balcony sides and at each corner. Adjacent to the Stage is a set of sound equipment manned by an elderly man (the DJ) who plays the music and who is often overwhelmed by the technology of the music and sound systems, which are under his control. He plays the pre-selected music for the Line Dancing Class and requested dancing tunes during intervals and 'free-dancing periods'.

This initial geography confronts the newcomer and over a number of attendances can be mapped into areas where different groups of regulars would normally be expected to be found. That is, if they are not in their usual place, this would be a matter for comment and explanation as other regulars arrive to occupy the space, irrespective of their being standing, sitting, or leaning-at-the-bar types of spaces. The spatial distribution of groups, to put this more formally, does have an achieved structure but that structure is constructed, achieved, reproduced and sustained as the process of each session occurs. It is a further matter for wonder that although there is no spatial or social necessity for this ordered arrangement of just those groups in just those spaces, these autochthonous ordered properties recur session after session. On looking to find similar recurrences, I have noted them in hospital dining rooms where grades of nurses and doctors occupy 'their tables'; in the crowds at soccer games where formal 'supporters' occupy different spaces on the open terraces or seating areas, separate from other groups of fans of the team; at larger discotheques 'locals', visitors, outsiders (e.g. 'townies' v students) occupy different spaces at or near the bars and on the dance floors; or in university car parks where office and teaching staff who arrive 'early' occupy spaces nearest to buildings isolating late comers to parking areas 'away' from entrances and access points to buildings.[13] It appears that where recurrent social constructions occur, space-occupancy becomes a necessary property in establishing and sustaining order.

The occupation of 'our space' which in other social locations, like 'my seat' at the pub or local working men's club, at the Bingo Hall, or school classroom, might otherwise be a matter of challenge and dispute, here, results in arrivals occupying the nearest, alternative, suitable seating or standing area. The first arrival takes up station and others fill the surrounding space much like water filling the channels of an estuary as the tide comes in. Extra chairs are located. People 'squeeze' up, occupying a smaller individual space to make room for others to sit and draw near. That 'outsiders' may not do this is a clear signal to new arrivals that this area has not been reserved for them or that they are not expected to be occupants, i.e. members of this group. The spaces, the groups and occupants seem to be decided session by session, by the earliest arrivals, by the claim for membership being made by an arrival at any particular session, by the numbers who have already arrived and by the density of occupation of the space. Some individuals always seemed to warrant a space being found, these being identified and proclaimed (invited and included) by some person or persons already in the space. This identification and proclamation, although rarely challenged, always seemed to require some kind of confirmation in the response of 'squeezing up a bit closer to make way'. Space is occupied and defined in an ordered way rarely leading to or producing disputes. Occupying space is an ordered activity. In a Line Dancing class, the wonder is that the same spatial arrangement seems to emerge at each and any event – with occasional exceptions.

---

13   Laurier, Whyte and Buckner (2001) describe the consequences of a sign ordering that customers should queue for food before taking up seats at tables in a café. A pink sign, loosely attached to the entry door, has sufficient prominence to announce the rule that is recognized and generally obeyed by regulars. The rule, which is most significant when the café is busy at lunchtime, can otherwise be ignored without recrimination when sufficient empty seats are available.

Social Fixtures: Staffing the Venue

A doorman collects an entrance fee and wears the requisite cowboy hat and boots with jeans and an appropriate shirt. He sometimes wears a six-gun with belt and holster, although this is non-threatening. Although not always a paid member of the staff, he arrives early, pays no admission fee, drifts away from his duties as the evening passes beyond its mid-point when the door is 'quiet' and will participate in the free dancing intervals between and after the class sessions. On busy nights when there is a guest 'star', he may attend the door throughout the evening and may be assisted by a doorman of heavier build and with a more threatening demeanour. The assisting doorman will usually wear Stetson and cowboy boots. Throughout the 18 months of observation, the assistant doorman was never called upon to use his build and demeanour to bar entry or to eject anyone from the premises. This may be because attendees are conscious of the requirement to travel to this venue by coach or car unlike other more accessible venues that rely more on passing or pedestrian trade. More likely, this was an attended event where people chose to attend and would avoid behaviour or identification, which would preclude their current or future admission, like group rowdiness or prior excessive drinking. The assistant doorman's presence had more to do with reassuring attenders of their safety and security and protecting them from a 'general public' (just like them) who might make fun of their attire or activities. Several other venues had noticeably much looser arrangements at the door to collect entry fees or 'membership' and none of these were witnessed to require 'door staff' to vet admissions or eject troublemakers.

In the food preparation area and behind the bar, there are two bar staff and a cook, not in cowboy gear and one or two young men (C&W gear optional) who collect empty glasses, used plates, dishes and cutlery from the tables and the bar area. The young men dance when not busy with their work and appear quite accomplished suggesting that they have graduated from being child-attenders to casual employees, learning their dancing skills and acquiring their dancer status along the way. When accomplished dancers gather for a 'demonstration' of how-it-is-done, the glass collectors cease to be that and become members of the accomplished troupe. Those who join in the dancing demonstrations are suitably attired in C&W dress. One or other of these young men may take or share the job as doorman for some part of the evening.

The DJ is a paid member of the staff and will be involved in other activities during the evening, like arbitrating the Shoot-Out or drawing the raffle tickets. He stands down during the Line Dancing Class only reappearing when called upon to play the music for the first run through of the rehearsed set of steps. He has an encyclopaedic knowledge of his CD and record collection, which is called into play between Line Dancing Class sessions when he will respond to requests for particular dances and their associated music or with original suggestions to attach particular dances to music not usually associated with it. This is where professional expertise comes into play because the DJ is often called on to pre-judge music suggestions as appropriate for particular dances or to suggest dances that might match an original music request.[14] The limits of his technical expertise are often displayed when guest groups or Line Dancing instructors have problems with their sound equipment or microphones and he is called upon to affect repairs or modulate and balance the sound system. In any session some minutes may be taken up with these technical difficulties especially in the switching from instruction to dancing or from dancing to performance by a guest band. Peculiarly, when this 'resident' DJ is absent, the evening is less enjoyable, quieter, dancing is less strident, the evening flows less smoothly from dance to dance, to instruction to dancing and so forth. How the DJ achieves this smoothness of flow or what the missing ingredient is that he contributes to a successful evening, is not obvious. His professionalism, his contribution can only be described, as he is, by members. 'He's a crackin' good DJ, him.' How that conclusion is arrived at, what is being accounted for, lies somewhere in the completed event.

A Scottish, woman, dance instructor wears a cowboy hat, short skirt, cowboy boots and has a mobile microphone attached to a head band, fitted to sit in front of the mouth. The microphone operates through a belt pack to the sound system operated from the Stage and maintained by the DJ. Her role in maintaining the social order that is a Line Dancing Class is pivotal and will be described later in some detail. Although circulating and conversing with many individuals and groups when not giving instruction, during the classes all attention is focused on her. She has the stage, front and back.

The Sheriff is an elderly man with long tresses of silver hair and drooping silver moustache. He is generally fully attired in cowboy gear with holster, guns and Sheriff's star and is possibly a member of the owner's family. He will assist in any number of small tasks from collecting empty glasses, clearing tables after food, collecting raffle monies and drawing the raffle, filling in for the DJ and attending the DJ when technical problems surface. There is an audible and tangible expression of disappointment from regular attenders when he announces that he will be the DJ for the evening.

Two elderly women pass around during the evening selling raffle tickets. One of them appears to be related to the Sheriff. They are generally attired in a version of what might be described as 'bar-girls' dresses' copied from watching Western movies, shown when these women themselves would have been much younger. There is a certain incongruity between their age and the appropriate age for wearing such dresses but nobody seems to notice this or comment on it. As they pass among the tables occupied by dancers and their friends or guests, greetings

---

14   'We have playing's *in vivo* developingly phenomenal details, a locally produced, locally accountable phenomenon of order*, *making the time we need*, carried on to satisfy' in Garfinkel's example, a metronome, achieved in this case in the rhythms of particular Country and Western tunes. In this case, the DJ provides in identifying tune-dance combinations, 'marking time, in its commensurable FA alternate' (Garfinkel 2002: 99).

are exchanged along with items of gossip. Being recognized and greeted by them distinguishes regulars from strangers or guests. They feature in the evening's entertainment by drawing the raffle at the end of the dancing class and presenting prizes commensurate with the number of tickets sold. Compared with other venues, like Labour clubs and social clubs, the raffle is more of a ritual than a prize-winning competition. The drawing of the winning tickets passes with relatively little disturbance to the free-flow of interaction. Since the music stops during the raffle, it seems most likely that this ritual has emerged as a small money making venture for the venue which justifies an intermission in dancing and watching in order to sell more drinks, food and other refreshments, the proper purpose of this version of the entertainment business. These two women do, however, spend the whole of their evening engaged in 'running the raffle' and spreading gossip or telling the 'news'.[15]

Social Texture: The Cowboys

The Cowboys are an important part of the cast who give meaning to the event. They feature in the evening and offer a standard of authenticity for an attender to measure their self against and also a contrast for those who wish to dress otherwise than to qualify for membership of this group. One in-group identity serves as a contrasting out-group/in-group identity for other groups. The cowboys are the benchmark identity for this occasion and give the venue and the event a depth of meaning not always achieved at other Line Dancing classes. Other places where classes are held are multiple-use facilities like village halls, leisure centres or social clubs. These other events are more like 'exercise classes' and lack some depth of commitment or meaning given these events by their sole and specific use and purpose and by the attendance of the Cowboys.

Their highlight of the evening, in the middle of the free dance period after the Line Dancing Class is finished, is the Shoot-Out with blank bullets and a sound-triggered timing machine.[16] It takes the form of a knock-out competition where the loser, the slowest to draw and fire, in each Shoot-Out, in each round, drops

---

15   Reported in many studies of 'institutions', an important 'role' occurs for individual inmates, for example, who carry messages, news, information, and so forth, because they have the ability to move between groups, or parts of physical environments in prisons or hospitals. Here in a much less restricted and structured environment, the 'role' was repeatedly recreated and recognized in the communicative facility associated with the two women moving between group locations to sell raffle tickets. Their approaching 'newcomers' also offered a generic conduit for information to be passed by the two women about 'how things go on', 'what's happening tonight', 'who's on next week' and other matters of interest.

16   Due to changes in UK Firearms Laws, this feature of the evening has been withdrawn. It has been reformed into a private gun fighting and re-enactment club with a private membership.

out. Starting with 16 participants gives four rounds, down to eight, then four, then the final between the surviving two. All participants are generally 'men' but one or two women occasionally participate, as do one or two youngsters. Women and youngsters are expected to lose or to win in one round against a less accomplished Shoot-Out cowboy. Youngsters or women who compete beyond the first round draw attention to the cowboys' embarrassment in defeat. This will be exploited by members of others groups, who pass derisive remarks or shouts of encouragement to the woman or youngster. Such remarks are reserved to senior or established members of other groups.[17] These participation rules are regenerated at each event depending on the numbers available to make up the complete 16 or 8 in the first round. Some events will also involve private challenges or re-contests at the behest of the gunslingers and their supporting group among the Cowboys. Winning women fighters have to be beaten by a Cowboy even after the formal Shoot-Out has been completed, and where the woman has won, challenges are laid down and respected by the Sheriff. Since the Shoot-Out takes place in the dancing area, it is surprising that no challenge to the Cowboys' rights to command the floor for the duration of their event are ever issued by dancers.

Full cowboy attire including guns and holsters is de rigueur. Leather 'chaps' (leggings worn by cow-punchers and herdsmen to protect their legs while herding cattle) are worn over the ubiquitous blue-jeans (Levi's) with leather cowboy boots. An important marker (categorization device) adopted by cowboys is that their leather looks worn and well-used either in the form of 'chaps' or boots.

Since, when new, these are supplied normally with a polished finish to the leather, cowboys share ways of ageing or distressing their leather attire. Cement dust will dry and crack leather. A wire brush can take off the polished finish and may soften the leather. Any abrasive substance, like sand or a tool, like a file or rasp, will enhance or authenticate the distressed, just-come-down-off-the-range look of the cowboys' leather attire.[18]

Each 'gunfighter' is known by an appropriate name, as in Slim Jim, the High Plains Drifter, Cool Hand and the like, using names drawn from popular Western movies of the past thirty or so years. Cowboys do not generally participate in the Line Dancing but stand around, proudly, cleaning their weapons and discussing matters of interest to them. The guns are replica or adapted versions of the Colt

---

17 Sacks (1992: 172ff) notes: 'To set up a type, then, like Hotrodder, or Surfer, or Beatnik, if it can be successfully done, is then to get for the collection of persons a very large gain. That is, the "they" group whoever it be – call them "adults" – come to use the type as well, but use it under the extremely important constraint that what it takes to be a member, and what it is that's known about members, is something that the members enforce' (p. 173).

18 Attendees at Gay Clubs in Manchester who sport leather clothing like the 'Stevedore' in the Village People de-novate or distress-finish their leather in similar ways to authenticate their 'gay-role' in contrast with their normal occupations as office-worker, teacher and so forth.

45 favoured by the movie heroes. Other types of six guns are used and much of
the evening for Cowboys is spent examining, cleaning, comparing and preparing
the gun and its holster and rehearsing for the Shoot Out. Cowboys demonstrate
technique to each other but firing the gun is strictly prohibited outside the Shoot-
Out itself. They occupy no particular space in the Hall but tend to congregate near
the corner of the dancing floor nearest to the bar, the food serving area and at one
end of the balcony. Benches and tables at that very end of the balcony may be used
as seating and surfaces for the cowboys when dissembling, cleaning or displaying
their six-guns.

Towards the end of the evening, marking that proceedings are drawing to a
close (commensurate with UK Licensing Laws), a Salute to the Confederate and
US flags involves raising and lowering the flags to the tune of 'Dixie' sung by
Elvis Presley ('The King'), ending with a three-shot salute. Participation in the
Salute, often kneeling, is required for all Cowboys. Most are men aged between
25 and 60 years. One or two sport complete, authentic 'American Indian' outfits
(as represented in classic Western movies and the image of 'Sitting Bull' displayed
on the surrounding wall), salute the flag but do not participate in the Shoot-Out.
Whether this is by design or whether these participants choose not to get involved
is unclear. Some kind of status ranking, paralleling the 'real' world, thus emerges
and is recognized. Cowboys are men. Candidate Cowboys are young men. Women,
no matter how authentically attired, rank third and may participate in the Shoot-
Out. Indians may not. But Indians are definitely part of the Cowboy grouping
because they do not participate in Line Dancing.

Dancers and Candidate Dancers, Accomplished Line Dancers

The Accomplished Dancers are a small troupe of regular attenders who engage
in displays of quite complex step combinations that make up Line Dancing.
Although of varying ages, this group divides roughly in two: a younger element
in their teens and 20s who perform with gusto and verve, adding extra spins and
flourishes to demonstrate their competence, and the older group mostly in their 40s
and 50s who demonstrate their abilities competently but with a more physically
economic and less energetic style. Some younger people participate more with this
second group as they are recent 'graduates' and are still nervous of their abilities.
One or two of the older women attempt to 'mix it' with the younger group only
to demonstrate the obvious physical restrictions that attend ageing. The younger
group is predominantly male with one or two younger women and teenagers.
Although with varying membership this group normally totals about 10. Also equal
in size and with revolving membership, the older group is predominantly women
who gather around two or three 'cool dudes' who were accomplished dancers in
their youth and have moved on to Line Dancing as their new interest. Various
of the accomplished dancers are often 'corralled' into assisting the learners by
demonstrating steps and combination moves during teaching sessions.

The skill that is their professed competence is more to do with shifting from one move or move combination to another in much the same way that keyboard players shift from playing individual notes with fingers to the physical moves required to prepare for chord changes in playing jazz piano or guitar. Sudnow demonstrated with a keyboard during his presentations but says in Ways of the Hand:

> My hands have come to develop an intimate knowledge of the piano keyboard, ways of exploratory engagement with routing, through its spaces, modalities of reaching and articulating, and now I choose places to go in the course of moving from place to place as a handful choosing. (Sudnow: 1978: xiii)

Like ballet dancers who pre-rotate their heads before their bodies to avoid dizziness while performing a pirouette or martial arts fighter who uses the opponent's body weight to throw them in combat, the accomplished Line Dancer moves with speed and confidence to have the body in motion to execute a full or half turn, with or without kick or leg extension. The beginner would stumble, making the same move, because their body lacked the necessary momentum to execute the move. As Sudnow says of the hands rather than individual fingers on keys of the piano, so accomplished Line Dancers shift bodyweight through feet movements where the Beginner is making individual steps and bodyweight movements as virtually separate actions.

These Teacher instructions demonstrate this point:

> Cross the right foot over the left shin while bending the knees.
> Step to the right on the right foot, close left foot up to the right, step to the right on the right foot.
> Hold position as you slide the left foot next to the right (Keep weight on the right foot).
> Stomp left foot down next to the right foot. (Shift weight from the right to the left foot)
> Stomp right foot down next to the left (Shift weight back on to the right foot).

(Note that the 'Step to the right' would not be possible with knees bent so the physiologically unavoidable, taken-for-granted straightening of the knees is not stated. Anyone doing this stuff would be expected to know this to be commonsense. Equally, once practised, the straightening and integrating from 'steps' into a 'movement' uses the straightening of the knees as a platform for the body to launch the 'Step to the right'.) (Note also that this illustrates Garfinkel's distinction between 'instructions' and 'instructions *in vivo*' when 'we are busied topically with the practical issues of locally and endogenously achieved completeness, consistency, followability, empirical correctness, univocality, definiteness of sense and reference, temporal and logical sequence, identity, notational uniformity, comparability, and the rest' (2002: 205), that is, that there is a lot more to performing (*in vivo*) a dance than that which appears in the written manual, chart, map, etc.)

The Accomplished Dancers tend to wear cowboy hats and boots with appropriate shirts or T-shirts and jeans, or C&W dresses. In direct contrast to the Cowboys who seek authenticity (e.g. the recent genre of Western movies which focuses on the arduous and primitive life-style of the California Gold-Rush, the Texas Range Wars and the 'real' life of the Mountain Hunters or Cattle Drive cowboys), the accomplished dancers wear attire common to a more recent generation of popular Country and Western singers of the USA and Canada (c.g. Garth Brooks, Vince Gill, or Reba MacIntyre). Their dress is more colourful and 'in fashion' with decorative adornments of feathers, leather tassels, metal studs, buttons and motifs (Classically, the Rhinestone Cowboy). This is in direct contrast to the Cowboys who must look worn, 'distressed' and authentically 'used'. This is resonant of the Mod-Rocker, Scooter-Boy-Biker contrast, which marked the youth of some of the older participants (Cohen 1973). Accomplished dancers will own and wear several different sets of 'smart gear'. Occasionally individual males in this group who have recently won competitions (British or European Championships) are given the floor for an individual performance, without formal ceremony, to 'strut their stuff'.

Regulars

The Regulars are 50 to 60 people who regularly attend the 'lessons' and divide more or less equally into 'beginners' and 'intermediates'. Since lessons during the Line Dancing Class are described as 'beginner dances' or 'intermediate', all regulars participate in the beginner dance lessons but the less experienced, less accomplished or slow learners do not take the floor for an intermediate lesson. This is a self-imposed order and beginners who have remained on the floor for an intermediate dance instruction will be tolerated and assisted by regulars. Their inability to implement instruction is simply ignored so long as they stay within their allotted 'space'. The space allocation achieved in the lines allows for the less able or less competent to offer a diminished performance without their interfering with other dancers. No sanction, punishment, ridicule or show of opprobrium by the instructor or other dancers was ever witnessed. Attention to their limited capabilities (e.g. not being able to make the turns while performing complex steps – the so-called 'kick-ball-change') would only be drawn when the teacher would climb down from the raised platform to take up an adjacent space and talk them through the steps while the performance was in progress.

The regulars are aged anywhere from about 10 years old to some in their 60s and 70s. Women outnumber men about three to one. The longer the regular attends, and some have been attending for a number of years, the more likely they are to sport the cowboy/cowgirl uniform. The emerging 'intermediate' will have previously been adding items (hat, boots, jeans, shirt, shoe-lace tie) to their attire but they are obvious in the group because their attire looks very new or recently acquired. Much show is involved in appearing for the first time in 'new gear' as it symbolizes a 'graduation' or membership claim. Admiring new gear, especially items bought while on holiday visits to Nashville, Memphis or Calgary, acknowledges the membership claim or celebrates and recognizes the graduation. Conferring membership in this way is by senior members of the dancer group or through the collective admiration of the dress items by numbers of accomplished or regular dancers recognized as 'intermediates'.[19]

Generally the participants wear T-shirts and blue jeans. Newest regulars wear an assortment of everyday going-to-the-pub attire. No one 'dresses up' for an evening out. Women's make-up and hairstyles are restrained and everyday men's attire is similarly subdued rather than showy, in sombre colours avoiding the glaring or garish. This is a self-imposed reticence and seems to reflect a 'Don't get noticed' rule. Members know that this rule works and obey it by degrees but there is no apparent policing or sanctioning if the rule is broken.[20] There is an equal rule that Line Dancing is serious business and criticism, evaluation or ridicule are not to be expressed about the dress or dancing competence of Regulars.

Visitors divide into three groups and complete the ensemble. Visiting parties make up this group on some Fridays and Saturdays coming in coaches from related clubs and dancing classes. Their attendance also includes a meal served before the evening dancing lessons get underway and they tend to fill the balcony-area tables and chairs. They can be excitable and rowdy. They are often the fan-following of the performer, or band, who will be the highlight later in the evening. These regular if infrequent events serve an important purpose in reinforcing boundaries around 'us' which are replayed at each visit. At the most extreme this works through a competitive dance display between 'their' Accomplished dancers and 'ours'. Offering different sets of dance steps to the same piece of music becomes a kind of 'turf-war' for space on the limited dance floor. Visitors often engaged in dance where the individual floor space required exceeded the nominal metre-square and filled up more of the dance floor than was their right. This obvious lack of cognizance of how much space is available, is to be used, is appropriate, that Regulars are naturally aware of, even though it is redefined at any session, clearly defines the Visitor's status as Visitor. It is not clear that exceeding the appropriate spaced-to-be-used is intended to establish Visitor-status but within the order that is the Line Dancing Class the lack of awareness of space allocation, here, serves as a clear category marker.

---

19   Again (Sacks 1992: 172ff) we see how members operate categorical membership rules: 'what it takes to be a member, and what it is that's known about members, is something that the members enforce' (p. 173).

20   'Now the first thing that one wants to be able to do, is to so construct appearances and to so let out information, that members can take it that when they're seen by whomsoever, they will be seen as a member of the category they want to be seen as a member of' (Sacks 1992: 173).

At the abutment between the two dancing groups this might involve trips, bumps, trodden toes, and a general interference with 'our' competent display. Because the music rarely exceeded a three- or four-minute track, the rivalry, which took some minutes to develop, will be short-lived. No struggle or conflict of this order ever erupted into anything more than a few bruised toes or an odd knock such that formal control officers like the second-doorman would be required to intervene and eject Dancers or Visitors. The turf-war however did its work in reinforcing membership for the home team. Revenge for being out-displayed on the dance floor was mooted and usually repaired at the next appropriate dance opportunity. Cowboys might comment or ridicule dancers using the opportunity to reinforce allegiance among themselves in return for previous slights when, in the Shoot-Out, Cowboys were beaten by youngsters or women.[21]

An interesting question concerns the degree to which the membership, categorial or allegiance processes were engineered by the personnel, whether such opportunities were seized by leaders or seniors to strengthen commitment or whether some device could be seen to be operating to this end. The ordering of dances after the class but before artists take the stage or at either side of the Shoot-Out, is the decision of the DJ with his encyclopaedic knowledge of the music and associated dances. At Visitor events, he would invariably be present to do his work. His success for that evening and for each tune selection would revolve around the number of dancers who took to the floor and the gusto with which they engaged in the dancing. Visitors, especially, and Dancers were encouraged to submit requests for favourite tunes. The favoured requests would reflect the programme of tunes-dances practised by accomplished dancers at the home class or venue – and would be their displays of their champions and their highest achievements. Although not obviously so, it is possible that part of the DJs competence was to select a sequence of tunes that built enthusiasm, competitiveness and, thus, membership commitment. Certainly the DJ would be aware of previously 'successful' sequences, which could be replayed if appropriate requests were forthcoming. These sequences would however have to be inherently flexible because the sequence once started would have to provoke requests for other 'successful' tunes for sequences to be appropriately played through. The DJ's role would reflect that of the support band for the rock star, or the warm-up comedian for the TV-show, or the person selecting hymn sequences for church services or meetings designed for reaffirmation of faith or commitment. His success would be reflected in the sense of 'having had a good time' this week, increasing the likelihood that most of the Dancers would be back next week.

---

21   'Have to pick your feet up and get on your toes to match them!' or 'Getting slow in your old age!' (to an accomplished dancer in his early 20s) or 'The kid's faster than you – must be the arthritis.'

Pre-class Preparation

The first problem occurs some time before turning up for the Line Dancing Class – 'What to wear?' This question is obviously not unique to Line Dancing or Line Dancers. It marks a category of events for those people preparing to attend where 'dress' is for them of categorial or criterial significance. For the Disco Dancer, the white suit, red shoes, open-necked black shirt, gold neck-chain with medallion and suitably styled, gelled or greased hair were items which sought to present the wearer as qualified to 'be someone' at the Disco. Equally, the dress suit, white shirt, black bow-tie, cummerbund, patent-leather shoes were qualifications for entry to a 'Black Tie' event for the male attender.

It is not always clear who imposes the code or how persons who breach the dress code are prevented from attending or are sanctioned when admitted to the event. Some events or nightclubs have doormen who can bar entry for inappropriate attire. This facility often functions to bar entry to unwanted guests – groups of single males, individuals or groups who show signs of drunkenness or likely unruly behaviour, those previously barred or refused entry – when the venue is busy or full, although admission may be granted on 'quiet nights' or early in the evening. The dress code can be self-imposed especially if it is clearly declared beforehand on the invitation or ticket to the event or venue. Sanctions are more often a matter of social interaction, or exclusion from it, inside the venue or as part of the proceedings of the event.

Events and venues like the Line Dancing class provide for learning-the-dress-code. One of the buildings associated with our Line Dancing venue, 'Fort San Antone', houses a shop, which is announced as being open during and at the end of the Line Dancing Class. Serving in the shop are one or more of the 'social fixtures'. Apart from standard commercial practices to do with retail buying and selling, their membership status gives extra value to their advice about purchases or outfits. The buyer will seek this advice or may leave and revisit the shop at another time if the server is not a Cowboy or Accomplished Dancer suitably qualified to give this technical advice. Working out how to join groups like this progressively involves understanding the dress code and choosing to fall in with it, or not. Adopting the attire is a membership claim and members seem to take some time in 'learning' how to make this claim appropriately before investing in the expensive dress of one or other of the groups.

This decision is also contingent on making the requisite progress towards competence in dancing or showing interest in the authenticity requirements of Cowboys, showing curiosity and engaging in 'gun-talk'. The progression toward becoming a Regular, and then an Accomplished Dancer would seem to be easier, or at least more obvious, than toward being recognized as a Cowboy. There is potentially an account available, here, but the 'observation' has not made that account 'visible' and it looks like much more time and attention would need to be devoted to looking to see what would be there. Getting inside enough to engage in talk with the Cowboys seems to involve a more elaborate process than that of joining the Line Dancing Class (Hilbert 2004). Being a Cowboy insider would seem to correspond more with the afficionados at a model railway exhibition, war games, battle reenactments, or recreations of the Celtic village or the American Homestead – relating to 'others' as an excluded audience. The difference, here, is that the categorization, Cowboy, is set against the equally significant category, Dancer, each category's existence and presence being dependent on that special relationship. Dancers, like Cowboys, will have pre-prepared their attendance by making available a range of suitable clothes or a choice of specialized attire.

Being constantly aware of how others, especially Visitors, breach rules and avoiding rule breaking while participating seriously in learning to dance by regularity and frequency of attendance, attracts the attention of the Teacher and other Accomplished Dancers and Regulars who assist in giving the Class. Accomplishing this effectively while a Learner will invite Banter with the Teacher and accepting that invitation by competent 'responding' occasions progressive recognition, the move from Learner to Regular, as in:

Teacher:	Have we all got that? (*After demonstrating a four-step sequence*)
D1:	We would, if we could see your feet?
D2:	Better to be done at our speed than yours.
D3:	Have a heed. That's no teachin' that's showin' off.
Teacher:	Again?
D2:	Yeah, just one more time, but slower.

Visitors or Others breach rules, do not competently recognize Banter and are not 'seen' to be regular attenders or to take seriously learning Line Dancing. The transition marker for recognition as a Regular is to 'accept' a kiss-greeting from the Instructor, and for recognition as an Accomplished Dancer, to participate in kiss-greeting with other Regulars and Line Dancers. The Big Move seems to be the moment for confidently and competently, without breaching rules, joining the dancing that goes on in the breaks between Lessons. Membership moves are occasioned, often by invitations from other Accomplished Dancers, to 'take the floor'. This is how becoming-a-Line-Dancer seems to be done. Observe in the class, practice the steps, become familiar with the tunes, appear competent and confident in 'line dancing'.

The Dancing Lesson

After an initial half hour of appearing, drinking and chat, the instructor using the microphone calls the dancers to the floor. Dancers array themselves into the appropriate number of lines for the space available given the numbers beginning to assemble. A small class might involve two lines of six or eight, arrayed towards the front of the floor, either side of some notional centre line. Spacing like this concentrates on learners being able to see the feet of the Instructor who now stands on a raised platform (a board set between two benches on the balcony). There may be some realigning of spaces to ensure this visibility once all those proposing to participate have taken the floor. A busy class might involve four or six lines of 10 or 12 who, magically, successfully occupy the same space. It is trying to understand the 'magic' of this achievement that is the wonder that the ethnomethodologist brings to this apparently simple task. This arrangement may involve anywhere from 12 to 60 or more dancers and yet is achieved in the same moments that are the beginning of the class. On rare occasions where new Learners are present, the Teacher may re-order the lines so that the Learners are towards the front and are attended by an accomplished dancer who can replicate the instruction for this individual learner.

The opening remarks of each lesson involve stating two general rules. The first is known as 'Dance Floor Etiquette' presented visually as:

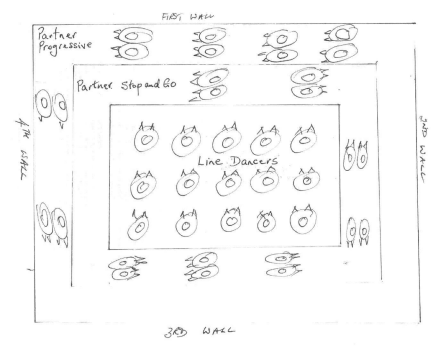

Figure 11.2   Dance floor etiquette: using space for partner dancing, continuous and stop-and-go, and for Line Dancing in free-dance sessions

The graphic represents the floor for general dancing and how 'Progressive' partner dances should occupy the outer edge of the floor. Partner dances are effectively lines of two, which move progressively in the same direction. Partners are normally husband and wife, man and his woman partner or pairs of women. No pairs of men entered seriously into a partner dance, although pairs of young men who are accomplished dancers, might join the ring for a few steps as a 'joke'. This gesture is about the recognition of the superiority of the accomplished Line Dancer and premier on the floor. A young man Accomplished Line Dancer joining the ring with a young woman would respect the propriety of the partner dance like any other couple. An inner ring moving in the same general direction (anticlockwise) is reserved for 'Stop and Go' partner dances where pairs may move forward, reverse, turn a full turn and turn back again, and then to proceed forward. Again if pairs do not proceed in step, in time and at the same pace, the result for their zone and the adjacent zones would be chaos. The primary and central zone is reserved for line dancers. Rarely, however, are all three zones to be seen in simultaneous action. One pre-announced, partner dance might circle the line dancers. This rule however operates more than effectively and its implementation, its *in vivo* recognition of spatial allocation, never fails in maintaining the unseen barrier between the circling partners and the central lines. A withdrawing line dancer will select the most appropriate space between partner pairs to cross from the central zone to leave the floor, thus respecting the partner dancers' zone.

A second, frequently stated rule concerns the supervision of children and their safety, especially when accomplished dancers are 'strutting their stuff'. Foot stomping in a heeled cowboy boot can cause serious injury to a child's foot. This rule is taken to state or reinforce the point that Line Dancing is serious business, not to be engaged in by 'children' or novice-learners. It also states the core 'order rule', that is, that successful Line Dancing means a group, sometimes large, of people, doing the same thing, at the same time, in the same way, lest the order* of the floor descends into chaos. Such chaos would ensue where avoiding the small child breaks up the even and ordered distribution of people across the floor space, as would the learner incorrectly turning to the left rather than the right, or making a quarter rather than a half turn. The partner dancer proceeding too quickly, or too slowly, would throw out the time being marked by the music, for all.

Other than this frequently announced 'safety regulation', rules are something that members become aware of. Being aware and recognizing rules by obviously not breaching them is also an affirmation of status and an acting-out of a membership claim by Regulars. And this not-breaching of rules is a further autochthonous order property of what it is to be at this Line Dancing class. This is a self-imposed reticence and seems to reflect a 'Don't get noticed' rule. Members know that this rule works and obey it by degrees but there is no apparent policing or sanctioning if the rule is broken. There is an equal rule that Line Dancing is serious business and criticism, evaluation or ridicule are not to be expressed about the dress or dancing competence of Regulars.

The line(s) are called to order, facing front. Line dancing involves a number of people formed into one or more 'lines', together, simultaneously, performing a series of steps that moves each individual and all the individuals in the line(s) in the same direction, in the same way. The combination of steps that makes up a line dance becomes increasingly complex, e.g. the Grapevine – walking sideways while crossing the feet, left in front or behind right, and vice versa, heel-toes and so forth. Turns (quarter and half) mean that the dancer probably uses no more than a square metre of the floor to complete a dance sequence. There is no division of the floor space by age or gender, although regulars tend to gather at the front or rear, usually in the central area. Line dancing instruction involves slowly demonstrating short sequences of steps, adding sequence to sequence, until the 'dance' is learned. This sequence of moves, with four repetitions of the sequence, constitutes a Line Dance: 'Hooked on Country', taught to beginners, it is a four-wall dance. Four-wall refers to the sequence of turns built in to the dance such that each dancer, and the line together, face each of the four walls surrounding the floor, in turn.

What follows are a set of instructions, available as hand-outs at a class, as dances in a handbook or magazine, instructions presented with a video or in a manual. They are supposedly sufficient in themselves. Quinn (1997), for example, describes itself on the front-cover as 'The most comprehensive line-dancing manual available.' The instructions presented should be complete and adequate to learn 'Hooked on Country'.

Beginners – Four Wall

Beats	**Movement**	**Direction**
Right Shuffle Back		
1	Step right foot back	▼
&	Step left foot back beside right	
2	Step right foot back	
Left Shuffle Back		
3	Step left foot back	▼
&	Step right foot back beside left	
4	Step left foot back	
Walk Forward		
5	Step right foot forward	▲
6	Step left foot forward	
7	Step right foot forward	
8	Kick left foot forward and clap	

Walk Backward and Ball Change

9	Step left foot back	▼
10	Step right foot back	
11	Step left foot back	
&	Step on ball of right foot	
12	Cross left foot over right, taking weight on left.	

Vine Right

13	Step right foot to right side	▶
14	Step left foot behind	
15	Step right foot to right side	
16	Kick left foot across right and clap	

Vine Left

17	Step left foot to left side	◀
18	Step right foot behind left	
19	Step left foot to left side	
20	Kick right foot across left and clap	

Step and Kick

21	Step right foot in place	●
22	Kick left foot across and clap	
23	Step left foot in place	
24	Kick right foot across and clap	

Taps

| 25, 26 | Tap right heel forward, twice | ● |
| 27, 28 | Tap right toe behind, twice | |

Heel Turn

29	Tap right heel forward	
30	Quarter turn to left	←
	(to face left wall, which becomes front)	
31	Stomp right foot	
32	Kick right foot	

Repeat from Step 1

The only apparent equipment required is an unencumbered floor space and some technology to play the recommended music (the metronome for marking time). As Garfinkel notes: nowhere in his set of instructions do what seem to be necessary steps appear. 'The idea is … that for me to deal with the question seeably, *in vivo*, of whether these instructions are complete, I now find that I'm making use of the *etcetera* provision' (2002: 202). Here 'Direction' indicates the direction of movement in Beats 1 and 2, then in 3 and 4. Reversed in 5, 6, 7 and 8 and reversed again in 9, 10, 11 and 12. Steps 13–16 are a move to the right. Note the significance of the 'clap', ostensibly marking the rhythm of moves in this sequence. Even though the first run-through, probably 4 steps at a time, is way off the *in vivo* rhythm of the tune to be played, the clap is included in the demonstration by the teacher and imitated by the dancers. It is will be the *in vivo* demonstration that 'we are all in step together'. Clapping, early or late, (hearably) draws attention to the dancer. An intermediate or accomplished dancer will be embarrassed by the attention drawn to this hearable error and ineptitude and will concentrate attention on avoiding such errors.

This sequence also carries a shorthand, 'Vine Right', which will be used in instructions, in future, in more complex and elaborate dances, was what someone learning such a dance will take-for-granted as something known to dancers like them. Steps 21–24, 25, 26, 27, 28 occur 'in place' and precede a quarter-turn whose synchronicity is hearably accomplished, by each and all in the 'stomp right foot'. 'Four Wall' in the rubric at the top of the instruction sheet tells the instructee that they will begin facing forward and at each quarter turn they will face the 'next wall' and on the fourth quarter turn, they will resume their starting position, having addressed each of the 'four walls' during the sequence.

The intermediate process between reading the written and diagrammatic instructions, Garfinkel's *etcetera*, and engaging with others in the *in vivo* practice that is line dancing involves *in corpo* demonstration by the Teacher. Other than repetition, no pedagogical theory or analysis is obviously engaged in. The Teacher selects the demonstrable step sequences into which she breaks the dance steps leaving the remainder, including achieving *in vivo* dancing to the emerging practical achievement of the instructees who have taken the floor.

Raised on a platform above the eyeline of the class, the Teacher demonstrates short step sequences (not in time, not according to the rhythm of the tune, not following the metronome), these are repeated once, maybe twice, in response to demands from the floor. The instructees are invited to reproduce these first four steps. Normally, this sequence is most simple and is easily reproduced. Teacher demonstrates the next sequence. The instructees continue adding these steps to those already reproduced. Some will comfortably, seeably add the *etcetera*, ready to add a further sequence and look like competent line dancers, others will struggle to find the *etcetera*. Teacher takes the whole floor, all participants, back to step 1 and puts the sequences together as one string of moves. A third sequence is added, Sequences 1 through 3 are repeated as a continuous string. More of the instructees manage to add the bodily movements, some rhythm, and flow of movement, the accruing *etcetera* that is this line dance.[22] Sequence 4 ends at Step 12 with the first significant shift of body weight from one foot to another (the dreaded kick-ball change). This step at the end of a sequence sets the dancer up to flow directly into the next sequence and is one flow of movement in the *in vivo* accomplishment. That the Teacher breaks the demonstration up in this way might meet all manner of requirements in writing and graphically presenting instructions but the body movements necessary here can only be realized in the *in vivo* version. To the instructee, the dance as several sequences merged into the *in vivo* flow that is a line dance actually is experienced as easier, less challenging, less difficult, more routine, as expected, than the demonstrated, divided up version missing the *etcetera*.

After all 32 steps have been demonstrated in sequences of 3 or 4, kick-ball changes have been accomplished, turns managed in unison, claps and stomps hearably marking the increasing coincidence of accomplished steps, the Teacher accompanied by the instructees will "walk through" (minus the *etcetera* of the instructions) the complete sequence. Most people will "have it" now. The music starts on a count of 3 and the steps, sequences, weight shift and turns, claps and stomps merge together into an accomplished line dance, achieved by nearly everyone on the floor, seeably, hearably, in sync, together … fun is had by all.

> … I mean to be talking about something awesome and beautiful, which is what I take it that Merleau-Ponty spoke of as the familiar miracles of ordinary society. … Obviously it's a miracle, a miracle being: Well, yeah, it happens like that. Don't ask me, I don't know. Nobody knows, it just happens like that. It's a kind of appreciation of the givenness of it. (Garfinkel 2002: 206)

The instruction finishes with the dance to music being repeated without talk. The Teacher may intersperse instruction sequences with banter with one or more of the Regulars regarding their accomplishment, lack of, or any other matter that comes to the instructor's attention (new clothes). In particular, Regulars who try to sit out a dance lesson may be identified from the floor and called to account ('Have you brought a sick note?'). The banter is friendly but the language sometimes reflects that of the bar-room. Regulars rarely return these 'attentions' although when directed at Accomplished Dancers or Cowboys, they often occasion replies in kind. Mild 'insult exchanges' are common. Teaching dances are interspersed with short breaks when the Accomplished Dancers take the floor to demonstrate. Learners who stay on the floor attempting to 'imitate' their peers are not always looked upon kindly. Although nothing is said, the non-verbal language can be loud.

---

22   King and de Rond (2011) report on how rhythm was achieved in the Cambridge boat in the Boat Race in a brief six-minute phase. Once this etcetera added to the crew's performance what looked like a losing row turned into a winning drive as rhythm was achieved.

Some Ethnomethodological Observations

So the methodological work is done. How well?, or badly?, is difficult to judge except to say that every effort has been made to follow the policy Garfinkel sets out (Garfinkel 1967: 1–11). The reflexivity, here, is attached to the attenders. Members go about doing the everyday-taken-for-granted-things that members do in doing a Line Dancing Class. Any formal structures identified are identified as:

> ... by formal structures we understand everyday activities (a) in that they exhibit upon analysis the properties of uniformity, reproducibility, repetitiveness, standardization, typicality, and so on; (b) in that these properties are independent of particular production cohorts; (c) in that particular-cohort independence is a phenomenon for members' recognition; and (d) in that phenomena (a), (b) and (c) are every particular cohort's practical, situated accomplishment. (Garfinkel and Sacks 1970: 346)

Attire is obviously a key to accomplishing group membership and categorization. This distinguishes, particularly, the Cowboys from the Accomplished Dancers and the more renowned Regulars. Attire also suspends the social life of the individual outside the class, and all that goes with it. One advantage of leisure pursuits like this is that a new set of categorizations are available both to the group to allocate and for the member to pursue. And such allocations or accomplishments are set aside as the cowboy hat, shirt, jeans and boots are returned to the clothes cupboard until next time. Within the venue, groupings are fairly discrete with inter-group interaction kept to a minimum, although the Instructor, the Sheriff and the Raffle Ticket Sellers traverse the prominent participant groups. That membership is not in one large amorphous group, as in some of the village hall Line Dancing classes, seems to strengthen both the commitment to the group one belongs to within the venue and, from the available contrasting memberships, to that venue as a whole. Members who may be discretely divided within this venue, on just this evening, may advertise their events under some collective rubric, like the 'Valley Stompers' or the 'Tush Pushers', to other clubs.

Becoming a Regular first involves frequent and/or noticeable attendance (as, for example, in being the subject of banter during instruction). Membership categorization among Regulars while sometimes marked by the acquisition of more appropriate membership attire, especially as the dancer appears to be near graduating to Accomplished Dancer when they participate competently in the between-teaching dancing, is actively marked by the Instructor. Greeting-kissing occurs where the Instructor can mark a Regular at any time in the evening she makes first direct interaction with a participant. At sometime in the evening all Accomplished Dancers and Regulars will be 'greet-kissed' by the Instructor although Accomplished Dancers will also greet-kiss each other. Man-to-Man is marked not with a greet kiss but with verbal greetings, handshakes or hugging and back-patting. Since this process of greeting occurs on arrival or on first contact with the Instructor, it serves the purpose of indicating categorization, or process of change in categorization, on, and as this evening progresses. Greetings like hugging, kissing and handshaking seem to do the work of announcing category allocation in this and a host of other settings.

This is a notable difference in the greeting and member recognition of the Cowboys. Cowboy-to-Cowboy recognition, claimed in the authenticity of the attire, is achieved with an intricate left-handed handshake. The left hand (not the 'gun-hand') is generally covered with a fingerless glove associated with pulling the 'gun-hammer' in the Shoot-Out. The gloved hand is offered and held in the greeting by grasping the base of the extended thumb and/or wrist. In this way, Cowboy visitors are recognized as category members and can participate in the Shoot-Out. It would appear that this form of hand-shake greeting is common to Cowboys throughout the network of Country and Western venues and is the recognition and categorization device for all 'competent' members. Aspirant 'Cowboys' (particularly teenagers or young boys) may possess all the attire attributes necessary for membership, although without the 'distress' of full authenticity, but are not proffered the hand-shake by full members.

Visitor membership can generally be recognized by contrast (and, consequently, self-exclusion) from the 'rituals' associated with being a competent member of other established categories. Occasionally 'outsider' status is marked by forms of sanction where visitors transgress the operating social order in attempting to participate in rituals or activities where their 'competent membership' has not been recognized. For example, Learners 'treatment' by Accomplished Dancers in between-classes dancing. Regulars, in contrast, when they have the floor, will accommodate Learners and assist them in 'practising' the dances. Occasionally, 'showy' Visitors may be 'marked' by clearing the floor leaving them exposed to scrutiny by 'members'. Visitor groups who 'take the floor' can call up a competitive member-group, including Accomplished Dancers with Regulars, who perform a 'different' dance and compete for control of the dance-floor space. These conflicts are rarely resolved because dances are relatively short (a few minutes per CD track) but the 'sanction' is clear. However, in the busy fervour of a Friday or Saturday night event, such 'sanction signals', although repeated, can be ignored and disputes are simply resolved by separation of the competing dancing groups into separate areas of the floor.

A footnote on ethnicity: all Cowboys are white, all Accomplished Dancers are white. All Regulars are white. No black or Asian people have ever attended. Two women of oriental origin have been Visitors. The 'Indians' are a small subset of Cowboys. One incident seems to point to the relevance or awareness of racial issues. On one very special occasion where attire was previously announced as significant for that event, two young men, Accomplished Dancers, appeared and drew attention to the apparently authentic Klu-Klux-Klan hoods and robes that they were wearing. Neither Cowboys nor Line Dancers, nor the frescoes on the surrounding walls recognized this as suitable attire for category membership. The two young men had obviously declared themselves 'outside' the established grouping. They were remonstrated with forcibly by some senior Regulars and asked to remove the offending robes before they were recognized as being appropriate to attend this Line Dancing event. This one example clearly demonstrates that there are a host of rules underlying any social gathering or social interaction which are taken-for-granted. It is only in the breach that such rules are brought into awareness by members, there, then. Garfinkel states:

> Fourth, the reported phenomena are only inspectably the case, They are unavailable to the arts of designing and interpreting definitions, metaphors, models, constructions, types, or ideals. They cannot be recovered by attempts, no matter how thoughtful, to specify an examinable practice by detailing a generality. Fifth, they were discovered. They are only discoverable and they cannot be imagined. (Garfinkel and Sacks 1970: 16)

The reported phenomena here are inspectably the case of a Line Dancing Class.

Chapter 12

Encounters at the Counter:
The Relationship between Regulars and Staff

Eric Laurier

What is a Regular?

Amongst the forms of relating to place, one that remains common enough yet seemingly overlooked by the social sciences is 'the regular' (though see, Morgan 2009: 70–72). While it is the name for a repetitive, definite and predictable pattern of things happening or being positioned, it is the regular, as one of the possible forms of relating to a place, that I want to concentrate on here. The regular is the person that goes to the same place recurrently. That there are regulars for shops, bars, cafes, sports clubs, parks and all manner of other places points towards the commonality of this figure. It is not an official, legal or other institutionally defined role and that perhaps begins to explain why it has not engendered much inquiry into its nature. Yet these are persons who are of significance both to the custodians of those places and to other regulars in those places.

Let's remind ourselves of some of the things we can say about those persons who are regulars. The regulars visit a particular place regularly without being its employees or its residents. Yet they are not all one thing, they could be customers, users, walkers, visitors and a series of other possible entities for a place that have the possibility of visiting it once, twice, irregularly or, of course, regularly. Their becoming regulars appears purposeless in that it is hard to imagine oneself saying 'I will become a regular of X'. Instead people find themselves becoming regulars as the after-effect of returning to the same place over and over again. It is not without consequence nor, perhaps, responsibility because in becoming regulars persons are recognizable and made recognizable by their regularity. They begin to belong in a place and make that place what it is. And once recognized as regulars, small tokens of cognizance of one another emerge in exchanged nods, smiles and greetings. Some of these tokens grow into the small talk of the acquainted and a tiny few transform into new friendships. What I want to begin to describe in what follows are the appearances of 'doing being a regular', to borrow and adapt that fruitful phrase of Harvey Sacks (1984).

Cavan's (1966, 1973) study of US bars provides the precursor for this chapter and touches indirectly upon the idea of the regular. Rather than the bar, the particular place that I will be using, for a number of reasons, not least that with

Chris Philo I undertook a two-year project into its part in city life,[1] is the cafe. In itself it is as common a place, as the regular is a common member of it. Cafes have not only regulars but also counter and/or waiting staff that are responsible for the cafe. Being a competent staff member of a cafe involves recognizing, orienting toward and, often, building relationships with regulars. The regulars are economically important to the cafe because of their repeat business, for spreading its reputation by word of mouth and establishing the crowd that constitutes much of the character of the cafe (Laurier and Philo 2007). It is useful to compare the cafe to the supermarket chain to begin to appreciate the special nature of the regular. Large supermarkets struggle to have the sort of relationship between staff and customers that could produce a high proportion of customers recognizable and treated as regulars. The loyalty card is an attempt to secure something of the regular's relationship but customers and staff are too interchangeable to sustain it. The problem of providing a place that can sustain regulars is one that Raffel (2004) highlights for Starbucks and other large cafe chains. However, in the study that Chris and I undertook what was striking was that individual Starbucks branches, and even the most anonymous cafes in places like airport departure lounges, had regulars. The situation where cafes struggled to have regulars, regardless of whether they were part of global chains or individually owned, was where they were dominated by tourists.

A central element of the regular in the cafe is that they have a 'usual' drink. Their 'usual' becomes a way of identifying them and perhaps making inferences about the character of the regular. For instance, those kinds of person who, in the face of the proliferation of espresso-based coffees in recent years, continue to ask for 'just plain old coffee' and thereby mark their generational allegiance and resistance to new-fangled frappuccinos and their like. Or, those other kinds of customers who ask what the coffee of the day is and discuss the altitude of a particular estate. Those customers that always have a half decaff' latte with soya milk. For each regular anyway, the staff are expected to know their tastes and usually end up inferring something more about them by their tastes. There is still more to the regular than their drink in the cafe and these aspects are shared with a number of other places. They have a time of day they turn up at. They have a rhythm of days of the week that appear on. They have preferred places to sit. In fact they begin to build biographies as Cavan notes of the bar regulars:

> While the patrons of public drinking places can exist without a valid biography (or without any biography at all) with respect to their lives in the outside world, some who patronize any given establishment regularly may create or have created for them a kind of biographical reputation within the bar. Regular patrons of a bar may find their presence and their activities within the bar being strung together in a kind of narrative, eventually to be read as a statement attesting to

1   The ESRC-funded 'The Cappuccino Community: cafes and civic life in the contemporary city' (R000239797).

the kind of person they are. Sometimes this biography is localized only within the bar, but sometimes it contains imputations of more generalized attributes. (Cavan 1966: 82)

Regulars can and do make small talk about the weather, the news of of the day and a host of other topics that are accessible to them as members of the same society relating to one another in public (Coupland 2000). The small talk between staff and customers formed a large part of Goffman's (1971) elaboration of the everyday encounters of, amongst others, customers and cafe staff, in what he called 'supportive' and 'remedial' interchanges (or what we might also call the maintenance and repair of relationships). Cavan's (1966) ethnographic study of bars predates the close attention to talk of Goffman's later work but nevertheless she documents the special nature of bars as 'open regions' where, by their very presence at the bar, patrons can be expected to be available for small talk. Picking up where Goffman's studies of the maintenance and repair of public relationships left off, Maynard and Zimmerman (1984) made an important early contribution to our understanding of how it is that despite seemingly only having general topics that they could talk about, unacquainted persons still successfully (and unsuccessfully) introduce 'their personal biographies' (Maynard and Zimmerman 1984: 301). Their study also brought to light how pre-topical talk amongst unacquainted persons sets up markers of the distance or intimacy between them before they got to the topic itself (see also, Svennevig, 1999). Rather than the exogenous studies common to many approaches from the psychology or sociology of relationships they described 'the work by which members may analyse and formulate a relationship as distant or intimate' (Maynard and Zimmerman 1984: 302).

Because of their repeated encountering of one another, regulars and staff, as Cavan (1966) noted earlier, become less and less like Maynard and Zimmerman's unacquainted persons. They acquire shared topics based on the past experiences of their encounters which means that pre-topical talk ought no longer to be required. Through repeated meetings they acquire other topical resources such each other's usual appearances and so can remark on departures from them (e.g. 'no tie today?') or elaborate on those usual features (e.g. 'another gorgeous handbag!'). Events of their lives that they report (such as parties, promotions, weddings etc.) can be tracked as part of building their relationship. So it is that, in the materials that follow, we will see and hopefully recognize that regulars and staff can become surprisingly intimate with one another while still sustaining the distance of their place-based relationship.

Distinguishing the Regular from the 'Stranger on a Train'

A stimulating comparison can be made between the regular, who expects repetition and ongoing relations with the places they have adopted, and the persons who meet each other once in their life. These persons are 'strangers on a train', persons whom we are brought together with for one extended period during their lives, strike up a conversation. In doing so, revealing parts of their mutual biographies that they would keep secret from many of their friends. It seems odd that persons who begin their encounter as strangers may reveal more than those in search of acquaintanceship (Svennevig 1999).

What can help us here it to look back to Simmel's (2009 (orig, 1908)) excursion on the social form that is the stranger:

> The stranger is fixed within a certain spatial area – or one whose delimitation is analogous to being spatially limited – but the position of the stranger is thereby essentially determined by not belonging in it from the outset, and by introducing qualities that do not and cannot originate from the stranger. The union of the near and the far that every relation among people contains is achieved here in a configuration that formulates it most briefly in this way: The distance within the relationship means that the near is far away, but being a stranger means that the distant is near. (Simmel 2009: 601)

The stranger, for Simmel, is the wanderer who has arrived in a place recently and then ceases their wandering and settles into the place. Where the community of the place might like to treat that person as external to them (as an 'outsider' to use a similar concept) Simmel notes that they are a member of the community, just as 'the poor' and its 'inner enemies' are. For strangers on a train there is no such residence in the place nor is there a community to which they will both belong. Through the lack of such connections to family, community or work they then also lack any shared relationals (persons to whom they are related as family or friend). By dint of their lack of persons to whom any of their stories could be retold to, they are, then, ideal recipients for private thoughts and secrets. A secret told to a stranger can travel no further since the secret is of no exchange value to them and so, under these exceptional circumstances it remains a secret.

Yet sharing a secret is the last step in realizing one of these special encounters. Before we become interested in what such a person's response might be to our secrets we have to find we have other things that we share such as music, ambitions, humour, hobbies, passions etc. To return to the regular, by the very nature of their relationship, there will be future meetings. In the repeated establishment of intimacy and distance, should they pursue intimacy in the way that strangers on a train can, then unlike them they will then face the repeated future encounters with that other. An intimacy at odds with the distance that is part of the idea of the cafe as a place for public sociability that mixes the already intimate, friends, enemies, acquaintances, regulars and staff.

Relationships as Ongoing in situ Accomplishments

What the cafe staff and their regulars pose for us is a social relationship that falls between relationships in public between either intimates or strangers. This then is part of the array of public relationships that Morgan (2009) collects as 'acquaintances'. Yet to say that a regular is an acquaintance of another regular, or of the staff, marks their membership of a wider more general set rather than tells us anything more about the specific nature of the ongoing lived relationship between regulars and staff. Starting from regular-staff relationships as they actually happen we can examine them in terms of their identifying particulars as being just this sort of relationship. This shift of perspective is toward treating a relationship as a form of togetherness constituted, displayed and analysed in the actions that support, maintain and repair it. In common with the rest of the chapters in this collection it is a turn toward lived orders of practice. Maynard and Zimmerman's work, as I noted earlier, pursued this through how the introduction of topics could be used to reproduce the relationship:

> practices for introducing a topic display and accomplish particular features of social relationships, such as the distance and intimacy of involved parties. We regard "relationship" as something that is subject to ongoing, step-by-step management within talk between persons, rather than as a state of affairs that underlies their talk. (Maynard and Zimmerman 1984: 302)

One set of materials through which relationships have been examined is in those occasions where relationships are explicitly formulated (Edwards 1995; Enfield and Stivers 2007; Schegloff 2007; Stokoe 2010). This focus on relationship reference overlaps with the material that follows but neither regulars nor staff were formulating their relationship explicitly as 'regular, friend, acquaintance' etc. While it is not explicit it remains relevant given that:

> participants relied on shared understandings of the activities, competencies, responsibilities, rights, and/or motives regarded as appropriate or inappropriate for incumbents of specific relationship categories to perform a conversational action. (Pomerantz and Mandelbaum 2005: 160)

Quite, then, what a regular does, is able to do, is accountable for, and the analysis of their motives in doing so, turns then on relationship categories and categories that in turn provide grammars for those relationships (Stokoe 2010). Identifying the relationship then does not determine what happens, though it can serve as a device to make sense of what is happening, what just happened and what will happen in the future. However the key difference here, to those that conceive of the relationship as something that members of society *have* and that what it is can thus be assumed, is that ethnomethodology and conversation analysis take the relationship between regulars and staff to be generated, regenerated and degenerated in practice. As Pomerantz and Mandelbaum continue, the intimacy and distance of any relationship is produced through a number of practices that make it recognizable to the persons constituting it:

1. tracking inquiries + providing further details on one's own activities,
2. discussing one's own personal problems + displaying interest in discussing the other's personal problems,
3. making oblique references to shared experiences + taking up the other's talk about shared experiences, and
4. using improprieties + taking up the other's improprieties by using additional, stronger improprieties, or laughter (Pomerantz and Mandelbaum 2005: 161).

Pomerantz and Mandelbaum's list of elements of how we maintain and monitor relationships is not an exhaustive one but it does begin to suggest some features for investigation. For the staff and regulars their recurrent encounter lends itself to picking up where each last left off (e.g. 'how was the concert?' 'feeling better today?'). Staff and customers can use improprieties that, by the polite norms of waiting service, may have all the more force. Where the regular-staff relationships may diverge is around the over-hearable quality of conversations between regulars and staff. An audibility that makes the cafe an unsuitable site for disclosing personal problems (though cafe staff did report this happening in the earlier study – Laurier and Philo 2003), it is the exceptional case). Also what the staff and the regular appear to lack is a set of shared experiences outside of their sharing of the cafe and its world to refer to or take-up when talking with others present (Mandelbaum 2003).

Regulars and the Order of the Service

What I have under-examined until now is that this distinct relationship of the regular emerges out of the background of the service encounter in shops and cafes. A related area of work we can thus look to is on how service encounters are accomplished. Early work by Merritt picked up on the use of questions/answers and requests/acceptances in adjacency pairs (Merritt 1976) and 'okay' as a marker of task completion (Merritt 1978). Though, as later studies pointed out, the service encounter in supermarkets has some peculiar adjacency properties in that 'how-are-you?'s can be happily ignored by customers (Coupland et al. 1992; Kuiper and Flindall 2000).

Beyond the verbal aspects of the sales encounter, the customer's movements around the space of shops or markets are themselves analysable by staff in terms of whether (and what) they are browsing, about to purchase, whether they are in need of assistance etc. (Brown 2004; Clark and Pinch 2009; Lamoureux 1988; Lee and Watson 1993). The cafe has an order of service distinct from that of retail shop spaces, one that bears closest resemblance to the restaurant and the bar (Cavan 1966). For both of the latter the idea of service is one that draws upon hosting more than it does the buying and selling of goods (though see, Traverso 2001). That said, the production of orders at the counter in cafes remains closely related to retail counters by the very fact of how transactions over the counter are organized (Brown 2004).

When making an order at the counter the regular has a distinct object – 'the usual' – which reshapes the order of service. With the rise of espresso variants on the 'cup of coffee' and the ever more elaborate frappuccinos, even a single order may take several lines to describe in sufficient detail and thus and by having a 'usual' makes the regular's order faster for staff (Bartlett 2005). Quite why this might be becomes evident when we see how their orders get done:

Encounter 13 (STAR)
1 S: Hi. The Americano?
2 C: Yeah
3 S: Anything else today?
4 C: No thanks (*hands over money*)
5 S: Three four five ten out of twenty. Thank you.

(Bartlett 2005: 321)

Here the member of staff already knows what the regular usually has and so can compress the full order into an opening first turn that does the greeting and shortcuts to the placing of the order (there are other ways in which the order is compressed see, Kuroshima 2010). This latter part merely needs confirmed by the regular. Moreover it also reverses the adjacency pair with the staff now asking the question and waiting on an answer from the customer, the usual request-response pairing disappearing. Becoming a regular can mean less rather than more is said between staff and customer. However the quality of that more is merely the adequate, for all practical purposes, description of the ordered drink. Returning to a concern with relationships it is the buying of the object (e.g. the usual form of coffee, tea etc.) that becomes the shared experience that indexes the relationship.

Jefferson and Lee (1981) raise the more intriguing issue of how one part of maintaining a relationship – discussing problems and displaying an interest in personal problems – misfits with the service encounter. In the diverse encounters they examined between troubles-teller and troubles-recipient, when the recipient of the troubles shifted to offering advice they then reconfigured the relationship from one of, for instance, friendship to, instead, a service encounter and found their advice rejected. Equally during a service encounter, problems also arose when one relationship contaminated the other. In part this is because the different relationships each generate different foci which then sit at odds with one another: 'while in a Troubles-Telling the focal object is the "teller and his experiences", in the Service Encounter, the focal object is the "problem and its properties"'

(Jefferson and Lee 1981: 411). For the encounters that we shall see the regulars are not bringing troubles for either sympathy from a friend or advice from a professional. Yet, as we shall see, their status as more-than-mere-customers does, at points, raise problems for both the staff and the regulars themselves.

The Study Site

The cafe that the data comes from was first studied as part of the earlier mentioned project on cafe and city life and the opportunity presented itself for a return study six years later when the cafe requested a follow-up recording of its daily custom.[2] It was selected in the initial study because it had a high proportion of regulars compared to other cafes involved in the project. In the intervening years the cafe had changed location to a brand, and grand, new premises. In doing so it had lost old regulars and gained new ones. It had also altered the order of its service. In its previous, fairly cramped premises, customers selected their tables on entry and then the waiting staff came to their tables to take their order. Customers could also place their orders at the counter but this was reasonably uncommon. In the new premises with varied table sizes and more complex lunchtime bookings the staff collected the majority of customers on entry and selected their tables for them and, at that point, the previous order of service resumed. What this means is that in distinction to the branches of Costa, Starbucks, Nero and many other contemporary cafes, customers did not usually place their order at the counter, the order was taken by the waiting staff once customers were seated. As a consequence the customers' order of service was organized into four broad parts: *table selection, placing the order, receiving the order and paying the bill*. In the fragments we will examine below the majority occur before the order of service gets underway, slipping in ahead of table-selection.

In the first study of the cafe, one camera had been used, during the second study, two cameras were used to record a working day in the life of the cafe. Customers were informed of the recordings via posters and flyers on the tables and were able to have their recordings deleted if they so wished (problems arising from this approach are discussed in Laurier and Philo, 2006). One camera roved around the cafe and the other was fixed above and behind the counter. The latter provided by far the best recordings for comparative purposes while also being the least problematic in terms of the sensitivity of topics discussed.[3] Because of the order of service in the cafe, the placing of orders was rarely recorded since they were almost all placed at individual tables. However, and as we shall see,

2   The video recordings of the initial study had turned out to be useful in marketing the cafe.

3   All customers were warned filming was taken place several days in advance and during the filming with posters and flyers. During that day (and afterwards) they could visit the project website and, if they wished, have their recordings erased by the researcher.

greetings, partings and other sociable elements of the cafe-going of regulars and other customers did occur at the cafe's counter.

Cafe Regulars Arriving

The episode below is typical of the arrival of customers who are not recognized as regulars. In this case there is an absence of greeting, though greetings are also used commonly enough, less as greetings, than to bring the arriving customers into the order of service:

Figure 12.1   Transcript 1: Non-regular arrives

In Transcript 1 (Fig. 12.1) 'is it a …' is used to form a question while also securing the customers' attention before then providing the matter in hand. By its very asking this question also establishes a form of entering the cafe where the waitress will be involved in table selection rather than the customers having free reign. The question itself also begins an order of service that is about matching group size to table size, hence the standard 'is it a table for two' generated from the appearance of a group of two. Here, my purpose is not so much to consider how the order of service is recognized by newly arrived customers as to provide a contrast with the arrival of a regular:

Figure 12.2   **Transcript 2: Regular arrives**

The waitress's first-pair part greeting in Transcript 2 in panel 3 is responded to with a second-pair part greeting in return. The doing of greetings in itself does not differentiate a regular's arrival in the cafe from that of other customers. What does differentiate the course of action from other customers is that the regular does not break stride and instead continues rapidly toward a table. As is noted in the caption in the fourth panel of Transcript 2, it is his 'usual table'. Where this regular usually sits is known in common by both other regulars and staff. His rapid and direct path to his table is quite different from the slow trajectory of the women in Transcript 1 who are then also caught by the waitress just as they reach the point where they might begin to survey the cafe in order to select a table. The very pace and trajectory of the regular is indicative of his rights to do so in this space, his desire to get straight to business and steer clear of any extended greeting sequences that might be expected by staff and regulars. It is not just the regular's pace and trajectory toward his table, the waitress herself checks to see who is entering the cafe in panel 2 of Transcript 2. Having identified the regular she does not change pace or alter course in ways that would prefigure intervening in his table selection. There is thus a paired relationship made observable and recognizable by the trajectory and pace of both parties. (Ryave and Schenkein 1974; vom Lehn 2006)

What this gives us is a place that is owned by and looked after by a staff, a place where a visitor can rush straight to a position within it and set themselves down after only the briefest greeting. It seems not that far from having rented a hotel room and is, indeed, not so far from that form of temporary tenancy since by buying drinks and food in cafes what you are always also doing is acquiring some rights to sit at a table for a while, to rest, read the news, meeting a friend or conduct some other business (Laurier et al. 2000). Part of the extra rights one acquires as a regular is to circumnavigate the order of service and go straight to one's usual table. When this cafe first opened customers could go directly to their tables, because that had been the order of service in its previous premises and it was only later when the staff realized they ended up with seating problems that the waiting staff began to direct customers to tables on their arrival. As part of introducing the new order of service the cafe placed a sign just ahead of the point where the two customers stopped in the first transcript saying 'wait here to be seated'; a sign, however, that regulars were told that they could ignore when it was introduced. Part of the rights of regulars then are to compress the order of service in this way as was the case with Bartlett's (2005) ordering sequences.

Partings with Regulars

The order of service ends with the payment of the bill and then partings are usually done. As we shall see more of below, it provides a further slot for small talk, the exchange of news and so on. One repeated feature that does make visible the ongoing nature of the relationship is the intermittent use of 'see you' rather than 'bye'. What the news delivery by regulars does often provide is when they are about to go on holiday or depart on business trips. In parting staff then keep track of regulars who are leaving the place for a while.

In this case one of the regulars has been talking to one of the owners about his holidays while she took his order. On leaving he he inquires at some length about where they get their pastries, he pays his bill and then:

Figure 12.3   Transcript 3: Regular departs

Having exchanged thanks with one another, the regular begins to walk away from the counter. The owner offers him wishes in panel 3 of Transcript 3 'have a good hols', though then self-repairing this wish given that it might be incorrectly placed in relation to another visit. In overlap the regular meantime provides a show of his commitment to the cafe 'I'll be straight back' in response to her holiday wishes (panel 4 of Transcript 3). Cafe staff (and many other service staff such as hairdressers, bank tellers) use 'have you been on holiday/are you going on holiday' as a topic for small talk. This then provides further resources for wishing their customers well for holidays, inquiring into them on their return. As McCabe and Stokoe (2010) note, inquiries about holidays are a constant prop for the unacquainted and acquainted alike. Here it signals how regulars' lives as regulars are set-up to be tracked by members of the staff (Pomerantz and Mandelbaum 2005).

The Intimacy of Regulars

As we have noted already regulars have greater rights to table selection and thus can compress this format of the order of service. What skipping the earlier slots of the order of service also results in, is missing the slot for extended greetings and the ritual 'how-are-yous' at the counter on arrival that generate the relationship beyond that of just another customer. In Transcript 4, a regular attends to this by approaching the counter later in the order of service.

By approaching the counter he also controls which members of staff he will greet. The staff's order of service is organized not only around the sequencing of orders but also the geography of the cafe. Each member of staff is responsible for a spatially proximate collection of tables. As a result regulars that stay at their table will, at that stage, only speak to the member of staff allocated to their table. To select which members of staff he will greet he thus has to make his way to the counter. By his very trajectory he is also displaying his availability and intent to make small talk with the staff.

Figure 12.4a   Transcript 4: Greeting a regular

Figure 12.4b   Transcript 4: Greeting a regular

When the waitress sees him approaching she does indeed repeat her 'hallo' (in the 3rd frame) thus providing an accentuated greeting displaying her pleasure at seeing him (Schegloff 1972). A greeting which he returns and then, in overlap, they continue their greeting moves with mutual 'how are yous' This second step in the sequence of greeting by its mutuality displays their relationship as one in which news updates are expected. 'How-are-yous' when only produced by the staff are part of the production of the service encounter and are not ordinarily returned (Kuiper and Flindall 2000).

In her response the waitress (Amy) adds a formulation of the identity of the regular in age and gender terms (i.e. 'how are you young man'). Clearly there are a number of possible related standardized relational pairs (e.g. staff-customer, friend-friend etc.). By addressing him as 'young man' then this positions her not just as older but as perhaps too old to be paired in a romantic relationship. It is also pursuing intimacy in being mildly provocative, where the 'young man' phrase has entered the British repertoire of quotes from comedy shows. It featured as a catchphrase in a series of sketches from the Harry Enfield's Television Programme (BBC 1990) where two elderly women tried to take advantage of various youthful men (i.e. 'The Lovely Wobbly Randy Old Ladies'). While playful it also succeeds in framing the upcoming hug as affectionate rather than serious. Initially its pursuit of intimacy is not taken up by the regular, verbally. That a hug is incipient is itself made apparent by the waitress coming out from behind the counter. The counter providing a variety of resources in the encounters between staff and customers, not least of which is as being a device for maintaining a minimal distance between the staff and the customers. Thus, by coming out from behind the counter Amy is making herself available for a greeting hug. The regular has however also set himself in place for potential hugging by standing back from the counter rather than walking right up and leaning over it.

The course of the greeting hug continues with the arms of both the regular and Amy going out for a hug in overlap. The greeting hug then comes off as a mutual hug rather than one person hugging the other. By accomplishing the hug as from both sides then the relationship also comes off as being mutual. The regular's 'You all right' in the 5th panel of Transcript 4 is also in close overlap with the hug being launched. In mid-hug Amy (6th panel) responds positively and returns the question. Opening questions provide the possibility of warning of some form of trouble ahead if they are not answered with positive responses (Sacks 1992). They also index the relationship of waitress and regular as having both the rights to inquire after one another's general state and the background knowledge of their being 'good' and 'all right' is (Sacks 1992).

Hugs themselves are key cultural objects during greetings (and elsewhere) in showing intimacy with others while also ripe for being awkward or misunderstood because their acceptance and appropriateness in whatever relationship varies by cultural background, generation, by family, by individual, by workplace, and so on. What is striking here is that the strength of relationships formed between regulars and staff in this cafe allows them to hug one another. How then is the hug done to express the relationship? Their gazes are kept apart from one another to avoid the intimacy of eye contact at such close quarters. In its duration, the hug is brief, punctual almost. It establishes a friendliness without further intimacy. In fact their gazes do not return to potentially reciprocal positions until the waitress is safely back behind the counter. For either to have picked up the gaze or watched the other could have produced a number of other stances toward the other from tenderness to unwanted attention.

After completing their greetings and checks on one another's status as without problems or troubles to be shared, the regular does move on to his status as 'with' someone. In the last frame of the strip:

> Regular: I'm with mammy so
> W'tress: [Wi your mammy
>   +
> Waiter: [((*look over shoulder and sees regular*))
> Regular: For a wee spot of dinner
> Waiter: Hullo
> Regular: There he is
> Regular: How are you handsome you all right
> W'tress: Aw:::

The regular's mention that he is 'with' somone brings him back into an order of service in that customers consistently attend to their with-ness on arriving if they are not together as they walk in (as we will see more of below). It's of interest as well in establishing his relationship with the older woman he is with for the benefit of the staff. One of things that is known about him as a regular is that he is usually with girlfriends. The waitress's voicing of her response is louder, catching the waiter's attention, and has an air of adult-child about it in its tone and repetition to check who he's with. It perhaps continues the earlier pursuit of intimacy, which if so, is not taken up directly by the regular. He continues with providing what they are the cafe for (e.g. 'a wee spot of dinner') and thus orienting to the order of service. At this time in the early evening/later afternoon the staff routinely ask new arrivals whether they are in for coffee or dinner. Where the waitress could take this as information she instead provides an assessment 'aw:::' as to the apparent sweetness of a son out for dinner with his mum.

Figure 12.5a   Transcript 5: (continues directly from 4) 'But you know what I'm like'

Figure 12.5b **Transcript 5: (continues directly from 4) 'But you know what I'm like'**

Having greeted the waitress the regular then moves on to the waiter. Bound up with the regular's greeting is the endearment 'how are you handsome', once again indexing their familiarity as does the regular's further use of 'pal' in his positive response to the waiter's inquiring 'are you well?'.

Having not prefigured any larger troubles during the greetings, the regular then does initiate a problem presentation 'I'm a bit worried' (*Transcript 5*, 5th panel). In this second slot, after initial greetings, the problem is likely less serious by its second position and is also further established as minor 'a <u>bit</u> worried'. In fact by being pre-formulated as a worry it indicates that this problem is not yet manifest, it is only potential and potentially personal. Once the regular's worry is elaborated 'I've got football this evening' it is immediately responded to with a sharp intake of breath by the waitress showing concern (*Transcript 5*, 5th panel). Coming in at this point her audible intake shows not only concern but an understanding – though of what it's hard to say, it might be that the customer has double-booked himself between cafe dining and football playing. What we do have though, in her response, is that display of interest we might expect of those persons building a relationship of intimacy with us (Pomerantz and Mandelbaum 2005). It stands in opposition with the indifference of requests for help to the emergency services noted by Jefferson and Lee later in their article.

However instead of revealing a personal worry, Amy's show of concern sets off a repairing restart from the regular that indicates his playing is not in question and the upshot of the problem ought not to have yet been inferable. This time Amy receipts, not as an immediate cause for concern, though still showing interest if in a less emotive tone, 'oh whereabouts?' As his concerns are elaborated – 'like if I eat dinner now' – he is in fact making the football relevant to Amy and the waiter as a problem for the cafe staff. 'I'm gonna get the worst stitch aren't I' (*Transcript 5*, 7th panel) should he end up eating too much, either through his own over-ordering or their powers of persuasion, then he'll suffer later when he plays football. He gets an appreciative laugh from the waiter in the pay-off of the mildly dramatic expectation of the worry being turned around as humorous. Taking up a solution to the worry as a problem relevant to the upcoming food order, the waitress offers general advice (which the manageress just-off-screen to the right in frame 3 agrees with). We can note the sensitivity to the agency of the customer and the accountability of selecting their specific dish in that staff member only provides the formulation 'light' rather than mentioning one of the dishes that is actually on the set or specials menu.

The regular accepts their advice and in a lovely orientation to his status as a regular and thus what the staff will know about him he adds 'but you know what I'm like.' Which is an interesting attribution of knowledge of his self to others which is on a parity with what family or close friends might otherwise know (i.e. what foods we like and how much we eat (Laurier and Wiggins 2011)). What we also have though is very close to the switching between relationships that Jefferson and Lee (1981) traced through troubles-tellings. What it does in this case is something perhaps more subtle, and related to order of service, by organizing the group of recipients involved. This regular been warmly greeted by Amy, rather than other members of staff. The shift to a worry that is related to his appetite, by its topic re-includes all of the staff as potential advice-givers. And indeed we have an appreciative laugh from the waiter, advice from Amy and an agreeing 'yeah' from the manageress. The 'but you know what I'm like' refocuses the attention on Amy and does then get an appreciative and almost motherly laugh from her.

What this begins to give us a sense of is the café-specific staff knowledge of their regulars. Knowledge that then can be used to build an intimacy with the regulars through shared access to their tastes, their likes and dislikes. While within the family this is part and parcel of eating together, here, within the cafe, it is both the nature of their transaction and also, we should not forget, asymmetrical since the staff, when they eat, eat quietly in a corner.

Accounting for Absence

One of the features of regular contact between family members and friends is that they seek and provide updates for one another (Drew and Chilton 2000). As was captured in the earlier extract the feature appears largely absent from cafe regulars and staff even though they see each other more often than many of their friends, family and work colleagues. Part of the reason for regulars and staffs not doing so is, of course, that those closer relationships come with expectations and rights about sharing and keeping track of one another's daily news, significant events and calendars (Brown et al. 2007; Pomerantz and Mandelbaum 2005; Sacks 1992). Nevertheless when the regular re-appears after a prolonged absence it does then make noticeable their absence, an absence that is an accountable matter. When regulars do not appear it is not of course a notifiable, and potentially serious, matter in the way that it is when a husband's wife fails to return home at the end of the day. When the regular reappears after their disappearance, their re-appearance is taken quite calmly with something like 'have you been away?' although inquiries into their absence are occasioned not so much by a desire to 'oil the wheels of social interaction' (McCabe and Stokoe 2010: 1128) as to genuinely account for their absence. It is here where we again reconnect to Jefferson and Lee's (1981) study of the rejection of advice. The trouble that may arise asking customers about their absence is related to two subtly different potential inquiries with different relationships in play. The first is around catching up with potential news that may account for an absence and the second is learning why a relationship has been transformed/ended. In the first case, the inquiry collects acquaintances and friends that we see regularly, for the second case, it is the relationship between the service and its customer.

In the following a regular has arrived, and in this case they have not been in the cafe in a while. After doing greetings and a hug:

Figure 12.6   Transcript 6: Absent regular returns

Before we move on to the regular accounting for their absence, we can pick up on the regular and Amy having a hug. The hug on this occasion is initiated by the regular. Before the transcript begin the mutual trajectory toward the hug was broken Amy telling a humorous story about him not noticing her outside the cafe. Arriving later the hug takes quite some work to bring it off and is preceded by a thanks that initially configures it as a thank you hug rather than a greeting. However as with the previous hug with the 'young man' the regular then combines it with a 'how are you', recovering the hug as a marker of friendship. Nevertheless it still catches Amy slightly off-balance. In *Transcript 6*, panel 2, the regular is then asked by Amy 'what you been doing' and then by the waitress in black 'have you been away'. In between he is apologizing to Amy for not having noticed her in the street. Amy picks up the previous question 'have you been away' with 'I know' in an emphatic tone and redoing it as 'where you been away'. This little flurry of questions nicely showing a joint and genuine interest over what has happened in his absence and doing 'making a fuss' over the regular. For his part he does then provide the preferred response here that he has been away.

'What you been doing' is interesting because it conforms with an invitation for news delivery between friends and acquaintances and is thus not quite the expected 'have you been away?' In one sense it indexes a greater degree of intimacy between this waitress and the customer. However it also perhaps marks a different sort of issue: that the customer has been absent because he has been busy. If we consider some of the alternative explanations for a regular's absence it is that the regular has in fact become a regular of a competing cafe or given up frequenting cafes altogether. Either of which would spell the transformation and potential death of this relationship and, like refusals, rejections and divorces, they are not what the other who is committed to the initial course of action usually hopes for. The second waitress's question is thus on safer territory in that it expects absence from their shared place to be the cause of his absence from the cafe. Indeed the regular orients to their relationship by including not only the preferred response, that yes he has indeed been away rather than started taking his business elsewhere, but also that he is going to be 'going away' in the future. These remarks preface the longer account he gives later of the various places his work has taken him that meant he wasn't in this part of the city and then following that, that he will be leaving the country for at least a couple of months with his work.

In terms of where they are placed in the unfolding arrival of the regular in the cafe these accounts for absence bear comparisons to how guests are greeted on arrival at the doorstep (Béal and Traverso 2010). In Béal and Traverso's study they documented how noticings of punctuality or lateness provided for teasing which thus was also an early way of re-establishing the intimacy of the hosts and their guests. These are not host-guest relations, they are staff-regulars though as I argued at the outset of the article, the cafe provides for relations of hosting as part of its good service. In terms of the regular's special status as a regular there is a similar desire to re-establish and re-examine their relationship from the first few minutes of their encounter. As such, providing the reasons for the regular's absence and the warning of his future absence orient toward their ongoing relationship that in a gentle way is marking that their relationship is likely coming to an end.

The regular talked with these two waitresses for a few minutes passing on his news of his job changes. An emergent asymmetry here is that the waitresses do not provide news of what has been happening with them because, by the fact that they are waiting on him in the cafe their job, they can be assumed to be roughly the same unless they indicate otherwise. It is the regular who has been absent and thus broken the very pattern of attendance that gave him his status. Should a member of the staff also disappear for an extended period of time, by the nature of their regularity of encounter, the regular is then entitled to notice their absence. The 'have you been away' or 'where have you been' is thus also used by regulars in pursuing accounts of the staff. However the staff member's accountability is asymmetrical in a further way because they are employed to reside there rather than customers that are visiting at their discretion.

Later in the encounter all the waiting staff orient to this departure by making sure that they either say goodbye to him or make a final date when they will goodbye. For the time being, when the greeting and news delivery are completed the regular then departs to eat/drink without the waitresses. The order of service in cafes (unless it's a take-away order) creates a gap in the middle of the encounter while the regular then sits at their table engaging in whatever activities (e.g. meetings, newspaper-reading, texting, daydreaming etc.). The encounter is closed by the regular's departure from the cafe at which point their relationship to the staff as a regular becomes a matter of potential concern again.

Concluding Thoughts

The ambition of many cafes (and other places of hospitality) is to build up relationships with its regulars that borrow from and sometimes come to appear like close acquaintanceships or friendships. What we have followed here are how those relationships are ongoingly generated and maintained, if asymmetrically, by both parties. Looking to Jefferson and Lee's (1981) original analysis of the conflicts between troubles-telling and problem-presenting, I traced out similar adjustments around what aspect of the staff-regular relationship was being made relevant. Whether they were pursuing the relationships as friends or returning to the order of service that divided them back into staff and customer. Other elements of the maintenance and repair of relationships were apparent in the tracking of customer activities and the use of improprieties.

While the regular finds themselves a regular, as I noted earlier, almost without motive or plan, they then find themselves in a relationship which creates commitments. This is made apparent to them when either party returns after an absence or the relationship is being altered or ended. On return after an absence the reasons for regulars' absence would be pursued and greetings would be upgraded, even up to the level of hugging. Equally, regulars mark their departure from daily attendance to the staff and have that departure responded to as a significant matter by the staff. In doing so our departure from this category within a public place becomes one of the practices of parting and departure that are oriented toward a community and to a shared place in the city. We discover in these farewells and wishes to visit again, our relationship to the staff that have been our hosts through the order of service.

What I have found myself returning to in considering how intimacy is generated, and absence accounted for, is an asymmetry around the regular. In fact they have a certain vulnerability because the staff come to know more and more about their lives and yet the regulars' knowledge of the staff is predominantly through their workplace life. This is part of the particular geography of this kind of public place because it has customers that enter within it and form relationships with its staff, relationships distinct from those between the staff themselves as fellow workers within a business. The vulnerability of the regular is in a developing intimacy; they are describable and memorable in terms of their daily habits. As we saw, some regulars delight in this 'but you know me', while others may be surprised to discover that they have lost the anonymity that public space appears to offer.

Acknowledgements

Moira, Rich, Lucy, Finton, Gemma. The members of SEDIT. Chris Philo. ESRC Ref 000239797.

Bibliography

Agyeman, J. and Neal, S. (eds) (2006a). *The New Countryside? Ethnicity, Nation and Exclusion in Contemporary Rural Britain.* Bristol: The Policy Press.

Allcock, J. (1988). Tourism as a sacred journey. *Loisir et Societé*, 11, 33–48.

Allen-Collinson, J. (2009). Sporting embodiment: sports studies and the (continuing) promise of phenomenology. *Qualitative Research in Sport and Exercise*, 1(3), 279–96.

Allen-Collinson, J. (2010). Running embodiment, power and vulnerability: notes towards a feminist phenomenology of female running, in E. Kennedy and P. Markula (eds) *Women and Exercise: The Body, Health and Consumerism.* London: Routledge, 280–98.

Allen-Collinson, J. (2011a). Feminist phenomenology and the woman in the running body, *Sport, Ethics & Philosophy*, 5(3), 287–302.

Allen-Collinson, J. (2011b). Intention and epochē in tension: autophenomenography, bracketing and a novel approach to researching sporting embodiment. *Qualitative Research in Sport & Exercise*, 3(1), 48–62.

Allen-Collinson, J. and Hockey, J. (2005). Autoethnography: self indulgence or rigorous methodology, in *Philosophy and the Sciences of Exercise, Health and Sport: Critical Perspectives on Research Methods*, edited by M.J. McNamee. London: Routledge, 187–202.

Allen-Collinson, J. and Hockey, J. (2009). The essence of sporting embodiment: phenomenological analyses of the sporting body. *International Journal of Interdisciplinary Social Sciences*, 4(4), 71–81.

Allen-Collinson, J. and Hockey, J. (2011). Feeling the way: notes toward a haptic phenomenology of distance running and scuba diving. *International Review for the Sociology of Sport*, 46(3), 330–45.

Anderson, B. and Harrison, P. (2010). The promise of non-representational theories, in Ben Anderson and Paul Harrison (eds), *Taking Place: Non-representational Theories and Geography.* Farnham, Surrey: Ashgate, 1–36.

Anderson, L. and Taylor, J.D. (2010). Standing out while fitting in: serious leisure identities and aligning actions among skydivers and gun collectors. *Journal of Contemporary Ethnography*, February 2010(39), 34–59.

Armour, D. (1997). A study of colour: Wittgensteinian and ethnomethodological investigations. Unpublished Ph.D. Thesis. Lancaster University: Sociology Department.

Atkinson, J.-M. (1978). *Discovering Suicide.* London: Macmillan.

Atkinson, P. and Delamont, S. (2006). Rescuing narrative from qualitative research. *Narrative Inquiry*, 16(1), 164–72.

Bærenholdt, J.O., Haldrup, M., Larsen, J. and Urry, J. (2004). *Performing Tourist Places*. Aldershot: Ashgate.

Bartlett, N.J.D. (2005). A double shot 2% mocha latte, please, with whip: service encounters in two coffee shops and at a coffee cart, in M.H. Long (ed.), *Second Language Needs Analysis*. Cambridge, Cambridge University Press, 305–43.

Bartlett, T. (2005). *RYA Navigation Handbook*. Southampton: The Royal Yachting Association.

Béal, C. and Traverso, V. (2010). 'Hello, we're outrageously punctual': front door rituals between friends in Australia and France, *French Language Studies*, 20, 17–29.

Beardsworth, A. (1997). *Sociology on the Menu*. London: Routledge.

Becker, H.S. (ed.) (1973). *Outsiders: Studies in the Sociology of Deviance*. New York: The Free Press (first published 1963).

Benford, S., Tolmie, P., Ahmed, A.Y., Crabtree, A. and Rodden, T. (2012). *Supporting Traditional Music-Making: Designing for Situated Discretion, Proceedings of CSCW'12*, February 11–15, Seattle, Washington, ACM.

Benson, D. and Hughes, J.A. (1983). *The Perspective of Ethnomethodology*. London: Longman.

Bittner, E. (1974). The concept of organization, in R. Turner (ed.), *Ethnomethodology*. Harmondsworth: Penquin Books, 69–81.

Bittner, E. (1967). The police on Skid Row. *American Sociological Review*, 2, 699–715.

Bjelic, D. (2004). *Galileo's Pendulum: Science, Sexuality and the Body-Instrument Link*. Albany, NY: State University of New York Press.

Bjelic, D. and Lynch, M. (1992). The work of a scientific demonstration: respecifying Newton's and Goethe's theories of color, in G. Watson and R. Seiler (eds), *Text in Context: Contributions to Ethnomethodology*. London and Beverly Hills: Sage Publications, 52–78.

Brekhus, W. (1998). A sociology of the unmarked: redirecting our focus. *Sociological Theory*, 16(1), 34–51.

Brown, B. (2004). The order of service: the practical management of customer interaction. *Sociological Research Online*, 9(4), 364–83.

Brown, B. and Chalmers, M. (2003). Tourism and mobile technology, in K. Kuutti and E.H. Karsten (eds), *Proceedings of the Eighth European Conference on Computer Supported Cooperative Work*. Helsinki, Finland: Kluwer Academic Press, 14–18 September 2003.

Brown B., Taylor, A., Izadi, S., Sellen, A. and Kay, J. (2007). Locating family values: a field trial of the whereabouts clock, in *Proceedings of UbiComp 2007*. Insbruck, Austria. Springer, 354–71.

Burke, S.M., Sparkes, A.C. and Allen-Collinson, J. (2008). High altitude climbers as ethnomethodologists making sense of cognitive dissonance: ethnographic insights from an attempt to scale Mt. Everest. *The Sport Psychologist*, 22, 336–66.

Butler, C. (2008). *Talk and Social Interaction in the Playground.* Aldershot, UK: Ashgate.

Button, G. (1991). Introduction, in G. Button (ed.), *Ethnomethodology and the Human Sciences.* Cambridge: Cambridge University Press.

Carr, N. (2008). Is Google making us stupid? What the Internet is doing to our brains. *Atlantic Magazine*, July/August 2008.

Carson, C. (1986). *Irish Traditional Music.* Irish Books and Media.

Carson, C. (1998). *Last Night's Fun: A Book about Irish Traditional Music.* New York: North Point Press.

Casey, S. (1998). *Set Phasers on Stun and Other True Tales of Design.* Santa Barbara, CA: Aegean.

Caton, C.E. (ed.) (1963). *Philosophy and Ordinary Language.* Urbana, IL: University of Illinois Press.

Cauldwell, J. (ed.) (2006). *Sport, Sexualities and Queer Theory.* London: Routledge.

Cavan, S. (1966). *The Liquor License, An Ethnography of Bar Behavior.* Chicago, Aldine.

Cavan, S. (1973). Bar sociability, in A. Birenbaum and E. Sagarin (eds), *People in Places: The Sociology of the Familiar.* London: Nelson, 143–54.

Charles, N. and Kerr, M. (1988). *Women, Food and Families.* Manchester: Manchester University Press.

Charmaz, K. (2006). *Constructing Grounded Theory.* London: Sage.

Clark, C. and Pinch, T. (2009). *The Socially Organized Basis of Everyday 'Economic' Conduct: Evidence from Video Recordings of Real-life Pre-verbal Salesperson-Shopper Encounters in a Showroom Retail Store.* Aberdeen: University of Aberdeen Business School.

Coakley, J. and Dunning, E. (eds) (2000). *Handbook of Sport Studies.* London: Sage.

Coates, S. (1999). Analysing the physical: an ethnomethdological study of boxing. *Ethnographic Studies*, 4, 14–26.

Cohen, E. (1998). Tourism and religion: a comparative perspective. *Pacific Tourism Review*, 2, 1–10.

Cohen, S. (1972). *Folk Devils and Moral Panics: The Creation of the Mods and Rockers.* London: MacGibbon and Kee.

Collins, N. (2011). E-readers 'too easy' to read. *Daily Telegraph*, 13 January 2011.

Constantine, M. and the Sound Approach (2006). *The Sound Approach to Birding: A Guide to Understanding Bird Sound.* Poole, Dorset, UK: Sound Approach.

Coulter, J. and Parsons, E.D. (1991). The praxiology of perception: visual orientations and practical action. *Inquiry*, 33, 251–72.

Coupland, J. (ed.) (2000). *Small Talk.* Harlow: Longman.

Coupland, J., Coupland, N. and Robinson, J.D. (1992). 'How are you?': negotiating phatic communion. *Language in Society*, 21, 207–30.

Coveney, J. (2006). *Food, Morals and Meaning: The Pleasure and Anxiety of Eating* (Second Edition). Abingdon: Routledge.

Crabtree, A., Nichols, D.M., O'Brien, J., Rouncefield, M. and Twidale, M.B. (1999). Ethnomethodologically-informed ethnography and information system design. *Journal of the American Society for Information Science*, 51(7), 666–82.

Crabtree, A., Rouncefield, M. and Tolmie, P. (2012). *Doing Design Ethnography*. London: Springer.

Crabtree, A., Twidale, M.B., O'Brien, J. and Nichols, D.M. (1997). Talking in the library. *Proceedings of the 2nd International Conference on Digital Libraries*, 221–8, ACM.

Crowley, A. (1980). *Book of Lies*. Newburyport MA: Red Wheel, originally published 1921.

Dant, T. and Wheaton, B. (2007). Windsurfing: an extreme form of material and embodied interaction? *Anthropology Today*, 23(6), December 2007, 8–12.

de Jong, A. and Mazé, R. (2010). *Cultures of Sustainability: 'Ways of Doing' Cooking*. In, ERSCP-EMSU Conference 'Knowledge Collaboration & Learning for Sustainabile Innovation', 25–9 Oct 2010, Delft, the Netherlands.

De Leseleuc, E., Jacquews, G. and Marcellini, A. (2002). The practice of sport as a political expression? Rock climbing at Claret, France. *International Sociology*, 17(1), 73–90.

de Vos, D. (2007). *Vogelzang in beeld* [Birdsong in the picture]. Zeist: KNNV Uitgeverij.

de Vos, D. and de Meersman, L. (2005). *Wat zingt daar?* [What's singing there?]. Utrecht: KNNV Uitgeverij.

Deem, R. (1986). *All Work and No Play?* Milton Keynes: Open University Press.

Dennis, N., Henriques, F. and Slaughter, C. (1956). *Coal is Our Life*. London: Eyre and Spottiswoode.

Donnelly, P. (1994), citing Dvorks, P. (1991). Take my word for it: trust in the context of birding and mountaineering. *Qualitative Sociology*, 17(3), 215–41.

Douglas, J.D. (ed.) (1971). *Understanding Everyday Life: Towards the Reconstruction of Sociological Knowledge*. London: Routledge and Kegan Paul.

Drew, P. and Chilton, K. (2000). Calling just to keep in touch: regular and habitualised telephone calls an environment for small talk, in J. Coupland (ed.), *Small Talk*. Harlow, UK: Pearson Education.

Dulin, K.L. (1974). The sociology of reading. *The Journal of Educational Research*, 67(9), Research in Reading (May–June, 1974), 392–6.

Edwards, D. (1995). Two to tango: script formulations, dispositions, and rhetorical symmetry in relationship troubles. *Research on Language and Social Interaction*, 28(4), 319–50.

Elias, N. (1969). *The Civilizing Process, Vol. I. The History of Manners*. Oxford: Blackwell.

Enfield, N. and Stivers, T. (eds) (2007). *Person Reference in Interaction: Linguistic, Cultural, and Social Perspectives*. Cambridge: Cambridge University Press.

Fele, G. (2008). The phenomenal field: ethnomethodological perspectives on collective phenomena. *Human Studies*, 31, 299–322.

Foy, B. (2009). *Field Guide to the Irish Music Session.* Seattle: Frogchart Press.

Francis, D. and Hester, S. (2004). *An Invitation to Ethnomethodology.* London: Sage.

Fuller, S. (2003). Creating and contesting boundaries: exploring the dynamics of conflict and classification. *Sociological Forum*, 18(1), 3–30.

Garfinkel, H. (Unpublished Manuscript 1). Ethnomethodology's rivalry with and succession to Husserl's programme for studies of the Lebenswelt origins of the sciences. UCLA: Department of Sociology and Anthropology.

Garfinkel, H. (Unpublished Manuscript 2). About the missed orderliness of ordinary activities. UCLA: Department of Sociology and Anthropology.

Garfinkel, H. (1967a). *Studies in Ethnomethodology.* Englewood Cliffs, NJ: Prentice-Hall.

Garfinkel, H. (1967b). 'Good' organizational reasons for 'bad' clinic records, in H. Garfinkel, *Studies in Ethnomethodology*. Englewood Cliffs, NJ: Prentice-Hall, 186–207.

Garfinkel, H. (ed.) (1986). *Ethnomethodological Studies of Work.* London: Routledge & Kegan Paul.

Garfinkel, H. (1988). Evidence for locally produced, naturally accountable phenomena of order, logic, reason, meaning, method, etc., in and as of the essential quiddity of immortal ordinary society, (I of IV): an announcement of studies. *Sociological Theory*, 6(1), 103–9.

Garfinkel, H. (1996). Ethnomethodology's program. *Social Psychology Quarterly*, 59(1), 5–21.

Garfinkel, H. (2002a). *Ethnomethodology's Program: Working Out Durkheim's Aphorism.* Lanham, MD: Rowman and Littlefield.

Garfinkel, H. (2002b). A study of the work of teaching undergraduate chemistry in lecture format, in H. Garfinkel, *Ethnomethodology's Program: Working Out Durkheim's Aphorism*. Maryland: Rowman & Littlefield Publishers, Inc., 219–44.

Garfinkel, H. (2007). Lebenswelt origins of the sciences: working out Durkheim's aphorism: Book Two: workplace and documentary diversity of ethnomethodological studies of work and sciences by ethnomethodology's authors. *Human Studies*, 30(1), 9–56.

Garfinkel, H., Lynch, M. and Livingston, E. (1981). The work of a discovering science construed with materials from the optically discovered pulsar. *Philosophy of the Social Sciences*, 11(2), 131–58.

Garfinkel, H. and Sacks, H. (1970). On formal structures of practical actions, in J.C. McKinney and E.A. Tiryakian (eds), *Theoretical Sociology: Perspectives and Developments.* New York: Appleton-Century Crofts, 337–66.

Garfinkel, H. and Wieder, D.L. (1992). Two incommensurable, asymmetrically alternate technologies of social analysis, in G. Watson and R.M. Seiler (eds), *Text in Context: Contributions to Ethnomethodology*. London: Sage, 175–206.

Gibson, J.J. (1979). *The Ecological Approach to Visual Perception.* Boston: Houghton Mifflin.

Giddens, A. (2006). *Sociology: 5th Edition*. London: Polity.

Girton, G.D. (1986). Kung Fu: toward a paradoxical hermeneutic of the Martial Arts, in H. Garfinkel (ed.), *Ethnomethodological Studies of Work*. London and NY: Routedge & Kegan Paul, 60–91.

Goffman, E. (1971). *Relations in Public: Microstudies of the Public Order.* London: Allen Lane.

Gold, R.L. (1958). Roles in sociological field observations. *Social Forces*, 36, 217–23.

Gombrich, E.H. (1960). *Art and Illusion: A Study in the Psychology of Pictorial Representation*. Princeton, NJ: Princeton University Press.

Goode, D. (1994). *A World without Words: The Social Construction of Children Born Deaf and Blind*. Philadelphia: Temple University Press.

Goode, D. (2007). *Playing with My Dog Katie: An Ethnomethodological Study of Dog-Human Interaction*. West Lafeyette, Indiana: Purdue University Press.

Goodwin, C. (1994). Professional vision. *American Anthropologist*, 96(3), 606–33.

Goodwin, C. (2003). Practices of seeing visual analysis: an ethnomethodological approach, in T. Van Leeuwan and C. Jewitt (eds), *Handbook of Visual Analysis*. London: Sage, 157–82.

Goody, J. (1982). *Cooking, Cuisine and Class: A Study in Comparative Sociology.* Cambridge: Cambridge University Press.

Green, E., Hebron, S. and Woodward, D. (1990). *Women's Leisure, What Leisure?* London: Macmillan.

Haldrup, M. and Larsen, J. (2006). Material cultures of tourism. *Leisure Studies*, 25(3), 275–89.

Hamilton, C. (1999). Session, in F. Vallely (ed.), *The Companion to Irish Traditional Music*. Cork: Cork University Press, 345–6.

Hanson, N.R. (1958). *Patterns of Discovery: An Inquiry into the Conceptual Foundations of Science*. Cambridge: Cambridge University Press.

Have, Paul ten (1999). Structuring writing for reading: hypertext and the reading body. *Human Studies*, 22, 273–98.

Heap, J.L. (1990). Applied ethnomethodology: looking for the local rationality of reading activities. *Human Studies*, 13(1), 39–72.

Hemphill, D. (2005). Deeper inside the beautiful game. *Journal of the Philosophy of Sport*, XXXII, 105–15.

Heritage, J.C. (1989). Current developments in conversation analysis, in *Conversation: An Interdisciplinary Approach*, edited by D. Roger and P. Bull. Clevedon: Multilingual Matters, 21–47.

Hess, A. (2007). The social bonds of cooking: gastronomic societies in the basque country. *Cultural Sociology*, November 2007, 1(3), 383–407.

Hetherington, K. (1997). In place of geometry: the materiality of place, in K. Hetherington and R. Munro (eds), *Ideas of Difference*. Oxford: Blackwell.

Heywood, I. (1994). Urgent dreams: climbing, rationization and ambivalence. *Leisure Studies*, 13, 179–94.

Hilbert, R. (2004). Coding, in *Ethno/CA List*, ETHNO@cios.org 24.11.2004.

Hockey, J. and Allen-Collinson, J. (2006). Seeing the way: visual sociology and the distance runner's perspective. *Visual Studies*, 21(1), 70–81.

Hockey, J. and Allen-Collinson, J. (2007a). Grasping the phenomenology of sporting bodies. *International Review for the Sociology of Sport*, 42(2), 115–31.

Hockey, J. and Allen-Collinson, J. (2007b). Public space and running-together: some ethnomethodological considerations, in, F. Jordan, L. Kilgour and N. Morgan, *Academic Renewal: Innovations in Leisure and Tourism Theories and Methods*. Eastbourne: Leisure Studies Association. P3-23.

Hockey, J. and Allen-Collinson, J. (2009). The sensorium at work: the sensory phenomenology of the working body. *The Sociological Review*, 57(2), 217–39.

Holden, P. and Cleeves, T. (2010). *RSPB Handbook of British Birds: Third Edition*. London: Christopher Helm.

Hollinshead, K. (2004). Tourism and the making of the world: the dynamics of our contemporary tribal lives. *Imperium* (http://imperiumjournal.com/).

Howe, P.D. (2004). *Sport, Professionalism and Pain*. London: Routledge.

Hughson, J. and Inglis, D. (2002). Inside the beautiful game: towards a Merleau-Pontian phenomenology of soccer play. *Journal of the Philosophy of Sport*, XXIX, 1–15.

Izhaki, R. (2008). *Mixing Audio: Concepts, Practices and Tools*. London: Focal Press.

Jefferson, G. and Lee, J.R.E. (1981). The rejection of advice: managing the problematic convergence of a 'troubles-telling' and a 'service encounter'. *Journal of Pragmatics*, 5(5), 399–422.

Jimerson, J.B. and Oware, M.K. (2006). Telling the code of the street. *Journal of Contemporary Ethnography*, 35(1), 24–50.

Kaufman, K. (2011). *Field Guide to Advanced Birding: Understanding What You See and Hear*. Boston, New York: Houghton Mifflin Harcourt.

Kaul, A.R. (2007). The limits of commodification in traditional Irish music sessions. *Journal of the Royal Anthropological Institute*, 13(3), 703–19.

Kelly, R.S. (1999). One step forward and two steps back: Woolgar, reflexivity, qualitative research and a line dancing class. *Ethnographic Studies*, 4, September 1999, 1–13.

Kew, F. (1986). Playing the game: an ethnomethodological perspective. *International Review for the Sociology of Sport*, 21(4), 305–21.

Kew, F. (1990). Constituting games: an analysis of game rules and game-processes. Ph.D. thesis, University of Leeds.

Kew, F.C. (1992). Game-rules and social theory. *International Review for the Sociology of Sport*, 27(4), 293–307.

King, A. and de Rond, M. (2011). Boat race: rhythm and the possibility of collective performance. *British Journal of Sociology*, 62(4), 565–85.

Kuhn, T.S. (1970). *The Structure of Scientific Revolutions*, 2nd edition. Chicago: University of Chicago Press.

Kuhn, T.S. (1974). Second thoughts about paradigms, in F. Suppe (ed.), *The Structure of Scientific Theories*. Urbana, IL: University of Illinois Press, 459–82.

Kuiper, K. and Flindall, M. (2000). Social rituals, formulaic speech and small talk at the supermarket checkout, in J. Coupland (ed.), *Small Talk*. Harlow: Pearson Education.

Kuroshima, S. (2010). Another look at the service encounter: progressivity, intersubjectivity, and trust in a Japanese sushi restaurant. *Journal of Pragmatics*, 42, 856–69.

LAgroup & Interarts (2005). *City Tourism & Culture: The European Experience.* Report produced for European Travel Commission (ETC) and World Tourism Organization (WTO).

Lamoureux, E.L. (1988). Rhetoric and conversation in service encounters. *Research on Language and Social Interaction*, 22, 93–114.

Laurier, E. (2004). The spectacular showing: Houdini and the wonder of ethnomethodology. *Human Studies*, 27(4), 377–99.

Laurier, E., Whyte, A. and Buckner, K. (2000). An ethnography of a neighbourhood café: informality, table arrangements and background noise. *Journal of Mundane Behaviour* (http://www.mundanebehavior.org/index2.htm).

Laurier, E. and Brown, B. (2004). *Cultures of Seeing: Pedagogies of the Riverbank*. Institute of Geography, Edinburgh University. Available at: http://www.ericlaurier.co.uk/resources/Writings/Laurier_cultures_of_seeing3.doc.pdf (accessed 18 December 2012).

Laurier, E. and Brown, B. (n.d.). *Method and Phenomenon: ".. .. ..", "V", "->"* = *a big fish*. Available at: http://web2.ges.gla.ac.uk/~elaurier/texts/seeing_fish.pdf (accessed 18 December 2012).

Laurier, E. and Philo, C. (2003). *The Cappuccino Community: Cafés and Civic Life in the Contemporary City*. Project Description, Swindon and Glasgow: ESRC and University of Glasgow.

Laurier, E. and Philo, C. (2006). Natural problems of naturalistic video data, in H. Knoblauch, J. Raab, H.-G. Soeffner and B. Schnettler (eds), *Video-analysis: Methodology and Methods, Qualitative Audiovisual Data Analysis in Sociology*. Oxford: Peter Lang.

Laurier, E. and Philo, C. (2007). 'A parcel of muddling muckworms': revisiting Habermas and the early modern English coffee-houses. *Social and Cultural Geography*, 259–81.

Laurier, E. and Wiggins, S. (2011). Finishing the family meal. The interactional organisation of satiety. *Appetite*, 56(1), 53–64.

Law, J. and Lynch, M. (1988). Lists, field guides, and the descriptive organization of seeing: birdwatching as an exemplary observational activity. *Human Studies*, 11, 271–303.

Le Breton, D. (2000). *Eloge de la marche*. Paris: Editions Metailie.

Lee, J.D. and Watson, D.R. (1993). *Interaction in Urban Public Space, Final Report – Plan Urbain*. Manchester, UK: University of Manchester.

Levi-Strauss (1970). *The Raw and the Cooked*. London: J Cape.

Liazos, A. (1972). The poverty of the sociology of deviance: nuts, sluts and perverts. *Social Problems*, 20(1), 103–20.

Livingston, E. (1987). *Making Sense of Ethnomethodology*. London: Routledge and Kegan Paul.

Livingston, E. (1995). *An Anthropology of Reading*. Bloomington, IN: Indiana University Press.

Livingston, E. (1999). Cultures of proving. *Social Studies of Science*, 29(6), 867–88.

Livingston, E. (2006). Ethnomethodological studies of mediated interaction and mundane expertise. *The Sociological Review*, 54(3), 405–25.

Livingston, E. (2008). *Ethnographies of Reason*. Aldershot: Ashgate.

Lupton, D. (1996). *Food, the Body, and the Self*. London: Sage.

Lynch, M. (1988). The externalized retina: selection and mathematization in the visual documentation of objects in the life sciences. *Human Studies*, 11(2/3), 201–34.

Lynch, M. (1993a). *Scientific Practice and Ordinary Action: Ethnomethodology and Social Studies of Science*. New York: Cambridge University Press.

Lynch, M. (1993b). Representing reference, or how to say 'fish'. *Social Epistemology*, 7(4), 355–8.

Lynch, M. (2001). Ethnomethodology and the logic of practice, in T.R. Schatzki, K. Knorr Cetina and E. Von Savigny (eds), *The Practice Turn in Contemporary Social Theory*. London: Routledge, 131–48.

Lynch, M. (2006). The origins of ethnomethodology, in M.W. Risjord and S.P. Turner (eds), *Philosophy of Anthropology and Sociology*. London: North Holland, 485–515.

Lynch, M. and Law, J. (1999). Pictures, texts, and objects: the literary language game of birdwatching, in M. Biagioli (ed.), *The Science Studies Reader*. London and New York: Routledge, 317–41.

Lynch, M., Livingston, E. and Garfinkel, H. (1983). Temporal order in laboratory work, in K. Knorr Cetina, and M. Mulkay (eds), *Science Observed: Perspectives on the Social Study of Science*. London: Sage, 205–38.

Lyng, S. (1990). Edgework: a social psychological analysis of voluntary risk taking. *American Journal of Sociology*, 95(4), 851–86.

Macbeth, D. (2012). Some notes on the play of basketball in its circumstantial detail, and an introduction to their occasion. *Human Studies*, 35(2), 193–208.

Maguire, J. and Young, K. (2002). *Theory, Sport & Society*. Oxford: JAI.

Mandelbaum, J. (2003). Couples sharing stories. *Communication Quarterly*, 35(2), 144–70.

Marr, A. (2007). Curling up with a good ebook. *The Guardian*, 11 May 2007. Available at http://books.guardian.co.uk/ebooks/story/0,,2077277,00.html (accessed January 2011).

Maynard, D. and Zimmerman, D. (1984). Topical talk, ritual and the social-organization of relationships. *Social Psychology Quarterly*, 47(4), 301–16.

McCabe, S. and Stokoe, E. (2010). Have you been away? Holiday talk in everyday interaction. *Annals of Tourism Research*, 37(4), 1117–40.

McHoul, A. (1978). Ethnomethodology and literature: preliminaries to a sociology of reading. *Poetics*, 7(1), 113–20.

McHoul, A. (1982). *Telling How Texts Talk: Essays on Reading and Ethnomethodology*. London: Routledge & Kegan Paul.

Mehan, H. (1979). *Learning Lessons: Social Organization in the Classroom*. Cambridge: Harvard University Press.

Merritt, M. (1976). On questions following questions in service encounters. *Language in Society*, 5(3), 315–57.

Merritt, M. (1978). On the use of 'OK' in service encounters. *Working Papers in Sociolinguistics*, 42 (Southwest Educational Development Laboratory).

Miller, T. (1998). Commodifying the male body, problematizing 'hegemonic masculinity?'. *Journal of Sport & Social Issues*, 22(4), 431–46.

Morgan, D. (2009). *Acquaintances. The Space Between Intimates and Strangers*. Milton Keynes: Open University Press.

Morley, J. (2001). Inspiration and expiration: yoga practice through Merleau-Ponty's phenomenology of the body. *Philosophy East and West*, 51(1), 73–82.

Mullarney, K., Svensson, L., Zetterstrom, D. and Grant, P.J. (1999). *Birds of Europe*. London: Harper Collins.

Murcott, A. (ed.) (1983). *The Sociology of Food and Eating*. Aldershot: Gower.

Murcott, A. (1995). Raw, cooked and proper meals at home, in D.W. Marshall (ed.), *Food Choice and the Consumer*. Glasgow: Blackie Academic & Professional, 219–35.

Neth, B. (2008). *Ecotourism as a Tool for Sustainable Rural Community Development and Natural Resources Management in the Tonle Sap Biosphere Reserve*. Kassel: Kassel University Press.

O'Shea, H. (2006–2007). Getting to the heart of the music: idealizing musical community and Irish traditional music sessions. *Journal of the Society for Musicology in Ireland*, 2, 1–18.

O'Shea, H. (2008a). 'Good man, Mary!' Women musicians and the fraternity of Irish traditional music. *Journal of Gender Studies*, 17(1), 55–70.

O'Shea, H. (2008b). *The Making of Irish Traditional Music*. Cork: Cork University Press.

Owsinski, B. (2008). *The Mastering Engineer's Handbook (2nd edn.): The Audio Mastering Handbook*. Boston, MA: Thomson Course Technology.

Paget, E. and Mounet, J.-P. (2009). La pratique de la raquette a neige dans la Reserve naturelle de la Haute-chaine di Jura: un egestion problematique. *Science & Motricite*, 67(2), 79–87.

Parker, S. (1971). *The Future of Work and Leisure*. London: MacGibbon and Kee.

Paul e Meehl (1957). When shall we use our heads instead of the formula? *Journal of Counselling Psychology*, 4, 268–73.

Peterson, R.A. (1997). *Creating Country Music: Fabricating Authenticity*. Chicago: University of Chicago Press.

Polanyi, M. (1958). *Personal Knowledge*. Chicago: University of Chicago Press.

Pomerantz, A. (1984). Agreeing and disagreeing with assessments: some features of preferred/dispreferred turn shapes, in J.M. Atkinson and J. Heritage (eds), *Structures of Social Action: Studies in Conversation Analysis*. Cambridge: Cambridge University Press, 57–101 [version previously in *Analytic Sociology*, 1979, 2(1)].

Pomerantz, A. and Mandelbaum, J. (2005). Conversation analytic approaches to the relevance and uses of relationship categories in interaction, in K.L. Fitch and R.E. Sanders (eds), *Handbook of Language and Social Interaction*. London: Lawrence Erlbaum, 149–71.

Quinn, Á. (1997). *Line Dancing*. Glasgow: Harper Collins.

Raffel, S. (2004). Baudrillard on simulations: an exegesis and a critique. *Sociological Research Online*, 9(2). Available at: http://www.socresonline.org.uk/9/2/raffel.html (accessed January 2010).

Randall, D., Harper, R. and Rouncefield, M. (2007). *Fieldwork for Design: Theory and Practice*. London: Springer Verlag.

Randall, D. and Sharrock, W. (2011). The sociologist as movie critic, in M. Rouncefield and P. Tolmie (eds), *Ethnomethodology at Work*. Farnham, Surrey: Ashgate, 1–18.

Revermann, C. and Petermann, T. (2002). Tourism in large nature reserves – interactions and possibilities for cooperation between nature conservation and regional tourism, TAB (Buro fur Technikfolgen-Abschatzung Beim Deustschen Bundestag) Report, Berlin.

Richards, A. (1932). *Hunger and Work in a Savage Tribe: A Functional Study of Nutrition among the Southern Bantu*. London: Routledge & Kegan Paul.

Ritzer, G. (2008). *The McDonaldization of Society*. Los Angeles: Pine Forge Press.

Robillard, A.B. (1999.) *Meaning of a Disability: The Lived Experience of Paralysis*. Philadelphia: Temple University Press.

Rooksby, J. (2011). Reading, in M. Rouncefield and P. Tolmie (eds), *Ethnomethodology at Work*. Farnham, Surrey: Ashgate, 173–90.

Rossiter, P. (2007). Rock climbing: on humans, nature, and other nonhumans. *Space and Culture*, 10(2), 292–305.

Rouncefield, M. and Tolmie, P. (eds) (2011). *Ethnomethodology at Work*. Farnham, Surrey: Ashgate.

Ryave, A.L. and Schenkein, J.N. (1975). Notes on the art of walking, in R. Turner (ed.), *Ethnomethodology: Selected Readings*. Harmondsworth: Penguin, 265–74.

Sacks, H. (1984a). Notes on methodology, in J.M. Atkinson and J.C. Heritage (eds), *Structures of Social Action: Studies in Conversation Analysis*. Cambridge: Cambridge University Press, 21–7.

Sacks, H. (1984b). On doing being ordinary, in J.M. Atkinson and J.C. Heritage (eds), *Structures of Social Action*. Cambridge: Cambridge University Press, 413–29.

Sacks, H. (1992). *Lectures in Conversation*. Volumes 1 and 2. Oxford: Basil Blackwell.

Sacks, H., Schegloff, E. and Jefferson, G. (1974). A simplest systematics for the organization of turn-taking in conversation. *Language*, 50, 696–735.

Sample, G. (2010). *Collins Bird Songs & Calls*. London: Collins.

Sanders-Bustle, L. and Oliver, K.L. (2001). The role of physical activity in the lives of researchers: a body-narrative. *Studies in Philosophy and Education*, 20, 507–20.

Schegloff, E.A. (1972). Sequencing in conversational openings, in J.J. Gumperz and D. Hymes (eds), *Directions in Sociolinguistics: The Ethnography of Communication*. New York: Holt, Rhinehart & Winston.

Schegloff, E.A. (1988). Presequences and indirection: applying speech act theory to ordinary conversation. *Journal of Pragmatics*, 12, 55–62.

Schegloff, E. (2007). Categories in action: person-reference and membership categorization. *Discourse Studies*, 9(4), 433–61.

Schuster, R.M., Thompson, J.G. and Hammitt, W.E. (2001). Rock climbers' attitudes toward management of climbing and the use of bolts. *Environmental Management*, 28(3), 403–12.

Schutz, A. (1967). *The Phenomenology of the Social World*. Translated by G. Walsh and F. Lehnert. Evanston, ILL: Northwestern University Press.

Schutz, A. (1976). Making music together: a study in social relationship, in A. Brodersen, *Collected Papers II: Studies in Social Theory*. The Hague: Martinus Nijhoff, 159–78.

Seater, B. and Jacobson, C. (1976). Structuring sociology: the prestige of sociological sub-fields in North America. *International Social Science Journal*, 28, 391–5.

Sharpley, R. and Jepson, D. (2010). Rural tourism: a spiritual experience? *Annals of Tourism Research*, doi:10.1016/j.annals.2010.05.002.

Sharrock, W.W. and Anderson, D.C. (1979). Directional hospital signs as sociological data. *Information Design Journal*, 1(2), 81–94.

Sharrock, W.W. and Anderson, D.C. (1986). *The Ethnomethodologists*. Chichester: Ellis Horwood.

Sharrock, W.W. and Coulter, J. (1998). On what we can see. *Theory & Psychology*, 8, 147–64.

Sharrock, W. and Ikeya, N. (2000). Instructional matter: readable properties of an introductory text in matrix algebra, in S. Hester and D. Francis (eds), *Local Educational Order*. Amsterdam: John Benjamins, 271–88.

Sharrock, W. and Watson, R. (1988). Autonomy among social theories; the incarnation of social structures, in N. Fielding (ed.), *Actions and Structure: Research Methods and Social Theory*. London: Sage, 56–77.

Short, F. (2006). *Kitchen Secrets: The Meaning of Cooking in Everyday Life*. Oxford: Berg.

Simmel, G. (2009). *Sociology: Inquiries into the Construction of Social Forms*. Leiden: Koninklijke Brill.

Simmel, G. (2009 (orig, 1908)). *Sociology: Inquiries into the Construction of Social Forms, Volume 1*. Danvers MA: Koninklijke Brill NV.

Skeggs, B. (1999). Matter out of place: visibility and sexuality in leisure spaces. *Leisure Studies*, 213–32.

Smith, G. (1997). Incivil attention and everyday intolerance: vicissitudes of exercising in public places. *Perspectives on Social Problems*, 9, 59–79.

Smith, S.L. (2000). British non-elite road running and masculinity: a case of 'running repairs'? *Men and Masculinities*, 3(2), 187–208.

Sparkes, A. (2000). Autoethnography and narratives of the self: reflections on criteria in action. *Sociology of Sport Journal*, 17(1), 21–43.

Sparkes, A.C. (2009). Ethnography and the senses: challenges and possibilities. *Qualitative Research in Sport and Exercise*, 1(1), 21–35.

Stebbins R.A. (1992). *Amateurs, Professionals and Serious Leisure*. Montreal: McGill-Queens University Press.

Stebbins, R.A. (1993). Social world, life-style, and serious leisure: towards a mesostructural analysis. *World Leisure and Recreation*, 35, 23–6.

Stebbins, R.A. (1997). Casual leisure: a conceptual statement. *Leisure Studies*, 16(1), 17–25.

Stebbins, R.A. (2011). The semiotic self and serious leisure. *American Sociologist*, 42(2–3), 238–48.

Stokoe, E. (2010). 'Have you been married, or …?': eliciting and accounting for relationship histories in speed-dating interaction. *Research on Language & Social Interaction*, 43(3), 260–82.

Stranger, M. (1999). The aesthetics of risk: a study of surfing. *International Review for the Sociology of Sport*, 34, 265.

Suchman, L. (1987). *Plans and Situated Actions*. Cambridge: Cambridge University Press.

Suchman, L.A. (2007). *Human-Machine Reconfigurations: Plans and Situated Actions*, 2nd Edition. Cambridge: Cambridge University Press.

Sudnow, D. (1972). Temporal parameters of interpersonal observation, in *Studies in Social Interaction*, edited by D. Sudnow. New York: Free Press, 259–79.

Sudnow, D. (1978). *Ways of the Hand: The Organization of Improvised Conduct*. London: Routledge & Kegan Paul.

Svennevig, J. (1999). *Getting Acquainted in Conversation: A Study of Initial Interactions*. Amsterdam: John Benjamins.

Tejada-Flores, L. (1986 (1978)). Games climbers play, in K. Wilson (ed.), *The Games Climbers Play*. London: Diadem Books.

Thompson, J.B. (2005). *Books in the Digital Age*. Cambridge: Polity Press.

Thurston, D. (2010). Irish music in Wellington: a study of a local music community, Ph.D. thesis. Victoria: University of Wellington.

Tomlinson, A. (1993). Culture of commitment in leisure: notes towards the understanding of a serious legacy. *World Leisure and Recreation*, 35, 6–9.

Traverso, V. (2001). Syrian service encounters: a case of shifting strategies within verbal exchange. *Pragmatics*, 11(4), 421–44.

Tunstall, J. (1962). *The Fishermen*. London: MacGibbon and Kee.

Turner, R. (1975). Words, utterances and activities, in R. Turner (ed.), *Ethnomethodology: Selected Readings*. Harmondsworth: Penguin, 197–215.

UNEP (2011). *Climate Change and Tourism Policies in OECD Countries*. United Nations Environment Programme.

Urry, J. (2001). *The Tourist Gaze*. London: Sage.

vom Lehn, D. (2006). Embodying experience – a video-based examination of visitors' conduct and interaction in museums. *European Journal of Marketing*, 40, 1340–59.

Walter, J.A. (1982). Social limits to tourism. *Leisure Studies*, 1, 295–304.

Watson, R. (1994). Harvey Sacks' sociology of mind in action. *Theory, Culture and Society*, 11, 169–86.

Watson, R. (2006). Tacit knowledge. *Theory, Culture & Society*, 23(2–3), 208–10.

Watson, R. (2009). *Analysing Practical and Professional Texts: A Naturalistic Approach*. Aldershot: Ashgate.

Webb, A.T. (2007). *A Father, a Son, and a Storybook: A Case Study of Discourse during Storybook Reading*. California: University of Southern California.

Weeks, P. (1990). Musical time as a practical accomplishment: a change in tempo. *Human Studies*, 13, 323–59.

Weeks, P. (1996a). A rehearsal of a Beethoven passage: an analysis of correction talk. *Research on Language and Social Interaction*, 29(3), 247–90.

Weeks, P. (1996b). Synchrony lost, synchrony regained: the achievement of musical coordination. *Human Studies*, 19, 199–228.

Wellard, I. (2002). Men, sport, body performance and the maintenance of 'exclusive masculinity'. *Leisure Studies*, 21, 235–47.

Wesely, J.K. and Gaarder, E. (2004). The gendered 'nature' of the urban outdoors: women negotiating fear of violence. *Gender & Society*, 18(5), 645–63.

Whyte W.F. (1943). *Street Corner Society*. Chicago: University of Chicago Press.

Wittgenstein, L. (2001). *Philosophical Investigations*, 3rd Edition. Oxford: Blackwell.

Zimmerman, D.H. and Pollner, M. (1971). The everyday world as a phenomenon, in J.D. Douglas (ed.), *Understanding Everyday Life: Towards a Reconstruction of Sociological Knowledge*. London: Routledge & Kegan Paul, 80–103.

Index